D1316037

TIME-LIFE BOOKS
GREAT MEALS
IN MINUTES

TIME-LIFE BOOKS
GREAT MEALS IN MINUTES

WINGS BOOKS
New York • Avenel, New Jersey

Selections from the *Great Meals in Minutes* series, reprinted by arrangement with Time-Life Books. *Great Meals in Minutes* was created by Rebus, Inc.

Rebus, Inc.

Publisher: Rodney Friedman
Editorial Director: Shirley Tomkievicz

Editor: Marya Dalrymple
Art Director: Ronald Gross
Managing Editors: Brenda Goldberg, Frederica A. Harvey
Senior Editors: Charles Blackwell, Cara De Silva, Ruth A. Peltason, Barbara Benton
Assistant Managing Editor: Cynthia Villani
Food Editor and Food Stylist: Grace Young
Photographer: Steven Mays
Prop Stylists: Cathryn Schwing, Zazel Wilde Lovén
Staff Writer: Alexandra Greeley
Associate Editors: Ann M. Harvey, Jordan Verner
Assistant Editor: Bonnie J. Slotnick
Editorial Assistants: Joan Michel, Jennifer Mah, Michael Flint
Assistant Food Stylist: Karen Hatt, Nancy Leland Thompson
Photography Assistant: Glenn Maffei
Recipe Tester: Gina Palombi Barclay
Production Assistant: Lorna Bieber
Editorial Board: Angelica Cannon, Sally Dorst, Lilyan Glusker, Kim MacArthur, Kay Noble, Joan Whitman

Time-Life Books Inc.
is a wholly owned subsidiary of
Time Incorporated

Founder: Henry R. Luce 1898–1967

Editor-in-Chief: Henry Anatole Grunwald
President: J. Richard Munro
Chairman of the Board: Ralph P. Davidson
Corporate Editor: Jason McManus
Group Vice President, Books: Reginald K. Brack Jr.
Vice President, Books: George Artandi

Time-Life Books Inc.

Editor: George Constable
Executive Editor: George Daniels
Editorial General Manager: Neal Goff
Director of Design: Louis Klein
Editorial Board: Dale M. Brown, Roberta Conlan, Ellen Phillips, Gerry Schremp, Gerald Simons, Rosalind Stubenberg, Kit van Tulleken, Henry Woodhead
Director of Research: Phyllis K. Wise
Director of Photography: John Conrad Weiser

President: William J. Henry
Senior Vice President: Christopher T. Linen
Vice Presidents: Stephen L. Bair, Robert A. Ellis, John M. Fahey Jr., Juanita T. James, James L. Mercer, Joanne A. Pello, Paul R. Stewart, Christian Strasser

SERIES CONSULTANT
Margaret E. Happel is the author of *Ladies Home Journal Adventures in Cooking, Ladies Home Journal Handbook of Holiday Cuisine,* and other best-selling cookbooks, as well as the translator and adapter of Rebecca Hsu Hiu Min's *Delights of Chinese Cooking.* A food consultant based in New York City, she has been director of the food department of *Good Housekeeping* and editor of *American Home* magazine.

WINE CONSULTANT
Tom Maresca combines a full-time career teaching English literature with writing about and consuming fine wines. He is the author of *Mastering Wine a Taste at a Time.*

This 1992 edition is published by Wings Books, distributed by Outlet Book Company, Inc., a Random House Company, 40 Engelhard Avenue, Avenel, New Jersey, 07001, by arrangement with Time-Life Books Inc. Printed and bound in the United States of America
Library of Congress Cataloging-in-Publication Data
Great meals in minutes.
    p.   cm.
Originally published: Alexandria, Va. : Time-Life Books, 1985.
    ISBN 0-517-07765-5
    1. Cookery.   2. Menus.
[TX652.G725 1992]
641.5′55—dc20
                                        91-36508
                                           CIP

8 7 6 5 4 3 2 1

Contents

Introduction

Recently, a new way of cooking and eating has developed in this country, spurred by the ever-increasing availability of fresh produce and high-quality imported ingredients, and enhanced by the sudden interest in American regional cuisines. More than ever before, American cooks are clearly stimulated by fresh food and unusual approaches to cooking it: Where Creole dishes could be found only in Louisiana a few years ago, they now appear on menus and dinner tables throughout this country; Italian radicchio and arugula are currently as ubiquitous in our salad bowls as Bibb lettuce; and raspberry vinegar—once obscure—is flavoring everything from chicken to mayonnaise. And yet, the cook of the 1980s has less time than ever to spend in the kitchen.

Great Meals in Minutes is tailored for the busy person—novice cook and gourmet alike—who enjoys serving meals that are different, tasty, and nutritious, but that do not take long hours to prepare. In this volume, twenty-seven of America's most talented and successful cooks contribute seventy-seven complete menus for all occasions. Every menu, which serves four people, is planned for ease and efficiency, and all can be prepared *in an hour or less*. The cooks draw upon recipes and quick-cooking techniques from many countries around the world (France, Italy, China, and Indonesia, among them) and adapt them to the American kitchen. They also provide shopping lists, utensil lists, and a step-by-step format that assures spectacular results every time you prepare a meal. Nothing is left to chance.

In *Great Meals in Minutes*, every recipe uses fresh produce, with no powdered sauces or other dubious shortcuts. The other ingredients (vinegars, spices, herbs, and so on) are all high quality yet widely available in supermarkets or occasionally in specialty food stores. The cooks and the test kitchen staff have planned and tested the meals for appearance as well as taste, as the accompanying photographs show: The vegetables are brilliant and fresh, the visual combinations appetizing. The table settings feature bright colors, simple flower arrangements, and attractive serving dishes.

For each menu, the Editors, with advice from the cooks, suggest wines and other beverages. And there are added touches, which are recipes for complementary appetizers, side dishes, and desserts, as well as ideas for what to do with leftovers. On each menu page, too, you will find a number of tips, from the easiest way to peel and seed a tomato to advice on choosing the freshest produce.

BEFORE YOU START
Great Meals in Minutes will work best for you if you follow these suggestions:

1. Read the guidelines on the following pages for selecting ingredients.

2. Refresh your memory by reviewing the few simple cooking techniques on the following pages. They will quickly become second nature and will help you produce professional-quality meals in minutes.

3. Read the menus before you shop. Each lists the ingredients you will need, in the order you would expect to shop for them. Many items will already be on your pantry shelf.

4. Check the equipment list on page 21. Good, sharp knives and pots and pans of the right shape and material are essential for making great meals in minutes. This may be the time to buy a few things.

5. Set out everything you need before you start to cook: The lists at the beginning of each menu tell just what is required. To save effort, always keep your ingredients in the same place so you can reach for them instinctively.

6. Follow the start-to-finish steps provided with each menu. That way, you can have the entire meal ready in an hour.

The menus in this book are grouped according to the primary ingredient in the main course: beef and veal, pork, poultry, fish and shellfish, eggs, pasta, and vegetables. For convenience, the information that follows on selecting and preparing these foods has been organized in the same manner. You will also find tips on storing and freezing food, and a discussion of cooking techniques.

BEEF AND VEAL
Both beef (the meat from fully grown cattle) and veal (the meat of newborn to three-month-old calves) are highly nutritious. They contain high-quality protein and are a complete source of the essential amino acids. Beef is an excellent source of B vitamins, particularly B-12, and iron, and contributes substantial amounts of phosphorus and zinc to the human diet. Furthermore, recent findings indicate that if eaten in moderation beef and veal do not pose a problem with cholesterol. Today, Americans eat more beef than any other meat, including chicken.

On the tabletop, a cornucopia of fresh, high-quality ingredients—the makings for many great meals in minutes.

To buy the best beef or veal for a particular dish, a cook should know how to choose it by grade and cut. For these menus, the meat must also be suitable for quick cooking. However, this does not necessarily mean you have to buy the most expensive grade and cut.

Selecting the Right Grade
In 1927, the United States Department of Agriculture established a federal grading system, a uniform method for appraising the quality of inspected meat. Not all meat is graded to USDA standards because meat grading is voluntary; however, in general, the consumer's best bet for quality is to buy USDA graded meat.

Meat grading indicates palatability, and the grades are set, in part, by two criteria: marbling and color. Marbling is the amount of interior fat that interlaces the meat, and one of the most important factors affecting tenderness, taste, and juiciness. The highest grades of beef are well marbled, with parallel flecks of fat resembling paint splatters. Since veal comes from tender young animals, it has little, if any, marbling from stored fat. Fresh beef should have bright red meat; good veal has light pinkish-white meat.

Of the eight official beef grades, only the highest three—prime, choice, and good—are widely available in retail markets. The other grades are usually reserved for ground beef products or processed meats. Of the six veal grades, only the two best grades, prime and choice, are available to consumers.

Prime: Because USDA prime beef is the highest quality and the most expensive, it is produced in limited quantities. Richly marbled throughout, prime beef is the tenderest and most flavorful of all grades. Prime veal is most readily available to consumers: The meat should have a soft, smooth, velvety texture, and feel firm to the touch.

Choice: USDA choice beef is the most popular grade and is available at most butchers and supermarkets. Less marbled than prime and slightly less flavorful, most choice beef contains enough fat to cook by dry heat and still be tender, though some choice-grade cuts require moist-heat cooking. Choice veal may be colored a darker reddish-pink than prime veal and have a coarser texture, signs that the meat is from larger animals and of lower quality.

Good: USDA good beef contains even less marbling than choice beef and is often sold under a store brand name or as economy meat. Although it is as nutritious as the higher grades, beef stamped *good* is lean, and most cuts require moist-heat cooking to become tender.

Selecting the Right Cut
Knowing where a cut of beef or veal is from is the best way to determine tenderness.

Most meat is muscle, and cuts from heavily exercised muscles (the muscles of locomotion) are tougher than cuts from rarely used ones (the muscles of suspension). For instance, rib and loin cuts are the most tender because they come from the little-used muscles along the backbone. Shoulder, leg, and neck cuts are tougher because these muscles are frequently used and have a higher concentration of connective tissue.

A knowledge of the source of cuts also helps in selecting the appropriate cooking methods. For example, leg, neck, and shoulder cuts require cooking at low temperatures, by a method such as braising, poaching, or stewing, to tenderize the meat and keep it moist. Tender rib and loin cuts can be roasted, broiled, pan broiled, grilled, or fried briefly to seal in juices and sharpen flavor.

Veal is relatively tender but has little marbling; therefore, to impart flavor, veal steaks, cutlets, scallops, and chops should be sautéed or braised rather than broiled. Cuts from the lower leg and shoulder require moist-heat cooking to make them more tender. Some of the delicate rib, loin, and rump cuts can be cooked by dry heat if the heat is kept low; otherwise the meat toughens and dries out. For more information on the cuts of beef and veal used in this volume, see the box on page 8.

PORK

Economical and widely available, pork plays an important role in most of the world's cuisines. From snout to tail, virtually every part of the pig is edible. According to USDA statistics, the pig of the 1980s is fifty percent leaner than the pig of the 1950s, and with just 198 calories in a three-ounce serving of fresh pork, dieters need no longer consider this a forbidden food.

Selecting and Cooking Fresh Pork
Pork carcasses are first split and then divided into primal cuts: Boston shoulder, picnic shoulder, side or belly, leg, and loin. These are subdivided into the various retail cuts, such as ribs, roasts, and chops. Nearly all pork cuts are consistently tender because pigs are slaughtered before they are a year old. Consequently, the USDA grades used to indicate beef tenderness are not applied to retail cuts of pork.

Although pork is tender throughout, it still helps to know which part of the carcass your cut is from so you know how to cook it. The forequarters of the pig have small muscles with many connective tissues; thus meat from this part, such as the boneless shoulder, tends to be more fibrous than meat from other parts of the pig and should be cooked by a moist-heat method such as braising. The hindquarters of the pig contain large muscles with few connective tissues, so the meat here, such as boneless leg, is more tender and suitable for roasting or frying. The less-developed back muscles, in the loin area, produce the tenderest cuts, which can be cooked by any method.

When purchasing fresh pork, look for firmly textured flesh with a moderate amount of marbling and a moderate layer of white exterior fat. Fresh pork ranges in color from grayish-pink to deep rose. Some cuts, particularly the loin, may have a slightly two-toned appearance (pearly white tinged with pink), which is also acceptable. Shoulder cuts and legs are generally darker, with a coarser texture. Any visible bones should be red and spongy at the ends, not white and hard. Avoid pork that looks dry, feels soft to the touch, or that has dark pink meat and yellowed fat. Fresh pork has no odor.

Pork is safe to eat when it has been cooked to an internal temperature of 140 degrees. However, cooking it to a higher temperature—170 degrees is often recommended—will result in juicier, more flavorful meat. Be careful not to overcook the meat: It should still be slightly pink inside. An instant-reading meat thermometer is an essential tool for cooking pork.

Ham
From the Old English word *hamm*, which meant thigh, ham today refers to the hind leg of a pig. Ham can be purchased fresh (called fresh leg of pork), but the word generally means a cured or cured and smoked product.

Most hams are cured by one of two basic methods: wet cure or dry cure. Although some wet-cured hams are simply immersed in a solution of salt, sugar, and preservatives to enhance their color and flavor and to prevent the growth of organisms, the more common wet-cure method in the United States is injection, or quick, curing. In this method, the meat is deeply injected with a curing solution and allowed to age for twenty-four hours to a week, then it

---

PORK AND HEALTH

Like all meats sold in the United States, pork is inspected for wholesomeness. Even so, inspection cannot determine the presence of *trichinae*, microscopic parasites that are the cause of trichinosis in humans. Although in recent years trichinosis has become quite rare, it is still absolutely necessary to observe certain precautions when handling and cooking raw pork and uncooked pork products.

Never taste raw pork, sausage, or bacon when cooking. If you must check ground pork or fresh sausage for seasoning, thoroughly cook a small amount first, taste it, and then season the rest accordingly.

Kitchen utensils—particularly wooden cutting boards and dishes, as well as your hands—should be thoroughly washed with hot, soapy water after coming into contact with raw pork.

Some processed pork products are cured or hot-smoked to USDA standards, which eliminates the danger of trichinosis, even without further cooking. Never assume, however, that any ham or sausage is safe to eat uncooked. Read the label carefully or ask your butcher for this information if the product is not labeled.

is heated. If the ham has been heated to an internal temperature of 155 degrees F, it needs no further cooking. The label will indicate this. Injection-cured hams are rarely smoked.

The second method, dry curing, produces the famous Smithfield and other American country hams, as well as renowned European hams such as prosciutto. Pigs intended for dry-cured ham are fed special diets to impart special flavoring to the meat. After slaughter, the meat is rubbed with salt, preservatives, sugar, and seasonings, and kept in a cool place until the seasonings penetrate the meat and the salt extracts much of the moisture. The hams are usually smoked and then aged for up to two years. Only a small percentage of hams are cured this way today, but they are sought after by connoisseurs for their firm texture and intense flavor.

Ham is sold in many different forms at supermarkets and butcher shops. It may be whole (bone-in) or have some or all of the bones removed (semi-boneless or boneless). Generally, the bone-in hams are most flavorful. Ham typically has a deep-pink color, finely textured meat, and firm white fat. If the ham is sealed in plastic or canned, check for an expiration date. The best insurance for quality ham is to buy it from a reliable butcher.

When buying a wet-cured ham, whether canned, vacuum packed in plastic, or by the pound or slice, look to see whether it is marked READY-TO-EAT, FULLY COOKED, or COOK BEFORE EATING. Ready-to-eat and fully cooked hams are safe to eat without further cooking; however, their palatability is greatly enhanced by heating, even if they are to be served cold later. Heat cook-before-eating hams to an internal temperature of 170 degrees, as you would fresh pork. American country hams, such as the Smithfield, usually come with special directions for soaking and cooking.

Sausage

Pork sausage originated from the economical salvaging of the trimmings left after butchering pigs, though today it is a product prized by many cuisines. The texture of the grind, the blend of seasonings, and the method of cooking, curing, or smoking give sausages their individual character. In general, sausage falls into three categories:

Fresh sausage: Made from fresh raw, uncured, chopped, or ground pork (or a combination of meats), this product is sold in bulk, in patties, or enclosed in natural or synthetic casings. All fresh pork sausage should be cooked until its center is no longer pink. Though some fresh sausage is smoked (usually at a low temperature), it still requires thorough cooking.

Cooked sausage: This type of sausage, made from cured or uncured meat, seasonings, and binders such as nonfat dry milk or flour, has been precooked and sometimes smoked for flavor, or it may have been smoked at temperatures high enough to eliminate the need for cooking. Though ready to eat, the flavor of many fully cooked sausages is enhanced by further cooking.

Dry sausage: Dry sausage originated in the warm countries of southern Europe, where the drying process was necessary to preserve the meat. Some varieties of dry sausage are still called summer sausage because they keep well. Dry sausages are ready to eat.

For more information on the types of fresh pork, ham, and sausage used in this volume, see the box on page 10.

POULTRY

When you want to cook a wonderful meal but do not have much time, poultry is the ideal choice for the main course.

You can cook it quickly, serve it hot, cold, or at room temperature, and it tastes equally delicious whether combined with elaborate sauces or just a few herbs. Plus it goes with any side dish.

Selecting the Right Chicken

You can find fresh chicken at any butcher or supermarket, thanks to modern shipping and refrigeration methods. Many birds reach the market twenty-four hours after they have been killed, and chickens kept in a properly cooled display case stay fresh for up to seven days. If possible, avoid chickens that have been frozen and then defrosted; a thawed chicken spoils quickly and is never as flavorful as a fresh one.

All supermarket poultry comes from mass producers who cage-raise birds by the tens of thousands. If you live near a farm and can buy fresh-killed, free-range chickens—birds that scratched around outside for their food— you know that these birds have a richer flavor than the commercial ones. Nevertheless, the advantages of the

DISJOINTING A CHICKEN

Disjointing a whole chicken takes only minutes and produces 8 or 10 portions (4 with breast meat) that you can quickly sauté or fry. You save money by doing your own disjointing, because whole chickens are fresher and cheaper per pound than chicken parts, and you have the added bonus of backbone, neck, and giblets for your chicken stock. The only tricks are to find all the joints—thigh, leg, and wing—and to cut through cleanly at those points. You need a sharp knife, and poultry shears are a great help too.

1. Set the bird on its back and pull one leg away from the body. Cut through parallel to the backbone at the joint. Then cut the thigh and leg apart at the joint. Repeat with the other leg. **2.** Pull the wing away and cut through, starting inward diagonally, at the shoulder joint; then slice toward the rear. Repeat with the other wing. **3.** Using a knife or poultry shears, cut through the ribs along either side of the backbone. **4.** Open up the body and cut between the breast and the backbone. Place the breast skin side down and push down with your hands to flatten it. **5.** Cut the breast in half lengthwise—and then into quarters if you want 10 serving pieces.

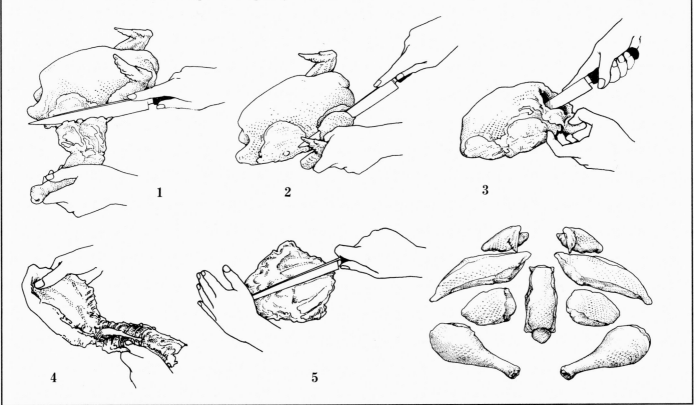

standard supermarket chicken—availability, ease of preparation, cleanliness, and low price—more than make up for its loss of flavor.

Whatever your source, you must pick out the right bird for your chosen menu. Markets sell chickens under different names and according to size and age. For most of the recipes in this volume, broilers or broiler-fryers are best. They weigh from one and a half to three pounds and are between seven and eight weeks old. Slightly larger chickens, called fryers, weigh up to four pounds and are just as tender and moist, but they take a little more time to cook. For one serving, allow three quarters of a pound of raw chicken with bone and skin, or a third to half a pound per person when the chicken is boned and skinned.

Despite their names, all these chickens can be roasted, sautéed, steamed, or poached—as well as broiled or fried. The bigger and older chickens, known as roasters, though usually better flavored, need more than an hour to cook and therefore are not called for in this book.

Whether you are buying whole birds or packages of parts, look for broiler-fryers with a USDA Grade A inspection stamp. This stamp means that the chicken is meaty, that it was healthy when slaughtered, and that both the chicken and the plant where it was processed were inspected.

Smell the chicken or the package. A fresh chicken has no odor, or almost none. A fresh-killed broiler-fryer will have a pliable breastbone and moist but not sticky skin. If the skin looks purplish, the bird is past its prime.

Game Hens and Quail
The Rock Cornish game hen, a cross between an English chicken from Cornwall and the American White Plymouth Rock, is all white meat. Its flavor is a little blander than a supermarket chicken and thus requires more seasoning or sauce. A Cornish hen should weigh less than a pound, which makes one hen about right for a single serving. Poultry growers have recently been marketing older game

---

FISH AND SHELLFISH IN THIS VOLUME

The fish and shellfish listed below are called for in this volume; however, many of the cooks specify substitutions. If the specified substitute is unavailable, you can usually substitute another fish and still get good results, whether it is a freshwater or a saltwater fish.

FISH
Cod: Atlantic cod and Pacific cod have lean, firm, white flesh. Cod may be called scrod when weighing less than two and a half pounds. Related fish may be substituted: haddock, whiting (silver hake), and pollock. Available fresh or frozen, whole, in steaks, and in fillets.

Flatfish: Flounders and halibuts. Some flatfish are called sole. Flatfish have lean, delicately flavored white flesh; some species are firmer fleshed than others. Related fish may be substituted: summer flounder (fluke); yellowtail flounder; petrale, lemon, gray, and rex soles; halibut; and turbot. Available fresh or frozen, whole, in steaks, and in fillets.

Halibut: See flatfish. Fine texture and flavor.

Mackerel: Mackerel has both dark and light fatty flesh. King mackerel is stronger flavored and fattier than Spanish mackerel. Related fish may be substituted: wahoo; bullet, chub, king, Spanish mackerels; and tunas. Another substitute is mullet, a good food fish, found in fresh water and salt water. Mackerel is available fresh or frozen, whole, in steaks, and in fillets.

Goosefish: Also known as monkfish or angler fish, it has firm, white flesh that tastes like lobster. The only good substitute is the more delicate cusk, related to cod, but both fish are restricted to the Atlantic coast. Only the tail section of goosefish is edible; it is usually marketed without the head.

Perch: A tasty, freshwater fish, averaging ten to twelve inches in length with greenish-brown back and yellow sides. Perch have firm white meat that becomes elastic when overcooked. A rare find in the fish market.

Salmon: Pink, chum, sockeye, and Atlantic salmon have

fatty, distinctively flavored firm flesh that ranges in color from white to deep coral. There is no substitute for salmon. It is available fresh or frozen, whole, in fillets, and in steaks.

Sea Bass: Lean, firm, white flesh. Related fish may be substituted: black sea bass, sand perch, grouper, scamp, sand bass, and striped bass. Sea bass is available fresh, whole, and in fillets.

Sole: See flatfish. All true sole (Dover sole) marketed in the United States is imported from Europe.

Swordfish: Coarse-textured, rich, delicately flavored. Mako shark may be substituted. Available fresh or frozen, in steaks.

Trout: Brook and rainbow; hatchery-bred most commonly available. Light meat, firm flesh, moderately fatty. They can be used interchangeably. Available fresh or frozen, whole, dressed, boned (with backbone and ribs removed).

SHELLFISH
Crab: Hard-shell crabs: blue, rock, Dungeness. Varieties differ from coast to coast, but the meat is delicate and moderately sweet. Available live, fresh, frozen, or cooked.

Shrimp and prawns (jumbo shrimp): Delicate, firm flesh. Available fresh, cooked or frozen, whole, in shell, or shelled.

Clams: Hard-shell: Littleneck, cherrystone, and chowder clams; soft-shell. Tender, sweet flesh. Available whole or shucked, fresh or frozen.

Mussels: Mollusks. Tender, sweet flesh. Low fat, high protein. Available live.

Oysters: Tender flesh, with delicate flavor. Low fat, high protein. Available year round, whole or shucked, fresh or frozen.

Scallops: Bay and sea. Both are tender, with delicately flavored ivory flesh. Available shucked, rarely whole, fresh or frozen.

Squid: Delicately flavored, firm (almost chewy) white flesh. Available whole or cut into pieces, fresh or frozen.

hens, and you may have trouble finding the convenient one-pound size. In that case, use the larger hens.

The quail, a tiny relative of the pheasant and common in the American South, weighs only five or six ounces and has almost no body fat. Plan on two quail per person—and reserve them for special occasions because they are expensive.

Most supermarkets carry fresh or frozen game hens, and also stock frozen, or even fresh, quail. The guidelines for selecting these birds are the same as for chicken.

FISH AND SHELLFISH

Approximately 250 varieties of fish and shellfish are now sold commercially in the United States. Whether boiled, broiled, fried, baked, or poached, and served hot or cold, fish and shellfish are indispensable to busy cooks, since their natural tenderness allows them to be cooked quickly.

Because all seafood is highly perishable, freshness is paramount. Unlike meat and poultry, fish and shellfish are not subject to mandatory federal or state inspections. Therefore, consumers should learn to recognize and select fresh seafood.

Judging Freshness

When choosing fish, look for the following: The eyes will be shiny and bulging; the gills will be bright red, not brown or rust colored; and the skin moist and shiny. Prime fish will feel firm and elastic to the touch, not flabby or soft. When cut up or filleted, the fish should still look moist; avoid dried-out or discolored pieces. Fresh fish has a mild, sweetish aroma and never smells fishy or sour.

Many supermarkets will sell fresh fish already packaged, and some date the package. After buying the fish, check the freshness of your purchase by opening the package before you leave the market. If the fish smells tainted, ask for a refund or an exchange.

Freshness is just as critical for shellfish, which spoil quickly out of the water. Fresh raw shrimp will be greenish-gray or pinkish, depending on their origin. The flesh should feel firm and slippery. Cooked shrimp are pinkish-white. Live oysters, mussels, and hard-shelled clams normally keep their shells tightly closed when out of the water. Do not purchase any that do not close when you tap them or that feel unusually light or heavy in the shell. Shucked shellfish should look plump and uniform in color.

What to Look for in the Market

A fish dealer cuts a fish according to its size, shape, and intended use. Flatfish, such as flounder, are sold whole, pan-dressed (without head or tail), or as fillets, although large flatfish, like halibut, may be cut into steaks. Round fish, such as trout, are sold whole, pan-dressed, in steaks and fillets. Fresh fish is marketed in these easy-to-identify forms:

Whole: The fish is whole, as it comes from the water. It may have been scaled but will need to be gutted.

Drawn: The fish is whole and has been gutted and scaled. Whole fish may be baked, grilled, steamed, poached, or fried.

Dressed or pan-dressed: The fish is whole but its head, tail, fins, scales, and viscera have been removed. Small pan-dressed fish are usually sautéed or deep fried.

Butterfly fillets: This fish, round or flat, has been cut into boneless twin fillets that are attached to each other by a strip of uncut skin along the back of the fish. The fillets are opened out and cooked as for ordinary fillets.

Fillets: The fish has been cut lengthwise along the backbone, into boneless, skinless pieces. These delicate cuts can be cooked by any method but usually need moist heat because they tend to dry out quickly.

Steaks: The fish, a large dressed round fish, has been cut into crosswise sections about one to one and a half inches thick. The backbone and skin have not been removed. Steaks can be cooked by any method but need added moisture if prepared by dry-heat cooking.

Fresh shellfish is usually sold in its natural form. Clams and oysters are obtainable either in the shell or shucked. Mussels are sold in the shell, but scallops are almost always sold shucked. Depending on their size, squid may be sold whole or cut into convenient serving portions. Shrimp and prawns are sold both raw and cooked, shelled and unshelled, and frequently the head has been removed.

Handling Fish and Shellfish

To save time, have your fish dealer draw and dress your fish for you if it hasn't been done already. Most of the recipes in this book call for fillets and steaks.

You may wish to purge live clams, mussels, and oysters to clear out their digestive systems before cooking. To do this, place them in a gallon of cold water with one teaspoon of sea salt and one cup of cornmeal, and let sit for at least three hours. Clams, mussels, shrimp, prawns, and squid all need further attention before cooking.

Clams: With a stiff brush, scrub the clams under cold running water. To shuck, hold each clam over a bowl to catch the liquor, and insert the blade of a clam knife or a wide, rounded-end knife between the shells opposite the hinge. Twist the blade to force the shell halves apart, then cut apart the muscles holding the shells together.

Mussels: With a stiff brush, scrub the mussels under cold running water to remove any surface mud. Remove the beard and pull off any strands that stick out of the shell. Using a stiff brush or knife, scrape off any surface encrustations.

SEASONING AN OMELET PAN

To produce perfect omelets, you need a well-seasoned or nonstick heavy-bottomed pan with sloping sides. Omelet pans range from 7 to 12 inches. You may choose an aluminum, steel, or cast-iron pan, but before using it you must clean and season it well unless it is nonstick. The "seasoning" is a coat of oil, which adheres permanently to the interior surface to prevent food from sticking. Ideally, the pan should be used only for omelets and not for cooking other foods. To season the pan, first wash it in hot water, scouring the inside surface with fine steel wool and soap. Rinse and dry the pan thoroughly.

If your pan has an ovenproof handle, pour in a tablespoon of cooking oil and spread it around with a pastry brush or paper towel to coat the interior, then heat the pan in a 375-degree oven for about half an hour. Cool it, then wipe it out with a paper towel. The pan is now seasoned.

If your pan does not have an ovenproof handle, put 1 inch of oil into the pan and heat it on the stove until the oil is very hot but not smoking (about 375 degrees). Carefully remove the pan from the heat and let it cool, then pour off the oil (if the oil has not been heated to the smoking point, it can be reused for cooking). Wipe out the pan.

Before using either type of omelet pan, sprinkle it with a little coarse salt, rub it with an oily paper towel, and wipe it out. To clean the pan after cooking an omelet, rub the pan with salt and a damp paper towel to remove any food residue. If you find it necessary to wash the pan, you may need to reseason it; avoid scouring or using harsh detergents. Always rub the interior of the pan with a few drops of oil before you put it away.

Shrimp and prawns: These are usually sold without the head, but if they are whole, twist off the head. To peel and devein, starting at the head end, slip your thumb under the shell between the feelers. Lift off two or three shell segments at once and, holding the tail, pull the shrimp out of the shell. If desired, pull off the tail shell, or leave it on for decorative appearance. With a sharp paring knife, slit down the back, and lift out the black vein.

Squid: Hold the head with one hand, the body with the other, and firmly pull the head from the body. Cut off the tentacles and discard the remainder of the head. Pull the transparent quill-like piece out of the body sac and discard it. Wash the squid thoroughly inside and out, and peel the skin away from the body and fins. Slice the body into rings, if desired.

For more specific information on the fish and shellfish used in this volume, see the box on page 12.

EGGS

Convenient, economical, and above all versatile, eggs are utilized by all the world's great cuisines. Used alone or in combination, they are the basis for hundreds of highly nutritious dishes.

Selecting Eggs

Before you buy eggs, look for the USDA shield on the carton. It means that the eggs are federally inspected and classified. Some small egg packers, who follow equally rigid state inspection standards, will mark their egg cartons with a state shield rather than that of the USDA.

Eggs are marketed by grade and size standards established by the USDA. Grade indicates the interior and exterior quality of the egg—the condition of the white and yolk, the size of the air pocket, and the cleanliness, smoothness, and shape of the shell. The grades in descending order are AA, A, B, and C. Both AA and A eggs are excellent for cooking, although some fastidious cooks prefer to use only AA eggs when appearance is important because they do not spread out when broken. The lower grades are just as nutritious but are better for scrambling or baking since the yolks tend to break easily. Grade B and C eggs are usually sold to bakeries or the food industry and rarely appear in supermarkets.

Size is determined by minimum net weight per dozen. There are six egg-weight classes set by the USDA, ranging from jumbo (thirty ounces per dozen) to peewee (fifteen ounces per dozen). Large eggs (twenty-four ounces per dozen) are the most commonly sold, and most recipes in this and other cookbooks call for them. If you are price conscious, a guideline to follow in buying eggs is that if there is more than a seven-cent difference between two sizes, the smaller size is the more economical.

Testing Eggs for Freshness

Egg freshness has no bearing on nutritional value, but freshness does affect both how an egg cooks and, ultimately, how it tastes. Very fresh eggs are best for poaching and frying because they hold their shape better. On the other hand, very fresh eggs, when hard-boiled, do not peel easily. Older eggs are fine for boiling, scrambling, or baking, when appearance is not important.

Measuring an egg's buoyancy is said to be one test for freshness. Put the whole egg in a bowl of cold water. A newly laid egg, with only a tiny air pocket, is heavy and will sink to the bottom of the bowl. A week-old egg, with a large air pocket, is more buoyant and will tilt, large-end up, in the water. An egg that is too old to eat will float to the surface.

Handling Eggs

Many cooks forget that for best results eggs need special handling. The following tips will improve your egg cookery:

Separating: Eggs separate more easily if they are thoroughly chilled. Set out two clean bowls, then separate the eggs one at a time. Break the egg in half over one bowl, allowing some of the white to drop into the bowl, but catching the yolk in one of the shell halves. Gently pour the yolk back and forth between the shell halves, allowing the rest of the white to slide into the bowl. When the white is completely separated, drop the yolk into the other bowl. Some cooks prefer to use an egg separator, available at most supermarkets.

Beating: Eggs will produce greater volume when beaten if they are at room temperature. Let the eggs sit at room temperature for half an hour or put the whole eggs into a bowl of warm water for a few minutes before beating. If a recipe calls for slightly beaten whole eggs, use a fork or whisk to beat the eggs until the yolks and whites are blended. For well-beaten whole eggs, use an electric mixer, egg beater, or whisk, and beat until the eggs are frothy and evenly colored. To beat yolks only, use an electric mixer at high speed, or beat rapidly with a fork or whisk until the yolks thicken.

When beating whites, use either a large glass, china, stainless-steel, or copper bowl (do not use plastic), and be sure that the bowl and beaters are free of any grease or yolk, which will keep the whites from expanding properly. To beat the whites with an electric mixer, begin at slow speed and beat until the whites produce small bubbles. Then beat at high speed until the whites are the required consistency. "Foamy" whites will be liquid and should flow easily. "Soft peak" whites are moist and shiny and form peaks that fold over when the beaters are removed. "Stiff peak" whites are still moist but form peaks that remain stiff when the beaters are removed. For the best results, beat the whites just before you need them so they do not deflate.

Incorporating: When adding whole eggs or egg yolks to a hot mixture, always add a small amount of the hot mixture to the eggs or yolks first to warm them—this "tempering" prevents the yolks from curdling. Then gradually add the warmed eggs to the hot mixture, stirring constantly.

Folding beaten egg whites into a mixture should be done at the last moment. Use a rubber spatula to gently cut the whites into the mixture, moving from the top center down to the bottom of the bowl and then up the sides. Turn the bowl slightly after each cut to ensure even dispersion.

Cooking with Eggs

The most important thing to remember when cooking with eggs is to use a low to medium temperature (except for omelets) and to monitor the cooking time. If you cook an egg at too high heat, or for too long at a low heat, the whites will shrink and become tough and rubbery, and the yolks will toughen and may turn greenish-gray.

If you cook an egg whole, the white firms more quickly than the yolk. If you blend the white and the yolk, they set at the same rate. If you stir the egg constantly while cooking, as you do for scrambled eggs, the egg remains soft and moist. Left unstirred, the egg thickens and becomes a cohesive whole, as in an omelet.

PASTA

Pasta has always been one of the most versatile foods. It can be served as an hors d'oeuvre, a soup course, a main course, a salad, a side dish, or a dessert. Simple to prepare, and nutritious, pasta is rich in protein and energizing carbohydrates, but virtually free of fat. Served in reasonable quantities, perhaps with a light sauce consisting of seafood or vegetables, it is far less fattening than comparable servings of meat.

Pasta is one food for which fresh does not necessarily mean best. A good quality, golden-colored commercial dried pasta made with 100 percent semolina flour from durum wheat is a better product than an inferior, pale-colored fresh one, either store-bought or homemade, that cooks too quickly and becomes gummy. If you buy fresh pasta, make sure that it is not matted or clumped together and that each pasta strand is coated with little specks of flour, which keep the noodles separate.

Cooking Pasta

Any pasta, fresh or dried, must be cooked in plenty of boiling water: Four quarts of water to each pound of pasta is the minimum, and some cooks recommend six to seven quarts. Keep the heat high. Use a large kettle, stockpot, or Dutch oven large enough to hold the water and a pound of pasta without boiling over. The pasta must have room to float: In too small a pot with too little water the pasta will stick together and may emerge partially overcooked and partially underdone. Never use a lid when you are cooking the pasta. A tablespoon of oil added to the water will help prevent sticking. Though most cooks in this volume recommend salting the water, follow your own preference.

When cooking pasta, timing is crucial; even if the pasta cooks only one or two minutes too long, the dish can be spoiled. The optimal cooking time for pasta depends on the brand as well as the type—but one thing to remember is that fresh pasta cooks much more quickly than dried. Although in general you should follow package instructions, always check about halfway through the allotted cooking time to see if the pasta is ready. The ideal state of doneness is *al dente* ("to the tooth"), which means the pasta is no longer hard but still firm to the bite. Pasta

BASIL AND ITS USES

Basil, an annual herb with a distinctive mint essence, is one of the most popular seasonings for pasta. Fresh basil is used as the basis for pesto—the Genoese sauce made of ground basil leaves, olive oil, cheese, and pine nuts—and is excellent for fresh tomatoes, sauces, salad dressings, soups, and salads. Fresh basil is always best, but frozen is also good—and one way to enjoy this pungent herb year round. Packaged dried basil has the least flavor, but it is useful nevertheless.

Today many supermarkets and greengroceries carry freshly cut basil during much of the year. However, basil grows easily in your garden or potted on a sunny windowsill. To plant outdoors, wait until the danger of frost has passed. Select a sunny plot and sow seeds two to four inches apart; thin them after two inches' growth to about ten to twelve inches apart. Basil plants flower quickly, and when they do, they put out fewer leaves. To increase leaf production, pinch off the flowering stems.

Freezing basil is an excellent way to preserve this herb. Pick unblemished leaves, wash them off, drain them, and pat them dry. Store the leaves in sealed plastic bags. When your recipe calls for basil, you do not need to thaw the leaves—you use them right from the freezer, either crumbling them or leaving them whole.

Packing basil leaves in olive oil is a traditional Italian method for preserving basil. First pick enough leaves to fill small preserving jars. After washing and drying them, layer the basil leaves in the jars and keep pressing them down as you pour in the olive oil. Fill the jars to the brim. The leaves will darken a bit but will remain pungent. Store the jars in the refrigerator indefinitely.

---

cooked past this point will stick together on the plate in a heavy mass. Instead of relying entirely on the clock, learn to rely on your eye. When the pasta loses its dry look and begins to soften and turn slightly translucent on the surface, use a wooden fork or a pair of long-handled tongs to retrieve a piece from the boiling water. Run it immediately under cold water and taste it. If the pasta is still hard in the middle, continue cooking. But if it is almost cooked through, taste again in thirty or—at most—sixty seconds. Remember that the pasta will continue to cook for another thirty seconds or so while you take it out of the water. When you decide it is *al dente*, take the kettle off the range at once.

Draining Pasta

By far the easiest, fastest way to drain pasta is to set a colander in the sink and pour the pasta into it. As soon as it is drained, immediately proceed with the recipe.

An alternative to draining pasta in a colander is to lift the pasta out of the water with a special wooden pasta fork (it looks like a brush with large wooden "bristles"), a regular wooden fork, a skimmer, tongs, or a slotted spoon, holding the pasta above the water to drain and transferring it directly to a serving dish. If you are very adept, and if you are working with a fairly manageable amount of

pasta (half a pound or less), this method can save time, since it eliminates a step between the stockpot and the serving dish. If you have difficulty handling wet pasta with a fork or skimmer, or you have to take it out in batches, you will risk overcooking the pasta that remains in the water longest. All of the recipes in this book call for a colander—certainly a practical draining method for most cooks.

Serving Pasta

Serve pasta as soon as it is done. It cools off quickly. Take time to warm the serving bowls or plates. Set them in a warm oven or even in a pan of hot water. If you have a dishwasher, plan to run it just before you serve dinner and take the clean warm plates directly out of it. There are various electrical plate-warming gadgets on the market, if you prefer. But whatever method you choose, warm dishes are a necessity for good pasta.

Leftover Pasta

Plain leftover pasta is useful for salads, side dishes, and casseroles. To store it, put the pasta in a container, toss it lightly in a small amount of olive oil (just enough to coat each piece very lightly), cover, and refrigerate. If you have cooked it *al dente*, you can reheat it. Bring a pot of water to a rolling boil, drop the pasta into the pot, and remove from the heat. Let it stand for about two minutes, or just until warmed through. It will no longer be considered *al dente*, but, on the other hand, most sensible cooks would be reluctant to throw it away. Or, if you have the extra minutes, reheat the pasta gently in a double boiler. You can toss it with a bit of oil or butter to prevent it from sticking.

Another method of reheating pasta is to transfer the pasta to a baking dish, cover it, and bake in a medium-warm oven just until the pasta is hot.

VEGETABLES

Today, Americans' attitudes toward eating vegetables have changed. They have rediscovered the joys of fresh vegetables and the value of fresh produce as an essential element in fine cooking as well as good nutrition. More than other foods, vegetables offer limitless variations in texture, taste, and color.

Vegetables are any edible portion of any plant with soft green stems. They are classified according to the part of the plant that is edible: roots and tubers (beets and potatoes); bulbs (the onion family); stems (asparagus and kohlrabi); leaves (lettuce and spinach); leafstalks (celery, rhubarb, and fennel); immature flowers (broccoli and cauliflower); seeds and seed pods (dried mature legumes and fresh young peas and beans). Another category is fruit-vegetables. Botanically, these are fruits because they contain one or more seeds surrounded by the flesh of the plant; but for purposes of cooking and eating, they qualify as vegetables because they are not as sweet as fruits and usually are not eaten out of hand. This group includes tomatoes, sweet peppers, eggplant, avocados, corn, squash, and cucumbers. Mushrooms, too, are treated as vegetables, although they really are fungi, those flowerless, rootless parasites that live on other plants.

Selecting Vegetables

The quality of vegetables is never guaranteed. Climate, soil, and sunshine affect vegetables as much as the care they get during harvesting, packing, and shipping. And the time lapse between picking and cooking affects appearance, taste, and nutritive value. Vegetables start to deteriorate as soon as they are picked. The best advice, therefore, is to buy produce locally during its natural growing season, either from a farmers' market or from a greengrocery supplied by local farmers. Or, choose a supermarket that offers seasonal and local items. Shop carefully, examining produce for any signs of age or decay, and select only crisp, firm, fresh-looking vegetables.

Canned or frozen vegetables are rarely as good as fresh picked. If the vegetable you want is out of season, try to find another with similar taste and texture. The notes or directions accompanying each recipe in this book often include suggestions for substitutions. In some cases, however, canned or frozen vegetables are acceptable alternatives to fresh: Canned tomatoes are as good as fresh for soups and sauces, and some frozen vegetables—for instance, black-eyed peas, lima beans, artichoke hearts, baby corn, spinach, and green peas—are good provided you do not overcook them.

Most growers wax vegetables to restore the natural sheen scrubbed off in a general cleaning process after harvest. This edible wax coating brightens vegetables, adds eye appeal, and retards decay by sealing in natural moisture and nutrients. Vegetables should be rinsed, of course, but there is no need to wash off this wax.

Roots and tubers: This category includes potatoes, beets, ginger, Jerusalem artichokes, carrots, radishes, sweet potatoes, turnips, and celeriac. The cooking method dictates the type of potato you buy. There are two basic types: waxy (low starch)—long white, round white, round red, and all new potatoes; and non-waxy (high starch)—long ovals with rough skins. To quickly determine potato type, slice a raw potato in two and rub the cut halves together. Starchy potato halves stick together, but low starch halves do not. Waxy potatoes are best boiled or steamed. Non-waxy potatoes are most desirable for baking, pan roasting, and mashing; they are ideal for French fries. All potatoes should be firm, without sprouts or green spots.

Bulbs: The allium family—onions, garlic, and so on—functions both as seasonings and as vegetables. Onions come in a considerable range: chive, scallion, pearl, Creole, Bermuda, leek, white boiling, shallot, and yellow globe. Mildly oniony chives (green shoots picked before a bulb forms) make tender garnishes; baby pearl onions are delicious pickled; the versatile yellow globe onion is a kitchen staple. Onions should be firm and well shaped. Old onions will have green sprouts and feel soggy.

Stems: Asparagus, the welcome harbinger of spring, comes in two different types: green and white. The familiar green spears are readily available in most markets, but the white ones are sold fresh only in select greengroceries or, more commonly, packaged in glass jars. Select spears that are crisp rather than spongy. Slightly limp spears firm up when soaked in cold water.

Leaves: Leafy greens—spinach, cabbage, lettuce, endive, kale, broccoli rabe, sorrel, and mustard greens—generally are available all year. The best tasting leafy vegetables are young, with bright crisp leaves and no bruises, yellowing spots, or wilt.

Leafstalks: These textured firm vegetables are erect stems with leafy tops; the category includes rhubarb, celery, fennel, Swiss chard, and *bok choy*, or Chinese cabbage. Tender young stalks are firm and unblemished; tough older stalks are coarse and pithy. Yellowed leaves or leaves with mushy brown spots indicate that the vegetable is old or has been overchilled and has thus become tasteless.

Immature flowers: Artichokes, broccoli, and cauliflower belong to this group. All have immature flower heads or clusters of heads surrounded by leaves and set on thick fleshy stalks. The globe artichoke, the unopened flower of a thistle, looks like a green-leafed crown circling a prickly choke and a saucer-shaped bottom. Artichokes with compact, hefty heads and firm green leaves are the ones to buy.

Fresh broccoli and its first cousin, cauliflower, have firm stalks and compact flowered heads. Broccoli should be dark green, and cauliflower should be white without any dark speckles. Neither should have any sign of yellowing.

Seeds and seed pods: This broad category encompasses seeds, peas, or beans in pods such as snow peas, and young shoots such as bean sprouts. Choose the smallest and youngest peas, with pods that are wrinkle free, moist, and firm. Dried legumes are the mature seeds of plants with pods, dried either before or after being shelled. These are available in boxes or plastic bags at most supermarkets and health food shops.

Fruit-vegetables: This category includes tomatoes, avocados, sweet peppers, eggplant, corn, squash, and cucumbers—warm-weather plants that are really fruits. Fruit-vegetables taste best when allowed to vine ripen; because they are delicate, plan to use them a day or two after purchase.

Out-of-season tomatoes must be picked hard and green for long-distance shipping, then artificially ripened. Your best bet are those labeled HOTHOUSE, because these are picked almost fully ripe, carefully packed in sturdy crates, then shipped to local markets. A tip for ripening hothouse tomatoes: Buy them several days before you plan to use them, and put them in a loosely closed paper bag with an apple. Unless tomatoes are on the verge of decay, never refrigerate them because this mars their full flavor.

Ripe avocados are slightly soft to the touch, with no bruises or dark spots. An underripe avocado ripens easily within a day or two if you wrap it in a brown paper bag and leave it at room temperature. To test for ripeness, stick a toothpick in the stem end. If the toothpick goes in and out easily, the avocado is perfectly ripe.

Sweet peppers should be firm, brightly colored, and well shaped. Eggplants should be firm, bright, heavy for their size, and shiny, with fresh green caps. Zucchini, yellow crookneck, pattypan, and all summer squash should look fresh, feel firm, and have tender skin. Winter squash—pumpkin, butternut, acorn, hubbard, and chayote—should have hard rinds and feel hefty.

As any enthusiast will agree, fresh sweet corn tastes best picked from the stalk, then immediately shucked and popped into a pot of boiling unsalted water. Most cooks obviously cannot follow such a plan. So, select ears with fresh green husks, plump juicy kernels, and silk that is free from decay.

Mushrooms: Fresh, standard, domestic mushrooms have tightly fitting caps that curve over the stems and cover the gills on the underside. If the caps flare open, exposing the gills, the mushrooms are old and dry. Some recipes in this volume use more unusual types of mushrooms such as Japanese *enokitake* and *shiitake*, Chinese oyster, and French chanterelles. Their cap shapes and colors differ from those of the standard mushroom varieties, so, when shopping, select mushrooms that feel firm and are not slimy.

STORING FOOD

Utilizing meat, fish, poultry, eggs, and vegetables as soon after purchase as possible assures maximum freshness. If you must store produce, or if you decide to freeze some items, the following guidelines will prove useful:

Meat

All fresh meat requires cold-temperature storage to prevent flavor deterioration and spoilage. If you plan to cook cuts of meat within a few days of purchase, you should store them preferably in the original store wrapper, or rewrap them and put them in the coldest section of your refrigerator. Do not rinse the meat before storing it. You can safely refrigerate large pieces for three to four days, and smaller pieces for two to three days. Because ground meats spoil very quickly, do not refrigerate them for more than a day or two.

To freeze meat properly, the freezer should be set at −10 degrees F, and the temperature raised to 0 degrees after the meat is frozen. The freezing compartment of a one-door refrigerator is not cold enough to freeze meat and should only be used to store meat in an emergency for up to two weeks, or for prefrozen meat. To freeze meat, enfold it in plastic freezer wrap, foil, or specially coated freezer paper. The wrapping must be airtight to seal in moisture and keep out air. This prevents freezer burn, which creates a brown, dried-out surface that must be cut off when the meat thaws. Label and date each package with a waterproof marker. Rotate meats so that older cuts do not get overlooked. The maximum freezing time for beef is twelve months, but for best flavor, you should use it in six to nine months. Freeze veal for no more than four to six months. Frozen pork cuts will keep for up to six months. You can freeze ground meat and variety meats for up to three months.

To thaw frozen meats, loosen the wrapping, but do not uncover completely, and set in your refrigerator for twenty-four to seventy-two hours in a tray or dish. Or unwrap them and thaw during cooking in a regular or microwave oven. If you intend to marinate frozen meat, unwrap it and let it thaw in the marinade. Cook meat as soon as possible after it thaws. Once meat has been defrosted, it is best not to refreeze it, since it loses juiciness and quality.

Seafood

Seafood should always be a last-minute purchase. Fresh fish should be drawn (cleaned) before being stored. Remove all blood, rinse the fish under cold water, and pat it dry with paper towels. Fish will keep best whole. Cover the fish loosely with plastic wrap. If you can provide drainage, store the fish in the refrigerator on ice. Otherwise, store the fish, preferably on an aluminum tray or a plate to maintain an even cold temperature, in the coldest part of your refrigerator.

Fresh clams, mussels, and oysters may be stored shucked or unshucked. If storing them in the shell, keep them dry and do not store them on ice. For shucked, store them in their liquor in a closed container, preferably set on ice. Store all shellfish in the coldest part of your refrigerator.

Poultry

Poultry tastes best when cooked and eaten as soon as possible, ideally within twenty-four hours after you buy it. (Make sure you use it within three days.) As soon as you get home, take the bird—whether it is a chicken, hen, or quail—out of the market package, put it on a platter, rewrap it loosely in waxed paper so that air can circulate around it, and refrigerate it. An airtight wrap makes poultry spoil more quickly.

When freezing poultry, wrap the whole bird or parts in heavy foil or freezer wrap, forcing out as much air as possible. Always label the package with the date. Poultry kept at 0 degrees can be safely frozen for six months, but two weeks or so is the sensible maximum if you want to preserve the flavor.

Thaw poultry slowly; quick thawing tends to reduce the flavor. The best method is to let the bird thaw in the regular food compartment of your refrigerator. This takes about two hours per pound (a three-pound chicken needs a long afternoon to thaw) but it helps the flavor and reduces the chance of bacteria forming as the temperature rises. Do not remove the freezer wrap until the bird is completely defrosted. To decrease cooking time, take the chicken from the refrigerator and let it come to room temperature before cooking. This should take no more than two hours—one hour if the room is very warm.

If you do not have the time for this preferred method, thaw the wrapped bird at room temperature, allowing about one hour per pound. In an emergency, you can unwrap poultry and thaw it fast in a bowl of cold water. To speed things along, pull the legs and wings away from the body as soon as you can pry them loose. A three-pound

Cooking at high temperatures will be less dangerous if you follow a few simple tips:

▶ Water added to hot fat will always cause spattering. If possible, pat foods dry with a cloth or paper towel before you add them to the hot oil.

▶ Place food gently into any pan containing hot fat, or the fat will spatter.

▶ If you are boiling or steaming some foods while sautéing others, place the pots on the stove top far enough apart so that the water is unlikely to splash into the hot fat.

▶ Turn pot handles inward, so that you do not accidentally knock over a pot containing hot foods or liquids.

▶ Remember that alcohol—wine, brandy, or spirits—may catch fire when you add it to a very hot pan. If this happens, step back for your own protection and quickly cover the pan with a lid. The fire will instantly subside, and the food will not be spoiled.

▶ Keep pot holders and mitts close enough to be handy while cooking, but *never* hang them over the burners or lay them on the stove top.

chicken should thaw in about an hour this way. Never defrost a frozen chicken in hot water—however great the temptation may be. The surface of the meat will begin to cook and will turn dry and tasteless in the recipe.

Be sure to wipe a defrosted bird inside and out before cooking.

Eggs

All fresh eggs require refrigeration. Eggs left out at room temperature will deteriorate more in one day than in one week of refrigeration. Never rinse eggs before storing them—you will wash away the light protective coating of tasteless mineral oil that is sprayed onto most eggs to seal their porous shells. Eggs stored large-end up in their carton in the coldest part of the refrigerator should keep for five weeks. Do not store eggs near onions or other aromatic foods or the eggs may absorb the aromas through their shells.

Hard-boiled eggs in their shells should be refrigerated as soon as possible after they cook and be used within a week. Peeled hard-boiled eggs placed in an airtight container or submerged in cold water will last two days in the refrigerator before becoming tough.

If a recipe calls for egg whites only, you can store any unbroken yolks in water in a covered container to use within a day or two. If a recipe calls for only the yolks, the unused whites may be stored in a covered jar for up to ten days.

Vegetables

Many fresh vegetables can be stored for up to a week if kept wrapped in plastic in the coldest part of the refrigerator. Exceptions are onions and garlic, potatoes, sweet potatoes, rutabagas, and hard-shell squash, which should be kept in a dry cool spot away from direct light. Onions should not be stored near potatoes because they absorb moisture from the potatoes, which causes them to decay.

GENERAL COOKING TECHNIQUES

Mastering the following techniques will help you prepare many of the main courses and side dishes in this volume.

Sautéing

Sautéing is a form of quick frying, with no cover on the pan. In French, *sauter* means "to jump," which is what vegetables or small pieces of food do when you shake the sauté pan. The purpose is to brown the food lightly and seal in the juices, sometimes before further cooking. This technique has three critical elements: the right pan, the proper temperature, and dry food.

The sauté pan: A proper sauté pan is ten to twelve inches in diameter and has two- to three-inch straight sides; it allows you to turn the food and still keep the fat from spattering. It has a heavy bottom that can be moved back and forth easily across a burner.

The best material (and the most expensive) for a sauté pan is tin-lined copper because it is a superior heat conductor. Heavy-gauge cast aluminum works well but will discolor acidic food like tomatoes. Another option is to select a heavy-duty sauté pan made of strong, heat-conducting aluminum alloys. This type of professional cookware is smooth and stick resistant. Be sure you buy a sauté pan with a handle that is long and comfortable to hold, and with a tight-fitting cover, since many recipes call for covered cooking following the initial sautéing.

Use a sauté pan large enough to hold the food without crowding, or sauté in two batches. The heat of the fat and the air spaces between the pieces facilitate browning. Crowding results in steaming, which releases juices.

Use a wooden spoon or tongs to keep the food moving in the pan as you shake the pan over the burner. If the food sticks, as it occasionally will, a metal spatula will loosen it best. Turn the food so that all surfaces come into contact with the hot fat. Do not use a fork when sautéing meat; piercing the meat will allow the juices to escape, causing the meat to become tough and dry.

The fat: Half butter and half vegetable oil is perfect for most sautéing. It heats to high temperatures without burning, yet imparts a rich butter flavor. For cooking, unsalted butter tastes best and adds no unwanted salt to the recipe.

If you prefer an all-butter flavor, clarify the butter before you begin. This means removing the milk solids (which scorch easily) from the oils. To clarify butter, heat it in a small heavy saucepan over medium heat and, using a cooking spoon, skim off and discard the foam as it rises to the top. Keep skimming until no more foam appears. Pour off the remaining liquid, which is the clarified butter, leaving the milky residue at the bottom of the pan. Clarify butter as you need it, or to save time, make a large quantity and store it in the refrigerator for up to three weeks.

Some sautéing recipes in this book call for olive oil, which imparts a delicious and distinctive flavor of its own and is less sensitive than butter to high heat. Nevertheless, even the finest olive oil has some residue of fruit pulp, which will occasionally scorch. Watch carefully when you sauté in olive oil; discard any scorched oil and start with fresh, if necessary.

To sauté properly, heat the fat until it is hot but not smoking. When you see small bubbles on top of the fat, lower the heat because it is on the verge of smoking. When using butter and oil together, add butter to the hot oil. After the foam from the melting butter subsides, you are ready to sauté. If the temperature of the fat is just right, the food will sizzle when you put it in the pan.

Searing
Searing is somewhat like sautéing, but you need slightly hotter fat. When you sear, you brown the meat without shaking or stirring the pan. Heat the oil until it is very hot, then brown the meat over high heat for a minute or two on each side. A metal spatula is essential, for the meat will tend to stick. Wait until the meat is very brown on one side before you turn it.

Deglazing
Deglazing is an easy way to create a sauce for sautéed, braised, or roasted food. To deglaze a pan, pour off all but one or two tablespoons of the fat in which the food has been cooked. Add liquid—water, wine, or stock—and reduce the sauce over medium heat, using a wooden spoon to scrape up the concentrated juices and brown bits of food clinging to the bottom of the pan.

Stir Frying
The basic cooking method for Chinese cuisine, this fast-cook technique requires very little oil, and the foods—which you stir continuously—fry quickly over a very high heat. Stir frying is ideal for cooking bite-size, shredded, or thinly sliced portions of vegetables, fish, meat, or poultry, alone or in combination.

Braising
Braising is simmering meats or vegetables in a relatively small amount of liquid, usually for a long period of time. Occasionally, foods that do not need tenderizing may be braised more quickly to impart flavor. Sometimes the food is browned or parboiled before braising. You may wish to flavor the braising liquid with herbs, spices, and aromatic vegetables, or use wine, stock, or tomato sauce.

Glazing
Glazing vegetables in their cooking liquid, butter, and a little sugar gives them a slight sheen as the butter and sugar reduce to a syrupy consistency. Glazing enhances the vegetables' flavor and appearance, and they need no additional sauce.

Steaming
Steaming is a fast and nutritious way to cook vegetables and other food. Bring water to a boil in a saucepan. Place the food in a steamer or on a rack over the liquid and cover the pan, periodically checking the water level. Keeping the food above the liquid preserves vitamins and minerals often lost in other methods of cooking.

Blanching
Also called parboiling, blanching is an invaluable technique. Immerse whole or cut vegetables for a few moments in boiling water, then "refresh" them—that is, plunge them into cold water to stop their cooking and set their colors. Blanching softens or tenderizes dense or crisp vegetables, often as a preliminary to further cooking by another method, such as stir frying.

Poaching
You poach meat, fish, chicken, fruit, and eggs in very hot liquid in a pan on top of the stove. You can use water or, better still, beef, chicken, or fish stock, or a combination of stock and white wine, or even cream as the poaching liquid. Bring the liquid to the simmering point and add the food. Be prepared to lower the heat if the liquid begins to boil.

Roasting and Baking
Roasting is a dry-heat process, usually used for large cuts of meat and poultry, that cooks food by exposing it to heated air in an oven or, perhaps, a covered barbecue. For more even circulation of heat, the food should be placed in a shallow pan or on a rack in a pan. For greater moisture retention, baste the food with its own juices, fat, or a flavorful marinade.

Baking applies to the dry-heat cooking of foods such as casseroles; small cuts of meat, fish, and poultry; vegetables; and, or course, breads and pastries. Some foods are baked tightly covered to retain their juices and flavors; others, such as breads, cakes, and cookies, are baked in open pans to release moisture.

Broiling and Grilling
These are two relatively fast ways to cook meat, poultry, and fish, giving food a crisp exterior while leaving the inside juicy. Whether broiling or grilling, brush the food with melted fat, a sauce, or marinade before you cook it. This adds flavor and moisture.

In broiling, the food cooks directly under the heat source. In grilling, the food cooks either directly over an open fire or on a well-seasoned cast-iron or stoneware griddle placed directly over a burner.

Equipment

Proper cooking equipment makes the work light and is a good cook's most prized possession. You can cook expertly without a store-bought steamer or even a food processor, but basic pans, knives, and a few other items are indispensable. Below are the things you need—and some attractive options—for preparing the menus in this volume.

Pots and pans
Large kettle or stockpot with cover
3 skillets (large, medium, small)
    with covers; one nonaluminum
2 heavy-gauge sauté pans, 10 to 12
    inches in diameter, with covers
    and ovenproof handles
3 saucepans with covers (1-, 2-, and
    4-quart capacities)
    Choose heavy-gauge enameled cast-
    iron, plain cast-iron, aluminum-clad
    stainless steel, and aluminum (but
    you need at least one saucepan that
    is not aluminum). Best—but very ex-
    pensive—is tin-lined copper.
Wok or Dutch oven with cover
Large, heavy-gauge roasting pan
    with rack
Broiler pan with rack
2 shallow baking pans
    (13 x 9 x 2-inch and 8 x 8-inch)
2 cookie sheets (11 x 17-inch and
    10 x 15-inch)
Large flameproof casserole with
    tight-fitting cover
Flameproof glass baking dish
Large heatproof serving bowl
2 heatproof serving platters
Four 4-ounce ovenproof ramekins
    or small custard cups
Four 8- to 12-ounce ovenproof
    ramekins or small custard cups
9-inch pie plate
Salad bowl

Knives
A carbon-steel knife takes a sharp
edge but tends to rust. You must
wash and dry it after each use; otherwise it can blacken foods and counter
tops. Good-quality stainless-steel
knives, frequently honed, are less
trouble and will serve just as well in
the home kitchen. Never put a fine
knife in the dishwasher. Rinse it, dry
it, and put it away—but not loose in
a drawer. Knives will stay sharp and
last a long time if they have their own
storage rack.

Small paring knife
10-inch chef's knife
Bread knife (serrated blade)
Sharpening steel

Other cooking tools
2 sets of mixing bowls in graduated
    sizes
Colander, with a round base
    (stainless steel, aluminum, or
    enamel)
2 strainers in fine and coarse mesh
2 sets of measuring cups and
    spoons in graduated sizes
    One for dry ingredients, another for
    shortenings and liquids.
Cooking spoon
Slotted spoon
Long-handled wooden spoons
Long-handled 2-tined cooking fork
Wooden spatula (for stirring hot
    ingredients)
2 metal spatulas, or turners (for
    lifting hot foods from pans)
Slotted spatula
Chinese metal wok spatula
Rubber or vinyl spatula (for folding
    in ingredients)
Rolling pin
Grater (metal, with several sizes of
    holes)
    A rotary grater is handy for hard
    cheese.
Small wire whisk
Balloon whisk
Pair of metal tongs
Wooden board
Garlic press
Vegetable peeler
Mortar and pestle
Vegetable steamer
Ladle
Pastry brush for basting (a small,
    new paintbrush that is not
    nylon serves well)
Vegetable brush
Stiff scrubbing brush
Cooling rack

Kitchen shears
Kitchen timer
Kitchen string
Aluminum foil
Paper towels
Plastic wrap
Waxed paper
Thin rubber gloves
Oven mitts or potholders

Electric appliances
Food processor or blender
    A blender will do most of the work
    required in this volume, but a food
    processor will do it more quickly and
    in larger volume. A food processor
    should be considered a necessity, not
    a luxury, for anyone who enjoys
    cooking.
Electric mixer

Optional cooking tools
Salad spinner
Salad servers
Citrus juicer
    Inexpensive glass kind from the
    dime store will do.
Nutmeg grater
Deep-fat thermometer
Metal skewers
Toothpicks
Roll of masking tape or white paper
    tape for labeling and dating

Pantry

A well-stocked, properly organized pantry is essential for preparing great meals in the shortest time possible. Whether your pantry consists of a small refrigerator and two or three shelves over the sink, or a large freezer, refrigerator, and entire room just off the kitchen, you must protect staples from heat and light.

In maintaining your pantry, follow these rules:

1. Store staples by kind and date. Canned goods, canisters, and spices need a separate shelf, or a separate spot on a shelf. Date all staples—shelved, refrigerated, or frozen—by writing the date directly on the package or on a bit of masking tape. Then put the oldest ones in front to be sure you use them first.

2. Store flour, sugar, and other dry ingredients in canisters or jars with tight lids. Glass and clear plastic allow you to see at a glance how much remains.

3. Keep a running grocery list so that you can note when a staple is half gone, and be sure to stock up.

ON THE SHELF:

Anchovies
Anchovy fillets, both flat and rolled, come oil-packed, in tins. If you buy whole, salt-packed anchovies, they must be cleaned under running water, skinned, and boned. To bone, separate the fish with your fingers and slip out the backbone.

Capers
Capers are usually packed in vinegar and less frequently in salt. If you use the latter, you should rinse them under cold water before using them.

Cornstarch
Less likely to lump than flour, cornstarch is an excellent thickener for sauces. Substitute in the following proportions: 1 tablespoon cornstarch to 2 of flour.

Flour
all-purpose, bleached or unbleached

Garlic
Store in a cool, dry, well-ventilated place. Garlic powder and garlic salt are not adequate substitutes for fresh garlic.

Herbs and spices
The flavor of fresh herbs is much better than that of dried. Fresh herbs should be refrigerated and used as soon as possible. The following herbs are perfectly acceptable dried, but buy in small amounts, store airtight in dry area away from heat and light, and use as quickly as possible. In measuring herbs, remember that one part dried will equal three parts fresh. *Note:* Dried chives and parsley should not be on your shelf, since they have little or no flavor; frozen chives are acceptable. Buy whole spices rather than ground, as they keep their flavor much longer. Grind spices at home and store as directed for herbs.

aniseed
basil
bay leaves
Cayenne pepper
cinnamon
cloves, whole and ground
coriander, whole and ground
cumin, whole and ground
dill
ginger
mustard (powdered)
nutmeg, whole and ground
oregano
pepper
   black peppercorns
   These are unripe peppercorns dried in their husks. Grind with a pepper mill for each use.
   white peppercorns
   These are the same as the black variety, but are picked ripe and husked. Use them in pale sauces when black pepper specks would spoil the appearance.
red pepper flakes (also called crushed red pepper)
rosemary
saffron
   Made from the dried stigmas of a species of crocus, this spice—the most costly of all seasonings—adds both color and flavor. Use sparingly.
salt
   Use coarse salt—commonly available as kosher or sea—for its superior flavor, texture, and purity. Kosher salt and sea salt are less salty than table salt. Substitute in the following proportions: three-quarters teaspoon table salt equals just under one teaspoon kosher or sea salt.
tarragon
thyme

Nuts, whole, chopped, or slivered
pine nuts (pignoli)
walnuts

Oils
corn, safflower, peanut, or vegetable
   Because these neutral-tasting oils have high smoking points, they are good for high-heat sautéing.
olive oil
   Olive oil ranges in color from pale yellow to dark green and in taste from mild and delicate to rich and fruity. Different olive oils can be used for different purposes: for example, lighter ones for cooking, stronger ones for salads. The finest olive oil is labeled extra-virgin or virgin.
sesame oil
   Dark amber-colored Oriental-style oil, used for seasoning; do not substitute light cold-pressed sesame oil.
walnut oil
   Rich and nutty tasting. It turns rancid easily, so keep it in a tightly closed container in the refrigerator.

Onions
Store all dry-skinned onions in a cool, dry, well-ventilated place.
red or Italian onions
   Zesty tasting and generally eaten raw. The perfect salad onions.
shallots
   The most subtle member of the onion family, shallots have a delicate garlic flavor.
Spanish onions
   Very large with a sweet flavor, they are best for stuffing and baking and are also eaten raw. Perfect for sandwiches.
yellow onions
   All-purpose cooking onions, strong in taste.

Potatoes, boiling and baking
"New" potatoes are not a particular kind of potato, but any potato that has not been stored.

Rice
long-grain white rice
   Slender grains, much longer than they are wide, that become light and fluffy when cooked and are best for general use.

Soy sauce

Chinese
Usually quite salty and richly flavored—for cooking.

Japanese
Less salty and more delicate than Chinese—for use as a table sauce and in cooking.

Stock, chicken and beef
For maximum flavor and quality, your own stock is best (see recipe page 13), but canned stock, or broth, is adequate for most recipes and convenient.

Sugar
light brown sugar
granulated sugar

Tomatoes
Italian plum tomatoes
Canned plum tomatoes (preferably imported) are an acceptable substitute for fresh.

tomato paste
Spoon single tablespoons of unused canned paste onto waxed paper and freeze them. Lift frozen paste off and store in plastic container. Sometimes available in tubes, which can be stored in the refrigerator after a small amount is used.

Vinegars
apple cider vinegar (also called cider vinegar)
Use for a mild, fruity flavor.
balsamic vinegar
Aged vinegar with a complex sweet and sour taste.
red and white wine vinegars
sherry vinegar
Somewhat less sharp than most wine vinegars, it has a deeper, fuller flavor.

Wines and spirits
Cognac or other brandy
sherry, dry
red wine, dry
white wine, dry

IN THE REFRIGERATOR:

Basil
Though fresh basil is widely available only in summer, try to use it whenever possible to replace dried; the flavor is markedly superior. Stand the stems, preferably with roots intact, in a jar of water, and loosely cover leaves with a plastic bag.

Bread crumbs
You need never buy bread crumbs. To make fresh crumbs, use fresh or day-old bread and process in food processor or blender. For dried, toast bread 30 minutes in preheated 250-degree oven, turning occasionally to prevent slices from browning. Proceed as for fresh. Store bread crumbs in an airtight container: fresh crumbs in the refrigerator, and dried crumbs in a cool, dry place. Either type may also be frozen for several weeks if tightly wrapped in a plastic bag.

Butter
Many cooks prefer unsalted butter because of its finer flavor and because it does not burn as easily as salted.

Cheese
Cheddar cheese, sharp
A firm cheese, ranging in color from nearly white to yellow. Cheddar is a versatile cooking cheese.
Gruyère
This firm cheese resembles Swiss, but has smaller holes and a sharper flavor. A quality Gruyère will have a slight "gleam" in its eyes, or holes.
Mozzarella
This favorite pizza cheese is bland and semi-firm in its packaged form; freshly made mozzarella is moister and more delicate. Both melt superbly.
Parmesan cheese
Avoid the pre-grated packaged variety; it is very expensive and almost flavorless. Buy Parmesan by the quarter- or half-pound wedge and grate as needed: 4 ounces produces about one cup of grated cheese. Romano, far less costly, can be substituted, but its flavor is considerably sharper—or try mixing the two.
Romano
This Italian grating cheese may be made from sheep's milk (pecorino Romano) or cow's milk.

Chives
Refrigerate fresh chives wrapped in plastic. You may also buy small pots of growing chives—keep them on a windowsill and snip as needed.

Coriander
Also called *cilantro* or Chinese parsley, its pungent leaves resemble flat-leaf parsley. Keep in a glass of water covered with a plastic bag.

Cream
heavy cream
sour cream

Eggs
Will keep 4 to 5 weeks in refrigerator. For best results, bring to room temperature before using, except when separating.

Ginger, fresh
Found in the produce section. Wrap in a paper towel, then in plastic, and refrigerate; it will keep for about 1 month, but should be checked weekly for mold. Or, if you prefer, store it in the freezer, where it will last about 3 months. Firm, smooth-skinned ginger need not be peeled.

Lemons
In addition to its many uses in cooking, a slice of lemon rubbed over cut apples and pears will keep them from discoloring. Do not substitute bottled juice or lemon extract.

Milk

Mint
Fresh mint will keep for a week if wrapped in a damp paper towel and enclosed in a plastic bag.

Mustard
The recipes in this book usually call for Dijon or coarse-ground mustard.

Parsley
The two most commonly available kinds of parsley are flat-leaved and curly; they can be used interchangeably when necessary. Flat-leaved parsley has a more distinctive flavor and is generally preferred in cooking. Curly parsley wilts less easily and is excellent for garnishing. Store parsley in a glass of water and cover loosely with a plastic bag. It will keep for a week in the refrigerator. Or wash and dry it, and refrigerate in a small plastic bag with a dry paper towel inside to absorb any moisture.

Scallions
Scallions have a mild onion flavor. Store wrapped in plastic.

Yogurt

BEEF & VEAL

Stevie Bass

When cooking for her own pleasure, food consultant Stevie Bass experiments with unusual ingredients and unexpected flavor combinations. Her goal is to create harmonious meals that balance color, texture, and flavor. Although the finished product may look complicated, Stevie Bass's recipes require minimal fuss. In Menu 1, an Oriental meal, she features two popular Vietnamese dishes. Asparagus (introduced to Vietnam by the French, and known there as "Western bamboo") is paired with crab meat to create a light, refreshing soup. The main course—beef balls and noodles seasoned with soy sauce and ginger and then wrapped in lettuce packages—is traditionally served as an appetizer in Vietnam. To accompany them, Stevie Bass offers a choice of sweet-spicy dipping sauces.

Both Menu 2 and Menu 3 are easy meals but elegant enough for guests. Menu 2 features a delicately seasoned veal and vegetable stew in a cream-puff pastry crust. In Menu 3, Stevie Bass combines steak and veal sweetbread kabobs with stir-fried fresh vegetables and a green salad dressed with a mustard-flavored glaze. Menu 4 features Stevie Bass's version of an Italian classic—pesto. Pesto is most often used for pasta; in this dish, it accompanies pan-fried sirloin steaks.

Serve this Oriental meal buffet fashion, and let your guests help themselves by ladling crab meat and asparagus soup into bowls, then removing the beef balls from the skewers and wrapping them in lettuce leaves, Vietnamese style. Maifun noodles, mint leaves, scallions, and a dipping sauce for the lettuce packages are also on the buffet table. Garnish the snow pea, mushroom, and cherry tomato salad with toasted sesame seeds.

Crab and Asparagus Soup
Vietnamese Lettuce-Wrap Beef
Snow Peas and Mushrooms with Tangy Dressing

Wrapping food in leaves is an ancient custom, particularly in Southeast Asia. For this version, each person takes the beef balls off the skewer, then puts one or two of the balls on a lettuce leaf, adds fresh mint leaves, scallions, and noodles to taste, and then folds the package up. It is then dipped in a sauce.

Mint is an integral part of the flavor balance here, but you may substitute fresh celery leaves or parsley. Also known as rice noodles or rice sticks, *maifun* are thin ivory-colored noodles made from rice flour. Chinese groceries and some supermarkets sell them. You can substitute Japanese ramen noodles, which are available in the soup section of most supermarkets.

The sauce shown here is made from apricot nectar combined with Chinese *hoisin* sauce. You will find *hoisin* in many supermarkets and in Chinese groceries.

WHAT TO DRINK

With the Oriental spices and the strong fruit flavor of the sauces, try a soft slightly sweet white wine such as a light German Riesling or a California Chenin Blanc.

SHOPPING LIST AND STAPLES

1¼ to 1½ pounds lean ground beef
¼ pound fresh crab meat, or 6-ounce can
1 pound asparagus
½ pound fresh snow peas, or two 6-ounce packages frozen
¼ pound mushrooms
1 pint cherry tomatoes
1 head iceberg lettuce (about 1 pound)
1 bunch scallions
Small bunch fresh coriander
1 bunch fresh mint
1¼-inch piece fresh ginger
3 large cloves garlic, plus 1 large clove (optional)
Small fresh peach (optional)
1 egg
3½ cups chicken stock, preferably homemade (see page 13), or canned
5½-ounce can apricot nectar
⅓ cup plus 2 tablespoons vegetable oil
½ cup *hoisin* sauce
4½ tablespoons soy sauce, plus 3 tablespoons (optional)
2 tablespoons white wine vinegar
7 ounces rice stick (*maifun*) or *ramen* noodles

2 tablespoons sugar, plus 1 tablespoon (optional)
3 tablespoons cornstarch
1 tablespoon sesame seeds
Freshly ground pepper

UTENSILS

Blender
Small heavy-gauge skillet
Large saucepan
Medium-size saucepan
Broiler pan
Large mixing bowl
Large salad bowl
2 small bowls
Colander
Salad spinner (optional)
Measuring cups and spoons
Chef's knife
Paring knife
Wooden spoon
Metal spatula
Grater
Whisk
Four 10-inch metal or bamboo skewers

START-TO-FINISH STEPS

At least 30 minutes ahead: If using bamboo skewers for lettuce wrap recipe, soak them in water to reduce charring.

1. Peel and mince garlic for soup and lettuce wrap recipes. Peel and grate ginger for lettuce wrap and snow peas recipes. Follow snow peas recipe steps 1 through 5.
2. Follow lettuce wrap recipe steps 1 through 6.
3. Chop coriander and follow crab and asparagus soup recipe steps 1 through 6. Serve soup.
4. Follow lettuce wrap recipe steps 7 and 8 and serve with snow peas.

RECIPES

Crab and Asparagus Soup

1 pound asparagus
Large clove garlic
2 scallions
2 tablespoons vegetable oil

¼ pound fresh crab meat, picked over, or 6-ounce can, well-drained
3½ cups chicken stock
3 tablespoons cornstarch
1 egg
Freshly ground pepper
2 tablespoons chopped fresh coriander

1. Wash asparagus. Trim and peel, if desired. In large saucepan, combine asparagus with ½ inch water, cover pan, and bring to a boil over high heat. Cook just until crisp-tender, 4 to 12 minutes; cooking time will vary with size. Drain, cut into 2-inch lengths, and set aside.
2. Peel and mince garlic. Wash, trim, and chop enough scallions to measure ¼ cup.
3. In saucepan used for asparagus, heat oil over medium-high heat. Add garlic and half the scallions and sauté until tender, about 2 minutes. Turn heat to high, add crab meat, and, stirring with wooden spoon, sauté about 3 minutes. Pour in chicken stock and bring to a boil.
4. In small bowl, blend cornstarch with 2 tablespoons cold water. Add mixture to boiling soup, stirring constantly, until soup thickens, 1 to 2 minutes. Rinse out bowl.
5. In rinsed bowl, whisk egg briefly and stir into boiling soup. Cook, stirring, about 1 minute. Add asparagus and cook just until heated through. Season to taste with pepper.
6. Transfer soup to serving bowl and sprinkle with coriander and remaining scallions.

Vietnamese Lettuce-Wrap Beef

The beef balls and wrap:
1 head iceberg lettuce (about 1 pound)
1 bunch mint
3 scallions
2 large cloves garlic, peeled and minced
1¼ to 1½ pounds lean ground beef
3 tablespoons soy sauce
¾ teaspoon peeled and grated fresh ginger

1 cup rice stick (*maifun*) or *ramen* noodles (without soup seasoning)

The apricot-hoisin sauce:
½ cup apricot nectar
½ cup *hoisin* sauce

The peach-ginger sauce (optional):
Small fresh peach
3 tablespoons soy sauce
¾-inch piece fresh ginger
Large clove garlic, peeled
1 tablespoon sugar

1. Core lettuce and separate into leaves. Wash lettuce leaves and mint, and dry in salad spinner or pat dry with paper towels. Strip enough leaves from mint stems to measure ¾ cup. Wash and trim scallions. Cut crosswise into ⅛-inch rounds. Put lettuce leaves, mint, and scallions in separate serving bowls and set aside.

2. In large bowl, combine beef, garlic, soy sauce, and ginger. Shape into 24 balls of uniform size, 1 to 1½ inches in diameter. String on metal or bamboo skewers.
3. In medium-size saucepan used for snow peas, bring 1 quart water to a boil. Add noodles. Return to a boil and cook 3 minutes. Drain noodles in colander and rinse with cold water to remove starchiness. Turn into serving bowl.
4. Preheat broiler.
5. For apricot-*hoisin* sauce, combine apricot nectar with *hoisin* sauce in small serving bowl and stir until blended.
6. For peach-ginger sauce, if using, wash and pit peach; do not peel. In blender, combine peach, soy sauce, ginger, garlic, and sugar. Process until smooth. Pour into small serving bowl.
7. Place skewers on broiler pan. Broil approximately 3 inches from heating element about 5 minutes, turning skewers once or twice. Transfer to serving platter.
8. Bring the beef balls, lettuce, scallions, mint, noodles, apricot-*hoisin* sauce, and peach-ginger sauce, if serving, to the table. Each person serves himself or herself by putting a beef ball on a lettuce leaf, adding the desired ingredients, wrapping the lettuce leaf around them, and then dipping the bundle into either sauce.

Snow Peas and Mushrooms with Tangy Dressing

1 tablespoon sesame seeds
2 tablespoons white wine vinegar
2 tablespoons sugar
1½ teaspoons soy sauce
1 teaspoon fresh ginger, peeled and grated
⅓ cup vegetable oil
2 cups cherry tomatoes
¼ pound mushrooms
½ pound fresh snow peas,
    or two 6-ounce packages frozen

1. In small skillet, toast sesame seeds over medium heat until they turn light brown, about 2 minutes. Stir with metal spatula and shake skillet frequently to keep seeds from burning.
2. For dressing, combine vinegar, sugar, soy sauce, and ginger in blender. With blender running at low speed, add oil in a slow, steady stream and blend until mixture is thick and smooth.
3. Wash cherry tomatoes and halve. Clean mushrooms with damp paper towels and halve.
4. If using fresh snow peas, trim stem ends, pulling along pod to remove "string." In medium-size saucepan, combine snow peas with 1 cup water. Cover pan, bring to a boil, and cook until crisp-tender, about 2 minutes. Drain in colander and refresh under cold running water. If using frozen snow peas, remove from package, place in colander, and hold under hot tap water just long enough to thaw.
5. In salad bowl, combine snow peas, tomatoes, and mushrooms. Sprinkle with toasted sesame seeds, and toss with dressing. Transfer to platter, cover with plastic wrap, and refrigerate until ready to serve.

Sweet Pea Soup
Veal in Gougère
Broccoli Caesar

Sautéed cubes of veal garnished with chopped parsley come to the table in individual pastry-lined baking dishes. They are complemented by a tart broccoli salad. Serve the pea soup for the first course.

T he pastry liner for each baking dish is a version of the French *pâte à chou,* or cream-puff pastry: it puffs up as it bakes and holds its shape when it cools. Line the sides of the dishes only, as pastry on the bottom will become soggy. You can bake the pastry several hours in advance, since the veal-and-vegetable filling will reheat it.

WHAT TO DRINK

A light, fruity red wine—a Bardolino or Valpolicella from Italy, or a Beaujolais from France—would be good here.

SHOPPING LIST AND STAPLES

1½ pounds boneless veal top or bottom round, or veal sirloin tip (leg round roast), cut into ¾- to 1-inch cubes
2 slices bacon (about 2 ounces)
1 bunch broccoli (about 1 to 1¼ pounds)
½ pound mushrooms
1 lemon
2 large cloves garlic
Small bunch scallions
Small bunch fresh parsley
Small bunch fresh thyme, or ½ teaspoon dried
Small bunch fresh dill, or ¾ teaspoon dried
3 eggs
5 tablespoons unsalted butter
½ pint heavy cream
½ pint sour cream (optional)
¼ pound Parmesan cheese
1-pound polybag frozen whole small onions
17-ounce can sweet peas
1 cup chicken stock, preferably homemade (see page 13), or canned
1 tablespoon tomato paste
½ cup olive oil or vegetable oil
3 tablespoons white wine vinegar
½ cup plus 2 tablespoons flour
¼ teaspoon dry mustard
Salt and freshly ground pepper
¾ cup dry red wine

UTENSILS

Blender
Large heavy-gauge skillet
2 medium-size saucepans with covers
Four 7½ x 4½ x 1½-inch oval ceramic gratin dishes

Large bowl
Large salad bowl
Medium-size bowl
Small bowl
Colander
Measuring cups and spoons
Chef's knife
Paring knife
Large metal spoon
Slotted spoon
Wooden spoon
Metal spatula
Flexible-blade spatula
Rubber spatula
Grater

START-TO-FINISH STEPS

1. Follow veal in gougère recipe steps 1 and 2.
2. While gougère is baking, follow broccoli recipe step 1.
3. While broccoli is cooking, follow soup recipe step 1.
4. Follow broccoli recipe step 2.
5. Remove gougère from oven and follow veal recipe steps 3 and 4.
6. Follow soup recipe steps 2 and 3, and serve.
7. Follow veal recipe steps 5 through 7, and serve with broccoli.

RECIPES

Sweet Pea Soup

¼ cup chopped scallions
17-ounce can sweet peas, drained
1 cup chicken stock
⅓ cup parsley sprigs, packed
1½ teaspoons chopped fresh dill or ½ teaspoon dried
½ cup heavy cream
Sour cream for garnish (optional)

1. In blender, combine scallions, peas, stock, parsley, dill, and heavy cream. Turning blender on and off, blend mixture until it is as smooth as possible. When blender clogs, turn it off to push ingredients down before proceeding.
2. Transfer mixture to medium-size saucepan used for broccoli. Heat over medium-low heat until piping hot, stirring often, but do not allow soup to boil.
3. Pour into individual bowls and garnish with a dollop of sour cream, if desired.

Veal in Gougère

5 tablespoons unsalted butter
½ cup plus 2 tablespoons flour
1 tablespoon freshly grated Parmesan cheese
2 eggs
2 slices bacon (about 2 ounces)
1½ pounds boneless veal top or bottom round, or veal sirloin tip, cut into ¾- to 1-inch cubes

1 cup frozen whole small onions, thawed
½ pound mushrooms, cleaned and halved
1 tablespoon tomato paste
Large clove garlic, minced
1½ teaspoons chopped fresh thyme, or ½ teaspoon dried
¾ cup dry red wine
Salt and freshly ground pepper
4 teaspoons chopped fresh parsley

1. Preheat oven to 400 degrees. In medium-size saucepan, bring ½ cup water and 4 tablespoons butter to a boil over medium heat. When butter has melted, remove pan from heat. Add ½ cup flour all at once and Parmesan cheese. Beat vigorously until mixture comes away from sides of pan and forms a ball. Stir in unbeaten eggs, one at a time, beating thoroughly after each addition.
2. Using flexible-blade spatula, spread mixture about ½ inch thick only against sides, not bottom, of baking dishes. Bake until richly golden, about 18 to 20 minutes.
3. Dice bacon and fry in large skillet until crisp. Using slotted spoon, transfer to paper towels.
4. In skillet with bacon fat, melt remaining tablespoon butter over high heat. Add half of the veal cubes and sauté, stirring frequently with metal spatula, until browned, but still pink inside, about 2 minutes. Transfer to large bowl. Repeat with remaining cubes. Cover bowl with foil.
5. For sauce, add onions, mushrooms, tomato paste, garlic, thyme, wine, ½ cup water, salt and pepper to taste to drippings in skillet. Bring to a boil over high heat, then simmer, uncovered, 5 minutes. Add veal and bacon.
6. In small bowl, blend remaining 2 tablespoons flour with ¼ cup water and gradually stir paste into veal mixture. Over medium-high heat, cook mixture, stirring, until thickened, about 2 minutes.
7. Spoon hot veal mixture into pastry-lined dishes, and garnish with parsley.

Broccoli Caesar

1 bunch broccoli (about 1 to 1¼ pounds)
Large clove garlic, peeled and minced
1 tablespoon lemon juice
¼ teaspoon dry mustard
¼ teaspoon salt
Dash of freshly ground pepper
1 egg
3 tablespoons white wine vinegar
½ cup olive oil or vegetable oil

1. Wash broccoli thoroughly and trim. Peel stems, if desired, and cut into spears. In medium-size saucepan, bring 1 inch water to a boil. Add broccoli, cover, and return to a boil. Boil gently 5 to 8 minutes, or until crisp-tender. Drain immediately in colander and refresh under cold running water.
2. In salad bowl, combine garlic, lemon, mustard, salt, pepper, egg, vinegar, and oil. With fork, stir until well blended. Add broccoli and toss gently but thoroughly with dressing. Cover and refrigerate until ready to serve.

Steak and Sweetbread Kabobs
Stir-Fried Vegetables
Green Salad with Mustard Glaze

Arrange the steak and sweetbread kabobs on a large platter, and serve the vegetables and tossed salad on the side.

Fresh veal sweetbreads should be plump and rosy, and encased in a shiny membrane. They are prepared by washing thoroughly, parboiling to firm them, and then removing the membrane. Since they are precooked, the sweetbreads broil as quickly as the steak cubes. Most supermarkets sell sweetbreads.

WHAT TO DRINK

The bright, straightforward flavors of this menu need a simple, robust red wine to accompany them. Try a young California Zinfandel or an Italian or California Barbera.

SHOPPING LIST AND STAPLES

1 pound veal sweetbreads
1 pound boneless beef sirloin (beef loin sirloin steak), cut into 1½-inch cubes
4 bacon slices (about 3 ounces)
1 head Romaine or iceberg lettuce
Large zucchini and large crookneck, or summer, squash (about 1¼ pounds total weight)
1 bunch celery
1 pint cherry tomatoes
2 lemons, plus 1 additional lemon (optional)
4 large cloves garlic

32

Small bunch fresh parsley (optional)
Small bunch fresh tarragon, or 2 teaspoons dried
1 stick unsalted butter
1 tablespoon Dijon mustard
½ cup plus 2 tablespoons vegetable oil
⅓ cup white wine vinegar
2 teaspoons soy sauce
5 teaspoons sugar
1¼ teaspoons salt
Freshly ground pepper

UTENSILS

Blender
2 medium-size heavy-gauge skillets
Large saucepan
Small saucepan
Broiler pan
Strainer
Salad spinner (optional)
Measuring cups and spoons
Chef's knife
Paring knife
Metal spatula
Basting brush
Four 12-inch metal or bamboo skewers

START-TO-FINISH STEPS

At least 30 minutes ahead: If using bamboo skewers for kabobs, soak them in water to reduce charring.

1. Follow salad recipe steps 1 and 2.
2. Follow kabobs recipe steps 1 and 2 and vegetables recipe step 1.
3. Follow kabobs recipe steps 3 through 5.
4. Follow vegetables recipe step 2.
5. Follow kabobs recipe step 6. Cut several strips of lemon peel for garnish, if using. Immediately after turning skewers, follow vegetables recipe step 3.
6. Follow salad recipe step 3.
7. Follow kabobs recipe step 7 and serve with stir-fried vegetables and salad.

RECIPES

Steak and Sweetbread Kabobs

2 lemons
1 pound veal sweetbreads
1 teaspoon salt
4 bacon slices
1 pound boneless beef sirloin (beef loin sirloin steak), cut into 1½-inch cubes
Freshly ground pepper
2 large cloves garlic, peeled and minced
1 stick unsalted butter
2 tablespoons chopped fresh tarragon, or 2 teaspoons dried, crumbled

1. Squeeze enough lemon to measure 5 tablespoons juice.

Strain to remove pits. Wash sweetbreads in cool water. In large saucepan, combine sweetbreads with 1 quart water, 1 tablespoon lemon juice, and salt. Bring to a boil and simmer, covered, 15 minutes.
2. While sweetbreads are simmering, sauté bacon in skillet just until it begins to brown but is not crisp. Drain on paper towels. Cut into 1-inch lengths.
3. Preheat broiler. Drain sweetbreads in colander and refresh under cold water. Remove white membrane and cut into 1- to 1½-inch chunks.
4. Thread meat onto skewers, alternating beef cubes, bacon, and sweetbreads. Sprinkle with pepper to taste and arrange on broiler pan.
5. In small saucepan, combine butter, tarragon, garlic, and remaining lemon juice. Heat, stirring, just until butter melts. Brush basting sauce lightly over meat.
6. Broil meat approximately 3 inches from heating element 2 to 3 minutes on each side.
7. Transfer kabobs to platter. Pour any remaining tarragon butter into small bowl and serve separately.

Stir-Fried Vegetables

4 celery stalks
Large zucchini and large crookneck, or summer, squash
1 pint cherry tomatoes
2 tablespoons vegetable oil
2 teaspoons soy sauce

1. Wash and dry celery, zucchini, squash, and cherry tomatoes. Cut celery diagonally into ⅛-inch-thick slices. Cut zucchini and squash diagonally into 2-inch pieces, then slice into ⅛-inch julienne. Halve cherry tomatoes.
2. In medium-size skillet, heat oil over medium heat. Add celery, zucchini, and squash, and stir fry until crisp-tender, about 5 minutes.
3. Add tomatoes and soy sauce, and continue cooking just until heated through.

Green Salad with Mustard Glaze

1 head Romaine or iceberg lettuce
2 large cloves garlic, peeled
⅓ cup white wine vinegar
1 tablespoon Dijon mustard
5 teaspoons sugar
¼ teaspoon salt
½ cup vegetable oil

1. Wash lettuce, separate leaves, and dry in salad spinner or pat dry with paper towels. Tear enough leaves into bite-size pieces to measure 6 cups. Place in salad bowl, cover with plastic wrap, and refrigerate until ready to serve.
2. In blender, combine garlic, vinegar, mustard, sugar, and salt, and blend until smooth. With blender running, add vegetable oil in a slow, steady stream and blend until dressing is thick and smooth.
3. When ready to serve, pour enough dressing over lettuce to coat leaves well and toss. Serve any leftover dressing on side.

Summer Squash Soup
Steak with Pesto and Sour Cream
Marinated Zucchini Salad

Serve the pan-fried steak, topped with a spoonful of pesto and sour cream, and the marinated zucchini salad separately.

Sirloin steaks topped with sour cream and pesto are the entrée for this light summer dinner. Traditionally, Italian cooks use a mortar and pestle to grind the basil leaves, but a blender or food processor is faster. If you cannot find fresh basil, substitute dried basil and fresh parsley. The pesto will lack the intense taste and aroma of fresh basil, but the sauce will be delicious nonetheless.

WHAT TO DRINK

Choose a red wine with good body: a California Pinot Noir or a French Moulin à Vent.

SHOPPING LIST AND STAPLES

2 top sirloin steaks (beef top loin steaks), cut about
   ¾ inch thick (about 2 pounds total weight)
2 medium-size crookneck, or summer, squash
2 small zucchini (about 8 ounces total weight)
1 large tomato
1 medium-size carrot
1 medium-size onion
4 large cloves garlic
Large bunch fresh basil, or large bunch fresh parsley
   and 1 tablespoon dried basil

Small bunch fresh thyme, or ¼ teaspoon dried
Small bunch fresh marjoram, or ¼ teaspoon dried
Small bunch fresh rosemary, or ¼ teaspoon dried
Small bunch fresh dill, or ½ teaspoon dried
1½ cups milk
½ pint sour cream
4 tablespoons unsalted butter
¼ pound Parmesan or Romano cheese
1 pint plain yogurt
6-ounce can whole pitted black olives
⅔ cup olive oil
½ cup vegetable oil
⅓ cup white wine vinegar
¼ cup sugar
1 teaspoon instant chicken stock base
Salt and freshly ground pepper
3 tablespoons dry sherry

UTENSILS

Blender
Large skillet with cover
Large heavy-gauge skillet
Medium-size saucepan
Large bowl
Medium-size bowl
Small bowl
Salad bowl
9 x 9-inch metal pan, or pan with large surface area
Colander
Measuring cups and spoons
Chef's knife
Paring knife
Metal spatula
Grater
Vegetable peeler

START-TO-FINISH STEPS

1. Follow soup recipe steps 1 through 3.
2. While soup mixture is cooling, follow salad recipe steps 1 through 3. Put 4 soup bowls in refrigerator to chill.
3. Follow soup recipe step 4.
4. While soup is chilling, follow steak recipe step 1.
5. Follow soup recipe step 5 and serve.
6. Follow steak recipe steps 2 and 3, and serve with salad.

RECIPES

Summer Squash Soup

2 cups plain yogurt
1½ cups milk
2 tablespoons unsalted butter
2 medium-size crookneck squash, thinly sliced
Medium-size carrot, peeled and grated
Medium-size onion, peeled and minced
3 tablespoons sherry
¾ teaspoon chopped fresh dill, or ¼ teaspoon dried
1 teaspoon instant chicken stock base

1. In blender, combine yogurt and 1 cup milk, and blend 1 minute. Transfer mixture to medium-size bowl, cover, and refrigerate until needed.
2. In large skillet, melt butter over medium heat. Add squash, onion, carrot, and sherry. Cover pan and cook until squash is very tender, about 10 minutes.
3. Transfer vegetables to blender. Add dill and chicken stock base, and blend until mixture is smooth. Transfer mixture to large bowl and let cool about 10 minutes.
4. To vegetable mixture add 1½ cups of yogurt-milk mixture and the remaining milk. Stir until well blended and pour into metal pan with large surface area. Place in freezer to chill, about 15 minutes. Stir occasionally.
5. Serve in chilled bowls topped with yogurt-milk mixture.

Steak with Pesto and Sour Cream

Large bunch fresh basil, or large bunch fresh parsley combined with 1 tablespoon dried basil
1 cup freshly grated Parmesan or Romano cheese
⅔ cup olive oil
3 large cloves garlic, peeled
2 top sirloin steaks, ¾ inch thick (about 1 pound each)
Salt and freshly ground pepper
2 tablespoons unsalted butter
½ cup sour cream

1. Wash fresh basil or parsley and dry thoroughly. Discard thickest stems. You should have about 2 cups leaves. In blender, purée herbs, cheese, olive oil, and garlic.
2. Cut each steak in two and season with salt and pepper to taste. In large heavy-gauge skillet, melt butter over medium-high heat. Add steaks and cook 3 minutes per side for rare, 4 to 5 minutes per side for medium rare, and 7 to 8 minutes per side for well done.
3. Place a dollop of sour cream and another of pesto on each steak, and serve.

Marinated Zucchini Salad

2 cups ¼-inch-thick zucchini slices
½ cup vegetable oil
⅓ cup white wine vinegar
¼ cup sugar
Large clove garlic, peeled and minced
¾ teaspoon salt
¾ teaspoon chopped fresh thyme, or ¼ teaspoon dried
¾ teaspoon chopped fresh marjoram, or ¼ teaspoon dried
¾ teaspoon chopped fresh rosemary, or ¼ teaspoon dried
¾ teaspoon chopped fresh dill, or ¼ teaspoon dried
Large tomato, cut into wedges
½ cup whole pitted black olives, halved

1. In medium-size saucepan, bring 1 quart water to a boil. Add zucchini and simmer 2 minutes, or just until crisp-tender. Drain in colander, then pat dry.
2. In small bowl, combine oil, vinegar, sugar, garlic, salt, thyme, marjoram, rosemary, and dill.
3. Combine zucchini, tomato, and olives in salad bowl. Pour just enough dressing over salad to coat lightly and toss gently. Cover and refrigerate until ready to serve.

Victoria Fahey

MENU 1 (Left)
Chilled Avocado Soup
Marinated Beef Salad
Fruit Dipped in White and Dark Chocolate

MENU 2
Hearts of Romaine with Walnuts, Roquefort, and Oranges
Oven-Barbecued Beef Back Ribs
Gingered Carrots in Foil
Roast Potatoes

MENU 3
Peppered Veal Chops
Sautéed Red Peppers with Pancetta
Pasta with Toasted Pine Nuts and Parmesan Cheese

Before Victoria Fahey became a professional cook, she studied art. Now, as she works with foods, she uses their colors, textures, smells, and tastes to produce meals of great appeal to all the senses. As a seacoast resident, she gathers her own shellfish, and she is also able to pick wild mushrooms from nearby woods. In addition, she has access to the fine restaurants, well-stocked grocery stores, and exotic specialty food shops in San Francisco. Thus, her menus exhibit both cosmopolitan and country touches.

A well-composed meal, Menu 1 is representative of how Victoria Fahey blends tastes and contrasts textures and colors. The avocado soup appears smooth, yet conceals diced avocado, tomato, and chives. The subtle flavor of the soup is counterbalanced by the highly spiced main-course beef salad.

For Menu 2, the cook presents an all-American entrée of oven-roasted beef back ribs basted with a spicy barbecue sauce and served with oven-roasted potatoes. To offset the basic quality of the meat and potatoes, she serves foil-baked gingered carrots and a Romaine salad with walnuts, walnut oil, and Roquefort cheese.

Menu 3 is a company meal of Italian-style peppery veal chops, served with sautéed red-pepper strips and pancetta (Italian bacon), and fresh pasta tossed with toasted pine nuts and Parmesan cheese on the side.

Serve the marinated beef salad on a bed of shredded lettuce with lime slices, sesame seeds, crushed red pepper, and a border of melon slices. Garnish the chilled avocado soup with whole chive stalks arranged in a pattern. Dessert is unhulled whole strawberries and dried apricots dipped in white and dark chocolate.

37

Chilled Avocado Soup
Marinated Beef Salad
Fruit Dipped in White and Dark Chocolate

The exotic chilled beef salad, the entrée for this summer meal, features flavorings often associated with Southeast Asian cuisines: lime juice, fresh ginger, coriander, mint leaves, sesame oil, and the optional red pepper flakes and sesame seeds. You can make the salad with thinly sliced rare roast beef from a delicatessen. Or, you can use leftover rare roast beef that was cooked at home. If you like raw beef, a high-quality sirloin steak (sometimes sold as beef loin sirloin steak) sliced very thin and used raw is another alternative.

In this light menu, the dessert is sweet as well as refreshing. Coating fruit with melted chocolate, as you do here, is a variation on a classic candy-making technique. Use semisweet or bittersweet chocolate, as you prefer. Real chocolate, used for most candy or baking, is made from chocolate liquor—part cocoa butter and part cocoa solids. Read labels carefully and avoid imitation chocolate products. White chocolate, which this recipe also calls for, is technically not a chocolate at all because it does not contain any chocolate liquor. Made with cocoa butter, sugar, vanillin, and other flavorings, white chocolate tastes like mellow milk chocolate. Victoria Fahey believes the best chocolate is from Belgium. It is generally available in specialty food stores, but if you have difficulty finding it buy baking chocolate from your supermarket, or use top-quality pure chocolate candy bars. Melt the chocolate slowly in the top of a double boiler to keep it from scorching, and keep it free from moisture; otherwise it becomes granular. Chop the chocolate into small pieces first to make the melting easier. And chill the fruit before you dip it, so that the chocolate will harden on it faster.

WHAT TO DRINK

You need a crisp, dry white wine with good body and flavor: a California or an Italian Sauvignon Blanc, or a good-quality French Sancerre.

SHOPPING LIST AND STAPLES

1½ pounds cooked rare roast beef or raw sirloin
Large head Romaine lettuce
3 medium-size avocados, preferably dark, knobby Haas variety (about 1½ pounds total weight)
Medium-size tomato
4 limes
1 lemon (if not using lime juice for soup)
2 small cantaloupes (½ to ¾ pound each)
1 pint strawberries
Small bunch fresh cilantro or parsley
Small bunch fresh mint, or 1 teaspoon dried
1 bunch fresh chives
1-inch piece fresh ginger
½ pint heavy cream
2 cups chicken stock, preferably homemade (see page 13), or canned
6 tablespoons peanut oil
1 teaspoon sesame oil
1 tablespoon Dijon mustard
4 ounces dark chocolate
2 ounces white chocolate
½ pound dried apricots or other fresh or dried fruit
1 tablespoon sesame seeds (optional)
Red pepper flakes (optional)
1½ teaspoons salt

UTENSILS

Food processor or blender
Electric mixer
Large heavy-gauge skillet or sauté pan
Small heavy-gauge skillet (optional)
2 double boilers or 2 heatproof mixing bowls to fit in separate saucepans
2 medium-size mixing bowls
Small bowl
Serving platter
Large flat plate or platter
Salad spinner (optional)
Measuring cups and spoons
Chef's knife
Paring knife
Slotted metal spatula
Rubber spatula
2 wooden spoons
Juicer (optional)
Grater

START-TO-FINISH STEPS

One hour and 15 minutes ahead: Follow fruit recipe step 1.

1. Follow fruit recipe step 2.

2. In small heavy-gauge skillet, toast sesame seeds for beef recipe, if using, over medium-high heat, until they smell toasty and turn a light brown. Shake skillet frequently to keep seeds from scorching.

3. Follow soup recipe steps 1 through 3.

4. Follow beef recipe steps 1 through 5.

5. Follow soup recipe step 4 and serve.

6. Follow beef recipe steps 6 and 7 and serve.

7. Serve chocolate-dipped fruits for dessert.

RECIPES

Chilled Avocado Soup

3 medium-size avocados, preferably dark, knobby Haas variety
1 lime or lemon
2 cups chicken stock
1 cup heavy cream
1 tablespoon Dijon mustard
1 teaspoon salt
Medium-size tomato
1 bunch fresh chives

1. Put soup bowls, medium-size mixing bowl, and beaters in freezer to chill.

2. Peel and pit avocados. Juice lime or lemon. In food processor or blender, purée 2 avocados, chicken stock, ½ cup cream, mustard, 1 to 2 tablespoons lime or lemon juice, and salt until very smooth.

3. Halve and seed tomato. Cut tomato and remaining avocado into ¼-inch dice. Mince enough chives to measure 1 tablespoon, reserving unchopped stalks for garnish. Remove soup bowls from freezer. Spoon a portion of avocado chunks, tomato, and minced chives into each bowl. Top with puréed soup. Cover with plastic wrap and refrigerate until ready to serve.

4. Just before serving, whip remaining ½ cup cream in chilled bowl, with chilled beaters. Garnish soup with whipped cream and whole chive stalks, decoratively arranged.

Marinated Beef Salad

Large head Romaine lettuce
3 limes
1-inch piece fresh ginger
Small bunch fresh cilantro or parsley
Small bunch fresh mint, or 1 teaspoon dried
6 tablespoons peanut oil
1 teaspoon sesame oil
½ teaspoon salt
1½ pounds cooked rare roast beef or raw sirloin
2 small cantaloupes (½ to ¾ pound each)
1 tablespoon sesame seeds (optional)
Red pepper flakes (optional)

1. Put serving platter in freezer to chill. Wash lettuce and dry in salad spinner or pat dry with paper towels.

2. Grate lime rind. Squeeze enough lime juice to measure 4 tablespoons, reserving any extra. Cut 1 lime into wedges for garnish. Peel and mince ginger. Wash, dry, and chop cilantro and mint, if using fresh, to measure 1½ tablespoons each. Reserve unchopped cilantro and fresh mint for garnish. For dressing, combine 4 tablespoons peanut oil, sesame oil, salt, ginger root, chopped cilantro, and mint in small bowl. Set aside.

3. With chef's knife, slice meat into strips ⅛ to ¼ inch wide, and 1 to 1½ inches long, if not already sliced.

4. To cook raw meat, unless you prefer to serve it raw, heat remaining 2 tablespoons peanut oil in large heavy-gauge skillet or sauté pan over high heat. Add meat and cook, stirring constantly, just until meat is no longer pink, 30 to 60 seconds.

5. Using slotted metal spatula, transfer meat to chilled platter. Arrange cooked sirloin, precooked roast beef, or raw sirloin in single layer. Pour dressing over meat, cover loosely, and refrigerate until chilled.

6. Transfer meat and dressing to medium-size bowl and clean platter. Peel, seed, and slice cantaloupe and arrange around edge of platter. Shred lettuce and form bed in center. Using wooden spoons, toss meat with dressing to coat well. Spoon meat over lettuce. Sprinkle with reserved lime juice to taste.

7. Just before serving, garnish with mint, cilantro, and lime wedges. Top with sesame seeds and sprinkle lightly with red pepper flakes, if desired. Serve additional red pepper flakes on the side.

Fruit Dipped in White and Dark Chocolate

1 pint strawberries, unhulled, or 2 Navel oranges
½ pound dried apricots, or other fresh or dried fruit
4 ounces dark chocolate
2 ounces white chocolate

1. Rinse strawberries briefly in cold water. Gently pat dry with paper towels and let stand for at least 1 hour, turning once, to make sure all moisture has evaporated. If using oranges, peel and remove as much white pith as possible. Section with sharp paring knife by cutting between membranes. Arrange on paper towels and proceed as for strawberries. Referigerate fruit until ready to use.

2. In 2 double boilers, one for dark chocolate and one for white, or in 2 bowls set in separate saucepans, melt chocolate over—not in—simmering water. Line large flat plate or platter with wax paper. When chocolate is melted, hold a strawberry by its hull and dip about two thirds of berry in chocolate, leaving some red showing. Lightly scrape one side of strawberry on edge of double boiler or bowl to prevent a puddle of chocolate from forming on wax paper. Set strawberry on wax paper, scraped side down. Repeat for remaining berries. Dip some of the strawberries in white and some in dark chocolate. If you like, dip berry first in one and, when that hardens, dip partially in the other. Or, with a teaspoon, drizzle chocolate of one color over the other. Repeat dipping process with fruits of your choice.

Hearts of Romaine with Walnuts, Roquefort, and Oranges
Oven-Barbecued Beef Back Ribs
Gingered Carrots in Foil / Roast Potatoes

Victoria Fahey provides an indoors alternative to barbecuing by oven-roasting beef back ribs in a barbecue sauce. More flavorful and less fatty than short ribs, these back ribs are roasted quickly at a high temperature so that they are crisp on the outside and slightly rare on the inside. The spicy sauce adds flavor and prevents the meat from drying out.

Wrapping food before cooking tenderizes it and protects it from burning. Foil-wrapped foods, such as the gingered carrots here, steam quickly. Cut the foil package open when you serve the carrots, releasing a burst of appetizing

Beef back ribs, glazed with barbecue sauce, are the focal point of this informal meal. Served family style, the ribs are accompanied by roasted potatoes, ginger-flavored carrots, and hearts of Romaine lettuce.

aroma. Fresh ginger is available in many supermarkets or in Chinese groceries. Select ginger that is hard, smooth-skinned, and tan in color. For information on storing it, see page 23.

Toasted walnuts and walnut oil give the salad a rich, nutty taste. Walnut oil, more expensive than extra-virgin olive oil, is sold in specialty food shops. It turns rancid easily; close it tightly after each use and store it in your refrigerator.

WHAT TO DRINK

The piquant spicing of this menu will taste best with a dry and fruity red wine: a California Zinfandel, a French Beaujolais, or an Italian Dolcetto.

8 to 12 beef back ribs (about 4 to 6 pounds total weight)

1½ pounds boiling potatoes, preferably, or red-skinned or baking potatoes

1½ pounds carrots

3 large or 4 small heads Romaine lettuce (about 2½ pounds total weight)

2 oranges

1 lemon

1-inch piece fresh ginger, or ½ teaspoon ground ginger

4 tablespoons unsalted butter

4 ounces Roquefort cheese

2 tablespoons walnut oil

2 tablespoons cider vinegar

1 cup catsup

4 ounces walnut halves

1 cup plus 1 tablespoon brown sugar

1 teaspoon dry mustard

½ teaspoon ground cumin

⅛ teaspoon celery seed (optional)

Cayenne pepper

Salt

Freshly ground pepper

UTENSILS

Small heavy-gauge saucepan

Two 9 x 12-inch shallow baking sheets

9 x 13-inch jelly-roll pan

Rectangular ovenproof baking dish

Large bowl

Medium-size bowl
Small bowl
Salad spinner (optional)
Measuring cups and spoons
Chef's knife
Paring knife
Spatula
Juicer (optional)
Scissors
Basting brush
Vegetable peeler

START-TO-FINISH STEPS

1. Follow potatoes recipe steps 1 through 3.
2. While potatoes are baking, follow carrots recipe steps 1 through 5 and Romaine recipe steps 1 and 2.
3. Follow ribs recipe steps 1 and 2, and carrots recipe step 6.
4. While ribs, carrots, and potatoes are cooking, follow Romaine recipe steps 3 and 4.
5. Follow potatoes recipe step 4.
6. Remove carrots and potatoes from oven, cover potatoes loosely with foil, and set on stove top to keep warm.
7. Follow ribs recipe step 3, Romaine recipe step 5, and then ribs recipe step 4. While ribs are browning, serve Romaine salad.
8. Follow ribs recipe step 5.
9. Just before ribs are done, check carrots and potatoes to see if they are hot enough. If necessary, return to oven briefly.
10. Follow ribs recipe step 6 and serve with potatoes and carrots.

RECIPES

Hearts of Romaine with Walnuts, Roquefort, and Oranges

½ cup walnut halves
2 oranges
3 large or 4 small heads Romaine lettuce
1 lemon
2 tablespoons walnut oil
Pinch of Cayenne pepper
Salt
4 ounces Roquefort cheese

1. Break walnut halves into smaller pieces. Arrange in single layer on baking sheet and toast in 375-degree oven 3 to 5 minutes.
2. While walnuts are toasting, cut several strips of orange rind. Cut lengthwise into julienne strips and then crosswise into ⅛-inch dice. Measure 1 tablespoon and set aside.
3. Remove tough outer leaves from Romaine and reserve for another use. Separate tender inner leaves. Wash, if necessary, and dry in salad spinner or pat dry with paper towels. Arrange on round platter, radiating out from center, with larger leaves on bottom, smaller on top. Cover and refrigerate.
4. Halve oranges and squeeze enough juice to measure ½ cup. Squeeze lemon to measure 1 to 2 tablespoons juice. In small bowl, combine orange juice, lemon juice, walnut oil, Cayenne, and salt to taste. Set aside until ready to serve.
5. Crumble Roquefort. Stir dressing to recombine and drizzle over greens. Sprinkle with walnuts, crumbled Roquefort, and reserved orange rind and serve.

Oven-Barbecued Beef Back Ribs

1 cup catsup
1 cup brown sugar
2 tablespoons cider vinegar
1 teaspoon dry mustard
½ teaspoon ground cumin
⅛ teaspoon celery seed (optional)
Cayenne pepper
Salt
Freshly ground pepper
8 to 12 beef back ribs
    (about 4 to 6 pounds total weight)

1. For barbecue sauce, combine catsup, sugar, vinegar, dry mustard, cumin, celery seed, if using, and Cayenne pepper to taste in medium-size bowl.
2. Line baking sheet with foil. Salt and pepper ribs, and arrange in single layer on foil-lined sheet. Bake 30 minutes at 375 degrees.
3. Remove ribs from oven and raise oven temperature to 450 degrees.
4. Stir barbecue sauce to recombine and brush ribs generously with it. Return ribs to oven for 10 minutes.
5. Brush ribs with sauce a second time and return to oven for another 5 to 10 minutes.
6. When ribs look shiny and crispy, remove from oven.

Gingered Carrots in Foil

1½ pounds carrots
1-inch piece fresh ginger, or ½ teaspoon ground ginger
1 tablespoon brown sugar
Salt
1 tablespoon unsalted butter

1. Peel carrots and cut on diagonal into ⅛- to ¼-inch-thick slices.
2. If using fresh ginger, peel and finely grate enough to measure 1 teaspoon.
3. In large bowl, combine carrots, ginger, brown sugar, and salt to taste, and toss to coat carrots evenly.
4. Cut four 12 x 20-inch sheets of aluminum foil. Butter foil and fold in half. With scissors, round corners.
5. Place a portion of carrots onto one half of each foil sheet and dot with about 1 teaspoon butter. Fold other half of foil over carrots and roll and crimp edges tightly so that no steam can escape.

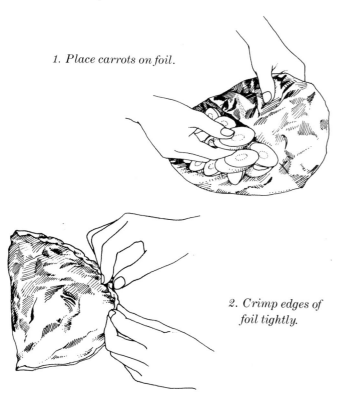

1. Place carrots on foil.

2. Crimp edges of foil tightly.

6. Place packages in ovenproof baking dish and bake 30 minutes in 375-degree oven.

Roast Potatoes

3 tablespoons unsalted butter
1½ pounds boiling potatoes, preferably, or red-skinned or baking potatoes
Salt

1. Preheat oven to 375 degrees. In small heavy-gauge saucepan, melt 1 tablespoon butter. Pour into jelly-roll pan, tilting pan to distribute butter evenly.
2. Wash potatoes and cut into 1-inch-thick slices. Do not peel. In jelly-roll pan, arrange slices in single layer. Dot with remaining butter. Pour ¾ cup water into pan. Salt potatoes to taste.
3. Place pan on bottom rack of oven and roast potatoes 30 minutes.
4. After 30 minutes, pour off any remaining water and return potatoes to oven. When bottoms of potatoes have browned, about 10 minutes, turn them over and roast until brown on other side, 10 to 15 minutes.

ADDED TOUCH

The cutting technique described in step 2 is an efficient way to work with juicy mangoes.

Mangoes with Whipped Cream and Crystallized Ginger

2 mangoes
1 tablespoon crystallized ginger
1 cup heavy cream
1 tablespoon sugar

1. In freezer, chill bowl and beaters for whipping cream.
2. Cut mangoes lengthwise down each side as close to the pit as possible. Gently pull apart and remove pit. With paring knife, being careful not to cut through skin, score mango so it separates into cubes. Now turn mango inside out by pushing on skin side until scored side curves outward. Over mixing bowl, carefully cut off protruding squares of mango, letting mango fall into bowl. Cover and refrigerate.
3. With chef's knife, chop ginger into tiny pieces, about ¹⁄₁₆ inch square.
4. Remove bowl and beaters from freezer and whip cream. Fold in sugar and ginger. Make nests of whipped cream on 4 plates. Spoon mango cubes into center.

Peppered Veal Chops
Sautéed Red Peppers with Pancetta
Pasta with Toasted Pine Nuts and Parmesan Cheese

Arrange this colorful company dinner of peppered veal chops, sautéed red peppers with pancetta, and pasta with pine nuts and Parmesan cheese on plain dinnerware. Garnish the red pepper strips with parsley.

These meaty veal chops are cut from the loin. For a more æsthetic-looking serving and for more even cooking, tie each chop securely with kitchen string: Cut string into 4 foot-long pieces. Tie 1 piece around each chop to make a tuck in the "tail" at the bottom of the T-shaped bone (see diagram on opposite page).

The sautéed red peppers are served with pancetta, an unsmoked Italian bacon cured in salt and spices. Pancetta is usually available in Italian grocery stores.

The salad dressing contains another Italian ingredient, balsamic vinegar. This dense, rich vinegar has a pungent aroma and a mellow sweet-sour taste. It is worth looking for in specialty food shops, though red wine or sherry vinegars are acceptable alternatives.

WHAT TO DRINK

To complement the flavors of this menu, choose a dry, medium-bodied red wine, either a Chianti Classico Riserva or a California Merlot.

SHOPPING LIST AND STAPLES

Four ¾-inch-thick veal loin chops (about ½ to ¾ pound each)
¼ pound pancetta (about 5 slices), or 2 ounces bacon
6 red bell peppers (about 1½ pounds total weight)
Small bunch fresh parsley (optional)
Small bunch fresh oregano, or 1 teaspoon dried
3 large cloves garlic
4 tablespoons unsalted butter
¼ pound Parmesan cheese
2 tablespoons olive oil
2 tablespoons balsamic vinegar
½ pound dry or fresh egg pasta, such as fettuccine
2 ounces pine nuts
Salt and freshly ground black pepper

UTENSILS

Large saucepan or stockpot with cover
Large heavy-gauge skillet or sauté pan with cover
Small heavy-gauge skillet or sauté pan
9 x 12-inch shallow baking sheet
Medium-size bowl
Small bowl or cup
Colander

Measuring cups and spoons
Chef's knife
Paring knife
Slotted spoon
Grater
Mallet or rolling pin (optional)
4 feet cotton string (optional)

START-TO-FINISH STEPS

1. For veal recipe, adjust pepper mill to coarse grind and grind enough pepper to measure 4 teaspoons. Or place peppercorns between 2 sheets of wax paper and crush with mallet or rolling pin. Follow veal chops recipe steps 1 and 2.
2. If using fresh oregano, strip leaves to measure 2 teaspoons. Follow red peppers recipe steps 1 through 4.
3. While peppers are cooking, follow pasta recipe steps 1 through 3 and veal recipe step 3.
4. Follow pasta recipe step 4 and veal recipe step 4.
5. Follow pasta recipe steps 5 and 6, and peppers recipe step 5.
6. Follow veal recipe step 5, pasta recipe step 7, peppers recipe step 6, and serve.

RECIPES

Peppered Veal Chops

Four ¾-inch-thick veal loin chops
4 teaspoons coarsely ground black pepper
Salt

1. Cut string into 4 foot-long pieces. Tie 1 piece around each veal chop to make tuck in "tail" at bottom of T-shaped bone. This step is optional but makes for a neater shape and slightly more even cooking.

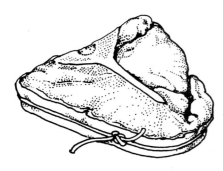

For a neat shape,
tie string around
each veal chop.

2. Rub approximately ½ teaspoon pepper into both sides of each chop. Sprinkle with salt to taste and set aside at room temperature.
3. Preheat broiler. Place oven rack approximately 4 inches from broiler element.
4. Arrange chops in single layer on shallow baking sheet. Place under broiler, leaving broiler door open, and broil approximately 3 minutes per side, until nicely browned on the outside and still pink on the inside.
5. Transfer chops to dinner plates and remove strings.

Sautéed Red Peppers with Pancetta

6 red bell peppers (about 1½ pounds total weight)
3 large cloves garlic
¼ pound pancetta (about 5 slices), or 2 ounces bacon
1 tablespoon olive oil
2 tablespoons balsamic vinegar
2 teaspoons fresh oregano, left in small leaves,
    or 1 teaspoon dried
1 teaspoon freshly ground black pepper
Oregano leaves or parsley sprigs for garnish (optional)

1. Wash, dry, and halve peppers lengthwise. Core, seed, and derib. With chef's knife, cut into ¼-inch-wide strips.
2. Peel garlic and, using paring knife, cut into thin slivers.
3. Briefly heat large heavy-gauge skillet or sauté pan over medium-high heat. Add pancetta and sauté until crisp. Using slotted spoon, remove and drain on paper towels.
4. Return pan to heat. Add olive oil and pepper strips. Sauté over medium-high heat until peppers are heated through, about 1 minute. Add garlic slivers, stir, and cover pan. Reduce heat to low and cook until peppers are tender, about 20 minutes. Remove from heat.
5. Crumble pancetta and add half of it to peppers along with vinegar, oregano, and pepper. Toss to combine.
6. Divide peppers among dinner plates and garnish each serving with a sprinkling of the remaining pancetta and a few oregano leaves or parsley sprigs, if desired.

Pasta with Toasted Pine Nuts and Parmesan Cheese

1 tablespoon salt
1 tablespoon olive oil
2 ounces Parmesan cheese
4 tablespoons unsalted butter
¼ cup pine nuts
½ pound dry or fresh egg pasta, such as fettuccine

1. In large saucepan or stockpot, bring 4 quarts water, 1 tablespoon salt, and 1 tablespoon olive oil to a boil over medium heat.
2. Grate Parmesan cheese and set aside.
3. In small heavy-gauge skillet or sauté pan, melt butter over medium heat. When it foams, add pine nuts and cook, stirring, until both butter and pine nuts turn golden brown. Remove from heat. Using slotted spoon, transfer half the pine nuts to a small bowl or cup and reserve for garnish.
4. Add pasta to the boiling water. Cook dry pasta 8 to 12 minutes, fresh pasta 3 to 5 minutes, or until *al dente.*
5. Place colander over bowl and drain pasta into it: The pasta water will heat the bowl. Empty the bowl of water, dry with paper towel, and fill with pasta.
6. Toss pasta with the remaining pine nuts and all the browned butter from skillet. Add Parmesan cheese and toss again.
7. Place a portion of pasta on each plate and garnish with reserved pine nuts.

Norman Weinstein

MENU 1 (Right)
Veal with Chestnuts
Ivory and Jade
Brown Rice with Pine Nuts and Raisins

MENU 2
Celestial Egg Flower Soup
Beef with Shredded Vegetables
White Rice, Chinese Style

MENU 3
Lemon-Flavored Steak
Braised Black Mushrooms with Snow Peas
Peppered Noodles

S ince the Chinese traditionally do not raise cattle for human consumption, the number of beef dishes in the Chinese repertoire is relatively small, and veal dishes are virtually nonexistent. But Norman Weinstein, a teacher of Chinese cooking, has devised three menus that show the adaptability of Chinese techniques to Western ingredients. In the majority of Chinese dishes, foods are cut into bite-size pieces and cooked rapidly in a small amount of oil over very high heat. This classic technique, called "stir frying," is fast and energy-efficient, and allows foods to retain basic nutrients, colors, and flavors. Deep frying and steaming are two other widely used Chinese cooking methods.

The veal and chestnut main course in the first menu combines two cooking methods. Norman Weinstein first deep fries veal cubes to give them a crisp texture and then simmers them slowly in a rich broth seasoned with soy sauce and sugar. The technique, which is close to the Western method of braising, is called "red cooking" and is common in eastern China, around Shanghai. This recipe is the cook's adaptation of a popular Shanghai chicken dish.

The beef with shredded vegetables of Menu 2 is a modified version of a Northern-style dish. Prepared like many of the dishes of that region, it is tossed and glazed with *hoisin* sauce, a sweet Chinese condiment made from soy beans, sugar, vinegar, chilies, and other spices.

Szechwan cuisine is from the western region of China. It is characterized both by fiery chili-flavored sauces and by beef dishes such as shredded beef and tangerine peel, of which the lemon-flavored steak in Menu 3 is a variation.

The balancing of opposites is important in Chinese cuisine; serving this meal on a white plate set on a larger, dark service plate dramatizes the contrasts of color and texture in these recipes. You can achieve the same effect with white plates on shiny black mats of wood, lacquer, or plastic.

Veal with Chestnuts
Ivory and Jade
Brown Rice with Pine Nuts and Raisins

For the main dish, the cook suggests using veal shoulder, which is more economical than loin or leg cuts and holds up well in moist cooking.

Dried chestnuts are available in most Chinese and Italian markets, but the cook prefers the Chinese variety for their slightly smoky taste.

Two types of soy sauce, light and dark, are called for here and in recipes for the following two menus. The dark is slightly darker and thicker than the light; it contains molasses and tastes saltier and sweeter than the light soy.

Most supermarkets now also stock fresh bean curd, or tofu, the soft, white, protein-rich cakes made from soybeans. For the Ivory and Jade recipe, use a firm variety; more fragile types will lose their texture.

WHAT TO DRINK

The ideal accompaniment to the medley of Oriental flavors would be well-chilled beer or ale, but you could also serve a German white wine, such as a *Kabinett*-class Riesling.

SHOPPING LIST AND STAPLES

1½ pounds lean boneless veal shoulder, cut into 1½-inch cubes
4 squares fresh bean curd, preferably firm variety (about 1 pound total weight)
1 pound fresh spinach
4 medium-size carrots (about 1 pound total weight)
4 scallions
2-inch piece fresh ginger
4 or 5 cloves garlic
2¾ cups chicken stock, preferably homemade (see page 13), or canned, plus 2½ cups (optional)
2 cups plus 3 tablespoons peanut oil or corn oil
2 tablespoons Oriental sesame oil
2 tablespoons light soy sauce
2 tablespoons dark soy sauce
1 cup brown rice
4 tablespoons cornstarch
4 ounces dried chestnuts
2 ounces pine nuts
½ cup dark raisins
Two 1½-inch lumps rock sugar, or 3 tablespoons light brown sugar
Salt and freshly ground black pepper
8 tablespoons dry sherry

UTENSILS

14-inch flat-bottom wok with cover
    or large cast-iron Dutch oven with cover
Large cast-iron Dutch oven
    or large heavy-gauge sauté pan
Medium-size heavy-gauge enamel-lined pot with cover
    (if using dried chestnuts)
2 medium-size heavy-gauge saucepans with covers
2 platters
Colander
Salad spinner (optional)
Large mixing bowl plus additional large bowl (optional)
2 small bowls
Cup
Measuring cups and spoons
Chef's knife or slicing cleaver
Paring knife
Chinese metal wok spatulas or 2 wooden spoons
Slotted metal spoon
Deep-fat thermometer (optional)
Vegetable peeler (optional)
Toothpicks

START-TO-FINISH STEPS

The night before: For veal and chestnuts receipe, bring 2 quarts water to a boil in heavy-gauge enamel-lined pot. Add dried chestnuts. Remove from heat, cover, and let stand overnight at room temperature.

1. Follow rice recipe step 1 and Ivory and Jade recipe step 1.
2. While bean curd is soaking and rice is cooking, follow veal recipe steps 1 through 3 and Ivory and Jade recipe step 2.
3. Follow veal recipe steps 4 through 6.
4. Follow Ivory and Jade recipe steps 3 through 5.
5. Follow rice recipe step 2.
6. While rice is cooking, follow veal recipe step 7.
7. While carrots are cooking, follow Ivory and Jade recipe steps 6 through 8.
8. Follow rice recipe step 3.
9. Follow Ivory and Jade recipe steps 9 and 10, and veal recipe step 8.
10. Follow Ivory and Jade recipe step 11, veal recipe step 9, and serve with rice.

Veal with Chestnuts

4 medium-size carrots (about 1 pound total weight)
2 tablespoons light soy sauce
2 tablespoons dark soy sauce
6 tablespoons dry sherry
Two 1½-inch lumps rock sugar, or 3 tablespoons light
    brown sugar
2 scallions
2 cups peanut or corn oil
Thin slice fresh ginger
1½ pounds boneless lean veal shoulder, cut into 1½-inch
    cubes
1 cup dried chestnuts, soaked overnight
1½ cups plus 5 tablespoons chicken stock
3 tablespoons cornstarch

1. Peel carrots and cut into 1½-inch pieces.
2. In small bowl, combine light and dark soy sauces and sherry. If using brown sugar, add it to soy-sherry mixture and stir to dissolve.
3. Cut off green part of scallions, reserving bulbs for another use. Wash, dry, and mince scallion greens.
4. Heat wok or Dutch oven over medium-high heat until it begins to smoke. Add oil and heat 2 minutes. Add ginger to pan. If it surfaces immediately, oil is ready (375 degrees on deep-fat thermometer). Remove ginger and discard. Add one third of the veal and deep fry, turning frequently with Chinese metal spatula, until cubes are browned, about 4 to 5 minutes. Transfer to paper-towel-lined platter. Repeat process for remaining 2 batches.
5. In colander, drain chestnuts and pat dry with paper towels. Using toothpick, remove any shell matter from crevices in chestnuts.
6. Pour off all but a film of oil from pan. Add soy-sherry mixture and bring to a boil. Add veal and stir to coat with sauce. Add 1½ cups chicken stock and bring to a boil. Reduce to a simmer, add rock sugar, if using, and dried chestnuts. Stir, cover, and simmer 10 minutes.
7. Add carrots and recover pan. Cook 20 minutes.
8. With slotted spoon, transfer veal, chestnuts, and carrots to serving bowl. In small bowl, combine cornstarch with remaining 5 tablespoons stock. Slowly add mixture to the simmering broth, stirring constantly. When sauce has reached desired consistency, stop adding mixture.
9. Pour sauce over veal mixture, and garnish with reserved minced scallion greens.

Ivory and Jade

4 squares fresh bean curd, preferably firm variety
    (about 1 pound total weight)
1 pound fresh spinach
2-inch piece fresh ginger
4 or 5 cloves garlic
2 scallions
¾ cup plus 3 tablespoons chicken stock
2 tablespoons dry sherry
3 tablespoons peanut or corn oil
½ teaspoon salt
1 heaping tablespoon cornstarch
Freshly ground black pepper
2 tablespoons Oriental sesame oil

1. In medium-size saucepan, bring 6 cups water to a boil. Add bean curd and boil 10 minutes. With slotted spoon, transfer bean curd to large bowl of ice water and let stand 20 minutes.
2. Fill kitchen sink or large bowl with cold water. Rinse spinach thoroughly. Remove and discard hard stems. Dry in salad spinner or pat dry with paper towels.
3. Peel ginger and cut crosswise into 10 or 12 slices. Tap garlic cloves lightly with flat blade of knife or cleaver to remove skins. Wash and trim scallions. With chef's knife or cleaver, cut into 1½-inch pieces.
4. In saucepan used for bean curd, combine ¾ cup stock, ginger, garlic, scallions, and sherry. Bring to a boil, cover, and simmer 10 minutes.
5. Cut each bean curd square in half, through widest part, then cut each half into 4 triangles.
6. With slotted spoon, remove ginger, garlic, and scallions from stock and discard. Transfer stock to Dutch oven or sauté pan and bring to a boil. Add bean curd and cook 3 minutes. With slotted spoon, transfer bean curd to large paper-towel-lined platter. Pour stock into small bowl and reserve.
7. Wipe pan dry. Return pan to stove and heat over medium-high heat until it starts to smoke. Add oil and heat 30 seconds.
8. Add spinach first and then add salt. With metal wok spatula, stir and press spinach until it is coated with oil and begins to wilt. Divide among 4 individual plates.
9. In cup, combine cornstarch with remaining 3 tablespoons stock.
10. Return reserved stock to pan, and bring to a boil. Lower heat to a simmer and slowly add cornstarch mixture, stirring constantly. When sauce has reached desired consistency, stop adding cornstarch mixture. Return bean curd to pan and simmer just until heated through.
11. Spoon bean curd and sauce over spinach, sprinkle with pepper to taste, and drizzle with sesame oil.

Brown Rice with Pine Nuts and Raisins

2½ cups chicken stock or water
1 cup brown rice
½ cup pine nuts (about 2 ounces)
½ cup dark raisins

1. In medium-size saucepan, bring stock or water to a boil. Add rice, stir once, reduce heat to low, cover, and simmer 35 minutes.
2. Remove cover and add pine nuts and raisins. Stir gently to mix, replace cover, and cook another 10 minutes.
3. Turn off heat and let rice stand, covered, until ready to serve.

Celestial Egg Flower Soup
Beef with Shredded Vegetables
White Rice, Chinese Style

The confetti effect of the soup complements the colorful beef with vegetables and the bowls of rice.

The very distinct grain of flank steak makes it easy to shred and ideal for the beef main course of this menu. Soaking the meat in egg whites and cornstarch is a common Chinese cooking technique used to preserve the juices during searing.

Leeks tend to be gritty, so be sure to rinse them thoroughly. The base for the Celestial Egg Flower Soup should be light and delicate so that it does not obscure the flavors of the other ingredients.

You will have egg yolks left over from the beef recipe and, if you choose to use eggs, from the soup recipe; save them for use in a custard dessert.

WHAT TO DRINK

Beer or ale, especially dark beer, is the first choice for this Chinese-style meal. A young and fruity Zinfandel is a good wine selection.

SHOPPING LIST AND STAPLES

1¼ pounds beef flank steak (trimmed weight)
¼ pound small shrimps
Large carrot
Small zucchini

2 medium-size green bell peppers
6 cherry tomatoes
3 leeks (each 1 inch in diameter)
2 large or 4 small scallions
4-inch piece fresh ginger
1 egg plus additional 3 eggs (optional)
10-ounce package frozen peas
6 cups chicken stock, preferably homemade
    (see page 13), or canned
7 to 9 tablespoons peanut or corn oil
1 tablespoon Oriental sesame oil (optional)
1 tablespoon dark soy sauce
1 tablespoon light soy sauce
½ cup *hoisin* sauce
6 dried Chinese black mushrooms (about 2 ounces total
    weight), or ½ pound fresh mushrooms
2 cups long-grain rice
¼ cup plus 1 tablespoon cornstarch
Pinch of sugar
3 tablespoons dry sherry plus additional sherry
    (if using canned broth)

UTENSILS

14-inch flat-bottom wok or 10- to 12-inch Dutch oven or
    heavy-gauge sauté pan
2 medium-size heavy-gauge saucepans, one with cover
2 platters
Medium-size bowl
5 small bowls
Measuring cups and spoons
Chef's knife or slicing cleaver
Paring knife
Chinese metal wok spatulas or 2 wooden spoons
Large slotted spoon
Wooden spoon
Whisk
Soup ladle
Vegetable peeler

START-TO-FINISH STEPS

1. Follow rice recipe steps 1 and 2.
2. Follow soup recipe steps 1 through 6.
3. Follow beef recipe steps 1 and 2.
4. While beef is in egg-white mixture, follow rice recipe

steps 3 and 4, and beef recipe steps 3 through 7.
5. Follow soup recipe steps 7 through 15 and serve.
6. Follow rice recipe step 5.
7. Follow beef recipe steps 8 through 10 and serve with rice.

RECIPES
Celestial Egg Flower Soup

6 dried Chinese black mushrooms (about 2 ounces total
    weight), or ½ pound fresh mushrooms
2 large or 4 small scallions
6 cups chicken stock
4 to 5 thin slices fresh ginger
Pinch of sugar
Dry sherry (if using canned stock)
¼ pound small shrimps
Small zucchini
1 leek (about 1 inch in diameter)
6 cherry tomatoes
¼ cup cornstarch
3 eggs (optional)
½ cup frozen peas
1 tablespoon Oriental sesame oil (optional)

1. If using dried mushrooms, place mushrooms in small bowl. Cover with boiling water and let soak 15 to 20 minutes, or until softened.
2. Wash scallions, trim off ends, and cut in half. In medium-size saucepan, bring chicken stock, ginger, scallions, and a pinch of sugar to a simmer. If using canned broth, add ⅔ can cold water and sherry to taste. Simmer 5 minutes. Using slotted spoon, remove scallions and ginger, and discard. Remove pan from heat and set aside.
3. Peel and devein shrimp. Rinse under cold water. Set aside.
4. Wash zucchini and cut enough into ⅜-inch dice to measure ½ cup.
5. Cut green portion from leek, reserving white for another use. Trim off tops of greens and discard. Slit remaining green portion lengthwise into 6 to 8 strips. Rinse thoroughly in cold water to remove any grit. With chef's knife or slicing cleaver, cut crosswise to yield ¼ cup.
6. Cut each tomato in half.
7. Drain mushrooms and discard tough stems. Cut mushrooms into quarters. If using fresh mushrooms, clean with damp paper towels and proceed as for dried.

8. In small bowl, mix cornstarch with ¾ cup stock.

9. If using eggs, separate them into 2 small bowls and reserve yolks for another use. With whisk, beat egg whites until frothy.

10. Return stock to a simmer. Add mushrooms and leeks, and simmer 2 minutes. Add zucchini and simmer 30 seconds.

11. Bring soup to a simmer. Stir cornstarch mixture to recombine. Stirring constantly, slowly add cornstarch mixture to the soup. When soup has reached desired consistency, stop adding cornstarch mixture.

12. Add tomatoes and shrimp to soup. Stir 30 seconds.

13. Reduce heat to low. Slowly pour egg white into thickened soup. Allow to set 10 seconds, then agitate soup slowly with a ladle to bring egg white to top.

14. Add peas to soup, stirring to break up frozen block.

15. Transfer soup to a tureen. Top with sesame oil, if desired, and serve.

Beef with Shredded Vegetables

1¼ pounds beef flank steak (trimmed weight)
1 tablespoon light soy sauce
3 tablespoons dry sherry
1 egg
1 tablespoon cornstarch
3-inch piece fresh ginger
Large carrot
2 medium-size green bell peppers
2 leeks (each about 1 inch in diameter)
½ cup *hoisin* sauce
1 tablespoon dark soy sauce
7 to 9 tablespoons peanut or corn oil

1. Lay steak on cutting surface. Holding sharp chef's knife or slicing cleaver at a very low angle, cut steak across grain into 3-inch slices. Then, cutting with, not against, the grain, shred the slices. (See diagrams below.)

2. Place shreds in medium-size bowl. Add light soy sauce and 2 tablespoons sherry, and toss. Separate egg, reserving yolk for another use. Add egg white to meat-sherry mixture and toss to coat shreds evenly. Dust surface with cornstarch and toss again. Let stand at least 15 minutes.

3. Peel ginger. Cut lengthwise into 8 thin slices. Make stacks of 3 to 4 slices each and cut into thin 3-inch shreds.

4. Peel carrot and cut into 3-inch sections. Cut a thin lengthwise slice from each section so it will lie flat. Place on cutting surface and, with chef's knife or slicing cleaver, cut each section into thin slices, then into shreds.

5. Core, seed, and derib peppers. Cut into 3-inch shreds.

6. Cut green portion from leeks. Reserve whites for another use. Trim off tops of greens and discard.

7. In small bowl, combine *hoisin* sauce, remaining tablespoon dry sherry, and dark soy sauce.

8. Heat wok, Dutch oven, or heavy-gauge sauté pan over high heat until it smokes. Add 5 tablespoons oil. Heat until a shred of ginger sizzles on contact. Remove ginger and discard. Add one third of the beef shreds. Using metal wok spatulas or 2 wooden spoons, stir fry beef until lightly browned, about 2 to 3 minutes. With slotted spoon, transfer beef to paper-towel-lined platter. Repeat process with remaining 2 batches.

9. Add 2 more tablespoons oil to pan if needed—do *not* use unless absolutely necessary—and heat 10 seconds. Add ginger shreds and carrots, and stir fry until carrots are slightly wilted, about 2 to 3 minutes. Add peppers and stir fry 15 seconds. Add leeks and stir fry another 15 seconds.

10. Transfer vegetables to another paper-towel-lined platter. Add 2 more tablespoons oil to pan and heat 15 seconds. Add *hoisin* mixture and stir until bubbly. Add beef and vegetables, and stir to mix well. When heated through, transfer to serving platter.

White Rice, Chinese Style

1. Place 2 cups long-grain rice in medium-size heavy-gauge saucepan. Add enough cold water to cover rice by 1 inch and bring to a boil over medium-high heat. Cover pan and reduce heat to very low.

2. Simmer rice 25 minutes.

3. Lift cover of saucepan and fork up a few grains of rice. Quickly replace cover. Rice is done when center of grain is still slightly firm.

4. Off heat, let rice stand, covered, for at least 15 minutes to absorb any liquid and steam still in pan. Rice will fluff up. (*Note:* If saucepan has sides thick enough to retain heat, rice can stand for as long as 30 minutes.)

5. When ready to serve, lift cover and fluff rice with fork. Turn into individual serving bowls.

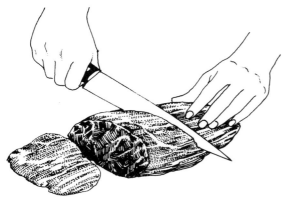

1. Cut steak across grain into 3-inch slices.

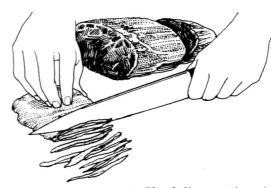

2. Shred slices, cutting with grain.

Lemon-Flavored Steak
Braised Black Mushrooms with Snow Peas
Peppered Noodles

The spicy noodles, which get their bite from serrano chilies, stand up to the tangy beef dish, flavored with lemon peel.

Shell steak (sometimes sold as strip steak or beef top loin steak) is used for this menu's main course. Both the ginger and the lemon peel in this dish are meant to be eaten, so slice the ginger very thin. Some of the white pith of the lemon should be included with the peel to add texture and bitterness.

Fragrant, meaty black Chinese mushrooms contrast dramatically with the crisp, fresh snow peas, and there really is no substitute for them in this vegetable dish. Dried Chinese mushrooms are available in Chinese markets and in many specialty food shops. If you cannot find fresh snow peas, substitute frozen ones. Thaw them before using.

The oyster sauce called for in this dish is a rich Cantonese condiment made from powdered fermented oysters and soy sauce. You can buy it in the Oriental-foods section of most supermarkets.

WHAT TO DRINK

These hot-and-sour flavors go well with an Alsatian or California Gewürztraminer, which is dry and spicy.

SHOPPING LIST AND STAPLES

2 boneless shell steaks, 1 inch thick, trimmed of fat, and
   tails removed (each about 1 pound)
½ pound snow peas
6 to 8 fresh serrano chilies, or fresh or canned jalapeño
   peppers
Large red bell pepper
Large bunch scallions
1 lemon
1½-inch piece fresh ginger
¾ cup chicken stock, preferably homemade (see page 13),
   or canned
3 cups plus 1 tablespoon peanut or corn oil
¼ cup Oriental sesame oil
3 tablespoons light soy sauce
2 tablespoons oyster sauce
3 tablespoons Worcestershire sauce
20 dried Chinese black mushrooms, of uniform size, or 1
   pound fresh mushrooms
¾ pound vermicelli
¼ cup cornstarch
2 tablespoons sugar
2 tablespoons coarse salt
Freshly ground black pepper
3 tablespoons dry sherry
3 tablespoons Cognac or brandy

UTENSILS

Large stockpot or kettle with cover
14-inch flat-bottomed wok or large Dutch oven or heavy-
   gauge sauté pan
Medium-size skillet with cover

Medium-size saucepan
Small enamel-lined saucepan
2 large mixing bowls
4 small mixing bowls
Large platter
Colander
Measuring cups and spoons
Chef's knife or slicing cleaver
Paring knife
Chinese metal wok spatulas or 2 wooden spoons
Slotted metal spoon
Small sharp scissors
Deep-fat thermometer
Rubber gloves

START-TO-FINISH STEPS

1. Follow mushrooms recipe step 1. While water is coming to a boil, follow steak recipe steps 1 and 2.
2. Follow mushrooms recipe step 2.
3. While mushrooms are soaking, follow steak recipe steps 3 through 6 and pasta recipe steps 1 through 4.
4. Follow mushrooms recipe steps 3 through 7.
5. While mushrooms cook, follow pasta recipe steps 5 and 6.
6. About 5 minutes before mushrooms are done, follow steak recipe step 7.
7. Follow pasta recipe step 7 and steak recipe steps 8 through 13.
8. Follow mushrooms recipe steps 8 and 9, pasta recipe steps 8 and 9, and serve with steak.

RECIPES

Lemon-Flavored Steak

2 boneless shell steaks, 1 inch thick, trimmed of fat, and
   tails removed (each about 1 pound)
¼ cup cornstarch
1 lemon
Large red bell pepper
4 scallions
1½-inch piece fresh ginger
1 tablespoon light soy sauce
3 tablespoons Cognac or brandy
2 cups peanut or corn oil
1 tablespoon sugar

1. With very sharp chef's knife, cut shell steaks in half lengthwise. Holding knife at as low an angle as possible to the meat, cut each half into six 1-inch-thick slices. Place in large mixing bowl and sprinkle with 3 tablespoons cornstarch. With your hands, toss slices to coat evenly with cornstarch. Shake off any excess starch. Let steak pieces stand for at least 15 minutes.
2. Cut lemon peel, including pith, into ½-inch strips. Squeeze lemon to measure 2 tablespoons juice. Set aside.
3. Core, seed, and derib pepper. Cut pepper lengthwise into quarters. On the bias, cut each quarter into 6 pieces.

4. Wash scallions and trim off ends. Remove green portions and reserve for another dish. With chef's knife, cut white portions, on the bias, into 1-inch sections.

5. Peel ginger and cut crosswise into ⅛-inch-thick slices.

6. For the sauce, combine remaining tablespoon cornstarch, lemon juice, soy sauce, and Cognac in small bowl.

7. Heat wok, Dutch oven, or sauté pan over high heat until it begins to smoke. Add oil and heat 2 minutes, or until a sliver of ginger rises immediately to the surface (375 degrees on deep-fat thermometer). Remove ginger and discard.

8. Add steak, 6 slices at a time. Deep fry until crusty, about 1 minute. With slotted metal spoon, remove steak, wait 15 seconds, and return to oil for another 10 to 15 seconds. Transfer steak to paper-towel-lined platter. Repeat process for remaining slices.

9. Pour off all but 3 tablespoons oil from pan and heat 10 seconds. Add ginger slices and lemon peel. Stir fry vigorously 1 minute.

10. Add scallions and peppers and stir fry another minute.

11. Return steak slices to pan. Add sugar and toss.

12. With spatula, move contents of pan to one side. Stir sauce mixture to recombine, and then pour it down side of pan into cleared space. Stir sauce with point of spatula until thickened. Incorporate remaining ingredients, stirring until they are evenly coated with sauce.

13. Transfer to serving platter and cover loosely with foil.

Braised Black Mushrooms with Snow Peas

20 dried Chinese black mushrooms, of uniform size, or 1 pound fresh mushrooms
½ pound snow peas
¾ cup chicken stock
2 tablespoons oyster sauce
3 tablespoons dry sherry
1 tablespoon sugar

1. In medium-size saucepan, bring 3 cups water to a boil.

2. If using dried mushrooms, place them in large bowl. Add the 3 cups boiling water and let soak at least 15 minutes. If using fresh mushrooms, clean with damp paper towels. Remove stems.

3. Remove caps, strings, and bottom tips from snow peas.

4. For sauce, combine remaining ingredients in small bowl.

5. When soaked mushrooms are soft and spongy, drain them and squeeze dry. With small sharp scissors, remove stems and discard.

6. In medium-size saucepan, bring 3 cups water to a boil.

7. In medium-size skillet, bring sauce to a boil over medium-high heat. Add mushrooms, and stir to coat with sauce. If using dried mushrooms, cover skillet and simmer 25 minutes; if using fresh, cover and simmer 10 minutes.

8. Place colander in sink. Add snow peas to the boiling water and stir. As soon as they turn bright green (no longer than 10 seconds), pour peas and water into colander. Rinse peas under cold running water. Shake colander a few times to drain. Pat peas dry with paper towels.

9. Remove skillet cover and add snow peas. Stir gently 10 to 15 seconds, just until peas are coated with sauce. Transfer to platter and serve immediately.

Peppered Noodles

4 scallions
6 to 8 fresh serrano chilies, or fresh or canned jalapeño peppers
1 cup plus 1 tablespoon peanut or corn oil
¼ cup Oriental sesame oil
2 tablespoons light soy sauce
3 tablespoons Worcestershire sauce
2 tablespoons coarse salt
¾ pound vermicelli
Freshly ground black pepper

1. Wash scallions and trim off ends. Mince green portions and reserve whites for another purpose.

2. Wearing thin rubber gloves, cut off and discard tops of chilies. With paring knife, split chilies lengthwise and, using tip of knife, remove seeds and membranes. Rinse under cold water and pat dry with paper towels. With chef's knife, cut chilies lengthwise into thin strips.

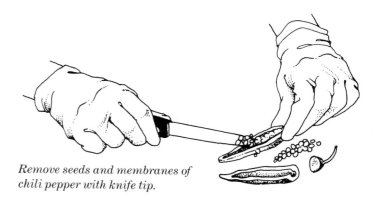

Remove seeds and membranes of chili pepper with knife tip.

3. In small bowl, combine peanut and sesame oils.

4. In small enamel-lined saucepan, heat 3 tablespoons of the oil mixture over medium-high heat. Add chili shreds and cook, stirring, 20 seconds. Remove pan from heat and reserve.

5. In large stockpot or kettle, bring 5 quarts water to a boil over high heat.

6. In small bowl, combine soy and Worcestershire sauces.

7. Add salt and 1 tablespoon oil mixture to the boiling water. Still over high heat, add vermicelli, one third at a time, waiting for water to return to a boil before adding each remaining third. Cook until *al dente*, about 5 minutes, testing frequently. In colander, drain and then rinse vermicelli under cold water. Shake colander a few times to drain thoroughly. Return pasta to pot and top with ¼ cup of the oil mixture. Toss until well coated, and cover.

8. For sauce, add chilies and soy sauce-Worcestershire mixture to remaining oil and stir to combine.

9. Add sauce to pasta. Top with minced scallions and freshly ground pepper to taste. Toss and serve immediately.

Victoria Wise

MENU 1 (Right)
Warm Tarragon-Mushroom Salad
Beef Roulade
Cottage Fried Potatoes

MENU 2
Asparagus and Tomatoes with
Shallot Vinaigrette
Veal Caponata
Fettuccine Oregano

MENU 3
Fresh Tomato Soup with Garlic-Basil Croutons
Cabbage Leaves with Beef Stuffing
Sour Cream with Chives and Dill
Parslied Potatoes

Victoria Wise, a California-based restaurateur and chef, joins classic French cooking techniques with a nonclassic approach to combining flavors and ingredients. A childhood spent in Japan and extensive travel in Europe have given her a broad cultural perspective for her menu planning. Working in California, where cooks have abundant seasonal produce and fresh aromatic herbs year round, has further enhanced her eclectic style.

Her first menu is a perfect example of how her travels have influenced her. She presents a Mediterranean-style flank steak that is first filled with chopped spinach and diced carrots, then rolled up jelly-roll style, and finally soaked in a rich and flavorful marinade of both Oriental and Western ingredients: soy sauce, fresh ginger, and fresh coriander with red wine, olive oil, and a bay leaf.

For Menu 2, Victoria Wise pairs two Italian-inspired dishes—an herbed veal caponata and a creamy Parmesan-sprinkled fettuccine. She serves these with a refreshing salad of tomato and crisp-tender asparagus dressed with a shallot vinaigrette. In Menu 3, Napa, also known as Chinese or celery cabbage, is used to wrap seasoned lean ground meat, making a lighter, exotic version of the Eastern European mainstay, stuffed cabbage.

A roulade of flank steak and spinach creates a pinwheel effect. The perfect companions to this elaborate-looking entrée are cottage fried potatoes seasoned with coriander and a tarragon-scented salad with mushrooms.

Warm Tarragon-Mushroom Salad
Beef Roulade
Cottage Fried Potatoes

Flank steak is a thick, flavorful cut of beef with a pronounced grain that makes it well suited for this roulade. Butterflying this—or other cuts of meat—is not difficult if you have a well-sharpened chef's knife. Simply make a smooth, even cut (with the grain) horizontally through the center of the meat, slicing almost, but not entirely, through the steak so that you leave a ½-inch "hinge" at one edge. Gently open the steak out like a book on a smooth surface and flatten it slightly with a wooden mallet. This will make it easier to roll after you spread the stuffing on the meat.

In the warm, tarragon-scented salad, the cook suggests combining fresh mushrooms with *shiitake*, which are thick, brown Japanese mushrooms with a distinct aroma and flavor. They are available in many specialty food stores and Oriental markets. If you cannot find fresh *shiitake*, substitute the dried variety, which is easily reconstituted by soaking for 15 to 20 minutes in hot water. If you cannot find butter lettuce, use red-leaf lettuce or watercress in the salad.

Fresh coriander, which is used in the roulade and cottage fries recipes, is a pungent herb that looks like parsley but doesn't taste like it. If you find the flavor of coriander too powerful, use fresh thyme or parsley instead.

WHAT TO DRINK
The cook suggests a Napa or Amador County Zinfandel to accompany this menu. A Cotes du Rhône or a Chianti would be good alternatives.

SHOPPING LIST AND STAPLES

1 beef flank steak (about 1¾ pounds trimmed weight), butterflied
5 russet potatoes (about 3 pounds total weight)
⅓ pound shiitake mushrooms, if available
⅔ pound fresh mushrooms, or 1 pound if not using shiitake
1 head butter or red-leaf lettuce
1 to 1½ pounds spinach
Medium-size carrot
2 large lemons
10 cloves garlic
1-inch piece fresh ginger
Medium-size bunch fresh coriander or parsley
Small bunch fresh tarragon, or 1 teaspoon dried

2 tablespoons unsalted butter
½ cup plus 3 tablespoons olive oil
½ cup vegetable shortening or oil
⅔ cup soy sauce
1 loaf French bread (optional)
1 bay leaf
Salt
Freshly ground peppper
2 cups dry red wine

UTENSILS

Food processor (optional)
2 large heavy-gauge non-aluminum skillets, one with ovenproof handle
Medium-size non-aluminum saucepan
Large non-aluminum roasting pan
Small roasting pan
Large platter
Colander or sieve
Salad spinner (optional)
Measuring cups and spoons
Chef's knife
Paring knife
Slotted metal spatula
Wooden spoon
Wooden mallet or rolling pin
Grater
Juicer (optional)
Vegetable peeler
Meat thermometer (optional)
Kitchen string

START-TO-FINISH STEPS

1. Chop fresh tarragon, if using, for mushroom salad and chop coriander or parsley for potatoes.
2. Follow roulade recipe steps 1 through 7.
3. While marinade is reducing and roulade is cooking, follow potatoes recipe steps 1 and 2.
4. Follow mushroom salad recipe steps 1 through 3 and place French bread, if serving, in 350-degree oven to warm.
5. Follow roulade recipe step 8 and potatoes recipe step 3.
6. Follow salad recipe step 4 and serve as first course with French bread.

7. Follow roulade recipe step 9 and potatoes recipe step 4, and serve.

RECIPES

Warm Tarragon-Mushroom Salad

⅓ pound shiitake mushrooms, if available
⅔ pound fresh mushrooms, or 1 pound if not using shiitake
6 cloves garlic
1 head butter or red-leaf lettuce
1 large lemon
1 tablespoon chopped fresh tarragon leaves, or 1 teaspoon dried
2 tablespoons unsalted butter
3 tablespoons olive oil
Salt
Freshly ground pepper
1 teaspoon chopped fresh tarragon for garnish (optional)
1 loaf French bread (optional)

1. Clean mushrooms with damp paper towels. Using paring knife, trim stem ends and cut each cap into 3 or 4 slices. Set aside.
2. Peel garlic and cut into slivers. Set aside.
3. Wash lettuce and dry in salad spinner or pat dry with paper towels. Divide among 4 salad plates. Set aside.
4. Juice lemon. Strain out pits and reserve juice. In large heavy-gauge non-aluminum skillet, heat butter and oil over high heat. When butter foams, add mushrooms and sauté, stirring with wooden spoon, 3 to 4 minutes. Add garlic, tarragon, and lemon juice, and stir 2 to 3 minutes longer, or until liquid is reduced by one third. Season with salt and pepper to taste and spoon over lettuce-lined plates while still warm. Garnish with chopped fresh tarragon and serve with warm French bread, if desired.

Beef Roulade

1 beef flank steak (about 1¾ pounds trimmed weight), butterflied
1-inch piece fresh ginger
4 cloves garlic
½ large lemon
2 cups dry red wine
⅔ cup soy sauce
½ cup olive oil
1 bay leaf
6 sprigs fresh coriander or parsley
1 to 1½ pounds spinach
Medium-size carrot
Salt
Freshly ground pepper

1. Have butcher butterfly flank steak, if possible. Otherwise, carefully do it yourself using sharp chef's knife. Gently open the steak out like a book on smooth surface and, using a wooden mallet or rolling pin, flatten it slightly, being careful not to tear hinges. Set aside.
2. Preheat oven to 475 degrees.
3. Peel and coarsely grate ginger. Peel and coarsely chop garlic. Juice lemon and strain out pits.
4. In large non-aluminum roasting pan, combine ginger, garlic, lemon juice, wine, soy sauce, olive oil, bay leaf, and coriander. Open butterflied steak and place in marinade, cut side down. Set aside 15 minutes.
5. Wash spinach in several changes of cold water. Remove stems and discard. Drain in colander or sieve; do not dry. Cut leaves into ½-inch wide strips. Peel and finely dice carrot. In medium-size non-aluminum saucepan, cook spinach and carrot, stirring with wooden spoon, over medium heat about 2 minutes, or until spinach is wilted. Drain in colander or sieve and press out excess liquid with wooden spoon. Set aside. Wipe pan.
6. Turn steak once in marinade to moisten outside and transfer to cutting surface, cut side up. Reserve marinade. Spread spinach-carrot stuffing over meat to within ½ inch of sides and moisten with 2 tablespoons marinade. Pour remaining marinade into pan used for vegetables and bring to a boil over high heat. Cook until reduced by about half, approximately 30 minutes. Remove bay leaf.
7. While marinade is reducing, roll flank steak up lengthwise (with the grain) and tie the roll at ½-inch intervals, starting in center. Tuck in ends of steak and tie 1 long piece of string lengthwise around the roll. Place in small roasting pan and put in oven. After 10 minutes, reduce temperature to 350 degrees and cook 20 minutes longer. Meat thermometer should register 135 to 138 degrees.
8. Turn off oven and place serving platter on oven rack to warm. Let roulade rest in oven until ready to serve (no longer than 15 minutes).
9. Transfer roulade to center of warmed serving platter and remove string. Reserve meat juices in roasting pan. Using chef's knife, cut roulade into ½-inch-thick slices and arrange on individual plates. Add reserved meat juices to the reduced marinade, skim off surface fat, and season with salt and pepper to taste. Reheat briefly and serve with the roulade.

Cottage Fried Potatoes

5 russet potatoes (about 3 pounds total weight)
½ cup vegetable shortening or oil
Salt
2 tablespoons chopped fresh coriander or parsley

1. Wash potatoes, but do not peel. Using chef's knife, cut into ¼-inch dice or coarsely chop in food processor.
2. In large heavy-gauge non-aluminum skillet, heat shortening over medium heat. When shortening begins to shimmer and has a faint blue haze, add potatoes and cook until golden, about 25 minutes, stirring occasionally with slotted metal spatula.
3. Transfer to paper-towel-lined platter and keep warm in turned-off oven.
4. To serve, season with salt to taste and sprinkle with chopped coriander or parsley. Divide among individual dinner plates.

Asparagus and Tomatoes with Shallot Vinaigrette
Veal Caponata
Fettuccine Oregano

Serve the tomato- and shallot-topped asparagus as a first course or as a side dish with this variation of veal scallopini.

This menu has a distinctly Italian flavor. Victoria Wise's veal scallopini dish is flavored with capers, white wine, and a touch of tomato paste. She recommends serving it with fettuccine, a flat, broad egg noodle that you can buy fresh in many specialty food shops. Or you can use a dried packaged fettuccine—choose an imported Italian brand or a domestic one made with durum semolina. If you are not using fresh oregano in the fettuccine recipe, use the best-quality dried oregano you can find. The cook recommends dried Greek oregano.

For the asparagus and tomato recipe, use Italian plum tomatoes, also known as egg tomatoes; they have a more intense flavor and lower water content than most commercial tomatoes. Most supermarkets stock them. If fresh asparagus are not in season, serve fresh artichokes in their place—but be sure to allow more time for cooking artichokes. The vinaigrette dressing for the vegetables features shallots; if they are not available, you can substitute chopped onion.

WHAT TO DRINK
The acidic elements in this menu call for a well-chilled white wine; choose a dry and flavorful Italian Pinot Grigio or California Sauvignon Blanc, or a French Muscadet to complement these dishes.

Eight to twelve ¼-inch-thick slices veal scallopini, or leg
   round steak (about 1¼ pounds total weight), preferably
   cut across grain from the top round, pounded thin
1 pound asparagus
4 medium-size ripe tomatoes (about 1 pound total weight)
3 large shallots
1 lemon
Small bunch fresh oregano, or 1 tablespoon dried oregano
Small bunch fresh parsley or chives (if not using fresh
   oregano)
1 to 2 tablespoons unsalted butter
1 pint heavy cream
¼ pound Parmesan cheese
½ cup plus 3 to 4 tablespoons olive oil
¼ cup red wine vinegar
3½-ounce jar capers
1 tablespoon tomato paste
12 ounces fettuccine, preferably fresh
1 loaf French bread (optional)
½ cup flour (approximately)
Salt and freshly ground pepper
1 cup dry white wine

UTENSILS

Food processor or blender (optional)
Large stockpot with cover
1 or, preferably, 2 large heavy-gauge non-aluminum
   skillets
Small saucepan
9-inch pie pan
Small bowl
Colander
Strainer or slotted spoon
Measuring cups and spoons
Chef's knife
Paring knife
Wooden spoon
Metal spatula
Grater (if not using processor)
Juicer (optional)
Tongs
Small whisk
Vegetable peeler (optional)
Kitchen string

START-TO-FINISH STEPS

1. If serving French bread with asparagus, preheat oven
to 350 degrees.
2. Follow asparagus recipe step 1. While water is coming
to a boil, chop fresh oregano or parsley, or snip chives,
juice ½ lemon, and slice remaining ½ lemon for veal recipe.
Grate Parmesan and chop fresh oregano, if using, for
fettuccine recipe.
3. Follow asparagus recipe steps 2 through 9.
4. Follow veal recipe step 1.
5. Follow fettuccine recipe step 1. While water is coming to
a boil, remove bread from oven, if serving, and lower oven
temperature to 200 degrees. Serve asparagus and warm
bread.
6. Follow fettuccine recipe step 2.
7. While fettuccine is cooking, follow veal recipe step 2.
8. Follow fettuccine recipe steps 3 and 4, veal recipe step
3, and serve.

RECIPES

Asparagus and Tomatoes with Shallot Vinaigrette

1 pound asparagus
4 medium-size ripe tomatoes (about 1 pound total weight)
1 loaf French bread (optional)
3 large shallots
½ cup olive oil
¼ cup red wine vinegar
Salt and freshly ground pepper

1. Fill large stockpot with water to within 3 inches of top,
cover, and bring to a boil over high heat.
2. Wash and trim asparagus. If spears are thick, peel
stems. Divide into 2 bundles and tie with kitchen string so
asparagus can be retrieved more easily. Set aside.
3. Drop tomatoes into boiling water, count slowly to 15,
and then, using slotted spoon, transfer them to colander.
Reserve boiling water for asparagus.
4. Carefully lower both asparagus bundles into the boiling
water. When water returns to a boil, cook asparagus 4 to 12
minutes, depending on size of spears. Be careful not to
overcook.
5. If serving French bread, place in 350-degree oven to
warm.

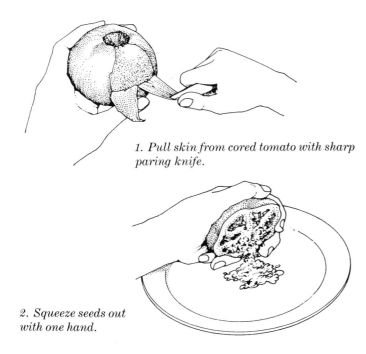

1. Pull skin from cored tomato with sharp paring knife.

2. Squeeze seeds out with one hand.

6. While asparagus are cooking, peel, seed, and dice tomatoes. Drain off juices. Peel and mince shallots.

7. Using tongs, transfer asparagus bundles to colander and rinse briefly in cold water. Reserve boiling water for fettuccine recipe.

8. For dressing, combine tomatoes, shallots, oil, vinegar, and salt and pepper to taste in small bowl.

9. Untie asparagus bundles and divide spears among 4 salad plates. With a fork, stir vinaigrette and pour over asparagus. Cover loosely and set aside until ready to serve.

Veal Caponata

2 tablespoons capers
1 to 2 tablespoons unsalted butter
2 to 3 tablespoons olive oil
Eight to twelve ¼-inch-thick slices veal scallopini, or leg round steak (about 1¼ pounds total weight), preferably cut across grain from the top round, pounded thin
½ cup flour (approximately)
1 cup dry white wine
Juice of ½ lemon
1 tablespoon tomato paste
1 tablespoon chopped fresh oregano or parsley or freshly snipped chives
½ lemon, thinly sliced

1. If using salt-packed capers, rinse in cold water and pat dry with paper towels. If using capers packed in vinegar, drain. Set aside.

2. In 1 or 2 large heavy-gauge non-aluminum skillets, heat butter and oil (if using 2 skillets, use a total of 2 tablespoons butter and 3 tablespoons oil) over medium-high heat. Warm serving platter under hot water. Put flour in pie pan and dredge each veal slice lightly. Shake off excess. When butter foams, add veal to pan and quickly

sauté about 1 minute per side. While veal is cooking, dry platter. Using metal spatula, transfer veal slices to platter as they are cooked. Keep warm in 200-degree oven.

3. Add white wine and lemon juice to skillet, stirring up any browned bits clinging to bottom. Add tomato paste and capers, whisking until blended. Pour sauce over veal, sprinkle with oregano, and garnish with lemon slices.

Fettuccine Oregano

12 ounces fettuccine, preferably fresh
1½ cups heavy cream
1 tablespoon olive oil
⅔ cup freshly grated Parmesan cheese
3 tablespoons chopped fresh oregano, or 1 tablespoon dried
Salt and freshly ground pepper

1. Add enough fresh hot water to asparagus cooking water to measure 3 quarts and return to a boil over medium-high heat.

2. Add fettuccine to pot and cook 3 to 5 minutes for fresh, 8 to 12 minutes for dried.

3. While fettuccine is cooking, gently heat cream in small saucepan over medium-low heat just until warm.

4. Drain fettuccine in colander and return immediately to pot. Add olive oil and toss to coat well. Add remaining ingredients and toss. Cover until ready to serve.

ADDED TOUCH

Anjou and Comice are two sweet and juicy varieties of pear, both recommended for this classic French dessert. Pears that seem a bit too firm, even underripe, will soften nicely when poached in the sweetened wine.

Warm Pears Poached in Red Wine

½ lemon
3 cups red wine
½ cup granulated sugar
1 stick cinnamon
4 slightly firm pears, preferably Comice or Anjou
1 cup heavy cream
4 sprigs fresh mint

1. Juice lemon half and strain out seeds. In medium-size non-aluminum saucepan, bring wine, sugar, lemon juice, and cinnamon stick to a boil over medium heat.

2. Peel, halve, and core pears. Lower into poaching liquid and cook 15 minutes, turning pear halves frequently. With slotted spoon, transfer pears to large bowl and set aside.

3. Over medium-high heat, reduce poaching liquid by half. This should take about 20 to 30 minutes. Liquid should be thick and syrupy.

4. To serve, briefly reheat pears in wine syrup. Spoon 2 pear halves with some syrup into each of 4 bowls. Pour cream over each and garnish with mint sprig.

Fresh Tomato Soup with Garlic-Basil Croutons
Cabbage Leaves with Beef Stuffing / Sour Cream with Chives and Dill
Parslied Potatoes

Fresh, thick tomato soup starts this meal of stuffed cabbage leaves with a dill-flavored sour cream sauce and new potatoes. You can garnish the soup with croutons or serve them on the side.

Napa cabbage (also know as celery cabbage), which is called for in this menu, is a mild Oriental cousin of green cabbage that comes in small compact, oblong heads of pale green and white leaves. Its flavor is delicate, combining that of cabbage, lettuce, and celery, and it gives off no strong cabbage odor during cooking. For this recipe, blanch the leaves, then cut out a small wedge from the spine of each leaf so that the leaf will roll up easily. Reserve the cut-out wedges, which you will chop and use as a bed for the stuffed leaves. If you cannot find Napa, use green cabbage instead.

The thick, fresh tomato soup can be made any time of the year, as long as fresh, flavorful tomatoes are available. The cook prefers Italian plum, or egg, tomatoes. (See page 62 for diagrams showing how to peel and seed tomatoes.) If fresh basil is out of season, use fresh or dried thyme, chervil, tarragon, or dill.

WHAT TO DRINK
The cook suggests a California Sauvignon Blanc or a hearty Provençal red—a Gigondas, for example, or a shipper's (rather than an estate-bottled) Châteauneuf-du-Pape. In warm weather, try a lightly chilled rosé from Provence or Anjou.

SHOPPING LIST AND STAPLES

1 pound ground round steak
2 pounds red potatoes
4 medium-size onions (about 2 pounds total weight)
4 pounds ripe tomatoes, preferably Italian plum
Medium-size head green cabbage, preferably Napa
4 cloves garlic
Small bunch fresh parsley
1 bunch fresh basil (enough to yield 16 good-size leaves)
Large bunch fresh oregano, or 1½ tablespoons dried
Large bunch fresh chives or small bunch scallions
Small bunch fresh dill, or 1 teaspoon dried
2 sticks unsalted butter
1 pint sour cream
½ cup plus 1 tablespoon olive oil
1½ tablespoons tomato paste
1 large loaf French bread or baguette
¼ teaspoon allspice
1 bay leaf
Salt
Freshly ground pepper

Food processor or blender
Large stockpot
Large heavy-gauge skillet
Large saucepan with cover
2 large non-aluminum saucepans with covers
Small saucepan
Medium-size bowl
Small bowl
2 large flat plates
Colander
Sieve
2 slotted spoons
Wooden spoon
Measuring cups and spoons
Chef's knife
Paring knife
Bread knife
Wooden spoon

START-TO-FINISH STEPS

1. Chop fresh oregano, if using, for cabbage recipe and chop parsley for potato recipe.
2. Follow cabbage recipe step 1.
3. While cabbage is being blanched, slice bread for soup recipe and follow steps 1 through 3.
4. Follow cabbage recipe steps 2 through 6.
5. Follow potatoes recipe steps 1 and 2.
6. While potatoes and cabbage are cooking, mince chives and fresh dill, if using, and prepare sour cream.
7. Follow soup recipe steps 4 and 5.
8. Follow cabbage recipe step 7 and potatoes recipe step 3.
9. Follow soup recipe step 6 and serve as first course.
10. Follow cabbage recipe step 8 and serve with sour cream sauce and potatoes.

RECIPES

Fresh Tomato Soup with Garlic-Basil Croutons

4 pounds ripe tomatoes, preferably Italian plum
2 medium-size onions (about 1 pound total weight)
½ cup plus 1 tablespoon olive oil
1 bay leaf

1 bunch fresh basil (enough to yield 16 good-size leaves)
4 cloves garlic
Four ½-inch slices from large loaf of French bread, or
  eight ½-inch slices from baguette
Salt
Freshly ground pepper

1. Peel, seed, and chop tomatoes. Peel and chop onions. In large non-aluminum saucepan, cook tomatoes, onions, 1 tablespoon olive oil, and bay leaf, covered, over medium heat 30 minutes.
2. While vegetables are cooking, wash basil and pat dry with paper towels. Strip leaves from stems and stack them so that they all point in same direction. Slice into strips and set aside.
3. Peel and chop garlic. Set aside.
4. In large heavy-gauge skillet, heat ½ cup olive oil over medium-high heat. Add garlic, stir, then add bread slices. Fry briefly on both sides until golden, about 1 to 2 minutes. Transfer croutons to paper-towel-lined plate.
5. Remove bay leaf from tomato mixture and discard. In food processor or blender, purée tomato mixture in batches, about one quarter of mixture at a time. Pour purée back into pan through a sieve, pressing through with wooden spoon, if necessary. Season with salt and pepper to taste. Cover and keep warm until ready to serve. If necessary, reheat before serving.
6. To serve, divide croutons among 4 bowls, sprinkle bowls with half the basil, fill with soup, and garnish each with remaining basil. Or, if you prefer, garnish soup with basil and serve croutons on the side.

Cabbage Leaves with Beef Stuffing

Medium-size head green cabbage, preferably Napa
2 medium-size onions (about 1 pound total weight)
1 pound ground round steak
4 tablespoons chopped fresh oregano, or 1½ tablespoons
  dried
¼ teaspoon allspice
1½ tablespoons tomato paste
Salt
Freshly ground pepper
1 stick plus 4 tablespoons butter
Sour Cream with Chives and Dill (see following recipe)

1. Fill large stockpot with water to within 3 inches of rim and bring to a boil over high heat. If using green cabbage,

blanch 15 minutes; if using Napa, blanch 5 minutes. Transfer cabbage to colander and drain.

2. Peel and mince onions. In small saucepan, cover onions with water, bring to a boil, and simmer 5 minutes. Pour through sieve and cool slightly.

3. In medium-size bowl, knead together ground round steak, blanched onions, oregano, allspice, tomato paste, and salt and pepper to taste.

4. One by one, gently peel leaves from cabbage. When you reach the core, reserve it. Using paring knife, trim core wedge from each leaf and reserve. Using chef's knife, roughly chop core and trimmings, and set aside.

5. Divide meat stuffing among cabbage leaves, placing 1 to 2 tablespoons stuffing in center of each leaf, and fold into neat "packages."

6. In large non-aluminum saucepan, melt butter over medium heat. Add chopped cabbage core and trimmings, and lay cabbage "packages" on top, folded side down. Season with salt to taste, cover, and simmer 20 minutes.

7. Remove pan from heat and keep covered until ready to serve.

8. To serve on platter, first remove cabbage rolls to plate and then transfer bed of chopped cabbage to platter. Place "packages" on cabbage bed and surround with parslied potatoes (see following recipe). Dot "packages" with a little sour cream sauce (recipe following) and serve remaining sauce on side.

Sour Cream with Chives and Dill

4 tablespoons minced fresh chives or scallions
1 tablespoon minced fresh dill, or 1 teaspoon dried
1 pint sour cream

In small bowl, combine all ingredients. Cover and set aside until ready to serve.

Parslied Potatoes

2 pounds red potatoes
Salt
4 tablespoons butter
4 tablespoons chopped fresh parsley
Freshly ground pepper

1. Wash but do not peel potatoes. Using chef's knife, cut potatoes in half if small, in quarters if large.

2. Place potatoes in large saucepan with water to cover

and 2 teaspoons salt. Bring to a boil and cook, covered, until knife inserted in center of potatoes penetrates easily, about 20 minutes.

3. Drain potatoes in colander. Return them to warm saucepan for 2 or 3 minutes to dry out. Return saucepan to medium heat and add butter. Gently toss potatoes in the melting butter until well coated. Add parsley and salt and pepper to taste. Toss gently, cover, and keep warm until ready to serve.

ADDED TOUCH

Prepare this refreshing minty lemon ice ahead of time and serve in scooped-out lemon halves garnished with mint sprigs. Freezing the lemon halves helps them to keep their shape and gives them an appealing frosty coat when they are served.

Lemon-Mint Ice

⅔ cup sugar
30 to 35 fresh mint leaves
4 to 5 lemons
1 cup sweet white wine or Champagne
Fresh mint sprigs for garnish

1. In small non-aluminum saucepan, bring sugar and ½ cup water to a boil over medium-high heat without stirring. Remove from heat and add mint leaves. Steep mint 5 minutes.

2. Juice enough lemons to measure ⅔ cup juice. Strain out pits. Cut thin slice of rind from outer curve of each lemon half so halves will sit flat. Using paring knife, remove remaining pulp from halves or, using teaspoon, press pulp flat against inside of rind.

3. Add lemon juice and wine to mint syrup in pan and stir to combine.

4. Strain out mint leaves and pour lemon mixture into ice-cube tray or glass bowl. Place in freezer for about 6 hours, or until frozen. To ensure proper texture, occasionally stir mixture, pushing edges down and in along sides of tray or bowl.

5. Remove lemon-mint ice from freezer 30 minutes before serving time. When softened, scoop ice into reserved lemon halves.

6. Return to freezer briefly, just until ready to serve. Garnish each lemon half with a fresh mint sprig and serve with chocolates, if desired.

PORK

Lucy Wing

MENU 1 (Right)
Thai Pork with Coriander and Garlic Chives
Braised Red Bell Pepper and Eggplant
Steamed Rice
Tropical Fruit Salad

MENU 2
Indonesian Pork Satay
Golden Rice
Vegetables with Peanut Sauce

MENU 3
Broiled Chinese Butterflied Pork
Sesame Noodles
Stir-Fried Broccoli
Honeydew with Crystallized Ginger

Although Lucy Wing grew up eating traditional Chinese food, she describes herself as an eclectic cook with an international palate. "I particularly enjoy simplifying recipes from many lands and experimenting with exotic ingredients," she says, "and I like to cook quickly to preserve the natural flavors of the food." The three Asian menus she presents here are all easy to prepare and are distinguished by their unusual seasonings and dramatic colors.

Menu 1 offers Thai dishes. The cook marinates thin slices of pork loin in a sauce flavored with coriander roots and garlic chives, then browns the pork quickly in a wok. Braised red bell pepper and eggplant strips and steamed rice accompany the pork.

In Menu 2, she prepares Indonesia's national dish, *satay*, in which marinated cubes of meat are threaded on bamboo skewers and then grilled. Every one of Indonesia's thousands of islands has its own version of *satay*, but only the Hindu island of Bali serves pork *satay* (all of the other islands are Islamic). Rice flavored with coconut and turmeric (*nasi kuning*), and vegetables with peanut sauce (*gado-gado*) are the colorful side dishes.

Chinese specialties make up Menu 3: broiled pork, stir-fried broccoli, and sesame noodles. Traditionally the Chinese marinate the pork for this dish for several hours, then roast it for another hour. Lucy Wing's streamlined version uses already-tender boneless pork loin, which is broiled for about 25 minutes.

Lightly browned slices of pork loin are garnished with fresh coriander and served with braised vegetables and fluffy steamed rice for this company meal. Offer the tropical fruits on individual plates or in a large bowl.

Thai Pork with Coriander and Garlic Chives
Braised Red Bell Pepper and Eggplant / Steamed Rice
Tropical Fruit Salad

Coriander roots and garlic chives flavor the sauce for the pork. Garlic chives, also called Chinese chives, are more strongly flavored than the Western type and somewhat garlicky. The narrow, flat leaves are cut to about 8 inches long and sold in bunches in Chinese and Japanese markets. Sometimes you will find them with small white flower heads intact; these are edible as well.

The eggplant dish calls for *nam pla*, a Thai sauce made from fermented fish. (Southeast Asians often use fish sauce in place of salt.) You may omit the *nam pla*, but if you do, increase the soy sauce as indicated.

WHAT TO DRINK

The cook suggests a piña colada as a refreshing accompaniment to this menu. If you prefer wine, choose a California Pinot Blanc or Alsatian Sylvaner.

SHOPPING LIST AND STAPLES

2-pound boneless center pork loin roast, trimmed
Large eggplant (about 1½ pounds)
Medium-size red bell pepper
Medium-size bunch coriander with roots
Large bunch garlic chives, or small bunch scallions
Large clove garlic
Small ripe pineapple
Medium-size ripe mango or papaya (about 1 pound)
1 kiwi
2 small or 4 tiny bananas
¾ cup peanut or vegetable oil
12-ounce bottle nam pla, Thai fish sauce, or other Oriental fish sauce (optional)
2 or 3 tablespoons light soy sauce, preferably Chinese
1 cup long-grain rice
4 teaspoons sugar
1 tablespoon plus 2 teaspoons cornstarch
½ teaspoon ground ginger
Dash of crushed red pepper
Salt and freshly ground pepper

UTENSILS

Large wok or Dutch oven
Large skillet with cover
2 large saucepans, 1 with cover
Large bowl
Medium-size bowl
Small bowl
Strainer
Measuring cups and spoons
Chef's knife
Paring knife
Slotted spoon
2 wooden spoons
Rubber spatula
Vegetable peeler

START-TO-FINISH STEPS

One hour ahead: Place pineapple, mango, or papaya if using, and kiwi in coldest part of refrigerator to chill.

1. Follow rice recipe step 1 and pork recipe steps 1 and 2.
2. Follow rice recipe step 2 and pork recipe steps 3 and 4.
3. Follow eggplant recipe steps 1 and 2.
4. Follow fruit salad recipe steps 1 and 2.
5. Follow eggplant recipe steps 3 and 4.
6. Follow rice recipe step 3.
7. Follow pork recipe steps 5 through 7, rice recipe step 4, and serve with eggplant.
8. For dessert, follow fruit salad recipe steps 3 and 4.

RECIPES

Thai Pork with Coriander and Garlic Chives

Large bunch garlic chives, or small bunch scallions
Medium-size bunch coriander with roots
Large clove garlic
2-pound boneless center pork loin roast, trimmed
2 teaspoons salt
2 teaspoons sugar
2 teaspoons cornstarch
Freshly ground pepper
½ cup peanut or vegetable oil

1. Preheat oven to 200 degrees. Place 4 dinner plates in oven to warm.
2. Rinse garlic chives and coriander, and dry with paper towels. Cut enough garlic chives into 1½-inch lengths to measure ½ cup. Cut off coriander roots and chop enough to measure 1 tablespoon. Reserve coriander leaves for garnish. Peel garlic and mince enough to measure 1 tablespoon.
3. Cut pork crosswise into 2 x 3 x ¼-inch-thick slices.

4. In large bowl, combine chopped coriander roots, garlic, salt, sugar, cornstarch, pepper to taste, and ¼ cup oil. Add pork, toss until coated, and set aside 10 minutes.

5. In large wok or Dutch oven, heat the remaining oil over medium-high heat until it begins to sizzle. Add half the pork and sauté, stirring occasionally, until lightly browned, 3 to 4 minutes. Transfer pork to a plate and cover loosely with foil to keep warm. Sauté remaining pork until lightly browned.

6. Return first half of pork to wok and stir together. Warm pork briefly, about 30 seconds, stirring constantly. Add garlic chives and stir to combine.

7. Divide pork among 4 warm dinner plates and garnish with coriander leaves.

Braised Red Bell Pepper and Eggplant

Large eggplant (about 1½ pounds)
Medium-size red bell pepper
1 tablespoon cornstarch
2 teaspoons sugar
Dash of crushed red pepper
½ teaspoon ground ginger
2 or 3 tablespoons light soy sauce, preferably Chinese
1 tablespoon nam pla, Thai fish sauce, or other Oriental fish sauce (optional)
¼ cup peanut or vegetable oil

1. Rinse eggplant and red bell pepper, and dry with paper towels. Trim eggplant and cut into 3 x ½ x ½-inch-thick strips. Halve bell pepper, core, seed, remove membranes, and cut into ¼-inch-thick strips.

2. In small bowl, combine cornstarch, sugar, crushed red pepper, ginger, 2 tablespoons soy sauce and 1 tablespoon nam pla, if using, or 3 tablespoons soy sauce. Stir mixture until blended and set aside.

3. In large skillet, heat oil over medium-high heat until hot. Add eggplant and pepper strips, and sauté, stirring constantly, until vegetables begin to wilt, 3 to 4 minutes.

4. Stir cornstarch mixture to recombine and pour over vegetables, tossing until thoroughly combined. Reduce heat to low, cover skillet, and cook, stirring occasionally, about 5 minutes, or until eggplant is tender. Remove from heat and keep covered until ready to serve.

Steamed Rice

1 cup long-grain rice

1. In large saucepan, bring 6 cups water to a boil over high heat.

2. Add rice and stir. Keeping liquid at a boil, cook rice uncovered, stirring occasionally, until tender, about 20 minutes.

3. Just before rice is done, bring about 1 inch of water to a boil in another saucepan. Turn rice into strainer and place over pan of water, making sure bottom of strainer does not touch boiling water. Cover pan and allow rice to steam until ready to serve.

4. Fluff rice with fork and divide among dinner plates.

Tropical Fruit Salad

Small ripe pineapple, chilled
1 kiwi, chilled
Medium-size ripe mango or papaya (about 1 pound), chilled
2 small or 4 tiny bananas

1. Remove stem, then halve pineapple lengthwise; reserve one half for another use. Quarter remaining half lengthwise, core each quarter, and cut flesh away from rind with paring knife. Remove pineapple eyes, cut each quarter into spears, and place in medium-size bowl.

2. Peel kiwi, quarter, and cut into bite-size pieces. Add to bowl. Peel mango: Using chef's knife, make 4 or more evenly spaced lengthwise cuts through mango flesh, pressing knife against pit; then score firmly several times crosswise and gently dislodge mango pieces with point of knife. Discard pit. Add mango pieces to bowl, cover with plastic wrap, and refrigerate.

3. Just before serving, peel bananas. Cut small bananas crosswise into bite-size slices, or, if using tiny bananas, leave whole. Remove fruit from refrigerator and add bananas.

4. Divide fruit salad among 4 salad plates and serve.

ADDED TOUCH

Canned coconut milk is readily available in Oriental markets and well-stocked supermarkets.

Coconut Chicken Curry Soup

1 chicken breast half (about ½ pound)
Small onion
1 tablespoon peanut or vegetable oil
1 teaspoon cornstarch
1 teaspoon curry powder, approximately
½ teaspoon salt
1 cup canned unsweetened coconut milk

1. In medium-size saucepan, bring chicken breast half and 1½ cups water to a boil over high heat. Cover, reduce heat to low, and cook until chicken is fork tender and flesh is white throughout, about 15 minutes.

2. Meanwhile, peel onion and chop enough to measure ½ cup.

3. Drain chicken, reserving stock; wipe out pan with paper towels. Remove skin and bone from chicken, cut meat into ½-inch cubes, place on plate, and cover with foil to keep warm.

4. In dry saucepan, heat oil over medium heat. Add onion and cook, stirring frequently, 4 to 5 minutes, or until soft.

5. Add cornstarch, 1 teaspoon curry powder or slightly more, if desired, and salt; cook 1 minute, stirring until blended.

6. Add coconut milk and 1 cup reserved chicken stock to pan, and cook soup over medium heat, stirring until slightly thickened, 3 to 4 minutes.

7. Add cubed chicken to soup, stir, and heat through, about 1 minute.

8. Divide soup among 4 bowls and serve immediately.

Indonesian Pork Satay
Golden Rice
Vegetables with Peanut Sauce

Crisscross skewers of pork in the center of each plate, then mound the rice and vegetables with peanut sauce on either side.

Chinese green beans and Napa cabbage are two common Oriental vegetables. Similar in taste and color to the American green bean, the Chinese variety usually measures 12 inches long and has a slightly chewy texture. Napa cabbage has an oblong head of broad, frilled, pale green leaves and a delicate flavor. Both are available year-round in many supermarkets and Chinese groceries.

WHAT TO DRINK

Ice-cold beer or ale is a good partner for these dishes, or try an India Pale ale for an interesting change of pace.

SHOPPING LIST AND STAPLES

2-pound boneless blade Boston pork roast
Medium-size head Napa cabbage (about 1½ pounds)
3 medium-size carrots (about ¾ pound total weight)
½ pound Chinese green beans or regular green beans
Small onion
Medium-size clove garlic
Small lemon
1¾ cups chicken stock, preferably homemade (see page 13), or canned
3 tablespoons peanut or vegetable oil

1 tablespoon rice wine vinegar or white wine vinegar
5 tablespoons light soy sauce, preferably Chinese
6-ounce jar creamy peanut butter
1 cup long-grain rice
2 tablespoons sugar
6-ounce package unsweetened shredded coconut
1 teaspoon ground coriander
1 teaspoon ground ginger
½ teaspoon turmeric
Dash of crushed red pepper
Salt

UTENSILS

Large skillet with cover
Medium-size saucepan with cover
Small heavy-gauge saucepan
Large bowl
2 large platters
Colander
Measuring cups and spoons
Chef's knife
Paring knife
Wooden spoon
Slotted spoon
Pastry brush
Vegetable peeler
Eight 10-inch bamboo skewers

START-TO-FINISH STEPS

1. Follow pork recipe steps 1 through 3.
2. Follow rice recipe steps 1 and 2.
3. Follow pork recipe steps 4 and 5.
4. Meanwhile, remove rice from heat and follow vegetables recipe steps 1 through 9.
5. Follow rice recipe step 3 and serve with pork and vegetables with peanut sauce.

RECIPES

Indonesian Pork Satay

2-pound boneless blade Boston pork roast
2 teaspoons minced garlic
¼ cup light soy sauce, preferably Chinese
1 tablespoon rice wine vinegar or white wine vinegar
1 tablespoon peanut or vegetable oil
2 tablespoons sugar
1 teaspoon ground coriander
1 teaspoon ground ginger
1 teaspoon salt

1. Cut pork into 1-inch cubes.
2. In large bowl, blend all ingredients except pork. Add pork, stir until evenly coated, and set aside 15 minutes.
3. Preheat broiler.
4. Using slotted spoon, transfer pork to large platter, reserving marinade. Divide pork evenly among 8 skewers

and place on rack in foil-lined broiler pan.
5. Broil meat 6 to 7 inches from heat source, turning skewers occasionally and brushing pork with marinade, until meat is a rich brown, about 20 minutes.

Golden Rice

2 tablespoons peanut or vegetable oil
½ cup chopped onion
1 cup long-grain rice
½ teaspoon salt
½ teaspoon turmeric
⅓ to ½ cup unsweetened shredded coconut
1¾ cups chicken stock

1. In medium-size saucepan, heat oil over medium-high heat. Add onion and sauté, stirring occasionally, until lightly browned, about 2 minutes. Stir in rice, salt, turmeric, and coconut to taste. Add chicken stock, stir, and bring to a boil over high heat.
2. Cover pan, reduce heat to low, and simmer rice until tender, about 20 minutes. Stir rice once with fork while cooking. Keep covered until ready to serve.
3. Fluff rice with fork and divide among 4 dinner plates.

Vegetables with Peanut Sauce

3 medium-size carrots (about ¾ pound total weight)
½ pound Chinese green beans or regular green beans
Medium-size head Napa cabbage (about 1½ pounds)
¼ cup creamy peanut butter
1 tablespoon light soy sauce, preferably Chinese
2 teaspoons lemon juice
Dash of crushed red pepper

1. Peel carrots, trim, and cut into ⅛-inch-thick rounds.
2. In large skillet, bring ½ inch water to a boil over medium-high heat. Add carrots, cover, and cook until crisp-tender, 3 or 4 minutes.
3. Meanwhile, trim stem ends of beans and cut enough beans into 2-inch lengths to measure about 2 cups.
4. Using slotted spoon, transfer cooked carrots to a large platter, leaving water at a boil. Cover carrots loosely with foil to keep warm. Place beans in boiling water, cover, and cook until crisp-tender, 3 or 4 minutes.
5. While beans are cooking, cut cabbage in half, reserving one half for another use. Cut remaining half crosswise into ½-inch-wide slices; wash and drain in colander.
6. Transfer cooked beans from pan to platter, keeping them separate from carrots. Keep water in pan at a boil.
7. Place cabbage in boiling water, cover, and cook just until wilted, about 1 minute. Turn cabbage into colander, drain, and transfer to platter with carrots and beans. Keep vegetables covered with foil.
8. Combine peanut butter, soy sauce, lemon juice, and red pepper in small heavy-gauge saucepan, and cook over low heat, stirring constantly, until sauce is smooth and creamy, about 2 minutes.
9. Divide vegetables among dinner plates, top with peanut sauce, and serve with remaining sauce.

Broiled Chinese Butterflied Pork / Sesame Noodles
Stir-Fried Broccoli
Honeydew with Crystallized Ginger

For an easy buffet, present the glazed pork on the same platter as the sesame noodles, and serve the stir-fried broccoli separately. Chilled honeydew wedges sprinkled with crystallized ginger are the dessert.

Visit the Oriental food section of your supermarket or an Oriental grocery to stock up on the ingredients for this menu. Rich, mahogany-colored *hoisin* sauce is a sweet-pungent mixture made with soybeans, ground chilies, garlic, and spices, which is often used in China as a condiment. *Hoisin* sauce is sold in cans or jars; any unused sauce can be stored in a covered jar in the refrigerator, where it will keep for several months. There are no substitutes.

WHAT TO DRINK

Tea, whether fresh-brewed or iced, is the time-honored drink to have with a Chinese meal. Well-chilled Chinese beer would also be very satisfying.

SHOPPING LIST AND STAPLES

2-pound boneless pork loin top loin roast, butterflied
1 bunch Chinese broccoli, preferably, or regular broccoli (1¼ pounds)
½ pound medium-size mushrooms
Large onion
Small bunch scallions for garnish (optional)
2 large cloves garlic
1 honeydew melon (about 4 pounds), or 1 cantaloupe (about 2 pounds)
Large lime (optional)
2 tablespoons peanut or vegetable oil
8-ounce bottle Chinese sesame oil
⅔ cup catsup
15-ounce jar hoisin sauce
12-ounce jar sesame paste (tahini), or 3 tablespoons creamy peanut butter
10-ounce bottle light soy sauce, preferably Chinese
9-ounce bottle oyster sauce
½ pound fresh Chinese egg noodles, or dry spaghetti, spaghettini, or vermicelli
1 teaspoon sugar
4¼-ounce package crystallized ginger
Dash of crushed red pepper
Salt
1 tablespoon dry sherry

UTENSILS

Large skillet

Large saucepan
Small saucepan
Small bowl
Colander
Measuring cups and spoons
Chef's knife
Paring knife
Wooden spoon
Wok spatula (optional)
Pastry brush
Cutting board

START-TO-FINISH STEPS

1. Follow pork recipe step 1 and noodles recipe step 1.
2. Follow honeydew recipe step 1.
3. Follow noodles recipe steps 2 through 4.
4. Follow pork recipe steps 2 and 3.
5. Follow broccoli recipe steps 1 through 3.
6. Follow pork recipe step 4 and broccoli recipe steps 4 through 6.
7. Follow pork recipe step 5, noodles recipe step 5, and serve with broccoli.
8. For dessert, follow honeydew recipe step 2.

RECIPES

Broiled Chinese Butterflied Pork

2-pound boneless pork loin top loin roast, butterflied
2 tablespoons minced garlic
⅔ cup catsup
⅓ cup hoisin sauce
1 tablespoon light soy sauce, preferably Chinese
1 tablespoon dry sherry
½ teaspoon salt

1. Preheat broiler.
2. Open loin, spread out to resemble butterfly wings, and press gently to flatten. Place pork on rack in broiling pan and place pan in broiler. Broil meat 6 inches from heat source, turning occasionally, about 20 minutes.
3. Meanwhile, make sauce for glazing: In small saucepan, combine remaining ingredients and bring to a boil over medium-low heat. Stir sauce and turn heat down as low as possible.
4. Brush pork with sauce and continue to broil, basting with sauce and turning, until completely glazed, 3 to 4 minutes. Transfer pork to serving platter and cover loosely with foil to keep warm.
5. When ready to serve, carve 4 or more slices of pork and transfer to platter. Serve remaining sauce separately.

Sesame Noodles

½ pound fresh Chinese egg noodles, or dry spaghetti, spaghettini, or vermicelli
2 tablespoons finely chopped scallions (optional)
3 tablespoons sesame paste (tahini) or creamy peanut butter

3 tablespoons.light soy sauce, preferably Chinese
2 tablespoons Chinese sesame oil
Dash of crushed red pepper

1. In large saucepan, bring 3 to 4 quarts water to a boil over high heat.
2. Place noodles in boiling water and cook until just tender, 2 to 5 minutes.
3. Meanwhile, blend remaining ingredients with 2 tablespoons water in small bowl.
4. Turn noodles into colander to drain and then return to warm saucepan. Add sesame sauce, toss noodles until evenly coated, and set aside to cool to room temperature.
5. Just before serving, toss again, and transfer to serving platter. Garnish with scallions, if desired.

Stir-Fried Broccoli

1 bunch Chinese broccoli, preferably, or regular broccoli, (1¼ pounds)
Large onion
½ pound medium-size mushrooms
2 tablespoons peanut or vegetable oil
¼ cup oyster sauce
1 teaspoon sugar
Salt

1. Wash broccoli and dry with paper towels. Remove florets and any large leaves, and set aside. Cut stems diagonally into 1- to 1½-inch lengths.
2. Peel onion, slice thinly, and separate into rings. Wipe mushrooms with damp paper towels and cut into ¼-inch-thick slices.
3. Bring ½ inch water to a boil in large skillet over medium-high heat. Add broccoli stems and cook about 2 minutes, or until almost tender. Add florets and leaves and cook another 30 seconds. Turn broccoli into colander to drain; dry skillet.
4. Heat oil in skillet over medium-high heat. Add onions and stir fry just until wilted, about 2 minutes.
5. Add mushrooms to skillet and stir fry until tender, about 1 minute.
6. Stir in broccoli, oyster sauce, sugar, and salt to taste, and stir fry mixture just until heated through, about 2 minutes. Transfer to serving platter and cover loosely with foil to keep warm.

Honeydew with Crystallized Ginger

1 honeydew melon (about 4 pounds) or cantaloupe (about 2 pounds)
2½ tablespoons finely chopped crystallized ginger
1 lime for garnish, thinly sliced (optional)

1. Cut honeydew in half, reserving one half for another use. Remove seeds from remaining half and cut lengthwise into 4 wedges; remove rinds. Place wedges on serving platter, sprinkle with ginger, cover, and refrigerate.
2. Just before serving, remove melon from refrigerator and garnish platter with lime slices, if desired.

Meryle Evans

An authority on American regional cooking, Meryle Evans feels that two important factors shaped this country's cuisine: the presence of indigenous ingredients such as pumpkins, cranberries, sweet corn, and maple syrup, and the arrival of immigrants bringing traditional recipes from many countries. Two of this cook's menus reflect her strong interest in American food, and the third is Scandinavian, a cuisine she has been studying recently.

Menu 2 is a traditional southern meal that can be prepared in very little time. It features ham steak glazed with maple syrup and bourbon, and individual cornmeal spoonbreads. With the pork Meryle Evans serves ambrosia, a sweet concoction of fruit and coconut that was created in the nineteenth century.

She offers a Creole dinner from New Orleans in Menu 3. The main course, jambalaya (the name comes from the French *jambon*, meaning ham), is a blend of French, Spanish, African, and American influences, as is most Creole food. This jambalaya includes ham, sausage, shrimp, vegetables, and rice, and is served with artichoke hearts and Creole *rémoulade*.

Menu 1 focuses on Scandinavian dishes. Pork chops stuffed with prunes is a variation on a Swedish specialty, prune-stuffed pork loin. It is served with Finnish spinach pancakes, smoked salmon (preferably Norwegian), and a refreshing cucumber salad.

Prune-stuffed pork chops with zesty sautéed apples spooned on top and spinach pancakes make an ample main course for this Scandinavian meal. Offer the sliced-cucumber salad with sprigs of fresh dill, and the smoked salmon rolls with a spoonful of crème fraîche.

Smoked Salmon with Dilled Crème Fraîche / Cucumber Salad
Prune-Stuffed Pork Chops with Apples
Spinach Pancakes

Smoked salmon is an elegant first course by itself or is equally delicious served, as here, with a cucumber salad. Buy top-quality salmon, such as Norwegian, Scotch, Irish, or Nova Scotia, and have it sliced paper thin. Salmon is perishable, so refrigerate it and use it quickly. *Crème fraîche*, which tops each serving of salmon, is thick, naturally fermented cream (see the start-to-finish steps for a simple recipe). It is occasionally available in the dairy section of well-stocked supermarkets. Sour cream is an acceptable substitute.

Try some *crème fraîche* on the spinach pancakes, or top them with melted butter.

WHAT TO DRINK

Cold aquavit is a fitting aperitif here. With the meal, offer Riesling—a lightly sweet *Kabinett* from Germany, a dry balanced bottle from Alsace, or a full-bodied one from California.

SHOPPING LIST AND STAPLES

Four ¾-inch-thick loin pork chops (about 2 pounds total weight) with pockets cut in sides for stuffing
12 thin slices smoked salmon, preferably Norwegian (about ⅓ pound total weight)
2 large cucumbers
Small head Boston or Bibb lettuce
½ pound fresh spinach
Large bunch dill
2 large firm tart apples, such as Granny Smith
1 lemon
2 eggs
1¼ cups milk
½ cup crème fraîche, preferably homemade, or commercial
1 stick plus 2 tablespoons unsalted butter
⅔ cup red or white wine vinegar
1 tablespoon Dijon mustard
8-ounce box medium-size pitted prunes
1 cup all-purpose flour
2 tablespoons plus ½ teaspoon granulated sugar
2 tablespoons light brown sugar
Ground nutmeg
Ground cloves
Salt

Freshly ground white pepper
Freshly ground black pepper

UTENSILS

Food processor or blender
Large heavy-gauge skillet with cover plus additional skillet (if not using griddle)
Griddle (optional)
Small heavy-gauge saucepan or butter warmer
13 x 9-inch shallow, ovenproof casserole or baking dish
Large bowl
2 medium-size bowls
Small bowl
Large sieve or strainer
Measuring cups and spoons
Chef's knife
Paring knife
2 wooden spoons
Slotted spoon
Metal spatula or pancake turner
Rubber spatula
Tongs
Wooden toothpicks or small metal skewers

START-TO-FINISH STEPS

The day before: If using homemade crème fraîche for salmon recipe, prepare as follows: Whisk ½ pint heavy cream into ½ pint sour cream at room temperature. Pour mixture into glass jar and cover tightly; let stand in warm place for 6 to 8 hours, then refrigerate.

Thirty minutes ahead: Soak prunes in hot water to cover.

1. Wash, dry, and mince dill for salmon and cucumber salad recipes.
2. Follow cucumber salad recipe steps 1 and 2.
3. Follow pork chops recipe steps 1 through 7.
4. Follow cucumber salad recipe step 3.
5. Follow pork chops recipe step 8 and pancakes recipe steps 1 through 4.
6. Follow salmon recipe steps 1 and 2, cucumber salad recipe step 4, and serve as appetizer.
7. While chops are still baking, follow pork chops recipe step 9 and pancakes recipe step 5.
8. Follow pork chops recipe step 10, and serve with pancakes.

RECIPES

Smoked Salmon with Dilled Crème Fraîche

½ cup crème fraîche, preferably homemade, or
    commercial
1 tablespoon minced dill plus 4 dill sprigs for garnish
    (optional)
12 thin slices smoked salmon, preferably Norwegian
    (about ⅓ pound total weight)

1. In small bowl, blend crème fraîche and minced dill.
2. Roll up slices of smoked salmon and arrange 3 rolls on each of 4 salad plates, leaving room for cucumber salad. Top each serving with spoonful of dilled crème fraîche and garnish each with dill sprig, if desired. Cover and refrigerate until ready to serve.

Cucumber Salad

⅔ cup red or white wine vinegar
2 tablespoons sugar
1 teaspoon salt
½ teaspoon freshly ground white pepper
2 large cucumbers
¼ cup minced dill plus 4 dill sprigs for garnish (optional)
Small head Boston or Bibb lettuce

1. In medium-size bowl, combine vinegar, sugar, salt, pepper, and ⅓ cup ice water.
2. Peel cucumbers and slice thinly. Add slices to bowl and stir. Sprinkle cucumbers with dill, cover, and refrigerate until ready to serve.
3. Wash lettuce and dry with paper towels. Wrap in paper towels and refrigerate until ready to serve.
4. Arrange lettuce leaves on plates with salmon and top with cucumbers; garnish with dill sprigs, if desired.

Prune-Stuffed Pork Chops with Apples

8 medium-size pitted prunes, soaked in hot water for 30
    minutes
Four ¾-inch-thick loin pork chops (about 2 pounds total
    weight) with pockets cut in sides for stuffing
Salt and freshly ground black pepper
1 lemon
2 large firm tart apples, such as Granny Smith
6 tablespoons unsalted butter
2 tablespoons light brown sugar
½ teaspoon ground nutmeg
Pinch of ground cloves
1 tablespoon Dijon mustard

1. Preheat oven to 350 degrees.
2. Stuff 2 soft prunes into each pork chop pocket and secure pocket with toothpick or small skewer. Rub both sides of each chop with salt and pepper.
3. Grate enough lemon zest to make 2 teaspoons and set aside. Cut lemon in half and squeeze juice from both halves into large bowl. Wash apples under cold running water. Halve 1 apple, core, and cut into 8 thin slices. Peel, core, and coarsely chop remaining apple. Toss apple slices

and chunks in lemon juice to prevent discoloration, and set aside.
4. In large heavy-gauge skillet, melt 2 tablespoons butter over medium-high heat until frothy, about 1 minute. Add chops and sauté, turning once, until well browned, 3 to 4 minutes per side.
5. Transfer chops to shallow, ovenproof casserole or baking dish; set aside. Wipe out skillet with paper towels.
6. In skillet, melt remaining butter over medium heat. With slotted spoon, remove apple chunks from lemon juice and dry with paper towels; reserve the apple slices. Add chunks to skillet, tossing until evenly coated with butter. Cover and cook until apples are slightly soft, 2 to 3 minutes.
7. Stir in lemon zest, light brown sugar, nutmeg, cloves, and pinch of salt, and cook about 5 minutes, or until ingredients are combined. Stir in mustard.
8. Spoon half of apple mixture over chops and bake 30 to 40 minutes, or until no pink shows at the bone and apples are golden brown. Cover remaining apple mixture and set aside.
9. Place 4 dinner plates under hot running water to warm.
10. Dry plates. Divide chops among warmed plates and top each serving with spoonful of remaining apple mixture. Garnish each with 2 slices of reserved raw apple slices and serve immediately.

Spinach Pancakes

½ pound fresh spinach
4 tablespoons unsalted butter, approximately
1 cup all-purpose flour
1 teaspoon salt
½ teaspoon sugar
1¼ cups milk
2 eggs

1. Remove tough stems from spinach and discard. Wash spinach thoroughly; do not dry. Transfer to large skillet, cover, and steam over medium heat 4 to 5 minutes, or until wilted.
2. Meanwhile, in small heavy-gauge saucepan or butter warmer, melt butter over low heat.
3. Turn spinach into sieve or strainer and squeeze out as much moisture as possible. Chop finely.
4. In food processor fitted with metal blade or in blender, combine flour, salt, sugar, milk, eggs, and 2 tablespoons melted butter; process until blended. Transfer to medium-size bowl and fold in spinach. Set batter aside.
5. In large skillet or griddle, warm ½ tablespoon melted butter over low heat. When butter begins to foam, pour out about 2 tablespoons batter per pancake, making four 3-inch pancakes. Cook until undersides begin to brown, 2 to 3 minutes. Using metal spatula or pancake turner, turn pancakes and cook other side another minute. Transfer to plate, place square of waxed paper between pancakes, and cover loosely with foil. Repeat with remaining batter, adding butter to pan as needed, to make a total of 12 to 16 pancakes.

Ham Steak with Maple-Bourbon Glaze
Ambrosia
Individual Spoonbreads

Slices of ham steak with maple-bourbon glaze and sweet ambrosia are the basis of an easy informal supper (the ambrosia could also be served for dessert). Serve the spoonbreads in their individual ramekins.

Maple-flavored syrup is sold in most supermarkets, but it lacks the intense flavor of pure maple syrup, which is preferred for the ham. Although costly, pure maple syrup is worth the extra money. Store the syrup in the refrigerator once opened because it spoils quickly if left at room temperature.

The spoonbreads, made with cornmeal, milk, and eggs, are more like pudding than bread. The cook prefers using white stoneground meal, available at health food stores and some supermarkets, but regular yellow cornmeal is an acceptable substitute.

WHAT TO DRINK

The cook suggests a dry rosé to accompany this dinner. Try a varietal Cabernet rosé from California or a fine French Tavel.

SHOPPING LIST AND STAPLES

1½-inch-thick center-cut ham steak (about 2½ pounds)
4 medium-size navel oranges
Small bunch seedless green grapes (about ¼ pound)
4 eggs
1 cup milk
4½ tablespoons unsalted butter
¼ cup pure maple syrup
1 teaspoon all-purpose flour
1 cup white or yellow cornmeal, preferably stoneground
Three 4-ounce bags sweetened shredded coconut
2 tablespoons sugar, approximately
Pinch of ground cloves
¼ teaspoon dry mustard
Salt
2 tablespoons bourbon
¼ cup plus 2 tablespoons dry red wine

UTENSILS

Large heavy-gauge skillet
Medium-size heavy-gauge saucepan
Four 10- to 12-ounce ramekins or other small ovenproof
  dishes
2 medium-size bowls
Small bowl
Measuring cups and spoons
Chef's knife
Paring knife

Wooden spoon
Spatula
Egg beater or electric mixer (optional)
Tongs

START-TO-FINISH STEPS

1. Follow ambrosia recipe steps 1 and 2.
2. Follow spoonbreads recipe steps 1 through 5.
3. Follow ham recipe steps 1 through 4. (If ham is ready before spoonbreads, leave in skillet and reheat briefly just before serving.)
4. Follow ham recipe step 5, ambrosia recipe step 3, and serve with spoonbreads.

RECIPES

Ham Steak with Maple-Bourbon Glaze

1½ tablespoons unsalted butter
1½-inch-thick center-cut ham steak (about 2½ pounds)
Pinch of ground cloves
¼ teaspoon dry mustard
1 teaspoon all-purpose flour
¼ cup plus 2 tablespoons dry red wine
2 tablespoons bourbon
¼ cup pure maple syrup

1. In large heavy-gauge skillet, melt butter over medium heat. Brown ham on both sides, 6 to 7 minutes per side, and transfer to platter. Remove skillet from heat and reserve.
2. In small bowl, combine cloves, dry mustard, flour, and 2 tablespoons water.
3. Return skillet to low heat. Add spice mixture, red wine, bourbon, and maple syrup, and stir until blended. Cook slowly, stirring constantly, until glaze begins to thicken, 1 to 2 minutes.
4. Return ham to skillet and heat through, turning once or twice, about 8 minutes.
5. Transfer ham to cutting board and slice crosswise. Arrange 3 to 4 slices on each of 4 dinner plates and top with glaze.

Ambrosia

4 medium-size navel oranges
Small bunch seedless green grapes (about ¼ pound)
2 tablespoons sugar, approximately
1½ cups sweetened shredded coconut

1. With paring knife, peel oranges and remove white pith. Cut crosswise into ¼-inch-thick rounds. Wash grapes and dry with paper towels.
2. Place orange slices and grapes in medium-size bowl. If oranges are tart, sprinkle with a little sugar. Cover and refrigerate until ready to serve.
3. Just before serving, overlap 3 to 4 orange slices on each dinner plate and sprinkle with coconut. Scatter grapes over the slices.

Individual Spoonbreads

1 cup white or yellow cornmeal, preferably stoneground
1 teaspoon salt
3 tablespoons unsalted butter
4 eggs
1 cup milk

1. Preheat oven to 425 degrees. Lightly grease four 10- to 12-ounce ramekins or other ovenproof dishes.
2. In medium-size saucepan, combine cornmeal and salt. Add 2 cups boiling water and stir well. Cook over medium heat, stirring constantly, 1 to 2 minutes, or until thickened.
3. Remove pan from heat and add butter, stirring until melted.
4. In medium-size bowl, beat eggs until frothy and lemon colored. Add milk and stir until blended. Add egg mixture to cornmeal mixture and stir until batter is smooth.
5. Divide batter among ramekins and bake about 25 minutes, or until tip of knife inserted in center comes out clean.

ADDED TOUCH

For this quick-to-assemble hearty salad, you can use canned black-eyed peas instead of frozen, but be sure to drain them well.

Black-Eyed Pea Salad

10-ounce package frozen black-eyed peas
Small head Boston or Bibb lettuce
2 medium-size tomatoes (about 1 pound total weight)
2 stalks celery
Small red onion (optional)
⅓ cup corn oil
3 to 4 tablespoons red or white wine vinegar
½ teaspoon dry mustard
Salt
Freshly ground pepper

1. In medium-size saucepan, cook peas as directed on package. Drain, transfer to medium-size bowl, cover, and refrigerate until chilled.
2. Meanwhile, wash lettuce and dry in salad spinner or with paper towels. Wrap in paper towels and refrigerate.
3. Wash tomatoes and celery, and dry with paper towels. Core, halve, and coarsely chop tomatoes; finely chop enough celery to measure 1 cup. Set aside.
4. If using red onion, peel and mince enough to measure 1 tablespoon; set aside.
5. In small bowl, whisk corn oil, vinegar, dry mustard, and salt and pepper to taste until blended.
6. Add tomatoes, celery, and onion, if using, to peas and toss to combine. Add vinaigrette and toss until evenly coated.
7. Divide lettuce among salad plates, top with salad, and serve.

Oysters on the Half Shell
Jambalaya
Artichoke Hearts with Creole Rémoulade

Oysters on the half shell introduce the hearty jambalaya, accompanied by artichoke hearts on a bed of watercress.

Raw oysters on the half shell require little preparation. Buy them as close to serving time as possible to preserve their freshness.

WHAT TO DRINK

With this meal, serve a fruity but firm red wine such as a young California Zinfandel or an Italian Barbera or Dolcetto.

SHOPPING LIST AND STAPLES

4 spicy link sausages, such as Polish or Italian (about 10 ounces total weight)
½ pound precooked ham
½ pound medium-size shrimp
12 oysters
Large bunch watercress
Large green bell pepper
Large stalk celery
2 medium-large onions
Small bunch scallions
2 cloves garlic
Small bunch parsley
1 lemon plus additional lemon (optional)
3 tablespoons unsalted butter, bacon fat, or lard
16-ounce can Italian plum tomatoes
2 cups chicken stock, preferably homemade (see page 13), or canned
Two 14-ounce cans water-packed artichoke hearts
⅓ cup vegetable oil
⅓ cup olive oil
¼ cup red or white wine vinegar
1 tablespoon Creole or Dijon mustard
1 tablespoon prepared horseradish
1 cup long-grain rice
¼ teaspoon dried thyme
1 teaspoon paprika
¼ teaspoon Cayenne pepper
Pinch of ground cloves
Salt and freshly ground black pepper
2 tablespoons anise-flavored liqueur, such as Pernod

Food processor or blender (optional)
Large heavy-gauge skillet with cover
Small bowl
Salad spinner (optional)
Measuring cups and spoons
Chef's knife
Paring knife
Serrated knife
Wooden spoon
Tongs
Oyster knife (optional)
Pastry brush

START-TO-FINISH STEPS

Two hours ahead: Refrigerate artichoke hearts.

1. Wash parsley and watercress; dry in salad spinner or with paper towels. Remove stems from watercress and discard. Wrap in paper towels and refrigerate. Mince enough parsley to measure 6 tablespoons; set aside. Rinse 1 lemon, dry with paper towel, and cut crosswise into 8 rounds; set aside. Juice remaining lemon.
2. Follow oysters recipe steps 1 and 2.
3. Follow jambalaya recipe steps 1 through 7.
4. While jambalaya is cooking, serve oysters.
5. Follow artichoke hearts recipe steps 1 through 3.
6. Follow jambalaya recipe step 8 and serve with artichoke hearts.

RECIPES

Oysters on the Half Shell

12 oysters
2 tablespoons anise-flavored liqueur, such as Pernod
1 lemon for garnish
Watercress for garnish

1. Shuck oysters, reserving liquor and bottom shells.
2. Arrange 3 oysters on each of 4 salad plates, top with a spoonful of reserved liquor, and brush lightly with anise liqueur. Garnish each serving with 2 lemon slices and watercress, cover, and refrigerate until ready to serve.

Jambalaya

4 spicy link sausages, such as Polish or Italian, (about 10 ounces total weight)
½ pound precooked ham
Large green bell pepper
Large stalk celery
2 medium-large onions
2 cloves garlic
3 tablespoons unsalted butter, bacon fat, or lard
¼ cup minced fresh parsley
¼ teaspoon dried thyme
¼ teaspoon Cayenne pepper
¼ teaspoon freshly ground black pepper
Pinch of ground cloves
½ pound medium-size shrimp
2 cups canned Italian plum tomatoes, with juice
2 cups chicken stock
1 cup long-grain rice

1. Cut sausages into ½-inch pieces and dice enough ham to measure 1 cup; set aside.
2. Wash bell pepper and celery; dry with paper towels. Halve, core, seed, and coarsely chop pepper; chop celery. Peel and chop onions; peel and mince garlic.
3. In large heavy-gauge skillet, melt butter over medium heat. Add sausages and ham, and sauté 5 to 7 minutes, or until sausage is browned.
4. Meanwhile, peel and devein shrimp: Starting at head end, slip thumb under shell between feelers. Lift off 2 or 3 shell segments at once and, holding tail, pull shrimp out of shell. Pull off tail shell. With sharp paring knife, slit down back and lift out black vein.
5. Add green bell pepper, celery, onions, garlic, and 2 tablespoons of the parsley to skillet, and cook, stirring frequently, until onions are soft and translucent, about 5 minutes.
6. Stir in thyme, Cayenne, black pepper, cloves, and shrimp. Add tomatoes and chicken stock, and bring to a boil.
7. Add rice, reduce heat to a gentle simmer, cover, and cook, stirring occasionally, until rice is tender, 25 to 30 minutes.
8. Divide jambalaya among dinner plates and garnish with remaining parsley. Serve at once.

Artichoke Hearts with Creole Rémoulade

Small bunch scallions
1 tablespoon Creole or Dijon mustard
1 tablespoon prepared horseradish
¼ cup red or white wine vinegar
Juice of 1 lemon
1 teaspoon paprika
⅓ cup vegetable oil
⅓ cup olive oil
2 tablespoons minced parsley
Salt and freshly ground pepper
Large bunch watercress
Two 14-ounce cans water-packed artichoke hearts, chilled

1. Wash scallions and dry with paper towels. Trim off root ends and chop enough to measure ½ cup; set aside.
2. In food processor or blender, combine mustard, horseradish, vinegar, lemon juice, and paprika. Process, adding vegetable and olive oils in a slow, steady stream, until sauce is thick and smooth. Turn sauce into small bowl and stir in scallions and parsley. Add salt and pepper to taste, cover, and chill in freezer until ready to serve.
3. Divide watercress among 4 dinner plates. Drain artichoke hearts, cut in half, and arrange on top of watercress. Top each serving with a spoonful of Creole rémoulade.

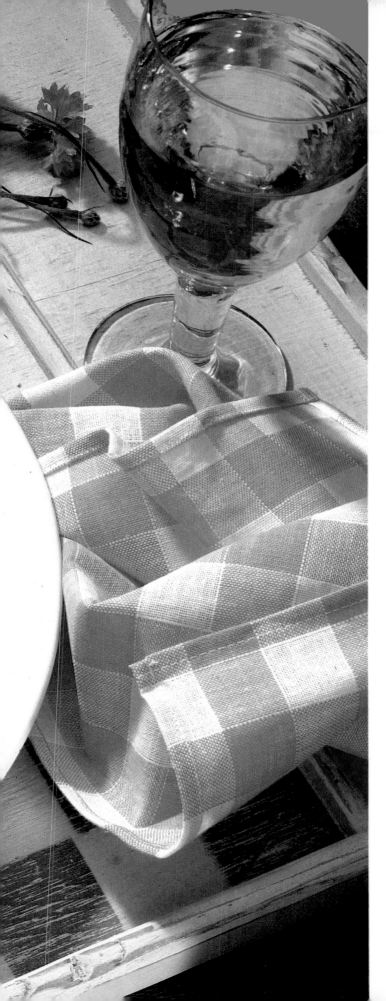

Dennis Gilbert

Dennis Gilbert describes himself as a man who cooks for the love of it and cites his travels through Europe and his experiences as a restaurant chef as the major influences on his culinary style. "Over the years," he says, "I have learned that recipes are really just guidelines and that the best meals can be made by experimenting with the ingredients at hand or by adapting a method to suit the situation." All three of his menus offer cooks the opportunity to be adventurous with a wide range of foods.

In Menu 1, he creates an unlikely—yet delicious—marinade for the country-style ribs by adding orange juice, cumin, coriander seeds, garlic, ginger, and jalapeños to a Japanese plum wine base. The ribs are served with sweet potatoes sautéed in a mildly spiced butter.

He stuffs and rolls slices of pork loin in Menu 2, then braises the rolls in a rich stock with sherry, tomatoes, and okra. For an unusual salad, he combines cucumbers and grapes with a dressing of sour cream, mustard, Japanese green horseradish, and rose water.

Menu 3 is perhaps a bit more traditional but no less interesting. Here Dennis Gilbert sautés medallions of pork tenderloin and tops them with orange sauce for the main course (he says freshly squeezed orange juice is important). The pork goes well with mixed vegetables with green peppercorn sauce and brown rice flavored with scallions, tamari, and sesame oil.

For a casual meal for friends or family, serve country-style ribs with a plum sauce containing red peppers and snow peas. Accompany the ribs with slices of sautéed sweet potato.

85

Country-Style Ribs with Plum Sauce
Sautéed Sweet Potatoes

Japanese plum wine, used in the sauce for the ribs, is a clear, very sweet wine with a delightfully subtle aftertaste of plums. If you prefer, you can substitute a German Gewürztraminer or a sweet Riesling; however, because of their lower alcohol content, these wines do not permit flambéing as the plum wine does. If firm, sweet Italian prune plums are out of season, pitted prunes are an acceptable alternative. They need no prior soaking or softening for this recipe.

Fresh hot jalapeño or the milder Anaheim chilies are increasingly available nationwide. The best are plump and wrinkle-free, without blemishes or soft spots. If you can't find fresh chilies, use red pepper flakes rather than canned chilies.

WHAT TO DRINK

If you choose a Gewürztraminer or Riesling to flavor the pork, serve the same wine with dinner as well. Or try a German *Kabinett*-class Mosel.

SHOPPING LIST AND STAPLES

8 country-style pork ribs, each 1¼ to 1½ inches thick (about 5 pounds total weight)
¼ pound snow peas
2 large red bell peppers (about 1 pound total weight)
2 jalapeño or Anaheim chilies (about 2 ounces total weight), or 1 tablespoon red pepper flakes
4 medium-size sweet potatoes (about 3 pounds total weight)
2 medium-size onions
2 small cloves garlic
Small piece fresh ginger (optional)
4 Italian prune plums, or 6 to 8 pitted prunes
6 tablespoons unsalted butter
3 cups chicken or veal stock, preferably homemade (see page 13), or canned
1 cup fresh orange juice
⅔ cup safflower or sunflower oil, approximately
2 tablespoons arrowroot or cornstarch
½ teaspoon ground cumin
2 teaspoons ground coriander
½ teaspoon ground cardamom
Freshly ground black pepper

¾ cup Japanese plum wine, German Gewürztraminer, or sweet Riesling
¼ cup Scotch whiskey (optional)

UTENSILS

Food processor or blender
Medium-size heavy-gauge saucepan with cover
Large sauté pan with cover
Small sauté pan
Large roasting pan with rack
2 medium-size bowls
3 small bowls
Measuring cups and spoons
Chef's knife
Paring knife
Wooden spoon
Spatula
Fine sieve
Pastry brush
Tongs
Vegetable peeler
Rubber gloves

START-TO-FINISH STEPS

1. Follow ribs recipe step 1.
2. Peel and chop onions for ribs and sweet potatoes recipes. Peel garlic. Mince one clove for ribs recipe and crush remaining clove with chef's knife for sweet potatoes recipe.
3. Follow ribs recipe steps 2 through 5.
4. Follow sweet potatoes recipe step 1.
5. Follow ribs recipe steps 6 and 7.
6. Follow sweet potatoes recipe step 2.
7. Follow ribs recipe steps 8 through 11.
8. Follow sweet potatoes recipe steps 3 through 5.
9. Follow ribs recipe step 12, sweet potatoes recipe step 6, and serve.

RECIPES

Country-Style Ribs with Plum Sauce

⅔ cup safflower or sunflower oil, approximately
1 cup fresh orange juice
8 country-style pork ribs, each 1¼ to 1½ inches thick (about 5 pounds total weight)

Freshly ground black pepper
2 large red bell peppers (about 1 pound total weight)
¼ pound snow peas
Small piece fresh ginger (optional)
Medium-size onion, peeled and chopped
¾ cup Japanese plum wine, German Gewürztraminer, or sweet Riesling
3 cups chicken or veal stock
½ teaspoon ground cumin
2 teaspoons ground coriander
2 jalapeño or Anaheim chilies (about 2 ounces total weight), or 1 tablespoon red pepper flakes
4 Italian prune plums, or 6 to 8 pitted prunes
2 tablespoons arrowroot or cornstarch
1 teaspoon minced garlic

1. Preheat oven to 450 degrees.
2. In small bowl, combine ¼ cup of the oil and ⅓ cup of the orange juice.
3. Brush each rib with about 1 teaspoon of remaining oil and season with pepper. Place ribs on rack in roasting pan and cook, turning ribs with tongs 3 or 4 times and basting them with juice mixture, 40 minutes.
4. While ribs are cooking, wash red bell peppers and dry with paper towels. Halve, core, and seed peppers. Cut one pepper into strips and chop remaining pepper. Trim and string snow peas. If using ginger, peel and mince enough to measure 1 teaspoon.
5. Heat 2 tablespoons oil in medium-size heavy-gauge saucepan over medium heat. Add onion and chopped red bell pepper, and sauté until onion is translucent and pepper is soft, about 5 minutes.
6. Remove pan from heat. Add ¼ cup of the plum wine and, averting your face, carefully ignite. When flame subsides, return pan to heat, add stock, remaining ⅔ cup orange juice, cumin, and coriander, and bring to a boil over high heat, skimming off any froth. Reduce heat to low and simmer until reduced to about 2½ cups, about 15 minutes.
7. While sauce is reducing, wearing rubber gloves, cut chilies, if using, into ½-inch-thick rings and remove seeds. Halve and pit plums or prunes, then cut into wedges. In medium-size bowl, combine plums or prunes with chilies, if using, and pepper strips, and toss mixture with ¼ cup plum wine.
8. When sauce is reduced, pass it through fine sieve set over medium-size bowl, pressing on solids to extract as much liquid as possible; discard solids. Return sauce to pan, set over low heat, and add snow peas.
9. Meanwhile, blend arrowroot or cornstarch with remaining ¼ cup plum wine in small bowl and slowly add to sauce, stirring, until sauce thickens, about 1 minute.
10. Add minced garlic and red pepper flakes and ginger, if using, and stir in pepper and plum mixture. Cover pan and set aside in warm place.
11. Place dinner plates under hot running water to warm.
12. Dry plates. Remove ribs from oven. Divide ribs among plates and top each serving with sauce, fruit, and vegetables.

Sautéed Sweet Potatoes

4 medium-size sweet potatoes (about 3 pounds total weight)
6 tablespoons unsalted butter
Medium-size onion, peeled and chopped
Small clove garlic, crushed
½ teaspoon ground cardamom
¼ cup Scotch whiskey (optional)

1. Peel sweet potatoes and cut into ¼-inch-thick rounds.
2. In large sauté pan, melt 2 tablespoons butter over medium-high heat until sizzling. Add sweet potatoes and sauté, turning frequently, until brown on both sides, 8 to 10 minutes.
3. While sweet potatoes are sautéing, melt 2 tablespoons of the butter over medium-low heat in small sauté pan. Add onion and garlic, and cook, stirring, until soft, 3 to 4 minutes.
4. Add remaining butter to onion mixture, sprinkle with cardamom, and carefully pour in Scotch, if using. Cook just until butter melts, about 2 minutes.
5. Transfer onion mixture to food processor or blender and purée. Pour purée over sweet potatoes and cover pan. Reduce heat to very low and cook 3 to 5 minutes, or until fork-tender.
6. Divide sweet potatoes among plates and top each serving with onion purée.

ADDED TOUCH

The knobby Jerusalem artichoke, or sunchoke, a native American vegetable, is the root of one type of sunflower. Available year-round at health food stores and many supermarkets, Jerusalem artichokes are at their best in winter. Before using, scrub them with a brush under cold water.

Stir-Fried Celery and Mushrooms with Jerusalem Artichokes

6 to 8 large celery stalks
½ pound small white mushrooms
½ pound Jerusalem artichokes
2 large shallots
2 tablespoons peanut oil
1 tablespoon clarified butter (see page 20)
¼ cup good-quality dry sherry

1. Trim celery stalks; wash, and dry with paper towels. Cut stalks into crescents ½ inch wide and 2 inches long.
2. Trim mushrooms and wipe clean with damp paper towels.
3. Scrub artichokes well and cut into ¼-inch-thick slices. Peel and chop shallots.
4. In wok or medium-size sauté pan, heat peanut oil over high heat until smoking. Add clarified butter, celery, and mushrooms, and stir fry until mushrooms are golden and celery is bright green, 2 to 3 minutes.
5. Add shallots and sherry, and cook 1 minute. Add artichokes, toss briefly, and serve.

Tangy Cucumber and Grape Salad
Stuffed Pork Rolls with Tomatoes and Okra

Let your guests help themselves to the cucumber and grape salad and ham- and mushroom-filled pork rolls.

The pork dish contains okra, a popular southern vegetable brought to America by African slaves in the eighteenth century. A tapered green or white seed pod, okra exudes a thick liquid while cooking that gives substance to sauces. The cook offers a general rule of thumb: The fresher the okra, the greater its thickening potential. Buy tender pods that are no longer than 4 inches and that snap easily. If fresh okra is out of season or not readily available in your area, use frozen okra; however, it may be necessary to thicken the sauce with arrowroot.

An unusual combination of *wasabi* (Japanese green horseradish), rose water, and two types of mustard enriches the sour cream dressing for the refreshing salad. *Wasabi* has a potent flavor, so be careful not to use too much. It is sold as a paste or powder, but the powdered form is preferable because it does not deteriorate (mix with a small amount of water or other liquid or wet ingredient as you need it). Rose water, a distillation of fresh rose petals, is used frequently to perfume Indian and Middle Eastern dishes. Add it sparingly to the dressing. Many liquor stores, pharmacies, and specialty food shops carry rose water.

WHAT TO DRINK

For this meal, select a young California Zinfandel or a Gamay Beaujolais. If you prefer an imported wine, either a young Chianti or a French Beaujolais would be ideal.

SHOPPING LIST AND STAPLES

Eight 1-inch-thick center loin pork scallops (about 2 to 2½ pounds total weight), pounded thin
¼ pound Westphalian ham
½ pound mushrooms
1½ pounds firm Italian plum tomatoes, or 28-ounce can whole peeled tomatoes
1 pound fresh okra, or two 10-ounce packages frozen
2 large cucumbers

Small bunch chives or scallions
Medium-size onion
2 large shallots
Medium-size clove garlic
½ pound seedless red or green grapes
1 stick unsalted butter, approximately
½ pint sour cream or crème fraîche
½ cup chicken stock, preferably homemade (see page 13),
    or canned
2 teaspoons rose water (optional)
1 tablespoon Dijon mustard
⅔ cup fresh or dried bread crumbs
2 tablespoons arrowroot or cornstarch (optional)
1 teaspoon wasabi or white horseradish
1 teaspoon dried thyme
1 teaspoon dry mustard
½ teaspoon ground sage
1 bay leaf
Ground nutmeg
Salt
Freshly ground black pepper
½ cup good-quality dry sherry

UTENSILS

Food processor (optional)
Large heavy-gauge skillet or sauté pan with cover
Large saucepan
Small saucepan
Medium-size sauté pan
Serving platter
Small bowl
Colander
Measuring cups and spoons
Chef's knife
Paring knife
2 wooden spoons
Metal tongs
Melon baller (optional)
Vegetable peeler (optional)
Kitchen string or wooden toothpicks

START-TO-FINISH STEPS

One hour ahead: If using frozen okra for the pork recipe, remove from packages and set out at room temperature to thaw.

Fifteen minutes ahead: Clarify enough butter (see page 20) to measure ¼ cup for pork recipe.

1. Follow salad recipe step 1.
2. Follow pork rolls recipe steps 1 through 7.
3. Follow salad recipe step 2.
4. Follow pork rolls recipe step 8.
5. While pork rolls are cooking, follow salad recipe steps 3 through 5.
6. Follow pork rolls recipe steps 9 and 10, and serve with salad.

RECIPES

Tangy Cucumber and Grape Salad

2 large cucumbers
2 to 3 tablespoons salt
½ pound seedless red or green grapes
Small bunch chives or scallions
1 cup sour cream or crème fraîche
1 teaspoon dry mustard
1 tablespoon Dijon mustard
1 teaspoon wasabi or white horseradish
¼ cup chicken stock
2 teaspoons rose water (optional)
Ground nutmeg

1. Halve cucumbers lengthwise and remove seeds with melon baller or teaspoon. Peel cucumbers or score decoratively, if desired, and slice into ½-inch-thick crescents. Place cucumbers in colander, sprinkle with salt, and toss to coat. Place colander in sink to drain cucumbers.
2. Wash grapes and dry; remove stems and discard. Wash chives, dry with paper towels, and chop enough to measure 2 tablespoons.
3. In small bowl, blend sour cream, dry and Dijon mustards, and wasabi. Add stock and rose water, if using, and stir until smooth.
4. Rinse cucumbers under very cold running water. Place them in clean dish towel and gently press out as much liquid as possible; set aside.
5. In serving bowl, combine cucumbers and grapes with sour cream dressing and toss until well coated. Sprinkle with nutmeg and set aside until ready to serve.

Stuffed Pork Rolls with Tomatoes and Okra

1 pound fresh okra, or two 10-ounce packages frozen,
    thawed
½ pound mushrooms
2 large shallots
Medium-size clove garlic
¼ pound Westphalian ham
Medium-size onion
1½ pounds firm Italian plum tomatoes, or 28-ounce can
    whole peeled tomatoes, drained
¼ cup clarified unsalted butter, plus 2 tablespoons
    unclarified
1 teaspoon dried thyme
½ teaspoon ground sage
½ cup dry sherry
⅔ cup fresh or dried bread crumbs
Eight 1-inch-thick center loin pork scallops (about 2 to 2½
    pounds total weight), pounded thin
1 bay leaf
¼ cup chicken stock
Freshly ground black pepper
2 tablespoons arrowroot or cornstarch (optional)

1. Remove okra stems and cut crosswise into 1-inch-long pieces. In large saucepan, bring 1 quart water to a boil over high heat. Blanch okra in boiling water 1 to 2 minutes. Turn into colander and set aside.

2. Trim mushrooms and wipe clean with damp paper towels. Peel shallots and garlic. Combine mushrooms, shallots, and garlic in food processor fitted with steel blade and process briefly until minced. Or, mince these ingredients with chef's knife.

3. Chop ham finely. Peel and chop onion. If using fresh tomatoes, rinse and pat dry. Core, halve, and chop tomatoes. If using canned tomatoes, drain and reserve liquid for another use.

4. In medium-size sauté pan, heat 2 tablespoons clarified butter over medium heat. Add mushroom mixture and sauté, stirring occasionally, until mushrooms are browned and most of liquid has evaporated, about 3 minutes. Add thyme, sage, and ¼ cup sherry. Increase heat to high and cook 1 to 2 minutes, stirring until blended. Remove pan from heat and stir in bread crumbs and ham.

5. Mound about ¼ cup of filling in center of each pork scallop. Fold in sides and roll pork into cylinder, totally enclosing filling. Secure rolls with kitchen string or wooden toothpicks.

6. In large heavy-gauge skillet or sauté pan, heat remaining 2 tablespoons clarified butter over medium-high heat. Add pork rolls and brown quickly on all sides, turning with tongs, about 5 minutes.

7. Stir in onion, tomatoes, 2 tablespoons sherry, bay leaf, and stock. Season with generous grinding of pepper and bring to a boil. Cover pan, reduce heat to low, and cook 5 minutes.

8. Add okra and cook another 10 minutes.

9. Transfer pork rolls to serving platter and remove strings or toothpicks. If cooking liquid is thin, blend 2 tablespoons arrowroot with remaining 2 tablespoons sherry in a cup and gradually stir mixture into sauce. If cooking liquid is sufficiently thick, add remaining 2 tablespoons sherry only and stir until blended.

10. Remove pan from heat and swirl in 2 tablespoons unclarified butter, one at a time. Spoon tomatoes, okra, and sauce over pork rolls.

ADDED TOUCH

For this dish, wild rice is served with carrots and celeriac, a gnarled bewhiskered brown-skinned root that tastes like strong celery. Select a small firm root, scrub it well, and use a sharp paring knife to peel away the tough skin.

Wild Rice with Sautéed Carrots and Celeriac

1 cup wild rice
Medium-size onion
2 tablespoons tamari or soy sauce
1 orange
Small bunch carrots (1 pound total weight)
Small-size celeriac (about 1 pound)
2 tablespoons walnut oil or vegetable oil
½ teaspoon dried marjoram
½ teaspoon ground cumin seeds
¼ cup veal or chicken stock, preferably homemade (see page 13), or canned
3 tablespoons sugar
2 tablespoons unsalted butter
Freshly ground black pepper

1. In medium-size heavy-gauge saucepan, bring 5 cups water to a boil.

2. Meanwhile, place wild rice in strainer and rinse thoroughly under cold running water. Peel onion.

3. Place rice, tamari, and whole onion in pan of water. When water returns to a boil, reduce heat to maintain a brisk simmer and cook rice 30 to 40 minutes, or until tender but slightly *al dente*.

4. While rice is cooking, cut orange in half, reserving one half for another use. Squeeze juice from half of orange and set aside. Peel carrots and cut crosswise on the diagonal into long flat slices. Scrub and peel celeriac. Halve celeriac lengthwise and cut each half into wedges. If center is hollow, trim away any discolored flesh. Cut wedges crosswise into ½-inch-thick slices.

5. In large sauté pan, heat walnut oil over medium heat. Add carrots and celeriac, and sauté, stirring, until color of vegetables begins to deepen, about 3 minutes.

6. Add marjoram, cumin, stock, and orange juice to pan; cover, and cook until vegetables are just tender, about 10 minutes.

7. Remove cover from pan and increase heat to medium-high. Sprinkle sugar over vegetables and stir with wooden spoon. Cook, stirring, about 5 minutes, or until liquid reduces to a glaze. Remove pan from heat and cover to keep warm.

8. Drain wild rice in strainer and discard onion. In medium-size bowl, combine rice with half of vegetables. Add butter and pepper to taste and toss rice mixture until butter melts. Add remaining vegetables to rice and serve.

Pork with Orange Sauce
Braised Leeks, Corn, and Carrots with Green Peppercorn Sauce
Oriental Brown Rice

The rich textures of glazed pork medallions, brown rice, and braised vegetables look appealing on plain dinnerware.

Green peppercorns are available packed in brine or vinegar and require refrigeration after opening. The former will keep for about a week, the latter two to three weeks. If the peppercorns turn dark, it means oxidation has occurred, and they should be discarded. Freeze-dried peppercorns do not have the right texture for this recipe.

WHAT TO DRINK

A fruity, slightly off-dry white wine, such as a California Chenin Blanc or a German Riesling from the Rhine valley, is a good choice for this menu.

SHOPPING LIST AND STAPLES

2 pork tenderloins (4 to 5 pounds total weight), trimmed and cut into 1-inch-thick medallions
¼ pound cultivated mushrooms
8 medium-size leeks (about 2 pounds total weight)
3 carrots (about ¾ pound total weight)
Small bunch celery
1 ear of corn, or 10-ounce package frozen corn kernels
1 bunch scallions
Small bunch parsley (optional)
2 medium-size cloves garlic

91

2 large shallots
6 medium-size oranges
2 lemons
½ pint heavy cream
1 stick plus 2 tablespoons unsalted butter, approximately
1 cup beef or veal stock, preferably homemade, or
    canned, plus ½ cup chicken or veal stock
2-ounce can green peppercorns, packed in brine
2 teaspoons sesame oil
3 tablespoons tamari or soy sauce
2 tablespoons honey
1½ cups short-grain brown rice
2 teaspoons ground coriander
½ teaspoon dried tarragon
½ teaspoon dried thyme
1 bay leaf
Dash of Cayenne pepper
¼ cup dry white wine
2 tablespoons Madeira

UTENSILS

Large heavy-gauge skillet or sauté pan
2 medium-size heavy-gauge saucepans, 1 with cover
Small saucepan
Medium-size sauté pan with cover
Large bowl
Large sieve
Strainer
Measuring cups and spoons
Chef's knife
Paring knife
2 wooden spoons
Spatula
Juicer
Vegetable peeler
Zester (optional)
Tongs

START-TO-FINISH STEPS

One hour ahead: If using frozen corn for leeks recipe, remove from package to thaw.

Fifteen minutes ahead: Clarify enough butter (see page 20) to measure 2 tablespoons for pork recipe.

1. Scrape carrots for pork and leeks recipes.
2. Follow pork recipe steps 1 through 4.
3. While stock is reducing, follow leeks recipe steps 1 and 2.
4. Follow rice recipe steps 1 and 2.
5. Follow pork recipe step 5 and rice recipe step 3.
6. Follow pork recipe steps 6 through 8.
7. While pork is cooking, follow leeks recipe steps 3 through 5.
8. Follow pork recipe step 9 and leeks recipe steps 6 and 7.
9. Follow pork recipe step 10, rice recipe step 4, and serve with leeks.

RECIPES

Pork with Orange Sauce

6 medium-size oranges
¼ pound cultivated mushrooms
1 carrot, scraped
1 celery stalk
2 large shallots
Medium-size clove garlic
Small bunch parsley for garnish (optional)
1 cup beef or veal stock
1 bay leaf
2 teaspoons ground coriander
Dash of Cayenne
1 cup heavy cream
2 tablespoons clarified butter
2 pork tenderloins (4 to 5 pounds total weight), trimmed
    and cut into 1-inch-thick medallions
¼ cup dry white wine

1. Halve 5 oranges and squeeze enough juice to measure 2 cups. In medium-size heavy-gauge saucepan, boil orange juice over medium-high heat until reduced by half, about 10 minutes.
2. While orange juice is reducing, trim mushrooms, wipe clean with damp paper towels, and chop. Chop carrot. Trim celery, wash, dry with paper towels, and chop. Peel and finely chop shallots. Peel garlic and crush lightly under blade of chef's knife. Peel remaining orange and cut into segments. Wash parsley, if using for garnish, and dry with paper towels. Reserve 4 sprigs and refrigerate remainder for another use.
3. Add stock, mushrooms, celery, shallots, garlic, bay leaf, coriander, and Cayenne to orange juice and continue boiling over medium-high heat until liquid is reduced to about 1 cup, 10 to 15 minutes.
4. Preheat oven to 200 degrees.
5. Add cream, reduce heat to medium, and cook 5 to 7 minutes, or until sauce thickens slightly.
6. Strain sauce into large bowl, pressing on solids with back of spoon to extract as much liquid as possible; discard solids and reserve sauce.
7. Place 4 dinner plates in oven to warm.
8. In large heavy-gauge skillet or sauté pan, heat clarified butter over high heat just until it begins to smoke, about 1 minute. Add pork and brown quickly on all sides, turning with tongs, about 2 minutes. Reduce heat to medium and sauté, turning occasionally, until pork is cooked through, 8 to 10 minutes.
9. Transfer medallions to warm plates. Add white wine to pan and boil over medium-high heat, scraping up any browned bits clinging to bottom of pan, 3 to 4 minutes, or until reduced to about 2 tablespoons.
10. Add reserved sauce and orange segments to pan, and cook sauce over medium heat, stirring frequently, until slightly thickened. Spoon sauce over medallions and garnish each serving with orange segment and parsley sprig, if desired.

Braised Leeks, Corn, and Carrots with Green Peppercorn Sauce

8 medium-size leeks (about 2 pounds total weight)
2 carrots, scraped
2 lemons
Medium-size clove garlic
1 ear of corn, or 10-ounce package frozen corn kernels, thawed
7 tablespoons unsalted butter
½ cup chicken or veal stock
2 tablespoons Madeira
½ teaspoon dried tarragon
½ teaspoon dried thyme
1 tablespoon green peppercorns, packed in brine
2 tablespoons honey

1. Trim green stems from leeks and reserve for another use. Split white parts lengthwise, wash thoroughly in cold water, and dry with paper towels. Cut leeks into 3-inch sections, and cut each section into ¼-inch-thick strips. Cut carrots into fine julienne. Remove zest from lemons and cut into thin strips. Juice lemons and strain juice. Peel and mince garlic.
2. If using fresh corn, remove husks and silk. Trim stem end so upended ear will rest flat on work surface. Holding ear upright, press base against surface and, with chef's knife, cut off kernels by pressing blade against cob and slicing downward. Turn corn and repeat process until all kernels are removed (see illustration on page 102).
3. In medium-size sauté pan, heat 3 tablespoons butter over medium heat until sizzling, about 1 minute. Add leeks and sauté, shaking pan occasionally, until they begin to wilt and are cooked evenly, 3 to 4 minutes.
4. Add lemon juice and zest, stock, Madeira, tarragon, and thyme. Reduce heat to low, until liquid barely simmers, then add corn and carrots. Cover pan and braise vegetables just until tender, 4 to 5 minutes.
5. Meanwhile, place peppercorns in strainer and rinse under cold running water to remove brine.
6. Transfer leeks to warm plates. Remove any tough outer layers of leek strips. Add honey to pan, increase heat to medium-high, and boil 1 to 2 minutes, or until sauce begins to shine.
7. Remove pan from heat and add garlic and green peppercorns. Still off heat, swirl in remaining butter, one tablespoon at a time. Spoon sauce over leeks and serve.

Oriental Brown Rice

1½ cups short-grain brown rice
3 tablespoons tamari or soy sauce
2 teaspoons sesame oil
1 bunch scallions

1. Place rice in large sieve and rinse well under cold running water.
2. In medium-size heavy-gauge saucepan, combine rice, 2⅔ cups water, tamari, and sesame oil. Cover pan and bring to a boil over high heat. Reduce heat to medium-low so water maintains a brisk simmer and cook until rice is tender but not soft, about 35 minutes.
3. Trim scallions, wash, and dry with paper towels. Chop enough scallions to measure ½ cup.
4. Just before serving, toss rice with chopped scallions and divide among warm plates.

ADDED TOUCH

You can use fresh raspberries rather than frozen ones for the sauce: Macerate 1 cup of fresh berries with 3 tablespoons of sugar and 1 tablespoon of Drambuie for an hour or two, then purée the berries and strain out the seeds.

Lemon Mousse with Tropical Fruits and Raspberry Sauce

3 lemons
1 orange
3 tablespoons Drambuie
1 package (1 tablespoon) unflavored gelatin
1 ripe mango
1 large kiwi, or 2 small
3 eggs
½ cup plus 3 tablespoons sugar
1 cup heavy cream
8-ounce package frozen raspberries, thawed

1. Place large bowl and beaters in refrigerator to chill. Grate zest of 2 lemons and orange into small saucepan. Squeeze enough lemon juice to measure ½ cup and strain juice. If necessary to make ½ cup juice, squeeze orange and add to lemon juice. Add juice, Drambuie, and gelatin to pan and set aside to soften.
2. Peel mango and remove flesh. Chop fruit into small dice and set aside in strainer to drain. Peel kiwi, cut crosswise into ¼-inch-thick slices, and set aside.
3. Bring juice mixture to a simmer over low heat until gelatin dissolves, 1 to 2 minutes. Pour mixture into medium-size bowl, cover, and refrigerate until cooled, about 10 minutes.
4. Meanwhile, separate eggs, placing yolks and whites in separate bowls.
5. With whisk, beat egg yolks with ½ cup sugar until thick and lemon colored. Wash and dry whisk.
6. Add remaining 3 tablespoons sugar to egg whites and whisk until stiff.
7. When gelatin mixture is cool but not set, add to yolks and stir to combine.
8. In large chilled bowl, beat heavy cream with electric mixer set at high speed until it holds a soft shape.
9. With rubber spatula, fold yolk mixture into whites. Gently fold this mixture into cream until no streaks show.
10. Divide mango among 4 stemmed glasses and top with spoonful of mousse. Cover with slices of kiwi and top with remaining mousse. Cover with plastic wrap and refrigerate until chilled and set, at least 1 hour.
11. Just before serving, purée raspberries in blender or food processor and then strain them. Top each mousse with a spoonful of raspberry sauce.

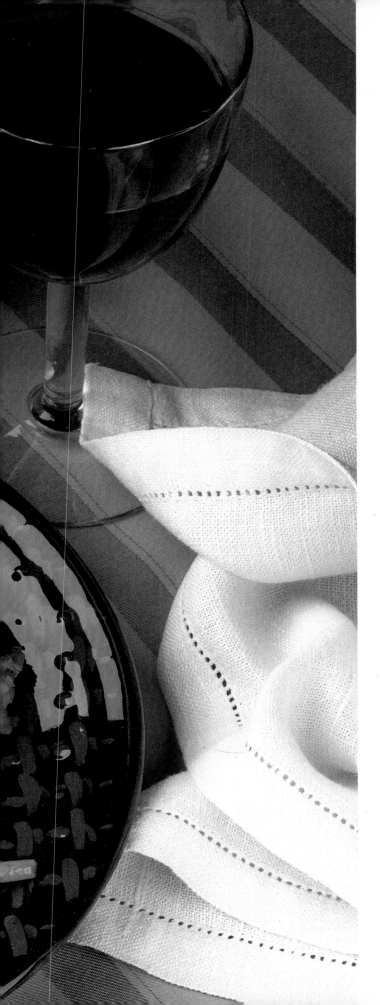

Holly Garrison

A ccording to Holly Garrison, there have been three major influences on her cooking style: the Pennsylvania Dutch country where she spent her childhood; her southern grandmother and mother; and her father, who worked with the French diplomatic corps in the United States and gave her an appreciation of French food at an early age. Her three menus reflect these influences.

In Menu 1 she re-creates a meal reminiscent of Pennsylvania Dutch cooking. Hollowed-out Golden Delicious apples are stuffed with a sweet-and-sour combination of ground pork, sausage, seasonings, and apple cider. She serves the stuffed apples with green beans and mushrooms, and offers French bread slices spread with walnut-garlic butter on the side.

Menu 3 begins with sweet corn soup (ideally made from freshly picked corn), followed by Virginia's famous Smithfield ham, sliced and sautéed with zucchini, jícama, and red bell pepper. Tangy Cheddar cheese biscuits complete this festive dinner.

In Menu 2, Holly Garrison modifies a dish often eaten in Alsace in northeastern France—*choucroute garnie,* or sauerkraut garnished with sausage and pork. She lends an American touch to the meal by adding fruity California wine and a Red Delicious apple to the *choucroute* and serving roasted yams as an accompaniment.

Golden Delicious apples filled with lean ground pork, mild pork sausage, and bread crumbs make a substantial entrée. Serve the green beans and sautéed shiitake mushrooms with the apples, and the French bread warm from the oven

95

Pork-and-Sausage-Stuffed Golden Apples
Green Bean and Mushroom Sauté
French Bread with Walnut-Garlic Butter

Golden Delicious apples work best here because they retain their shape and texture during baking. You can substitute Rome Beauties, although Golden Delicious are generally available all year round. To prepare this meal within an hour, stuff the apples first and, as they bake, prepare the rest of the meal.

Fresh Japanese *shiitake* mushrooms are sold at specialty food shops and some supermarkets specializing in imported delicacies. Discard their tough stems or reserve them for flavoring vegetable soups or meat stocks. As an alternative, you can use fresh golden oak mushrooms, a member of the *shiitake* family. If fresh mushrooms are unavailable, use dried *shiitake*.

WHAT TO DRINK

Try a light, fruity red wine with this menu. A good choice would be a French Beaujolais or Beaujolais-Villages.

SHOPPING LIST AND STAPLES

1 pound lean ground fresh pork
½ pound mild fresh pork sausage or link sausages
1 pound green beans
¼ pound fresh shiitake or other cultivated mushrooms,
   or ¼ pound dried shiitake
Small onion
2 small cloves garlic
Small bunch parsley
4 Golden Delicious apples (each about ½ pound)
Small red apple for garnish (optional)
Large lemon
1 stick plus 1 tablespoon unsalted butter
1 cup apple cider
11½-ounce bottle walnut oil, or 3 tablespoons
   vegetable oil
2 slices home-style white bread
1 long loaf French bread
4-ounce can walnut halves or pieces
1 teaspoon dried sage
Salt and freshly ground pepper

UTENSILS

Food processor or blender
2 large skillets, or 1 large skillet and 1 large wok
Medium-size saucepan
8 x 8-inch baking dish
Large bowl
Medium-size bowl
Small bowl
Colander
Measuring cups and spoons
Chef's knife
Paring knife
Wooden spoon
Slotted spoon
Teaspoon
Metal spatula
Juicer (optional)
Garlic press
Pastry brush
Apple corer (optional)

START-TO-FINISH STEPS

Thirty minutes ahead: Follow sauté recipe step 1 and bread recipe step 1.

1. Peel garlic cloves and set aside. Juice lemon for apples and sauté recipes.
2. Follow apples recipe steps 1 through 8.
3. Follow sauté recipe steps 2 through 5.
4. Follow bread recipe steps 2 through 4.
5. Follow apples recipe step 9 and bread recipe step 5.
6. Follow sauté recipe step 6.
7. Follow sauté recipe steps 7 and 8, apples recipe step 10, and serve with bread.

RECIPES

Pork-and-Sausage-Stuffed Golden Apples

Small onion
2 slices home-style white bread
Small bunch parsley
½ pound mild fresh pork sausage or link sausages
1 pound lean ground fresh pork
4 Golden Delicious apples (each about ½ pound)
Small red apple for garnish (optional)
¼ cup lemon juice plus 1 teaspoon (optional)
1 teaspoon dried sage
½ teaspoon salt
Freshly ground pepper
1 cup apple cider

1. Preheat oven to 350 degrees.
2. Peel and finely chop enough onion to measure ½ cup. Tear bread into pieces and process in blender to make about 1 cup crumbs. Rinse, dry, and chop enough parsley to measure ¼ cup, reserving 4 sprigs for garnish, if desired.
3. If using link sausages, remove from casings and cut into small pieces. In large skillet, cook sausage and pork over medium heat, stirring well with wooden spoon, 5 to 7 minutes, or until no trace of pink remains. With slotted spoon, transfer to large bowl.
4. Add onion to fat remaining in skillet and cook over medium heat, stirring until softened, about 3 minutes. Add onion to pork and sausage.
5. Wash and dry apples. Set aside red apple, if using, for garnish. With apple corer or paring knife, remove cores from whole yellow apples. Cut a thin slice from top of each apple. With paring knife and teaspoon, carefully hollow out apples, leaving ¼-inch-thick shell. Reserve pulp for stuffing mixture. Brush inside of each shell with lemon juice to prevent discoloration. Place apples in baking dish, spacing evenly.
6. Coarsely chop reserved apple pulp. Reserving 1 teaspoon, combine remaining lemon juice and pulp in small bowl. Add pulp mixture, bread crumbs, parsley, sage, salt, and pepper to taste, to skillet with pork and sausage and stir to combine.
7. Fill each apple with stuffing, mounding slightly. Place remaining stuffing around apples in baking dish; baste with a little apple cider.
8. Place apples in oven and bake 40 minutes, basting with cider about every 10 minutes.
9. Just before apples are done, halve red apple, if using, for garnish, reserving one half for another use. Core remaining half, cut into 4 thin wedges, and brush with reserved lemon juice.
10. Using spatula, carefully transfer apples from baking dish to 4 dinner plates and divide remaining stuffing among plates. Top each serving with a red apple wedge and parsley sprig, if desired. Serve immediately.

Green Bean and Mushroom Sauté

¼ pound fresh shiitake or other cultivated mushrooms, or ¼ pound dried shiitake
Salt
1 pound green beans
3 tablespoons unsalted butter
3 tablespoons walnut or vegetable oil
Small clove garlic, peeled
1 tablespoon lemon juice
Freshly ground pepper

1. If using dried shiitake, place in medium-size bowl with enough water to cover and set aside 20 to 30 minutes to soak.
2. In medium-size saucepan, bring 2½ quarts water and 2½ teaspoons salt to a boil over high heat.
3. Meanwhile, trim green beans and rinse in cold water. Place beans in boiling water and cook until crisp-tender, about 3 minutes.
4. Turn beans into colander, refresh under cold running water, and set aside to drain.
5. Remove mushroom stems, reserving for another use, and wipe caps with damp paper towels. Or, drain reconstituted shiitake and strain soaking liquid, reserving for another use; dry with paper towels and trim stems. Cut mushrooms into ¼-inch-thick slices.
6. In large skillet or wok, heat butter and oil over medium-high heat. When butter-oil mixture is hot, put garlic through press directly into pan. Add beans and mushrooms, and sauté, stirring, until mushrooms are limp and beans are hot and just tender, about 3 minutes.
7. Add lemon juice and salt and pepper to taste, tossing to combine.
8. Divide vegetable sauté among 4 dinner plates.

French Bread with Walnut-Garlic Butter

6 tablespoons unsalted butter
1 cup walnut halves or pieces
Small clove garlic, peeled
1 long loaf French bread

1. Cut 6 tablespoons butter into small pieces and set aside in small bowl to soften.
2. Coarsely chop walnuts in food processor fitted with steel blade or in blender.
3. Put garlic through press, stirring into softened butter to blend. Add walnuts and mix.
4. Cut bread in half lengthwise and spread each half with butter mixture. Place buttered halves together and wrap loaf in aluminum foil. Bake loaf in 350-degree oven about 20 minutes.
5. Just before serving, remove foil, cut bread crosswise into 4 pieces, and place in napkin-lined basket.

American Choucroute Garnie
Pan-Roasted Yams
Beet and Lettuce Salad with Mustard Vinaigrette

Colorful yams brighten a plate of pork loin, Polish sausage, and sauerkraut. Offer the beet and lettuce salad separately.

For the American *choucroute garnie*, buy a smoked center loin pork roast and have it prepared by your butcher for easy slicing into chops. Because this dish is quite salty, rinse the sauerkraut to remove its brine before cooking. If you wish to reduce the saltiness further, simmer the loin roast in water for about 20 minutes and drain before adding it to the sauerkraut. To add a slightly sweet flavor of anise to the pork, use the caraway seeds. Pungent mustard would be fitting with this entrée.

WHAT TO DRINK

This hearty menu deserves a lightly chilled California or Alsatian Riesling or Gewürztraminer. You can also use either type of wine in preparing the *choucroute garnie*.

SHOPPING LIST AND STAPLES

Smoked center loin pork roast (2½ to 3 pounds), chine
   bone sawed so roast carves easily
½ pound precooked kielbasa
4 yams (about 2½ pounds total weight)
Small head Bibb lettuce
Small head Boston lettuce
Small bunch arugula
4 small beets
Medium-size onion
Large clove garlic
Large Red Delicious apple
Large lemon, or ¼ cup white wine vinegar
Large egg
2 tablespoons unsalted butter
1 pound sauerkraut
¾ cup olive oil or vegetable oil, plus vegetable oil for
   pan roasting
2 tablespoons Dijon mustard
1 or 2 teaspoons caraway seeds (optional)
Coarse (kosher) salt (optional)
Salt
Freshly ground pepper
½ cup California Riesling or other fruity white wine

UTENSILS

Food processor or blender
12 x 9-inch roasting pan or ovenproof baking dish
4-quart enameled Dutch oven or heavy-gauge
   nonaluminum pan with tight-fitting cover
Medium-size saucepan with cover
Medium-size bowl plus additional bowl (optional)
Colander
Salad spinner (optional)
Measuring cups and spoons
Chef's knife
Paring knife
Wooden spoon
Metal tongs
Juicer

Vegetable peeler
Rolling pin (if using caraway seeds)

START-TO-FINISH STEPS

1. Follow yams recipe step 1 and salad recipe steps 1 and 2.
2. Follow choucroute recipe steps 1 through 3.
3. Follow yams recipe steps 2 through 4.
4. Follow vinaigrette recipe steps 1 and 2.
5. Follow salad recipe step 3 and turn yams.
6. Follow vinaigrette recipe step 3 and salad recipe step 4.
7. Follow choucroute recipe step 4, yams recipe step 5, and serve with salad.

RECIPES

American Choucroute Garnie

1 pound sauerkraut
½ pound precooked kielbasa
Medium-size onion
Large Red Delicious apple
1 or 2 teaspoons caraway seeds (optional)
2 tablespoons unsalted butter
Freshly ground pepper
½ cup California Riesling or other fruity white wine
Smoked center loin pork roast (2½ to 3 pounds), chine
   bone sawed so roast carves easily

1. Place sauerkraut in colander to drain. Cut kielbasa into ½-inch-thick slices and set aside. Peel and chop enough onion to measure 1 cup. Wash and dry apple. Halve, core, and coarsely chop enough apple to measure 1½ cups. Place caraway seeds, if using, between 2 sheets of waxed paper and crush with rolling pin.
2. Melt butter over medium heat in Dutch oven. When butter is bubbly, add onion and cook, stirring, until onion is softened, about 3 minutes. Stir in drained sauerkraut, caraway seeds, if using, pepper to taste, and wine.
3. Add pork to sauerkraut mixture and surround with kielbasa slices. Cover tightly, reduce heat to medium-low, and cook 45 minutes, or until pork is fork tender.
4. Transfer pork to cutting surface and slice into 4 chops. Divide among dinner plates and top each serving with sauerkraut and kielbasa slices.

Pan-Roasted Yams

4 yams (about 2½ pounds total weight)
Vegetable oil
Coarse (kosher) salt (optional)

1. Preheat oven to 375 degrees.
2. Peel yams and cut crosswise into 2-inch-thick pieces.
3. Pour vegetable oil about ¼-inch deep into roasting pan or ovenproof baking dish. Add yams and turn to coat with oil. Sprinkle with coarse salt, if desired.
4. Bake yams, turning once with tongs after 25 minutes, until tender and lightly browned, about 40 minutes.
5. Divide yams among 4 dinner plates.

Beet and Lettuce Salad with Mustard Vinaigrette

4 small beets
Small head Bibb lettuce
Small head Boston lettuce
Small bunch arugula
Mustard Vinaigrette (see following recipe)

1. Remove beet tops, leaving about 1-inch of stems. Wash beets and drain in colander. Place beets in medium-size saucepan, cover with water, and bring to a boil over medium-high heat. Reduce heat and simmer beets 30 minutes, or until tender when tested gently with point of knife. (Do not test beets too often or color will bleed.)
2. Meanwhile, separate lettuce leaves; wash lettuce and arugula, and dry in salad spinner or with paper towels. Trim off arugula stems and place greens in medium-size bowl. Cover with plastic wrap and refrigerate until ready to use.
3. When beets are cooked, turn into colander and refresh under cold running water; slip skins off with your fingers. Trim off beet stems and cut beets crosswise into ¼-inch-thick slices.
4. Divide salad greens among 4 side plates, drizzle with mustard vinaigrette, and top each serving with beets.

Mustard Vinaigrette

Large lemon, or ¼ cup white wine vinegar
Large clove garlic
Large egg
2 tablespoons Dijon mustard
¾ cup olive oil or vegetable oil
½ teaspoon salt
Freshly ground pepper

1. Squeeze enough lemon juice to measure ¼ cup. Peel garlic.
2. Place all ingredients in food processor fitted with steel blade or in blender and process 1 minute.
3. Just before using, process vinaigrette briefly to recombine.

ADDED TOUCH

Single layers of this cake may be split and served with whipped cream and strawberry or raspberry sauce.

Tennessee Black Cake

Cake:
2 sticks unsalted butter, approximately
2 teaspoons cocoa powder
4 squares unsweetened chocolate
   (4 ounces)
2½ cups all-purpose flour
¼ teaspoon salt
2 cups granulated sugar
2 teaspoons baking soda
4 large eggs
1 cup buttermilk
2 teaspoons vanilla extract

Frosting:
1 stick unsalted butter
4 squares unsweetened chocolate
   (4 ounces)
½ cup evaporated milk
1-pound box confectioners' sugar
1 teaspoon vanilla extract
Salt

Optional garnishes:
1 cup heavy cream
1 pint strawberries
1 tablespoon sugar

1. To make cake: Preheat oven to 350 degrees and place rack in middle of oven. Lightly grease two 8½-inch-round baking pans and dust each with 1 teaspoon cocoa powder. Cut 2 sticks butter into 8 pieces each.
2. Combine 4 squares chocolate and butter in top of double boiler set over, not in, barely simmering water and stir occasionally until melted, 1 to 2 minutes. Remove chocolate from heat and set aside to cool.
3. Sift flour, salt, granulated sugar, and baking soda into medium-size bowl. Break eggs into large bowl and beat with buttermilk and 2 teaspoons vanilla.
4. Gradually add flour mixture to egg mixture, stirring until well blended. Slowly pour in melted chocolate, stirring until smooth. Divide batter between pans.
5. Place pans in oven and bake 25 to 30 minutes, or until toothpick inserted in center of cake layers comes out clean. Be careful not to overbake.
6. Cool cake in pans on wire racks, about 10 minutes. Layers may sink slightly in center.
7. Remove layers from pans, place on racks, and allow to cool completely before frosting.
8. To make frosting: Cut 1 stick butter into 8 pieces. Place chocolate and butter in top of double boiler set over, not in, barely simmering water and stir occasionally until melted, 1 to 2 minutes. Remove chocolate from heat and set aside to cool.
9. Combine milk, confectioners' sugar, vanilla extract, and a pinch of salt in medium-size bowl, and stir until blended. Stir in cooled chocolate and beat mixture vigorously with wooden spoon until frosting thickens to spreading consistency.
10. If using heavy cream for garnish, place bowl and beaters in refrigerator to chill.
11. With icing spatula or table knife, generously frost one layer of cake. Top with second layer and frost top and sides of cake.
12. Wash strawberries, if using, hull, and dry with paper towels. Halve strawberries and arrange on top of cake.
13. Pour heavy cream into chilled bowl, add 1 tablespoon sugar, and with electric beater at high speed, beat until cream holds soft shape, about 1 to 2 minutes. Spoon whipped cream into small bowl, and serve with cake.

Corn Chowder
Sauté of Smithfield Ham and Vegetables
Cheddar Cheese Biscuits

Serve corn chowder in soup bowls or mugs, followed by sautéed ham and vegetables and a basket of cheese biscuits.

For the corn chowder in this traditional southern meal, select ears with clean green husks and golden-brown silk. Pull back the husks and check the kernels; they should be plump, not dry looking. Cook fresh corn as soon as possible after buying it.

For the main course, Smithfield ham is sautéed with jícama and other vegetables. Genuine Smithfield ham is often hard to obtain, but you can substitute another smoked country ham or, for a milder, less-salty flavor, use prosciutto (stir fry prosciutto quickly or it will toughen).

Although the tropical root vegetable jícama looks similar to a brown-skinned turnip, its crisp white flesh tastes like a combination of apple and water chestnut. Jícama is available in well-stocked supermarkets, either whole or in pieces, and can be refrigerated for a week or two. (Store small cut pieces in water to preserve their crispness and prevent drying.) You may substitute turnips for jícama.

WHAT TO DRINK

A very crisp, very dry white California Sauvignon Blanc would be ideal with these dishes. Or try a Sancerre or Pouilly-Fumé.

½- to ¾-pound slice Smithfield ham, smoked country
    ham, or prosciutto
2½ pounds jícama, or 2½ pounds turnips
3 medium-size zucchini (about 1½ pounds total weight)
3 or 4 ears fresh corn or two 12-ounce cans corn
    kernels
Small bunch celery
Large red bell pepper
Small onion
Small bunch parsley for garnish (optional)
Large lemon
2 cups milk, plus 1 or 2 tablespoons (optional)
½ pint heavy cream
½ pint light cream
1 stick unsalted butter plus 7 tablespoons salted
2 ounces Cheddar cheese
1 cup plus 2 tablespoons all-purpose flour,
    approximately
½ teaspoon sugar (optional)
1½ teaspoons baking powder
Salt
Freshly ground pepper

UTENSILS

Food processor or blender
Large wok or sauté pan
Small skillet or butter warmer
Large heavy-gauge saucepan with cover
Small heavy-gauge saucepan
Medium-size bowl
15 x 10-inch baking sheet
Wire rack
Measuring cups and spoons
1½-inch biscuit cutter
Chef's knife
Paring knife
2 wooden spoons or wok spatulas
Spatula
Metal tongs
Vegetable peeler
Whisk
Grater
Juicer
Cutting board or pastry board

START-TO-FINISH STEPS

1. Follow biscuits recipe step 1.
2. Follow sauté recipe steps 1 through 4.
3. Follow chowder recipe steps 1 through 6.
4. Follow biscuits recipe steps 2 through 4, and chowder recipe step 7.
5. Follow biscuits recipe steps 5 and 6, and chowder recipe steps 8 and 9.
6. Follow biscuits recipe step 7.
7. Follow sauté recipe steps 5 through 7, biscuits recipe step 8, chowder recipe step 10, and serve.

RECIPES

Corn Chowder

3 or 4 ears fresh corn or two 12-ounce cans corn kernels
Small onion
1 stalk celery
4 tablespoons salted butter
½ teaspoon sugar (optional)
Small bunch parsley for garnish (optional)
2 tablespoons all-purpose flour
1 cup light cream
2 cups milk
Salt
Freshly ground pepper

1. Remove husks and silk from corn. With chef's knife, trim off stem end. Holding 1 ear of corn upright, press base against table and, with chef's knife, cut off kernels by

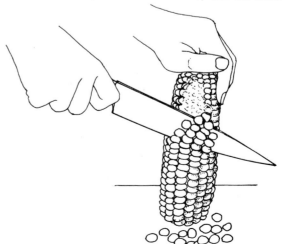

pressing blade against cob and slicing downward (see illustration). Turn corn and repeat process until all kernels are removed. Repeat process for remaining ears.

2. Peel onion and mince enough to measure ½ cup. Trim celery and mince enough to measure ¼ cup.

3. In large heavy-gauge saucepan, melt butter over medium heat until bubbly. Add onion, celery, and corn, and cook, stirring constantly with wooden spoon, until onion is soft and translucent, about 5 minutes.

4. Taste corn; if it does not seem naturally sweet, add sugar. Lower heat, cover pan, and cook another 5 minutes, or until onion and celery are very soft and corn is tender.

5. Meanwhile, if using parsley for garnish, rinse and dry with paper towels. Set aside 4 sprigs, reserving remainder for another use.

6. Add flour to corn mixture, reduce heat to medium-low, and cook, stirring, 1 or 2 minutes. Add cream and milk all at once and continue to cook, stirring occasionally, until simmering, about 7 minutes.

7. Stir in salt and pepper to taste. Set soup aside to cool slightly before puréeing.

8. Place soup in food processor fitted with steel blade or in blender and pulse once or twice to purée coarsely. Return soup to saucepan; set aside.

9. Place soup bowls under hot running water. Gently reheat soup over low heat.

10. Dry bowls, divide soup among them, and, if desired, garnish each with a parsley sprig.

Sauté of Smithfield Ham and Vegetables

Large red bell pepper
3 medium-size zucchini (about 1½ pounds total weight)
2½ pounds jícama, or 2½ pounds turnips
½- to ¾-pound slice Smithfield ham, smoked country
    ham, or prosciutto
Large lemon
1 stick unsalted butter
Freshly ground pepper

1. Rinse red bell pepper and zucchini; dry with paper towels. Halve, core, and seed pepper; trim zucchini. Peel jícama. Cut vegetables into ¼-inch-thick julienne.

2. Trim fat from ham and discard. Cut enough ham into ¼-inch-thick julienne to measure 2 cups; reserve remainder for another use.

3. Squeeze lemon and place juice in small heavy-gauge saucepan. Bring to a boil over medium heat, and reduce to

about 1 tablespoon, 2 to 3 minutes. Remove pan from heat and allow to cool slightly.

4. Cut 6 tablespoons butter into small pieces. Add to lemon juice, piece by piece, beating after each addition until incorporated. It may be necessary to warm mixture briefly, over very low heat, but butter must soften, not melt, in juice. When thoroughly combined, set aside.

5. Melt remaining 2 tablespoons butter in large wok or sauté pan over medium heat. When butter foams, add red pepper, zucchini, jícama, and ham, and sauté, stirring and tossing with wooden spoons, until vegetables are well coated with butter and starting to cook. Add 2 tablespoons water and continue to sauté, stirring and tossing until vegetables are crisp-tender, about 4 minutes.

6. If more than 2 or 3 tablespoons liquid remain in pan after vegetables are done, pour off.

7. Remove pan from heat, add lemon butter, and toss vegetables until evenly coated. Add pepper to taste and transfer to serving platter.

Cheddar Cheese Biscuits

3 tablespoons salted butter
2 ounces Cheddar cheese
1 cup all-purpose flour, approximately
1½ teaspoons baking powder
½ teaspoon salt
½ cup heavy cream
1 or 2 tablespoons milk (optional)

1. Preheat oven to 425 degrees.

2. Melt butter over low heat in small skillet or butter warmer and set aside.

3. Grate enough cheese to measure about ½ cup.

4. Combine grated cheese, 1 cup flour, baking powder, and salt in medium-size bowl. Stir in cream with fork, mixing just until moistened. Add 1 or 2 tablespoons milk to dough if too crumbly.

5. On lightly floured surface, knead dough 8 to 10 times. With fingers, press out to a scant ½-inch thickness. Cut dough into 1½-inch rounds with biscuit cutter.

6. With tongs, dip biscuits in melted butter to coat and place on ungreased baking sheet. Transfer to oven and bake 12 to 15 minutes, or until biscuits are golden.

7. Remove baking sheet from oven and place on wire rack to cool slightly.

8. With spatula, transfer biscuits from baking sheet to napkin-lined basket.

POULTRY

Perla Meyers

MENU 1 (Right)
Cauliflower with Roquefort Vinaigrette
Basque Sauté of Chicken Breasts
Creamy Lemon Pilaf

MENU 2
Zucchini, Tuna, and Tomato Salad
Sauté of Chicken with Mushrooms
Broccoli Purée

MENU 3
Game Hens with Green Peppercorn Sauce
Sweet and Sour Turnips
Green Salad with Lemon Mustard Vinaigrette

Perla Meyers grew up in Catalonia, the northeastern region of Spain, which used to be an independent kingdom and still has its traditional cuisine. She learned to cook from the family cook, who was Spanish, as well as from her Alsatian-born father and her Viennese mother. From them she acquired the habit of cooking by the season, choosing a main course, vegetables, and salads only after a trip to the market to see what is freshest and best.

She likes to begin a meal with a vegetable appetizer, such as the cauliflower vinaigrette at right—a custom in Catalonia as well as in other Mediterranean regions. A vegetable first course not only satisfies the appetite but also makes sense for the busy cook, since not all the dishes need to be ready at the same time. The cook and the guests can enjoy the first course while the main dish finishes or stays warm for a few minutes.

Today Perla Meyers continues to borrow techniques and ideas from abroad. The chicken breasts sautéed with sausage and zucchini in Menu 1 is a Basque dish—from northwestern Spain. In Menu 2, which offers a sauté of chicken and mushrooms as the main course, the salad is an Italian mix of zucchini, tuna, and tomato. And the green peppercorn sauce in Menu 3 is originally French.

This family meal will turn out best when cauliflower and zucchini are at their peak, in late summer and early fall. You can serve the cauliflower appetizer as a first course, garnished with cherry tomatoes, salami, and black olives. Then bring on the sliced chicken breasts cooked with sweet Italian sausages, red pepper, and sliced zucchini, and—to fill out the meal—a lemony rice pilaf and perhaps French bread.

106

Cauliflower with Roquefort Vinaigrette
Basque Sauté of Chicken Breasts
Creamy Lemon Pilaf

For the hors d'oeuvre, choose the whitest cauliflower you can find, avoiding any spotted or yellowish heads or any with open flower clusters. The recipe calls for a cup of milk to be added to the cooking water with the cauliflower. This keeps the cauliflower white without changing the taste. The oil-cured black olives, which are imported, are not as salty as those packed in salt and brine.

Crème fraîche, an increasingly popular ingredient in American kitchens, is very different from plain sweet cream or commercial sour cream. A staple of French cooking, it is a raw cream that has matured naturally and is slightly sour tasting. Look for *crème fraîche* in the dairy department. It will cost more than sour cream, which you may also opt for in the cauliflower recipe, but is worth trying. Leftover *crème fraîche* has many uses—as a topping for fresh fruit, cakes, or baked potatoes.

For the Basque sauté of chicken, you may want to roast your own red peppers rather than buying them in a jar. If so, select one large, unblemished pepper. To skin it, set it on a low flame on range top (or under the broiler of an electric oven if you do not have a gas stove), and allow the skin to blacken in the heat. Remove the blackened skin, core the pepper, and chop it.

WHAT TO DRINK

The strong flavors of this menu call for a wine with enough body to support them. Choose a not-too-expensive, white Graves, a California Sauvignon Blanc (sometimes labeled Fumé Blanc), or a white Spanish wine from the Rioja region.

SHOPPING LIST AND STAPLES

4 skinless, boneless chicken breast halves
¾ pound sweet Italian sausages
¼ pound Genoa salami, thinly sliced (optional)
1 large head cauliflower
1 pint cherry tomatoes (optional)
2 medium-size zucchini
1 hot dried chili pepper or crushed red pepper (optional)
3 large cloves garlic
3 tablespoons minced fresh chives, or 1 tablespoon
   freeze-dried
1 bunch fresh parsley
1 lemon
2 ounces Roquefort cheese

¼ pound Parmesan cheese
2 tablespoons *crème fraîche* or sour cream
¼ cup heavy cream
1 cup milk
3 tablespoons butter
2 extra-large eggs
3⅓ cups chicken broth
2 or 3 anchovy fillets (optional)
7-ounce jar roasted peppers
½ pound oil-cured black olives (optional)
¾ cup olive oil
3 tablespoons sherry wine vinegar or red wine vinegar
1½ cups long-grain white rice
½ cup flour
Salt and pepper
¼ cup dry white wine

UTENSILS

Blender or food processor
Large skillet with cover
Heavy saucepan
Large saucepan with cover
Small bowl
Measuring cups and spoons
Chef's knife
All-purpose knife
Rubber spatula
Slotted spoon
Grater
Tongs
Whisk
Waxed paper
Juicer

START-TO-FINISH STEPS

1. Mince chives for Roquefort vinaigrette. Slice zucchini and garlic for chicken recipe. Grate Parmesan cheese for pilaf recipe.
2. Follow vinaigrette recipe steps 1 and 2.
3. Juice lemon and follow lemon-cream sauce recipe.
4. Follow chicken recipe step 1.
5. Follow pilaf recipe steps 1 and 2.
6. Follow cauliflower recipe steps 1 and 2.
7. Follow chicken recipe steps 2 through 6.
8. Follow cauliflower recipe step 3 and serve cauliflower

with Roquefort vinaigrette as the first course.

9. Follow pilaf recipe step 3 and serve with chicken.

RECIPES

Cauliflower with Roquefort Vinaigrette

2½ quarts salted water
1 large head cauliflower
1 cup milk
Roquefort vinaigrette (see following recipe)
¼ pound Genoa salami, thinly sliced for garnish (optional)
½ pound oil-cured black olives for garnish (optional)
1 pint cherry tomatoes for garnish (optional)
Parsley sprigs for garnish (optional)

1. In large covered saucepan, bring 2½ quarts salted water to a boil.
2. Trim cauliflower. Add cauliflower and milk to boiling water. Cook over medium heat 8 minutes, or until cauliflower is crisp but tender. Test by inserting blade of knife near core end—it should come out easily.
3. Remove and drain cauliflower. Place on round serving platter. Serve with Roquefort vinaigrette and surround with salami, black olives, cherry tomatoes, and parsley as desired.

Roquefort Vinaigrette

1 large clove garlic, mashed
½ cup olive oil
2 ounces Roquefort cheese
3 tablespoons sherry wine vinegar or red wine vinegar
2 tablespoons *crème fraîche* or sour cream
2 or 3 rinsed anchovy fillets (optional)
Freshly ground black pepper
3 tablespoons minced fresh chives, or 1 tablespoon
    freeze-dried

1. Combine all ingredients except pepper and chives, including anchovy fillets if desired, in container of blender or food processor and blend until smooth. Season carefully with pepper. You will probably not need salt since both Roquefort and anchovies are salty.
2. Using rubber spatula, stir minced chives into dressing and set aside until serving time. Stir again just before serving and spoon over cauliflower.

Basque Sauté of Chicken Breasts

4 skinless, boneless chicken breast halves
Salt and freshly ground pepper
½ cup flour
2 to 4 tablespoons olive oil
2 medium-size zucchini, cut into 1½-inch matchsticks
¾ pound sweet Italian sausages
1 tablespoon butter
1 hot dried chili pepper, or ½ teaspoon crushed red
    pepper (optional)
¼ cup dry white wine
2 large cloves garlic, thinly sliced
⅓ cup chicken broth

7-ounce jar roasted peppers, drained and finely sliced
1 tablespoon finely chopped fresh parsley

1. Remove fillets (see page 8, step 7) from chicken breasts and remove and discard all fat and gristle. Cut chicken breasts crosswise into ½-inch slices. Season with salt and pepper and dredge lightly in flour. Set aside.
2. Place skillet over high heat. Add 2 tablespoons olive oil to skillet and, when hot, add zucchini. Sauté zucchini 3 minutes, or until nicely browned. Season with salt and pepper, remove with slotted spoon, and reserve.
3. Add sausages and sauté over medium heat until nicely browned on all sides. Add more oil if needed. When done, remove sausages and set aside. Discard all but 1 tablespoon of the fat from skillet.
4. Add butter and hot chili to skillet. When fat is hot, add chicken slices and sauté them over high heat 2 to 3 minutes, until browned. Add wine to skillet, bring to a boil, stir, and reduce for 2 to 3 minutes.
5. Add garlic and broth and simmer chicken, partly covered, 2 to 3 minutes more.
6. Slice sausages crosswise into ¼-inch slices. Add sausage slices, zucchini, and roasted red peppers to skillet. Toss with chicken and simmer over low heat 2 to 3 minutes. Taste for seasoning and sprinkle with chopped parsley.

Creamy Lemon Pilaf

2 tablespoons butter
1½ cups long-grain white rice
3 cups chicken broth
Salt
Lemon-cream sauce (see following recipe)
3 tablespoons freshly grated Parmesan cheese
3 tablespoons finely chopped parsley
Freshly ground black pepper

1. Heat butter in heavy saucepan.
2. Add rice and cook 1 minute, or until rice turns opaque. Add chicken broth and season with salt. Bring to a boil, reduce heat, and simmer, covered, 20 to 25 minutes.
3. Just before serving, add lemon-cream sauce to rice and fold in gently. Add Parmesan cheese and parsley. Taste, and season with salt and pepper. Serve immediately.

Lemon-Cream Sauce

1 tablespoon lemon juice
1 teaspoon grated lemon peel
2 yolks from extra-large eggs
¼ cup heavy cream

Combine lemon juice, lemon peel, yolks, and cream in small bowl. Whisk until well blended. Reserve for rice.

ADDED TOUCH

For a light, sweet dessert, chill, peel, and thinly slice four oranges. Sprinkle a teaspoon of orange liqueur (Grand Marnier and Triple Sec are both good with oranges) and a teaspoon of confectioners' sugar over each portion.

Zucchini, Tuna, and Tomato Salad
Sauté of Chicken with Mushrooms
Broccoli Purée

The right season for this meal is late summer, when the tomatoes and zucchini in the first-course salad are at their peak. The chicken and mushroom sauté with a cream sauce arrives at the table with an appetizing-looking broccoli purée.

You can make the sauté of chicken dark meat with mushrooms in any season, since the mushrooms here are dried. The broccoli, pureed to accompany the chicken, is also available year around. But the first course of this menu, which comes from northern Italy, depends upon the perfection of the zucchini and the tomatoes. Tuna packed in olive oil is another essential.

WHAT TO DRINK

Because of the fine textures of this meal, a light white wine would taste too acidic. Try instead a fuller wine, perhaps a white Burgundy from the Macon region or a moderately priced California Chardonnay—and serve lightly chilled.

SHOPPING LIST AND STAPLES

6 to 8 small chicken legs with thighs
1 bunch broccoli (about 1½ pounds)
3 small zucchini
1 pint cherry tomatoes
1 medium-size red onion
2 small yellow onions
1 green pepper
1 large clove garlic
1 bunch fresh parsley
¾ cup heavy cream
½ to ¾ cup sour cream
8 tablespoons butter (1 stick)
2 eggs (optional)
1½ cups chicken broth
7½-ounce can light tuna in olive oil
2 small dill gherkins
1 ounce Italian dried mushrooms
1 teaspoon vegetable oil
½ cup plus 1 tablespoon olive oil
3 tablespoons sherry wine vinegar or red wine vinegar
4 tablespoons flour
Coarse (kosher) salt
Salt and pepper

UTENSILS

Food processor
Large heavy skillet with cover
Small skillet
Large saucepan

Medium-size saucepan
Small saucepan with cover
Salad bowl
Small bowl
Measuring cups and spoons
All-purpose knife
Slotted spoon
Vegetable peeler
Whisk
Tongs

START-TO-FINISH STEPS

In the morning: hard-boil eggs for zucchini recipe, if egg garnish is desired.

1. Follow chicken recipe step 1. While mushrooms simmer, follow zucchini recipe steps 1 through 3.
2. Peel and cut onions for chicken recipe.
3. Follow chicken recipe steps 2 and 3. As chicken sautés, follow broccoli recipe steps 1 through 5.
4. Follow chicken recipe step 4.
5. Serve zucchini salad as the first course, followed by chicken and broccoli.

RECIPES

Zucchini, Tuna, and Tomato Salad

3 small zucchini
7½-ounce can light tuna in olive oil
½ cup thinly sliced red onions
½ green pepper, seeded and thinly sliced
2 small dill gherkins, thinly sliced
1 pint cherry tomatoes
Coarse (kosher) salt and freshly ground black pepper
1 large clove garlic, mashed
3 tablespoons sherry wine vinegar or red wine vinegar
½ cup plus 1 tablespoon olive oil
2 tablespoons finely chopped fresh parsley for garnish
    (optional)
2 sliced hard-boiled eggs for garnish (optional)

1. In medium-size saucepan, bring about 1 cup salted water to a boil. Add zucchini and poach 5 minutes, or until barely tender. Remove, cool under cold water, and slice thinly.
2. In salad bowl, combine zucchini, flaked tuna with its oil, onion, green pepper, and gherkins. Slice cherry tomatoes in half and add to bowl. Season with coarse salt and freshly ground black pepper.
3. Combine mashed garlic, vinegar, and olive oil in small bowl and blend thoroughly. Toss dressing with salad ingredients. Serve at room temperature or slightly chilled. Garnish with chopped parsley and hard-boiled egg slices, if desired.

Sauté of Chicken with Mushrooms

1 ounce Italian dried mushrooms
1½ cups chicken broth

6 to 8 small chicken legs with thighs
Salt and freshly ground black pepper
4 tablespoons butter
1 teaspoon vegetable oil
2 small yellow onions, cut in half crosswise
1 tablespoon flour
¾ cup heavy cream
Finely minced fresh parsley for garnish (optional)

1. Rinse mushrooms quickly under cold running water. Combine in small saucepan with 1 cup of the chicken broth. Bring to a boil. Reduce heat, cover, and simmer 20 minutes. Drain mushrooms, reserving liquid; dice them and set aside.
2. Rinse chicken pieces and dry thoroughly with paper towels. Season with salt and pepper. In large heavy skillet, heat 3 tablespoons of the butter with oil. Sauté chicken on both sides until it is nicely browned. Do not crowd pan.
3. Add onions to skillet and pour in ¼ cup of the remaining chicken broth. Lower heat and simmer, partially covered, 25 to 30 minutes, turning chicken once. Add some of the mushroom liquid if needed. Be sure not to drown chicken, or it will lose its nice color.
4. When chicken is done, use tongs to remove it from skillet and set it aside on platter. Remove onions with slotted spoon and discard.
5. Skim surface of pan juices of any fat. Add mushrooms and the remaining ¼ cup chicken broth to skillet. Cook until sauce is reduced to ½ cup.
6. Make *beurre manié* by combining flour with the remaining 1 tablespoon butter, working it together with your fingers until thoroughly blended.
7. Add cream to reduced sauce. Taste and season carefully with salt and pepper. Whisk in a little *beurre manié* until sauce is just thick enough to heavily coat spoon.
8. Return chicken to skillet and coat with sauce. Reheat, and serve garnished with parsley, if desired.

Broccoli Purée

1 bunch broccoli (about 1½ pounds)
4 tablespoons butter
3 tablespoons flour
½ to ¾ cup sour cream
Salt and freshly ground black pepper

1. Remove all leaves from broccoli stalks. Peel stalks with vegetable peeler or sharp knife and cut broccoli into 1-inch pieces.
2. In large saucepan, bring salted water to a boil. Add broccoli and cook 7 to 8 minutes, until tender.
3. Drain thoroughly and puree in food processor.
4. In small skillet, heat butter. Add flour and cook mixture, whisking constantly, until it turns pale brown. Add brown butter to broccoli puree, together with ½ cup sour cream, and stir to blend. If puree seems too thick, add a little more sour cream. Taste and correct seasoning.
5. Transfer to shallow covered serving dish. Keep warm in 200-degree oven until ready to serve.

Game Hens with Green Peppercorn Sauce
Sweet and Sour Turnips
Green Salad with Lemon Mustard Vinaigrette

Turnips glazed in brown sugar, wine vinegar, and chicken stock match the golden tones of roasted game hens. A light salad of two greens with sliced fresh mushrooms contrasts with the rich tastes of the entrée and vegetable.

Game hens need herbs, seasonings, and care. Here Perla Meyers combines them with rosemary, thyme, paprika, mustard, and green peppercorns—which are pepper berries picked before they ripen and turn black. Jars of green peppercorns preserved in brine or vinegar are on the shelf in most supermarkets and specialty shops. Always buy the brine-packed kind because vinegar overwhelms the peppery flavor. Be sure to add green peppercorns to the sauce at the last minute.

Take time to truss the game hens before you roast them: see the trussing diagrams on the following page. A trussed hen is easier for the cook to turn. And because the skin stays whole and the legs will cook close to the body, a trussed bird will look better after it has been untrussed and carved.

Small white turnips, far from being bitter, taste like a cross between a tart apple and radish: they hold their own in a full-flavored meal such as this one. They have a firm, clean texture, if not over cooked. Avoid large turnips, which do tend to turn woody and bitter.

Salad tip: most produce markets cut off turnip tops and discard them, but fresh green turnip tops make an interesting addition to any green salad, including the Boston lettuce and spinach salad in the recipe here.

Also known as butterhead, Boston lettuce is pale and leafy and a perfect companion to deep-green spinach. The whole head should be loosely packed when you buy Boston lettuce; also, check the inside leaves to make sure they are light yellow. Look for very green leaves that are not split or damaged. If bagged spinach is the only kind available, buy a bag that springs back to the touch.

Buy the greens the day you serve them and wash them just before assembling the salad. Boston lettuce needs only two or three washings, but you must wash spinach with special care in order to remove all grit. First cut off the stems, then fill a large pan or bowl with water and immerse the greens. Rinse and drain at least three times, and taste a leaf. If necessary, rinse again. Drain the spinach on paper towels and pat it dry. A salad spinner will save trouble and cut preparation time. In any case, be sure to dry the leaves thoroughly, for otherwise the dressing will not cling and the salad will taste watery.

You can save time by making the vinaigrette in the bottom of the salad serving bowl, then adding the mushrooms—which thus get the benefit of a marinade—and piling the greens on top. But do not toss the salad until you are just ready to serve.

WHAT TO DRINK

The rich sauce of this menu needs a full-bodied wine. Perla Meyers suggests the berry flavor of a California Zinfandel, an unusual pairing of red wine and chicken. Alternatively, you might try an imported brut rosé Champagne.

SHOPPING LIST AND STAPLES

4 Rock Cornish game hens
8 medium-size white turnips
1 head Boston lettuce
¼ pound fresh spinach
6 large fresh mushrooms
2 heads garlic (about 18 large cloves)
1 bunch fresh parsley
2 tablespoons chopped fresh dill, or 2 teaspoons dried
1 lemon
1 cup heavy cream
6 tablespoons butter
1 teaspoon green peppercorns
2 cups chicken broth
6 tablespoons olive oil
1 teaspoon vegetable oil
¼ cup sherry wine vinegar or red wine vinegar
1 tablespoon flour
4 teaspoons sugar
2½ tablespoons dark brown sugar
1 tablespoon chopped fresh thyme, or 1 teaspoon dried
1½ teaspoons chopped fresh rosemary, or
    ½ teaspoon dried
1 teaspoon paprika
2 tablespoons Dijon mustard
Coarse (kosher) salt
White pepper
Salt and pepper

UTENSILS

2 large heavy skillets with covers, one with
    oven-proof handle
Small saucepan
Salad bowl
2 small bowls
Measuring cups and spoons
Chef's knife
Slotted spoon

Tongs
Whisk
Trussing string
Vegetable peeler
Poultry shears
Juicer

START-TO-FINISH STEPS

1. Follow game hen recipe step 1.
2. Chop herbs for game hen and salad recipes.
3. Follow game hen recipe steps 2 through 6.
4. Juice lemon and follow salad recipe steps 1 through 3.
5. Follow turnip recipe steps 1 through 4. Keep warm.
6. Follow game hen recipe steps 7 through 11.
7. Follow salad recipe step 4 and serve with game hens and turnips.

RECIPES

Game Hens with Green Peppercorn Sauce

18 large cloves garlic
1 tablespoon Dijon mustard
1 teaspoon paprika
1 tablespoon chopped fresh thyme, or 1 teaspoon dried
1½ teaspoons chopped fresh rosemary, or
  ½ teaspoon dried
4 Rock Cornish game hens
Coarse (kosher) salt and freshly ground black pepper
3 tablespoons butter
1 teaspoon vegetable oil
1½ cups chicken broth
1 tablespoon flour
1 cup heavy cream
1 heaping teaspoon green peppercorns, crushed
Parsley sprigs for garnish (optional)

1. Preheat oven to 400 degrees.

2. Mash 2 of the garlic cloves. Combine in small bowl with mustard, paprika, thyme, and rosemary. Blend mixture into a paste and rub hens well with it. Season hens with coarse salt and freshly ground black pepper. Truss hens (see diagrams at right).

3. In skillet with oven-proof handle, heat 2 tablespoons of the butter and oil until foam subsides. Add game hens and sauté over moderate heat on both sides until they are lightly browned.

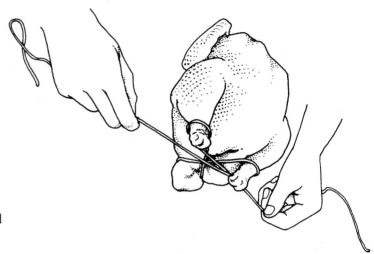

Tuck tips of wings under back securely. Tie legs and tail together, crossing string over cavity and pulling tight.

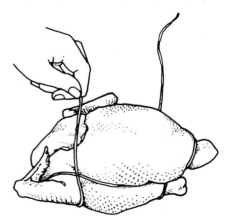

Run string under legs; turn game hen over, run string through wings. Tie securely in back, with knot over skin flap.

4. Meanwhile, bring about 1 cup water to a boil. Add the remaining 16 cloves garlic and blanch 1 to 2 minutes. Drain and slip skins off. Scatter garlic around hens and add half of the broth. Place uncovered in oven.

5. Baste hens every 10 minutes with the remaining chicken broth. Turn them once during their cooking time and make sure pan juices are not burning.

6. Cook 30 to 35 minutes, or until tender. Remove hens and set them aside. With slotted spoon, remove garlic

cloves and reserve.

7. Skim surface of pan juices of any fat. Place pan over high heat and reduce liquid by half.

8. Combine flour with the remaining 1 tablespoon butter and work together with your fingers until thoroughly blended, making *beurre manié*.

9. Add cream to reduced sauce. Taste and season with salt and pepper. Whisk in a little of the *beurre manié*, just enough for sauce to thicken. Taste and correct seasoning.

10. Return garlic cloves to skillet. Add crushed green peppercorns and heat sauce through. Keep warm.

11. Remove trussing string, and quarter game hens with poultry shears. Place on serving platter and spoon sauce over them. Garnish with sprigs of parsley, if desired.

Sweet and Sour Turnips

8 medium-size white turnips
3 tablespoons butter
Salt and freshly ground white pepper
1 teaspoon sugar
½ cup chicken broth
2½ heaping tablespoons dark brown sugar
¼ cup sherry wine vinegar or red wine vinegar

1. Peel turnips. Cut them crosswise into ¾-inch slices and then into ¾-inch cubes.

2. In skillet, melt butter. Add turnips. Season with salt, white pepper, and sugar. Cook turnips over medium-low heat, tossing them in pan until they are glazed and nicely browned. Lower heat and add a little of the chicken broth. Cover pan and cook 15 minutes. You may need to add a little more of the broth. Do not over cook.

3. While turnips are cooking, combine brown sugar with vinegar in small bowl. Blend well and add to turnips after they have cooked 15 minutes.

4. Raise heat and cook until turnips are well glazed and pan juices are reduced to about 2 tablespoons. Remove to serving dish and pour pan juices over them.

Green Salad with Lemon Mustard Vinaigrette

¼ pound fresh spinach
1 head Boston lettuce
6 large fresh mushrooms
Juice of 1 lemon
1 tablespoon Dijon mustard
3 teaspoons sugar
Freshly ground black pepper

2 tablespoons chopped fresh dill, or 2 teaspoons dried
6 tablespoons olive oil

1. Trim stems from spinach. Wash and dry spinach and lettuce. Slice mushrooms.

2. In bottom of salad bowl, whisk lemon juice, mustard, sugar, pepper, dill, and olive oil together. Vinaigrette will be very thick.

3. Add sliced mushrooms to vinaigrette and toss to coat them. Add lettuce and spinach to salad bowl. Refrigerate until serving time.

4. Toss salad and serve.

ADDED TOUCHES

For a variation on the turnip recipe, use six small turnips instead of eight, but add two or three carrots, each cut into strips about an inch long. Then proceed with the recipe.

If you have time, prepare the following dessert before you begin to cook dinner. Complete the recipe but leave the pears and sauce in the skillet and let them cool. Reheat just before serving, being careful not to let the cream boil.

Sautéed Pears in Caramel Cream

4 large semiripe pears
2 tablespoons butter
½ cup plus 1 tablespoon sugar
¾ cup heavy cream
2 tablespoons water
Pinch of freshly grated nutmeg
1 pint vanilla ice cream (optional)

1. Peel pears, cut in half, core, and cut ⅛-inch-deep scores. Reserve.

2. In 10-inch heavy iron skillet, heat butter. Add pears and sauté over fairly high heat until lightly browned. Add 1 tablespoon of the sugar and continue sautéing pears until soft and caramelized, or about 4 to 5 minutes.

3. While pears are sautéing, heat cream in small saucepan and reserve.

4. In 2-quart heavy saucepan heat sugar and water. Cook sugar until it turns deep caramel color. Remove from heat and add hot cream. Whisk mixture until cream and caramel are well blended and sauce is smooth. Add pinch of nutmeg, and when pears are done, add cream to skillet and mix into pears. Transfer pears to serving plates and serve with a side dish of vanilla ice cream, if desired.

Anne Byrd

One of the richest traditions in American cooking flourishes below the Mason-Dixon line, where for generations good cooks have developed their special ways with chicken, pork, corn, game, and such hot-weather vegetables as okra. A native southerner, Anne Byrd grew up relishing and mastering the great meals of her region. At the same time, she added her own touches to the best of the down-home recipes, picking up ideas for side dishes, spices, and sauces from other regions of the United States as well as from other nations.

The three menus here reflect this new eclectic kind of cooking. Anne Byrd's fried chicken in the meal at left (see pages 118–119 for recipes) cooks more quickly than older versions. The corn pudding gets a simple but sophisticated dusting of dill or chervil. In Menu 2, where the main dish is flamed chicken, the side dish is bulgur, a vitamin-rich cracked wheat that came to America from the cuisine of the Middle East. Menu 3 centers on a southern classic—quail. These quail, however, come from the supermarket rather than the woods. Anne Byrd serves them with buttered asparagus and wild rice, which is a native American delicacy from the lake country of Minnesota.

This menu of Southern fried chicken, corn pudding, and sautéed okra is as traditional as a barn raising, but Anne Byrd's approach to old-time Southern cooking produces lighter results that suit modern appetites. The meal looks as good as it tastes, either outdoors on a picnic table, as at left, or in the dining room with bright cotton mats and assorted informal serving pieces to pass around the table.

117

Southern Fried Chicken
Herbed Corn Pudding
Sautéed Okra with Tomatoes and Herbs

The fried chicken recipe for this menu calls for less fat than the old-fashioned deep fry, and instead of taking an hour or more, the chicken cooks at high temperature in 30 minutes. Buttermilk moistens and flavors the raw chicken before it is dusted with flour.

For authentic deep-South taste, be sure to use lard for the frying, rather than some other oil or fat. The chicken will fry as nicely in vegetable shortening but will not taste the same. You can buy lard, which is rendered pork fat, in pound packages at a butcher shop or the supermarket meat counter. Combining butter with the lard adds flavor too, and the butter will not scorch in this mixture, even at high frying temperatures.

Two timesaving tips: remember to bring the disjointed chicken to room temperature before you cook. It fries faster. Second, create leftovers on purpose: buy two small chickens and fry them in separate skillets. You can handle two chickens almost as easily as one, and the next day you will have a delicious cold lunch.

Because dark meat takes longer to cook, put the legs and thighs in the pan first, then add the breasts, and finally the wings. Remember, too, to use tongs to turn the pieces—a fork pierces the skin and lets the juices run out, leaving the chicken tough and dry.

Freshly picked corn produces the best corn pudding. Buy small to medium-size ears and, after shucking and desilking them, stand each ear on end and cut off the kernels (about three rows at a time) with a sharp knife. Do not slice too deep—the outer half of the kernel is the tastiest. If you cannot find good corn, frozen white "baby" corn is a good alternative. The pudding dish should bake in a pan of boiling water, as the recipe directs. The water keeps the temperature constant so that the texture of the pudding will be smooth.

Okra, a traditional side dish in the summertime, grows only in the South and has to be shipped north. Buy tender pods no more than four inches long. (The larger pods may be slightly wooden in texture.) Okra contains a thick liquid characteristically used to thicken Creole gumbos and stews. To keep it in the pod, where it belongs, avoid cutting off its top (the top is the end that is not pointed). If okra is not in season, buy fresh green beans and stir fry them in the same way.

To peel and seed the tomatoes for the okra recipe, drop them in boiling water for 15 seconds and then drain. Starting at the stem, peel with a paring knife. (The skin will practically slip off without a knife.) Cut the tomato in half and squeeze out the seeds and most of the juice. You will have to use your fingers to remove the remaining seeds. The seeded, dejuiced tomato will provide the right texture and taste for the stir fry but will not liquefy it.

WHAT TO DRINK

Iced tea is an excellent companion for fried chicken. For best results, use tea leaves rather than tea bags. Since you want a strong mixture of tea, allow a heaping tablespoon per glass and use freshly boiled water—about a cup per glass. Steep for five minutes in a teapot and add fresh mint leaves to the brew if you have them. Strain the tea, cool it, and add it to an ice-filled pitcher. Dilute if necessary, add sugar to taste, and serve with lemon slices or wedges. A few mint leaves will look summery in each glass.

If you prefer wine, a good complement to the gentle spicing of this menu would be a dry California Riesling, a white wine with a hint of subdued spice. Serve very cold.

SHOPPING LIST AND STAPLES

2- to 2½-pound chicken, cut into serving pieces
4 ears fresh corn, or 2 cups frozen white corn
¾ pound small pods fresh okra
1 small tomato
1 bunch watercress (optional)
1 bunch fresh parsley
2 teaspoons chopped fresh dill or chervil, or 1 teaspoon dried chervil
1 tablespoon chopped fresh basil, or 1 teaspoon dried
1 small lemon (optional)
⅓ cup buttermilk
1 cup heavy cream
7 tablespoons butter
3 large eggs
⅓ cup lard
½ cup flour
Salt and pepper

UTENSILS

Large deep frying pan
Medium-size skillet
Medium-size saucepan

1½-quart shallow baking dish and larger dish to hold it
Medium-size bowl
Small bowl
Measuring cups and spoons
Chef's knife
All-purpose knife
Whisk
Tongs

START-TO-FINISH STEPS

1. Cut chicken into serving pieces. Cut kernels from corn ears for corn pudding. Trim okra and chop tomato for okra recipe. Chop herbs for okra and corn pudding.
2. Follow corn pudding recipe steps 1 through 7. While pudding bakes, follow chicken recipe steps 1 through 8.
3. Follow okra recipe steps 1 through 3.
4. Follow corn pudding recipe step 8.
5. Wedge lemon and follow chicken recipe step 9.
6. Serve okra and corn pudding with chicken.

RECIPES

Southern Fried Chicken

2- to 2½-pound chicken, cut into serving pieces
½ cup flour
⅓ cup buttermilk
⅓ cup lard
5 tablespoons butter
1½ teaspoons salt
½ teaspoon freshly ground black pepper
Lemon wedges and watercress for garnish (optional)

1. Rinse chicken pieces and pat dry with paper towels.
2. Put flour in paper bag.
3. Pour buttermilk into medium-size bowl and dip each chicken piece in it to coat. Place 1 or 2 chicken pieces in bag and shake to coat with flour. Place coated pieces of chicken on plate. Repeat until all chicken pieces are floured.
4. Melt lard and butter over high heat in frying pan.
5. Meanwhile, sprinkle chicken with salt and pepper.
6. When fat is hot, add thighs and legs, fleshy side down. Brown about 3 minutes. When golden, turn them with tongs and brown other sides. Add chicken breasts to pan. After about 3 more minutes, turn all chicken pieces. Add wings to pan.
7. Continue cooking and turning chicken pieces so that they brown evenly. Cook chicken on as high a temperature as possible. Reduce temperature to medium-high only if chicken is browning too fast. It should be done in 20 to 30 minutes from time thighs and legs were placed in pan. Chicken should be medium brown and the crust very crisp.
8. Spread doubled paper towels on warm serving platter and place chicken on top; then cover chicken with doubled paper towels. Allow chicken to drain 3 to 5 minutes in a warm spot. Remove towels.
9. Garnish chicken platter with lemon wedges and watercress, if desired.

Herbed Corn Pudding

2 cups kernels cut from 4 ears fresh corn, or frozen white corn, defrosted
2 teaspoons chopped fresh dill or chervil, or 1 teaspoon dried chervil
3 large eggs
1 teaspoon salt
1 cup heavy cream
Additional fresh dill for garnish (optional)

1. Preheat oven to 350 degrees.
2. Bring water to a boil to pour around baking dish.
3. Place corn kernels in lightly greased shallow baking dish and sprinkle dill on top.
4. Using whisk, beat eggs about 10 strokes in small bowl. Add salt and cream and beat to incorporate.
5. Pour custard over corn and dill and stir briefly.
6. Place baking dish with corn pudding in larger dish. Pour enough boiling water into larger dish so that water comes about halfway up side of pudding dish.
7. Place dishes on middle rack of oven. Bake 35 to 40 minutes, or until knife inserted 1½ inches in from edge of baking dish comes out clean. The center will set after pudding is removed from oven.
8. Garnish with additional fresh dill, if desired.

Sautéed Okra with Tomatoes and Herbs

2 tablespoons butter
¾ pound small pods fresh okra, rinsed and dried, with stems, but not end of pod, cut off
¼ teaspoon salt
1 small tomato, peeled, seeded, and chopped
1 tablespoon chopped fresh basil, or 1 teaspoon dried
1 tablespoon chopped fresh parsley

1. Melt butter in skillet over high heat.
2. Sauté okra 3 to 5 minutes, depending on size of pods. Stir okra frequently so that pods do not brown. They should be just tender and bright green.
3. Remove okra to warm serving platter and sprinkle with salt. Top with chopped tomato and herbs.

ADDED TOUCH

If you serve the meal in the backyard or on the patio, watermelon slices or assorted flavors of ice cream make the easiest and most appropriate desserts. The blueberry cobbler on page 125 is another possibility. Serve it warm and top each portion off with vanilla ice cream.

LEFTOVER SUGGESTIONS

Fried chicken is especially good the second day, when allowed to warm to room temperature. If any okra and tomato sauté is left over, it will make a nice addition in tomorrow morning's omelet.

Flamed Chicken with Mushrooms
Bulgur with Aromatic Vegetables
Tomatoes with Chopped Herbs

Mushrooms, chicken breasts, and bulgur make a rich, dark dish that looks even better if enhanced with a bright salad. In summer use fresh tomatoes and in winter an assortment of watercress and two or three other, paler greens.

The bulgur that goes with the brandy-flamed chicken breasts in this menu is simply unbleached cracked wheat with all the good flavor of whole-grain bread. Look for it in the supermarket next to the rice, dried beans, or breakfast cereals. Health food stores and specialty shops often sell it loose, by the pound. Buy an unrefined brand, since the nutrients are mostly in the dark husk.

During cooking, the wine and brandy in the sauce lose their alcoholic content but not their flavor. When you cook with wine or spirits, therefore, always use something that you consider genuinely fit to drink. Your guests and family will enjoy watching you flame the chicken, so invite them into the kitchen or finish the dish at the table if you are serving in the dining room. Unless the brandy is warm, it will not catch fire. Warm it on the stove for a moment before you bring it in, then ignite it with a match. Or warm it over a small open-flame burner at the table. Remember that the brandy may accidentally flame up without your putting a match to it. If so, you should cover the pan with a lid, taking care to stand at arm's length.

WHAT TO DRINK

A bright, slightly acidic white wine will make a nice counterpoint to the rich flavors of this menu. Try an Italian Pinot Grigio or Pinot Bianco from either Friuli or Trentino-Alto Adige. Whichever you select, buy enough to use in the sauce as well as at dinner.

If you prefer a Mideastern touch, in keeping with the bulgur, brew hot tea with mint leaves and sugar.

SHOPPING LIST AND STAPLES

8 skinless, boneless chicken breast halves
4 large shallots
½ pound fresh mushrooms
1 carrot
1 stalk celery
1 small onion
4 tomatoes
1 bunch fresh parsley
1 tablespoon chopped fresh marjoram, or 1 teaspoon dried
2 tablespoons chopped fresh basil, or 2 teaspoons dried
2 tablespoons chopped fresh chives, or 2 teaspoons freeze-dried
8 tablespoons butter (1 stick)
1 cup bulgur

1½ cups chicken broth
Salt and pepper
¼ cup dry white wine
¼ cup brandy

UTENSILS

Large skillet
Medium-size saucepan
Small saucepan
Measuring cups and spoons
Heavy cleaver or meat pounder
Chef's knife
Paring knife
Tongs
Waxed paper

START-TO-FINISH STEPS

1. Chop herbs, mushrooms, and shallots for chicken recipe. Chop vegetables and herbs for bulgur recipe. Chop herbs for tomato recipe.
2. Follow tomato recipe steps 1 through 4.
3. Follow bulgur recipe steps 1 through 4.
4. Follow chicken recipe steps 1 through 7.
5. Follow bulgur recipe step 5.
6. Follow tomato recipe step 5.
7. Serve chicken and bulgur with tomatoes.

RECIPES

Flamed Chicken with Mushrooms

5 tablespoons butter
¼ cup minced shallots
½ pound fresh mushrooms, sliced
1 tablespoon chopped fresh marjoram, or 1 teaspoon dried
2 tablespoons chopped fresh chives, or 2 teaspoons
    freeze-dried
Salt and freshly ground black pepper
¼ cup dry white wine
8 skinless, boneless chicken breast halves
¼ cup brandy
2 tablespoons chopped fresh parsley for garnish
    (optional)

1. Melt 3 tablespoons of the butter in skillet large enough to hold chicken in one layer. (It may be necessary to use two skillets to cook chicken.) Stir in shallots and cook over low heat for about a minute.
2. Add mushrooms and continue cooking for another minute. Stir in herbs, seasonings, and wine. Cook over moderately high heat about 3 minutes, or until wine has reduced to an essence.
3. Remove mushroom mixture and set aside on warm plate. Cover and keep warm.
4. Put chicken between sheets of waxed paper and pound until breasts are about ½ inch thick. Season with salt and pepper.

5. Add the remaining 2 tablespoons butter to skillet over medium-high heat. When butter is hot, sauté chicken breasts, without crowding pan, 3 to 4 minutes on 1 side until lightly browned. Reduce heat slightly, turn each breast with tongs, and brown other side—adding more butter if necessary. Place some mushroom mixture on top of each breast and turn off heat.
6. Slightly warm brandy in small saucepan. Standing back, hold a match just above brandy and set it aflame.
7. Pour flaming brandy over chicken. Shake pan gently until flames have subsided. Remove to platter and garnish with parsley, if desired.

Bulgur with Aromatic Vegetables

3 tablespoons butter
¼ cup chopped carrots
¼ cup chopped celery
¼ cup chopped onion
1 cup bulgur
1½ cups chicken broth
¼ teaspoon salt
2 tablespoons chopped fresh parsley

1. Melt butter over medium heat and add chopped vegetables. Cook, stirring, for 1 minute.
2. Add bulgur and toss for 3 to 5 minutes until vegetables have softened and bulgur is golden brown.
3. Add chicken broth and salt and bring to a boil.
4. Reduce heat to medium low. Simmer, uncovered, about 15 minutes, or until all liquid has been absorbed.
5. Stir in chopped parsley.

Tomatoes with Chopped Herbs

4 tomatoes
2 tablespoons chopped fresh parsley
2 tablespoons chopped fresh basil, or 2 teaspoons dried
Salt and freshly ground black pepper

1. Bring enough water to a boil to cover tomatoes.
2. Drop tomatoes into boiling water for about 15 seconds.
3. Drain tomatoes. With paring knife, slip off their skins.
4. Slice tomatoes and arrange on platter. Refrigerate.
5. Before serving, top tomatoes with chopped herbs and season with salt and pepper.

ADDED TOUCH

For a quick dessert, chill a honeydew melon and, just before serving, cut into slices. Then run a sharp knife between the melon and the rind and cut the melon into bite-size pieces. Garnish with fresh sprigs of mint.

LEFTOVER SUGGESTION

The bulgur-and-vegetable mixture makes a good cold dish, and you will find it worthwhile to double the recipe and have leftovers. Toss it lightly with a vinaigrette dressing and garnish it with tomato wedges.

Sautéed Quail
Steamed Asparagus with Chervil Butter
Herbed Wild Rice

Silver serving platters, if you have them, along with your best dishes, silverware, and table linen, will underline the elegance of sautéed quail, wild rice, and fresh asparagus. Garnish the main dish with sprigs of flat-leaf parsley.

In the South, where quail was once a favorite dish at fancy lunches, the preferred breed was the bobwhite, one of three recognized varieties. Bobwhite are now a protected game bird, to be hunted only for a few weeks in the fall. Almost identical in every respect, however, are commercially grown quail now available in most fine meat stores. They grow to full size (five or six ounces each) and are ready for market six to eight weeks after hatching. If you cannot find quail at your local market, ask the butcher to stock them or write Manchester Farms (one of the largest breeders) at Box 97, Dalzell, South Carolina 29040, for the nearest distributor in your area.

Quail, which are all white meat and virtually fat free, are so small that you must allow two per serving. Generally more flavorful than chicken, they cook very fast. Over cooking will spoil their flavor and even their looks, for if they are baked or roasted too long, they fall apart. This recipe calls for sautéing the birds about 20 minutes, an ideal technique, and then coating them with a bourbon-accented cream sauce. Because they are so small, they are hard to eat without using your fingers, particularly for the leg and thigh meat.

Wild rice, like quail, is a special occasion dish—and the two blend deliciously. Technically not a true rice, this nutty-flavored grain is a wild grass seed and is one of many American contributions to world cuisine. Originally harvested wild by Indians, it grows only in Wisconsin, Minnesota, a few other northern states, and Canada. Commercial growers now successfully cultivate it, but the crop is always small, and wild rice sells for about 10 dollars a pound. Fortunately, one cup of raw rice (equal to one half pound) yields enough for four. You can find wild rice in most supermarkets and specialty shops. Be sure the package you choose is not a combination of wild rice and regular white rice.

A sauce of butter and chervil complements the fresh asparagus in this menu. Chervil is a delicate herb that combines the flavors of parsley, dill, and a hint of anise. Dried chervil, sold in many supermarkets, is not as good as fresh, but it will do. And, if you enjoy gardening, remember that chervil is one of the easiest herbs to grow. Plant it either in full sun indoors or partial sunlight outdoors. Dried and put into jars, chervil keeps well over the winter, and you can also freeze it in small packets—really a better method of preserving chervil than drying it. The plant is a perennial. Whether you grow it or buy it, be sure to add chervil at the last moment before finishing and serving the dish. Heat destroys it.

If fresh asparagus is not in season, substitute fresh green beans or broccoli, either of which will combine deliciously with the chervil butter sauce.

WHAT TO DRINK

The special flavor of asparagus unfortunately acts to distort the flavor of many wines, but in this case the quail and the wild rice win out. For a meal that is this festive, the best choice would almost certainly be a French Champagne: a nonvintage brut, served very cold and kept on ice during the dinner.

SHOPPING LIST AND STAPLES

8 fresh or frozen quail
1 large onion
1 pound fresh asparagus
1 bunch fresh parsley
1 tablespoon chopped fresh chervil, or 1 teaspoon dried
1 tablespoon chopped fresh chives, or 1 teaspoon freeze-dried
1 tablespoon chopped fresh thyme, or 1 teaspoon dried
10 tablespoons butter (1¼ sticks)
1½ cups chicken broth
1 cup wild rice
2 tablespoons flour
Salt and pepper
1 cup bourbon

UTENSILS

Large skillet
Large sauté pan
Vegetable steamer
Medium-size saucepan with cover
Small saucepan
Measuring cups and spoons
All-purpose knife
Poultry shears
Whisk
Tongs

START-TO-FINISH STEPS

1. Chop onion for quail recipe. Chop herbs for asparagus

and rice recipes.

2. Follow rice recipe steps 1 through 3.

3. Follow asparagus recipe steps 1 through 3. As asparagus steams, follow quail recipe steps 1 through 3.

4. Follow asparagus recipe step 4.

5. Follow quail recipe steps 4 through 7.

6. Follow asparagus recipe step 5.

7. Follow quail recipe step 8 and serve with rice and asparagus.

RECIPES

Sautéed Quail

8 fresh quail, or 8 frozen quail, thoroughly defrosted
Salt and freshly ground black pepper
4 tablespoons butter
½ cup plus ⅓ cup bourbon
½ cup finely chopped onions
2 tablespoons flour
1½ cups chicken broth
Sprigs of parsley (optional)

1. Split quail with poultry shears down their backs, and spread open. Sprinkle lightly with salt and pepper.

2. Taking care not to let it burn, melt butter over high heat in sauté pan. Place quail, flesh side down, in hot butter and sauté 3 minutes. Turn and sauté on other side 3 minutes more, or until both sides are golden.

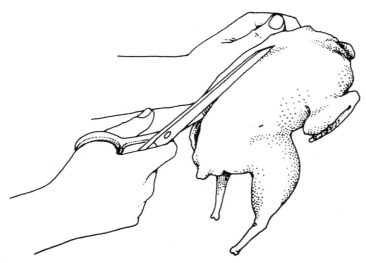

Using poultry shears, cut quail down the backbone.

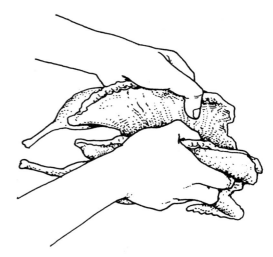

Spread each bird flat, with backbones outward.

3. Slightly warm ½ cup of the bourbon in small saucepan. Standing back, hold a match just above bourbon and set it aflame. With quail off heat, carefully pour flaming bourbon over quail.

4. Reduce heat to medium. Turn birds again, flesh side down, and cook 7 minutes. Turn flesh side up and cook 7 more minutes.

5. Remove quail to warm serving platter and place in 200-degree oven to keep warm.

6. Set heat under sauté pan to medium high. With whisk, stir chopped onions into juices in pan and cook 2 to 3 minutes. Whisk flour into mixture. Whisk the remaining ⅓ cup bourbon and chicken broth into flour mixture. Bring to a boil, stirring frequently.

7. When sauce has thickened, remove from heat. Taste and season with salt and pepper.

8. Lightly coat quail with sauce and serve the remaining sauce separately; garnish with parsley, if desired.

Steamed Asparagus with Chervil Butter

1 pound fresh asparagus
4 tablespoons butter
1 tablespoon chopped fresh chervil, or 1 teaspoon dried
½ teaspoon salt

1. Wash asparagus and trim stalks.

2. Fill vegetable steamer with water to just below steamer rack. Place asparagus in steamer and steam, covered, 8 to 15 minutes, depending on size of stalks.

3. Test asparagus stalks with tines of fork. When they are tender, but still resist with slight crunch, remove asparagus from heat.

4. Plunge asparagus into cold water to stop cooking and to set color. Drain and set aside until 5 minutes before serving.

5. Melt butter in skillet. Add asparagus and toss in hot butter. Add chervil and salt. Serve immediately.

Herbed Wild Rice

2 tablespoons butter
¼ cup chopped onion
1 cup wild rice
1 tablespoon chopped fresh parsley
1 tablespoon chopped fresh chives, or 1 teaspoon freeze-dried
1 tablespoon chopped fresh thyme, or 1 teaspoon dried
½ teaspoon salt
Freshly ground black pepper
2½ cups water

1. In medium-size saucepan, melt butter over medium-high heat. Add onion and cook about 2 minutes until soft.
2. Stir in wild rice and mix until coated with butter. Add parsley, herbs, salt, pepper, and water.
3. Bring mixture to a boil. Reduce heat to medium-low and cook, covered, 30 to 35 minutes, or until all liquid has been absorbed, and kernels are tender but still have some crunch. Keep warm until serving time.

ADDED TOUCHES

For a celebratory dinner you may want to take a few extra minutes to make a special dessert. To accompany quail, Anne Byrd serves either iced lemon cream or blueberry cobbler. An advantage of the iced lemon cream is that you can make it any time. It keeps a month in the freezer. Make the blueberry cobbler ahead on the same day and warm it before serving.

Iced Lemon Cream

4 egg yolks
½ cup sugar
Zest of 1 lemon, chopped or cut into julienne strips
Juice of 1 large lemon
1 cup heavy cream
Lemon twists for garnish (optional)

1. Beat yolks and sugar with electric mixer about 2 minutes.
2. Add lemon zest (outer rind) and juice, and beat another

minute to incorporate.
3. In another bowl, whip cream. When it reaches same consistency as yolk mixture, pour yolks into cream and beat together about 1 minute. Scrape beaters to remove any lemon zest and stir back into cream.
4. Pour ¾ to 1 cup of the mixture into individual serving bowls and place in freezer for at least 1 hour. If you freeze the cream for more than a few hours, cover bowls with foil. Before serving, allow it to soften slightly in refrigerator.
5. At serving time, garnish with lemon twists, if desired.

Blueberry Cobbler

If using fresh blueberries for the cobbler, treat them gently, washing them in running water in a colander and then picking over them carefully to remove the stems. You should make the cobbler as near meal time as possible, because it is best served warm. Whip a pint of cream to top it off, or serve it with vanilla ice cream.

1 pint fresh blueberries (about 2 cups), or frozen unsweetened blueberries, well drained
⅔ cup sugar
1 lemon
1 cup flour, plus ¼ cup if using frozen blueberries
1 teaspoon baking powder
¼ teaspoon baking soda
¼ teaspoon salt
6 tablespoons butter
½ cup buttermilk

1. Preheat oven to 400 degrees.
2. Rinse and pick over blueberries. Thoroughly drain. Place them in greased 1½-quart baking dish and sprinkle ⅓ cup of the sugar on top, plus ¼ cup of the flour if using frozen blueberries.
3. Cut off zest of lemon, not bitter white part. Cut zest into very thin strips and sprinkle on top of blueberries.
4. Cut lemon in half and squeeze juice (about three tablespoons) through sieve over berries. Stir gently to combine berries with sugar and lemon mixture.
5. Sift the remaining 1 cup flour, the remaining ⅓ cup sugar, baking powder, baking soda, and salt into bowl.
6. Cut butter into flour mixture until coarse and crumbly.
7. Add buttermilk and stir until blended. Beat with spoon about 30 seconds, or until dough sticks together.
8. Spread dough on top of blueberries. Do not worry if there are holes; they will fill in as cobbler bakes.
9. Bake 1 hour, or until golden brown.

Mary Beth Clark

MENU 1 (Right)
Chicken Breasts Stuffed with Pâté
in Sauce Suprême
Celeriac Purée
Watercress Salad

MENU 2
Chicken Breasts Stuffed with Cheese
Steamed Asparagus with Tarragon Butter

MENU 3
Sautéed Chicken Breasts with Persian Rice
in Orange Butter Sauce
Stir-Fried Sugar Snap Peas
Steamed Baby Carrots

One of the oldest and most useful tricks in cooking chicken breasts is to stuff them under the skin. You can use a wide variety of stuffings — ground meats, rice, or cheese. Not only will these add different flavors to the chicken, but they also keep the breast meat moist as it cooks. And the results can be as beautiful to look at as they are appetizing—a valuable addition to your repertoire of company dinners and a boost to your reputation as a good cook.

The three menus that Mary Beth Clark creates here offer variations on this theme. In Menu 1, she stuffs the chicken breasts with a savory homemade pâté and finishes them with a Cognac sauce. In Menu 2, the stuffing is a mild but delicious combination of Parmesan and ricotta cheese. The third variation is chicken breasts with Persian rice, an unusual mixture of rice, fruit, and nuts topped off with an orange-flavored sauce. The vegetables include asparagus and baby carrots—familiar on every table—as well as such relative newcomers to American menus as celeriac— a turniplike root—and sugar snap peas.

Boneless—but unskinned—chicken breasts stuffed with your own mixture of ground veal, pork, and prosciutto make an impressive main course for an important small dinner. Slice the breasts about a half inch thick and serve them on a platter with celeriac purée. As you serve each plate at the table, spoon the creamy Cognac sauce onto each slice. The watercress salad should have a separate plate; you may wish to serve it as a second course.

Chicken Breasts Stuffed with Pâté in Sauce Suprême
Celeriac Purée
Watercress Salad

Celeriac, a standard vegetable on French menus, is a type of celery with a knobby and edible root that has only recently begun to appear in American markets and on American tables. Blanched, diced, and dressed with a mustard mayonnaise, it becomes *céleri rémoulade*, a popular appetizer or buffet dish. Brown celeriac root looks so unprepossessing that you may not have noticed it in the produce department, but most large supermarkets now stock it in the fall and winter. Buy firm, small to medium-size knobs and refrigerate until you are ready to peel and cook them; they will keep from one to two weeks.

If you do not wish to bone the chicken breasts yourself, you will probably have to get them from a butcher, since you need to have boneless breasts with the skin left on. Spicy, cured ham will do fine as a substitute for the prosciutto, which tends to be costly.

Watercress, which belongs to the nasturtium family, has long stems and small, spicy leaves—and is very good alone, as in this recipe, or when mixed with other greens. A good produce market will usually keep it on crushed ice. Store watercress in plastic in the coldest part of the refrigerator. It should keep three or four days. Wash it just before using.

Sherry wine vinegar, one ingredient of the salad dressing, is a comparatively new item in American kitchens. Imported from Spain, as are the finest sherries, this vinegar is rich, sweet, and fairly expensive. Moreover, you may have to shop for it in a specialty shop or gourmet store. If you cannot find sherry vinegar, then you should substitute a good red wine vinegar.

WHAT TO DRINK

This special dish calls for a white Burgundy—a Meursault or, for a really festive occasion, a Montrachet. A less expensive alternative is to serve a lightly chilled Beaujolais, which would go well with these robust flavors.

SHOPPING LIST AND STAPLES

2 whole unskinned boneless chicken breasts
6 ounces ground pork
4 ounces ground veal
2 ounces prosciutto
2 bunches watercress
2 to 3 knobs celeriac (about 2 pounds)
3 large shallots
1 clove garlic
1 bunch fresh parsley
1 teaspoon minced fresh thyme, or ½ teaspoon dried
1 lemon
2 teaspoons unsalted butter
10 tablespoons salted butter (1¼ sticks)
½ cup heavy cream
1 egg
½ cup chicken broth
4 ounces shelled walnuts
3 tablespoons plus 2 teaspoons olive oil
1 tablespoon sunflower oil
2½ teaspoons red wine vinegar
2 teaspoons sherry wine vinegar
Pinch of ground allspice
Whole nutmeg
White pepper
Salt and pepper
¼ cup plus 2 teaspoons brandy or Cognac

UTENSILS

Food processor or food mill
Vegetable steamer
Large skillet
Medium-size saucepan
Shallow baking pan
Cookie sheet
Large bowl
Small bowl
Measuring cups and spoons
Chef's knife
All-purpose knife
2 wooden spatulas
Nutmeg grater
Cake rack
Juicer
Whisk
Instant-reading meat thermometer
Metal skewers (optional)

START-TO-FINISH STEPS

1. Follow watercress salad recipe steps 1 through 4.
2. Mince shallots, prosciutto, parsley, garlic, and thyme for chicken recipe. Grate nutmeg for celeriac and sauce

suprême recipes. Juice lemon for sauce suprême.

3. Follow chicken recipe steps 1 through 6.
4. Follow celeriac recipe step 1.
5. Follow chicken recipe steps 7 through 11. As chicken roasts, follow celeriac recipe steps 2 and 3, and then follow chicken recipe step 12.
6. Follow salad recipe step 5.
7. Follow celeriac recipe step 4.
8. Follow chicken recipe step 13.
9. Serve chicken with puree and salad.

RECIPES

Chicken Breasts Stuffed with Pâté

The stuffing:

6 ounces ground pork
4 ounces ground veal
2 ounces prosciutto, minced
3 tablespoons minced shallots
1 tablespoon finely chopped fresh parsley
¼ teaspoon minced garlic
2 teaspoons brandy or Cognac
Pinch of ground allspice
1 teaspoon minced fresh thyme, or ½ teaspoon dried
⅓ teaspoon salt
Freshly ground white pepper
1 large egg, well beaten

The chicken:

2 whole unskinned boneless chicken breasts
2 teaspoons unsalted butter
2 teaspoons olive oil
Sauce suprême (see following recipe)

1. In large bowl, combine all ingredients for pâté stuffing. Mix ingredients well, cover, and let flavors blend.
2. With knife, trim and discard fat, sinew, and cartilage from chicken breasts, keeping skin intact.
3. To form pockets for stuffing, gently separate skin from flesh with your fingers where breastbone was, keeping skin and flesh intact around remaining edges. If necessary, use knife to cut out tissue where skin and meat are attached along center of each breast.
4. Fill pockets with pâté mixture.
5. Smooth skin over filling so it is completely covered, and pull skin down around filling, tucking all edges under flesh of breasts. Use metal skewers, if necessary, to keep skins attached.
6. Turn oven to 375 degrees.
7. Heat oil in large skillet and add butter.
8. Place breasts, stuffed side up, in skillet and sear over high heat 2 to 3 minutes. Turn, and sear 1 to 2 minutes more.
9. Holding each breast between 2 spatulas, tilt, and sear any raw edges.
10. Over moderate heat, sauté, stuffed side up, for additional 2 minutes.
11. Remove pan from heat. Transfer chicken to cake rack set on baking pan. Roast 18 to 22 minutes, or until meat thermometer registers 155° degrees. Turn off oven and leave breasts in it.
12. Drain off any fat from skillet and make sauce suprême.
13. Remove skewers, if used, and cut each breast into ½-inch slices. Spoon sauce over each portion.

Sauce Suprême

¼ cup brandy or Cognac
½ cup chicken broth
½ cup heavy cream
1½ teaspoons lemon juice
Salt and freshly ground white pepper
Freshly grated nutmeg
2 tablespoons frozen, salted butter

1. Place skillet used for sautéing breasts over high heat and add brandy. Deglaze pan by stirring and scraping bottom until liquid is reduced by half.
2. Turn heat to moderate, add broth and heavy cream, and cook—stirring—until reduced by half.
3. Add lemon juice and season with salt, white pepper, and nutmeg. Remove from heat and whisk in butter.

Celeriac Purée

2 to 3 knobs celeriac (about 2 pounds)
8 tablespoons salted butter (1 stick)
Salt and freshly ground white pepper
Freshly grated nutmeg
4 tablespoons finely chopped fresh parsley

1. Peel celeriac and cut into ½-inch slices. Place in vegetable steamer and steam over boiling water about 10 minutes, or until tender.
2. Chop steamed celeriac coarsely and puree it in food processor or food mill.
3. Melt butter and stir in puree. Add salt, white pepper, and nutmeg to taste. When heated through, cover and keep warm until serving time.
4. Sprinkle 1 tablespoon fresh parsley over each serving.

Watercress Salad

2 bunches watercress
4 ounces shelled walnuts
3 tablespoons olive oil
1 tablespoon sunflower oil
4½ teaspoons wine vinegar, preferably 2½ teaspoons red wine vinegar and 2 teaspoons sherry wine vinegar
Salt and freshly ground black pepper

1. Preheat oven to 350 degrees.
2. Wash watercress and dry thoroughly. Remove any tough stems. Refrigerate until serving time.
3. Toast walnuts on cookie sheet in oven about 5 minutes. Set aside until cool; then chop them.
4. In small bowl, mix together oils and vinegars with small whisk. Season to taste.
5. At serving time, toss watercress with vinaigrette and sprinkle toasted walnuts on top.

Chicken Breasts Stuffed with Cheese
Steamed Asparagus with Tarragon Butter

Stuffed chicken breasts make a lovely light weekend lunch. Fresh asparagus is a perfect accompaniment.

Ricotta (the word means "buttermilk curd"), the cheese for the stuffing in this chicken menu, is a close Italian cousin of cottage cheese but slightly sweeter. You can buy ricotta fresh from the kitchen in Italian markets or prepackaged at the supermarket.

Two savory herbs—marjoram and thyme—flavor this cheese stuffing. Both are part of the mint family, and both are easy to grow in a sunny window box.

Tarragon, the herb for the asparagus, is better fresh but acceptable dried. Its sharp aroma and licorice flavor give it many uses. Employ it judiciously. Too much of it will overpower asparagus.

WHAT TO DRINK

A crisp wine, either a California Fumé Blanc or a French Pouilly-Fumé, should accompany this meal. Both have a hint of smokiness to add to the flavors' harmony.

SHOPPING LIST AND STAPLES

2 whole unskinned boneless chicken breasts
1½ to 2 pounds fresh asparagus
2 medium-size yellow onions
2 cloves garlic

1½ tablespoons minced fresh marjoram,
   or 1½ teaspoons dried
2 teaspoons minced fresh thyme, or ½ teaspoon dried
3 tablespoons minced fresh tarragon, or
   3 teaspoons dried
2 medium-size lemons
¼ pound Parmesan cheese
⅓ cup ricotta cheese
8 tablespoons (1 stick) plus 2 teaspoons butter
1 large egg
2 teaspoons olive oil
Whole nutmeg
White pepper
Salt

UTENSILS

Large skillet
Broiler pan
Vegetable steamer
2 small saucepans
2 bowls
Measuring cups and spoons
Chef's knife
All-purpose knife
2 wooden spatulas
Nutmeg grater
Metal skewers (optional)
Vegetable peeler

START-TO-FINISH STEPS

1. Chop onion and garlic, julienne lemon peel, grate nutmeg, and Parmesan cheese, and mince herbs for chicken recipe. Mince tarragon for asparagus recipe.
2. Follow chicken recipe steps 1 through 12.
3. Follow asparagus recipe steps 1 and 2.
4. Follow chicken recipe steps 13 through 15.
5. Follow asparagus recipe step 3.
6. Serve chicken and asparagus.

RECIPES

Chicken Breasts Stuffed with Cheese

The stuffing:
2 tablespoons butter
¾ cup chopped onions
2 teaspoons minced garlic
Peel of 2 medium-size lemons, finely julienned
⅓ cup ricotta cheese
2 tablespoons freshly grated Parmesan cheese
1½ tablespoons minced fresh marjoram,
   or 1½ teaspoons dried
2 teaspoons minced fresh thyme, or ½ teaspoon dried
Freshly ground white pepper
Salt
Freshly grated nutmeg
1 egg yolk from large egg

The chicken:
2 whole unskinned boneless chicken breasts
2 teaspoons butter
2 teaspoons olive oil
4 tablespoons freshly grated Parmesan cheese

1. In saucepan, melt butter and sauté onion until soft but not brown.
2. Add garlic and lemon peel and mix quickly. Transfer to bowl and cool.
3. Put ricotta cheese, 2 tablespoons Parmesan cheese, herbs, and seasonings in another bowl and mix well. Add egg yolk and garlic mixture and mix until well blended. Cover and refrigerate.
4. With sharp knife, trim and discard fat, sinew, and cartilage from chicken breasts, keeping skin intact.
5. To form pockets for stuffing, gently separate skin from flesh with your fingers where breastbone was, keeping skin and flesh intact around remaining edges. If necessary, use knife to cut out tissue where skin and meat are attached along center of each breast.
6. Fill pockets with cheese stuffing.
7. Smooth skin over filling so it is completely covered, and pull skin down around filling, tucking all edges under flesh of breasts. Use metal skewers, if necessary, to keep skin attached.
8. Melt butter in skillet and add oil.
9. Add breasts, stuffed side up, and sear over high heat 2 minutes. Turn and sear 1 to 2 minutes.
10. Holding each breast between 2 spatulas, tilt, and sear any raw edges.
11. Over moderate heat, sauté breasts, stuffed side up, 15 minutes.
12. Meanwhile, place broiler pan 3 inches from heat source and turn broiler on.
13. Remove skillet from heat and sprinkle Parmesan cheese on top of each chicken breast. Press cheese down with spatula.
14. Transfer to broiler and broil about 5 minutes, or until cheese topping is light golden brown.
15. To serve, remove skewers, if used, and cut each breast in half.

Steamed Asparagus with Tarragon Butter

1½ to 2 pounds fresh asparagus
6 tablespoons butter
3 tablespoons minced fresh tarragon, or
   3 teaspoons dried
Salt
Freshly ground white pepper

1. Trim by breaking off at tender point, wash, and peel asparagus spears.
2. Place asparagus in vegetable steamer and steam over boiling water 4 to 6 minutes, or until barely tender.
3. Melt butter in saucepan and add tarragon. Remove from heat. Season to taste with salt and white pepper. Spoon over steamed asparagus.

Sautéed Chicken Breasts with Persian Rice in Orange Butter Sauce
Stir-Fried Sugar Snap Peas
Steamed Baby Carrots

In the Middle East, fruit, rice, and nut mixtures signal a feast—a wedding, for example. In this menu, rice laced with raisins and pecans forms a sweet, exotic stuffing for chicken breasts. When you soak the raisins, you can substitute port for Madeira, if you wish. The tart orange butter sauce called for in this menu is particularly good with the nuts and raisins. Using frozen butter creates a creamy, satiny sauce and helps reduce the risk of the butter separating from the sauce: a technique Mary Beth Clark has used for several years.

Flowered table linens and pure white china and serving pieces complement this Persian-inspired meal. The bright-green sugar snap peas and orange baby carrots are important elements in the visual appeal of this celebratory dinner.

The fresh vegetables around this festive dish are baby carrots—available all year round and sweeter than the larger cellophane-packed variety—and sugar snap peas, which are seasonal. These crisp, sweet peas with an edible pod resemble the Chinese snow pea but are a new and native American vegetable. Since 1978, when this vegetable was introduced, it has become a garden staple second only to tomatoes in popularity. If you have a garden, plant sugar snaps. They grow in almost any soil, need no care (they do require a fence or a few poles to climb on), and bear a crop 10 weeks after you put the seed in the ground. Since they do not mind cold weather, you can plant in early spring and replant in July for the fall.

If you have no garden, you can buy sugar snaps in good produce markets in season. When you are unable to find

them, use Chinese snow peas instead. In either case, buy bright, unblemished pods—you should be able to see the peas through the thin, green skin. Use them the same day if possible and wash just before cooking. Remove the stem and string from each pod.

Shallots, which you need for the orange butter sauce, are particularly useful onions. Milder than regular onions or garlic, shallots add a special pungency and full flavor to a sauce, but never taste too oniony. They look like miniature yellow onions and cost a great deal more per pound—but a little goes a long way. Buy firm bulbs: two or three often grow out of a single base. Large ones taste just as good as small ones and are much easier to peel and chop. Store as you would a regular onion and use before they sprout.

Baby carrots usually come in a plastic bag at the produce counter. If they are very young and tender, you probably will not need to use a vegetable peeler. Simply cut off the tops and scrub the carrots with a brush under running water to peel them. For steaming, select carrots that are of uniform size so that they will cook evenly.

WHAT TO DRINK

German wines often complement Oriental dishes surprisingly well. Their delicate touch of sweetness harmonizes very pleasingly with Eastern spices. For this menu, try a good German Riesling of the *Kabinett* classification or, for a slightly sweeter wine, one of the *Spätlese* class.

For an Oriental note, omit the wine and serve hot tea instead—Lapsang Souchong, or green tea, if you can find it. Otherwise, Earl Grey is always good.

SHOPPING LIST AND STAPLES

2 whole unskinned, boneless chicken breasts
1 pound baby carrots
¾ pound sugar snap peas
7 large shallots
1 large orange
11 tablespoons unsalted butter (1 stick plus 3 tablespoons)
5 tablespoons salted butter
1 large egg
½ cup long-grain white rice
4 ounces chopped pecans
¼ cup golden raisins
2 teaspoons olive oil
1½ tablespoons white wine vinegar
Whole nutmeg
Salt and white pepper
1 tablespoon dry white wine
2 tablespoons Madeira

UTENSILS

Vegetable steamer
Large skillet
Medium-size skillet
Heavy saucepan with cover
Nonaluminum saucepan
Small saucepan
Small bowl
Measuring cups and spoons
Chef's knife
All-purpose knife
Nutmeg grater
Vegetable peeler
2 wooden spatulas
Whisk
Juicer
Metal skewers (optional)

START-TO-FINISH STEPS

In the morning: freeze butter for orange sauce recipe.
1. Follow chicken recipe steps 1 and 2. As rice simmers, mince shallots, grate nutmeg, juice orange, and julienne orange peel for orange sauce recipe. Peel carrots for carrot recipe and trim peas for pea recipe. Chop pecans and grate nutmeg for chicken recipe.
2. Follow chicken recipe steps 3 through 12.
3. Follow orange butter sauce recipe steps 1 through 3.
4. Follow carrot recipe steps 1 through 3.
5. Follow pea recipe steps 1 through 4.
6. Follow chicken recipe step 13.
7. Serve carrots and peas with chicken.

134

RECIPES

Sautéed Chicken Breasts Stuffed with Persian Rice

The stuffing:
¼ cup golden raisins
2 tablespoons Madeira
½ cup long-grain white rice
⅔ cup water
4 tablespoons butter
4 ounces chopped pecans
⅓ cup minced shallots
6 strips orange peel, finely julienned
¼ teaspoon salt
Freshly ground white pepper
Freshly grated nutmeg
1 yolk from large egg

The chicken:
2 whole unskinned boneless chicken breasts
2 teaspoons butter
2 teaspoons olive oil
Orange butter sauce (see following recipe)

1. Soak raisins in Madeira in bowl.
2. Bring rice, water, and 1 tablespoon of the butter to a boil in heavy saucepan. Stir, scraping pan so rice does not stick. Reduce heat to low, cover, and cook 20 minutes, or until rice is just tender. Stir once during this time, scraping sides of saucepan. Add 2 tablespoons additional water if rice is too hard. Remove from heat and set aside.
3. Melt 3 tablespoons of the butter in medium-size skillet. Add chopped pecans and toss until lightly browned. Add minced shallots and sauté until barely soft but not brown. Add raisins with Madeira and orange peel and stir to mix well. Remove from heat and add mixture to rice. Stir well. Season to taste with salt, white pepper, and nutmeg. Cool.
4. When mixture is cool, stir in egg yolk. Set aside, covered.
5. With knife, trim and discard fat, sinew, and cartilage from chicken breasts, keeping skin intact.
6. To form pockets for stuffing, gently separate skin from flesh with your fingers where breastbone was, keeping skin and flesh intact around remaining edges. If necessary, use knife to cut out tissue where skin and meat are attached along center of each breast. Do not split breasts.
7. Fill pockets with rice stuffing.
8. Smooth skin over rice so it is completely covered, and pull skin down around filling, tucking edges under flesh of breast. Use metal skewers, if necessary, to keep skin attached.
9. Melt butter in large skillet and add oil.
10. Add breasts, stuffed side up, and sear over high heat 2 minutes. Turn and sear 2 more minutes.
11. Holding each breast between 2 spatulas, tilt, and sear any raw edges.
12. Over moderate heat, sauté breasts, stuffed side up, 10 to 12 minutes. Turn and cook 5 minutes.

13. Remove chicken to platter. Cut each breast in half and serve with orange butter sauce.

Orange Butter Sauce

2 tablespoons minced shallots
⅓ cup orange juice
1½ tablespoons white wine vinegar
1 tablespoon dry white wine
5 tablespoons frozen, salted butter
2 strips orange peel, finely julienned
Salt and freshly ground white pepper
Freshly grated nutmeg

1. Combine shallots, orange juice, vinegar, and wine in nonaluminum saucepan. Reduce until about 2 teaspoons of liquid remain with shallots.
2. Over very low heat, carefully whisk in frozen butter, 1 tablespoon at a time, until all is melted. The sauce should look opaque. Do not overheat or butter will separate. Remove from heat.
3. Stir in julienned orange peel and season to taste with salt, white pepper, and nutmeg.

Stir-Fried Sugar Snap Peas

¾ pound sugar snap peas
3 tablespoons butter
Salt and freshly ground white pepper

1. Remove strings from sugar snap peas.
2. Melt butter over high heat in skillet.
3. Stir fry peas about 2 minutes, or until just tender. Remove from heat.
4. Season to taste with salt and white pepper.

Steamed Baby Carrots

1 pound baby carrots
3 tablespoons butter, melted
Salt and freshly ground white pepper

1. Peel carrots and bring water to a boil in steamer.
2. Steam carrots 5 to 8 minutes, or until barely tender when pierced with fork.
3. Remove to serving dish and toss with melted butter. Season to taste with salt and white pepper.

ADDED TOUCHES

If you want to serve fresh fruit for dessert, apricots—when in season—are ideal in flavor and color for this menu. When apricots are not in season, make this dried apricot mousse the afternoon or the day before you cook the chicken. It needs to be chilled for at least two hours—and it can also sit overnight.

Apricot Mousse

6 ounces dried apricots
1 cup water
1 tablespoon sugar
1 teaspoon unflavored gelatin

2 teaspoons apricot brandy (or orange brandy, such as Cointreau, Triple Sec, or Grand Marnier)
¾ cup heavy cream
2 teaspoons confectioners' sugar
½ teaspoon vanilla extract

1. Combine apricots, water, and sugar in saucepan and simmer about 15 minutes, or until apricots are tender. Remove with slotted spoon. Reserve syrup. Cool apricots.
2. Puree apricots in food processor or blender.
3. Dissolve gelatin in 1½ tablespoons of reserved apricot syrup. Add gelatin and apricot brandy to puree and mix well. Cool.
4. Whip cream until it forms soft peaks. Add confectioners' sugar and vanilla and whip until stiff peaks form.
5. Using wooden spatula, fold in whipped cream until well blended.
6. Spoon mousse into serving bowl or individual sherbet glasses and chill 2 to 24 hours.

Grapefruit-Clove Ice

For a dessert as elegant as the main dish, try this citrus ice.

4 pink grapefruits (about 1 pound each)
2 cups plus 2 tablespoons sugar
1 cup water
½ teaspoon ground cloves

1. Roll grapefruits on hard surface to prepare for juicing. Peel grapefruits without removing membranes or white bitter pith. Slice peel of 1 grapefruit into four 3-inch-long strips, each about ¼ inch wide. Reserve peel. Slice grapefruits in half and squeeze juice.
2. Bring water and 2 cups of the sugar to a boil, stirring constantly until sugar is completely dissolved and syrup is clear.
3. Remove from heat, cover, and cool to room temperature. (Leftover syrup can be stored indefinitely in tightly sealed jar at room temperature.)
4. Mix grapefruit juice and ⅓ to ½ cup of the sugar syrup, according to taste. Freeze in ice cream machine according to manufacturer's instructions, or place mixture in 9-inch square metal cake pan and freeze about 2 hours, stirring twice to distribute ice crystals evenly.
5. Bring water to a boil and blanch grapefruit peel 1 to 2 minutes to remove bitterness. Taste after 1 minute for desired flavor.
6. Drain peel under cold running water to stop cooking. Drain again on paper towels.
7. Combine grapefruit peel with 2 tablespoons of the sugar syrup.
8. Combine the remaining 2 tablespoons of the sugar and ground cloves. Remove peel from syrup with fork and coat it well on both sides with sugar-clove mixture. Transfer to cake rack and twist peel into curls. Let dry.
9. To serve, place twist of candied peel on top of each serving of ice.

135

Paula Wolfert

MENU 1 (Left)
Sautéed Chicken with Tart Green Grapes
New Potatoes with Herbs
Tossed Green Salad

MENU 2
Chicken Breasts and Artichokes with Fettuccine
Green Salad Vinaigrette

MENU 3
Steamed Chicken Sausages
in Clementine Sauce with Broccoli
Rice

A cookbook author and a longtime resident of both France and Morocco, Paula Wolfert specializes in Mediterranean cooking. Of the three chicken dishes in the menus that follow, two are regional French and one distinctively modern French. In Menu 1, the chicken with green grapes and whole cloves of garlic is an adaptation of an old springtime specialty from southwestern France. The underripe grapes retain their tartness in cooking, but the garlic releases its flavor and turns sweet.

In Menu 2, chicken breasts combine smoothly with artichoke hearts and a cream sauce that takes its particular piquancy from sherry wine vinegar. Cream sauces thickened with egg yolks will curdle if you boil them, so use a gentle flame (or low setting on an electric range) as you add the cream to the sauté pan and follow the tip in the recipe: beat a tablespoon of cold water into the egg yolk before adding it to the hot sauce.

In Menu 3, the modern French one, Paula Wolfert flattens boned chicken breasts, steams them, and coats them with a rich creamy sauce strongly flavored with the juice from clementines. These small, intensely sweet relatives of tangerines (which you may substitute in this recipe if clementines are not available) are native to southern Spain, Morocco, and Algeria. They ripen only in the winter months, and even the largest market may not stock them regularly. Ask the produce manager to stock clementines when they are available.

Dished up together on a large platter, chicken with green grapes, and potatoes cooked in their skins, accompanied by a green salad, provide a celebratory dinner for spring, when the key ingredients—tart grapes and new potatoes—are fresh in the marketplace.

137

Sautéed Chicken with Tart Green Grapes
New Potatoes with Herbs
Tossed Green Salad

One of the great regional cooking traditions of France grew up in the southwest around the Dordogne River. Chicken with tart or sour green grapes is an old favorite there; cooks call the piquant liquid pressed from grapes *ver jus* ("green juice") and use it in other dishes besides chicken.

Since most grapes in American markets have been picked for eating, not cooking, you may have to search for really tart grapes. Be sure to taste them before buying. If the grapes you find are not tart enough, add a few drops of lemon juice to the dish just before you serve it; the sauce must not taste sweet if it is to be authentic.

Cooking with unpeeled garlic cloves is an eminently easy and useful technique that produces an agreeably different result from mincing or chopping the garlic. Cooked in its skin, the garlic tends to lose its characteristic strong flavor, and instead contributes a savory aroma and taste, finally turning mild—as unlike raw garlic as a cooked onion is unlike a raw one. You should encourage your guests to mash the cloves with their forks, releasing the creamy juices.

Properly cooked breast meat will be white with no sheen as you slice into it. It should be firm to the touch. Train yourself to test for doneness by touch; you will soon become infallible and will never need to pierce a thigh or breast. Piercing allows juices to escape.

When you buy new potatoes, avoid those with green spots—they taste sour. To keep green spots from forming after you have brought the potatoes home, store them away from heat, light, and dampness. Use new potatoes as soon as possible—they will not keep as long as baking potatoes. And, for easy cooking, pick out potatoes of a uniform size. Otherwise, they will not cook evenly.

WHAT TO DRINK

This spring dish with green grapes needs a very dry, crisp wine, such as a California Sauvignon Blanc. A Sancerre would also go well with this meal.

SHOPPING LIST AND STAPLES

3-pound chicken, cut into 4 or 8 pieces
1 to 1½ pounds small new potatoes
1 head Boston lettuce
8 cloves garlic
1 teaspoon chopped fresh chives, or ½ teaspoon

freeze-dried
1 bunch fresh parsley
¾ pound seedless tart green grapes
1 lemon
6 tablespoons butter
3 cups chicken broth
2¼ teaspoons sherry wine vinegar or red wine vinegar
2 tablespoons walnut oil
4 tablespoons olive oil
Salt and pepper
3 tablespoons dry white wine

UTENSILS

Blender or food processor
Large deep nonaluminum skillet with cover
Large heavy skillet with cover
Small saucepan
Small bowl
Strainer
Measuring cups and spoons
Chef's knife
Tongs
Vegetable brush
Whisk
Juicer

START-TO-FINISH STEPS

1. Juice lemon and follow salad recipe steps 1 and 2. Set aside.
2. Follow chicken recipe steps 1 through 6. As chicken cooks, follow potato recipe step 1. Chop parsley and chives.
3. Follow chicken recipe steps 7 and 8 and potato recipe step 2.
4. Follow chicken recipe steps 9 and 10.
5. Follow salad recipe step 3 and potato recipe step 3. Serve both with chicken.

RECIPES

Sautéed Chicken with Tart Green Grapes

2 cups chicken broth
3-pound chicken, cut into 4 or 8 pieces
Salt and freshly ground black pepper
1½ cups seedless tart green grapes (about ¾ pound)

3 tablespoons butter
8 plump cloves garlic, unpeeled
3 tablespoons dry white wine
2 teaspoons chopped fresh parsley

1. In saucepan, simmer chicken broth until it is reduced to ⅔ cup. Set aside.
2. While broth is simmering, cut away and discard any excess fat from chicken quarters. Rub chicken with salt and pepper and set aside.
3. Puree 1 cup of the grapes in blender or food processor for 20 seconds. Rub puree through strainer, using back of wooden spoon to press some of pulp through. You should have about ¼ cup green-grape juice. Discard pureed pulp.
4. In large deep nonaluminum skillet, heat 2 tablespoons of the butter over high heat. Add chicken pieces, skin side down, and unpeeled garlic cloves. Brown chicken pieces 1 minute on each side. Shake pan often to keep chicken pieces and garlic from sticking.
5. Lower heat, cover pan tightly, and cook 10 minutes.
6. Uncover pan, tilt it, and degrease juices. Turn chicken with tongs and add white wine to pan. Cover and cook over low heat 10 minutes longer.
7. Uncover pan and add 3 tablespoons of the grape juice. Cover again quickly so chicken pieces absorb all aroma and flavor. Cook chicken about 7 minutes more.
8. Test breast pieces for doneness and remove them from skillet. Cover them lightly to keep warm and moist. Add ½ cup of the reduced chicken stock to skillet. Continue to cook leg pieces and garlic, uncovered, 5 minutes more, or until done. There should be about ¼ cup of juice in skillet. Return breast pieces to pan. Turn chicken and garlic cloves in syrupy pan juices in order to glaze them. Remove chicken from skillet. Cover and keep warm in oven while you make sauce.
9. Raise heat and add the remaining chicken stock, the remaining 1 tablespoon of butter, the remaining juice, and the remaining ½ cup grapes. Swirl over heat to combine. Remove from heat and season with salt and pepper.
10. Arrange chicken, garlic, and grapes on serving platter. Spoon sauce over them. Sprinkle with parsley.

New Potatoes with Herbs

1 to 1½ pounds small new potatoes, unpeeled
1 cup chicken broth
3 tablespoons butter
Salt
1 teaspoon chopped fresh parsley
1 teaspoon chopped fresh chives, or ½ teaspoon
   freeze-dried

1. Scrub potatoes with brush. Arrange them in large heavy skillet in 1 layer. They must fit snugly. Pour in broth and bring to a boil. Cover tightly and cook about 4 minutes, shaking skillet over high heat until almost all liquid has evaporated.
2. Lower heat, add butter, and cook gently 10 minutes, uncovered, shaking skillet often. Test for doneness with fork. Partly cover and set aside; keep warm.

3. Sprinkle with salt, chopped parsley, and chives just before serving.

Tossed Green Salad

1 head Boston lettuce
2¼ teaspoons sherry wine vinegar or red wine vinegar
2¼ teaspoons lemon juice
¼ teaspoon salt
Freshly ground black pepper
6 tablespoons oil, preferably 2 tablespoons walnut oil and
   4 tablespoons olive oil

1. Wash and dry salad greens. Refrigerate.
2. Combine vinegar and lemon juice in bowl. Add salt and pepper. Whisk in oil.
3. Just before serving, toss lettuce with vinaigrette.

ADDED TOUCHES

For a simple first course, trim off ends and string a pound of snow peas, sauté them very briefly in butter, drain, and cool. Roast, peel, and seed one ripe, sweet red pepper and cut it into julienne strips. Slice four scallions thinly and arrange the vegetables on four serving plates. Make a vinaigrette according to the salad recipe on this page and add 1 tablespoon of Dijon-style mustard. Spoon over the vegetables and serve.

A sabayon is a rich, creamy sauce, based on egg yolks, that French cooks typically use for fruit desserts. This version is particularly good with strawberries and will be even better if the strawberries are fresh picked in spring. If you have to buy strawberries in a market, choose berries in a container with no red stains, which are a sign the berries may be old. And take a quick look at the berries at the bottom, to be sure they are not squashy and overripe. To wash strawberries quickly, immerse them in cold water for half a minute, then rinse under running water and drain thoroughly.

Strawberries with Sabayon

1 pint fresh strawberries
4 eggs yolks
¼ cup superfine sugar
Juice of ½ orange
1½ tablespoons Triple Sec or Grand Marnier
2 to 3 tablespoons heavy cream

1. Wipe strawberries with damp paper towels. Hull and set side by side in heat-proof serving dish, pointed side up.
2. Beat yolks in double boiler over simmering water. Add sugar and whisk until smooth, continuing until mixture starts to thicken. Never let mixture reach a boil.
3. Add orange juice and whisk mixture until it thickens again. Repeat with Triple Sec and cream.
4. Cool sauce pot on bed of ice, stirring sauce to keep it from getting lumpy.
5. Coat berries with sauce and run serving dish under broiler just to glaze sauce. Serve at once.

Chicken Breasts and Artichokes with Fettuccine
Green Salad Vinaigrette

The chicken breasts, artichoke hearts, fettuccine, and cream sauce should arrive at the table all together on one platter. You will want separate plates for the salad, however, which is a mixture of escarole, chicory, and radicchio.

Because it is time consuming to prepare fresh artichokes, Paula Wolfert suggests using forzen artichoke hearts. They will certainly save time, and their flavor is quite adequate if you buy a high-quality brand. But if you have an extra 15 minutes, substitute fresh artichoke hearts; they taste better than frozen. For a quick method of turning an artichoke into an artichoke heart, see the ADDED TOUCH on page 142.

The guiding principle of the salad here is to combine one or more crisp green with a pale leafy lettuce. The mix that Paula Wolfert specifies is chicory, escarole, and *radicchio*, but do choose any combination of available greens that appeals to you. Chicory, which the greengrocer may also call curly endive, has very curly outer leaves of dark green and a slightly bitter taste. Escarole has a flat-edged leaf with all the crispness of chicory—and its own slightly sharp taste. *Radicchio*, a red-leaved wild chicory, faintly bitter and pleasantly aromatic, is a garden favorite that does not travel well. Use it the same day you buy it.

The special oil and vinegar in this recipe may prove hard to find, and they are certainly expensive. But you should treat yourself and your guests to them if you can: walnut oil, pressed from green walnuts, has a taste that cannot be duplicated; buy in small quantities, and once you have opened the bottle or tin, refrigerate it. But if these ingredients are too hard to come by, you may safely substitute a good olive oil and a red wine vinegar.

WHAT TO DRINK

Like asparagus, artichokes do not combine well with wine, but the creamy sauce on the artichokes in this menu makes them compatible with a full-bodied wine, for example an Italian or Californian Chardonnay.

SHOPPING LIST AND STAPLES

4 skinless, boneless chicken breast halves
1 small head chicory
1 small head escarole
1 small head *radicchio*
1 bunch fresh parsley
1 lemon
6 tablespoons butter
½ cup heavy cream
1 egg
9-ounce package frozen artichoke hearts
1 pound fresh or packaged fettuccine or *tagliatelle*
1 cup chicken broth
2 tablespoons walnut oil
4 tablespoons olive oil
Sherry wine vinegar or red wine vinegar
Salt and pepper

UTENSILS

Large saucepan with cover
Large nonaluminum skillet with cover
2 small bowls
Measuring cups and spoons
Colander
All-purpose knife
Long-pronged fork
Whisk
Juicer

START-TO-FINISH STEPS

1. If fixing fresh artichokes, follow explanation on page 142; otherwise, defrost frozen artichokes. Chop parsley for chicken recipe and juice lemon for salad recipe.
2. Follow salad recipe steps 1 and 2.
3. Follow chicken recipe steps 1 through 8.
4. Follow salad recipe step 3, and serve with chicken.

RECIPES

Chicken Breasts and Artichokes with Fettuccine

4 skinless, boneless chicken breast halves
Salt and freshly ground black pepper
6 tablespoons butter
2 to 3 tablespoons sherry wine vinegar or red wine vinegar
9-ounce package frozen artichoke hearts, defrosted
1 cup chicken broth
½ cup heavy cream
1 pound fresh or packaged fettuccine or *tagliatelle*
1 egg yolk
1 tablespoon water
1 tablespoon chopped fresh parsley

1. In covered saucepan, bring salted water to a boil for pasta.
2. Thoroughly dry chicken breasts. Rub with salt and pepper. Heat 1 tablespoon of the butter in nonaluminum skillet over low heat. Add chicken breasts and sprinkle them with 1 tablespoon of the vinegar. Cover and cook over low heat 3 minutes on each side or until cooked through. Remove breasts from pan and transfer to plate; keep warm by covering with foil.
3. Add another tablespoon of the butter to skillet. Add artichoke hearts and sauté over medium-high heat 2 minutes, or until tender. Remove artichokes from skillet and set aside.
4. Deglaze pan by stirring 1 tablespoon of the vinegar into skillet. Add chicken broth and simmer, stirring, until broth is reduced by ½.
5. Add cream, stirring, and reduce liquid again by ⅓.
6. Add fettuccine to boiling water and stir several times with long-pronged fork. Cook 5 to 8 minutes. (If using fresh fettucine, cook according to maker's instructions.) Drain in colander and return to saucepan. Toss with the remaining 4 tablespoons butter. Season to taste.
7. Beat egg yolk in small bowl with 1 tablespoon cold water for 45 seconds, or until foamy. Then whisk it into hot sauce

in skillet. Immediately remove skillet from heat, whisking constantly. Sauce must not boil after eggs are added. Adjust seasoning with salt and pepper and, if desired, a drop more vinegar to taste. Stir in parsley.

8. Arrange chicken halves and artichoke hearts on bed of fettuccine. Spoon sauce over them.

Green Salad Vinaigrette

1 small head chicory
1 small head escarole
1 small head *radicchio*
2¼ teaspoons sherry wine vinegar or red wine vinegar
2¼ teaspoons lemon juice
¼ teaspoon salt
Freshly ground black pepper
6 tablespoons oil, preferably 2 tablespoons walnut oil and
   4 tablespoons olive oil

1. Wash and dry salad greens. Refrigerate.

2. Combine vinegar and lemon juice in small bowl. Add salt and pepper. Whisk in oil.

3. Just before serving, toss salad greens with vinaigrette.

ADDED TOUCHES

For an elegant dessert, try this croustade: butter, rum, and crushed walnuts in *filo*, or strudel, dough.

Walnut and Rum Croustade

1¼ cups freshly shelled walnut halves
½ cup dry, unflavored bread crumbs
½ teaspoon grated lemon rind
½ cup plus 1 tablespoon superfine sugar
8 tablespoons butter (1 stick), melted
¼ cup dark rum
8 *filo* pastry leaves

1. Grind walnuts in food processor. Add bread crumbs, lemon rind, and ½ cup of the sugar and process until well blended. Mix in 2 tablespoons of the melted butter and rum.

2. Preheat oven to 375 degrees.

3. Brush 8-inch round cake or pie tin with a bit of the remaining melted butter. Cover bottom of pan with 1 sheet of *filo* dough. Fit dough in pan and brush lightly with butter. Layer 5 more sheets of the dough on top, brushing each lightly with butter and scattering each with ⅕ of walnut mixture.

4. Cover with the 2 remaining sheets of dough, brushing each with butter. Tuck them in around edges. Brush top with butter and bake 35 to 45 minutes, or until golden in color and crisp.

5. Sprinkle the remaining 1 tablespoon of sugar on top and let stand on cake rack 15 minutes. Cut into wedges and serve warm.

Fresh Artichokes

Three or four large fresh artichokes—if you are going to use fresh rather than frozen—will be sufficient for this recipe. Make this the first of your START-TO-FINISH STEPS.

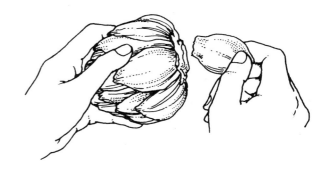

Cut off stem. Pull off the hard outer leaves from the bottom. Bring enough water to cover the artichokes to a boil in a large pot and, meanwhile, soak the artichokes in cold water. Cook the artichokes at a simmer for 15 minutes, or until you can remove a leaf easily. Drain and set aside until cool enough to handle.

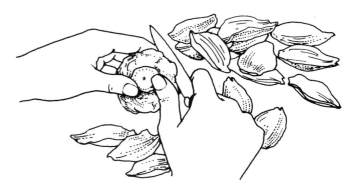

Pull away all remaining leaves above the bottom, and trim any remaining stem and leafy bit from the underside. Reserve leaves if desired.

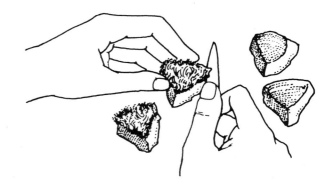

Cut the bottom into quarters. Carefully run the tip of a knife under the fuzzy choke or pull off the choke with your hands and discard. If desired, the tender edible portion of the leaves can be eaten if reserved leaves are boiled an additional 15–20 minutes. Set aside the quartered artichoke hearts until time to sauté them (step 3 of the chicken recipe).

Steamed Chicken Sausages in Clementine Sauce with Broccoli Rice

The sauce here takes its color from clementines—or from tangerines. The sections of either fruit make an attractive garnish.

The chicken sausages in this recipe are not sausages at all but boneless chicken breasts pounded thin and rolled into a sausage shape, with half a teaspoon of butter inside each roll. Like almost any form of steamed chicken, they present the opportunity to make a colorful, highly flavored sauce—in this case, a clementine sauce with a chicken broth and cream base.

Clementines come from Spain and Morocco and are a cross between a tangerine and a small variety of orange. American markets carry them only from November through February and not regularly even then. Like truffles, they are a rarity, usually expensive but with an unforgettable aroma and sweetness. If you can find them, be choosy when you select them. Look for those with a deep orange coloring and with thin, smooth skins. And avoid any fruit with soft spots or mold. Pick out clementines that seem heavy for their size, since those will probably be the juiciest.

If you cannot lay hands upon clementines, this recipe will be delicious—if not quite so unusual—with tangerines. And if fresh tangerines are not in season, or if you are really in a hurry, try frozen tangerine concentrate. Do not reconstitute it with water but, instead, use about a third of the can of concentrate and add no liquid except a teaspoon of lemon juice.

Although clementines and tangerines are both very sweet, they blend like magic with the cream, broth, butter, salt, and pepper, and after the sauce has cooked, you will discover that most of the sweetness has disappeared. The result is a complex, even mysterious, flavor.

Plain as they are, broccoli and rice make the best side dishes for this unusual main dish. Broccoli is available all year; buy green heads with firm stems and compact bud clusters. Store broccoli in plastic in the refrigerator. And since broccoli is an excellent source of two highly perishable vitamins (A and C), use it within three days.

WHAT TO DRINK

The sweet-tart flavors of the clementine sauce need a white wine with the slightest hint of sweetness to accompany them: a California Riesling or a German Riesling *Kabinett* or a California Chenin Blanc.

SHOPPING LIST AND STAPLES

12 to 14 skinless, boneless chicken breast halves
1 bunch broccoli
5 medium-size clementines or tangerines
1 lemon (optional)
1½ sticks unsalted butter
½ cup heavy cream
1 cup chicken broth
1 cup long-grain white rice
Salt and pepper

UTENSILS

Medium-size saucepan with cover
Small nonaluminum saucepan
Small saucepan
Large steamer or large saucepan with steaming rack
Measuring cups and spoons
Meat pounder or heavy cleaver
Chef's knife
Long-pronged fork
Waxed paper
Heat-proof plastic wrap
Tongs
Juicer

144

START-TO-FINISH STEPS

1. Cut broccoli into flowerets for chicken recipe.
2. Follow clementine sauce recipe steps 1 and 2.
3. Follow rice recipe steps 1 and 2. As rice simmers, follow chicken recipe steps 1 and 2. As chicken steams, follow clementine sauce recipe step 3.
4. Follow rice recipe step 3.
5. Follow chicken recipe steps 3 and 4.
6. Follow clementine sauce recipe step 4.
7. Follow chicken recipe step 5 and serve with rice.

RECIPES

Steamed Chicken Sausages with Broccoli

12 to 14 skinless, boneless chicken breast halves
Salt and freshly ground black pepper
6 to 7 teaspoons butter, softened
1 bunch broccoli, separated into flowerets, stems removed
2 tablespoons butter, melted
Clementine sauce (see following recipe)

1. Gently pound chicken breasts between sheets of waxed paper until they are uniform in size and thin enough to roll. Season each breast with salt and pepper, and spread each breast with ½ teaspoon of softened butter. Roll each breast, starting at narrow end, into shape of sausage, enclosing butter. Squeeze gently so that each rolled sausage adheres and stays rolled. Wrap each in heat-proof plastic wrap and twirl ends to seal.
2. Add small amount of water to steamer or large saucepan with rack. Do not let water touch rack. Bring water to a boil. Using tongs, carefully arrange chicken and broccoli on rack in 1 layer. Cover and steam 9 to 12 minutes, depending on size of breasts.
3. Remove chicken from plastic wrap and cut into 2 or 3 equal slices, or leave whole.
4. Remove broccoli to serving dish. Season and sprinkle with melted butter.
5. Arrange chicken on warmed serving plates. Coat with clementine sauce.

Clementine Sauce

5 medium-size clementines or tangerines (enough to make 1 cup strained juice), or ⅓ cup frozen tangerine concentrate
1 cup chicken broth

½ cup heavy cream
2 to 3 tablespoons butter
Salt and freshly ground black pepper
Lemon juice (optional)

1. Squeeze clementines and strain juice. In nonaluminum saucepan, reduce juice to ⅓ cup over low heat.
2. Add chicken broth to clementine juice (or frozen tangerine concentrate) and bring to a boil. Cook until reduced by ½.
3. Add cream and reduce again until sauce is just thick enough to coat spoon. Set aside.
4. Just before serving, reheat, and swirl butter into sauce. Adjust seasonings with salt and pepper and, if too sweet, a touch of lemon juice.

Rice

2 cups salted water
1 cup long-grain white rice
4 tablespoons butter
Salt and freshly ground black pepper

1. In medium-size saucepan, bring 2 cups salted water to a boil.
2. Add rice and bring water back to a boil. Stir with long-pronged fork to separate grains. Reduce heat to low, cover tightly, and simmer 20 minutes, or until all water is absorbed.
3. Add butter to cooked rice and toss. Season with salt and pepper. Keep warm until served.

ADDED TOUCHES

If you want a first course, serve a fresh fennel appetizer. Two small fennel bulbs will make four servings. Remove the tops and cut away the hard outer stalks. Trim each base and thinly slice. Cover the fennel with ice water and refrigerate until serving time. Then make a mustard cream dressing as follows:

1 lemon, juiced (about 3 tablespoons)
3 tablespoons heavy cream
1 tablespoon Dijon mustard
Salt and pepper to taste

Combine all ingredients in small bowl, using wire whisk. Drain fennel, and spoon dressing over each serving. Garnish with chopped parsley and walnut halves, if desired.

Since the main course is rather light, a substantial dessert might be welcome with this meal. This combination of pineapple, brioche, and ice cream is easy to make and a good complement to a meal that contains a distinctive fruit flavor also. Use only fresh pineapple, and look for the Hawaiian kind, which is better than other imports. Once picked, a pineapple will not continue to ripen, so be sure to buy a fruit that is at its peak. Pick it up and smell it—it should be fragrant and sweet; but if the bottom has a slightly fermented smell, then it is overripe.

Brioche, called for in this recipe, is a French cakelike bread of yeast dough that is baked in a high-walled, fluted pan. Good bakeries always sell them. This is a good way to use up day-old brioches, which will toast nicely and stay crisp in the rum-flavored sauce. If you use pound cake, toast it as you do the brioche.

Since the recipe calls for only half a pineapple, chill the rest and serve it for breakfast.

Sautéed Pineapple Slices with Toasted Brioches and Ice Cream

1 fresh pineapple
5⅓ tablespoons sweet butter
4 to 8 tablespoons granulated sugar
2 to 3 tablespoons rum
2 stale brioches, cut in half, or 4 slices pound cake
Confectioners' sugar (optional)
1 pint coffee ice cream

1. Cut pineapple in half lengthwise. Cut 1 half in half again; reserve other half for another meal. Remove core from pineapple quarters and discard core. Slide thin-bladed serrated knife between flesh and shell, and lift out flesh. Cut it crosswise into ¾-inch slices.
2. Heat 4 tablespoons of the butter in skillet and gently cook pineapple slices, on both sides, several minutes on medium-high heat. Sprinkle with 2 to 4 tablespoons of the granulated sugar, depending on sweetness of pineapple, and cook until lightly caramelized.
3. Heat rum and pour over pineapple. Flame rum and cook 1 minute longer, shaking pan. Cool slightly.
4. Toast brioches until golden. Sprinkle 1 side with the remaining granulated sugar and broil until caramelized. Watch to see corners do not burn.
5. Place slice of brioche on each serving plate. Spoon pineapple over it and sprinkle with confectioners' sugar, if desired. Serve at once with scoops of ice cream.

FISH & SHELLFISH

Elisabeth Thorstensson

MENU 1 (Right)
Fillets of Sole in Herb Butter
Riced Potatoes with Parsley
Sautéed Snow Peas with Water Chestnuts

MENU 2
Seafood Curry Chowder
Bibb Lettuce, Avocado, and Tomato Salad

MENU 3
Chicken Liver Mousse
Fillets of Brook Trout with Mushroom Sauce
Spicy Rice

S wedish cooking, like that of Scandinavia in general, is straightforward and down to earth. Swedish cooks use fresh produce, dairy products, subtle seasonings, and most important, just-caught fish. Elisabeth Thorstensson grew up at lakeside and often caught the family's fish for dinner. Very early, she learned how to prepare fish for poaching, pan frying, and baking, all techniques her family commonly uses and that she employs in her menus here.

She frequently returns to Sweden to gather cooking suggestions. In addition, she has also incorporated a variety of new ideas into these three menus. Menu 1 consists of three dishes: fillets of sole in herb butter, riced potatoes, and a vegetable dish of sautéed snow peas with water chestnuts. The presentation of the meal is designed for visual effect—the green herb butter contrasts with the white fish and sauce, and there is a similar color contrast in the vegetable dishes.

Elisabeth Thorstensson first tasted a version of Menu 2's curry chowder at her sister's house in Sweden. Here, the chef has varied her sister's recipe by adding chunks of fresh fish.

In Menu 3, she presents a chicken liver mousse flavored with Cognac, brandy, or sherry, and sautéed fillets of brook trout served with mushroom sauce. The rice is seasoned with turmeric, a spice often used in Indian and Asian recipes, which turns the rice a golden color.

Serve this dinner on individual plates for a pleasing appearance. The fillets of sole are topped with browned breadcrumbs and surrounded by a wine sauce, the riced potatoes are studded with parsley and chopped pimiento, and the snow peas are sautéed with sliced water chestnuts.

148

Fillets of Sole in Herb Butter
Riced Potatoes with Parsley
Sautéed Snow Peas with Water Chestnuts

Fillets of sole are ideal for rolling up, then baking, as in this recipe. The accompanying wine sauce is made with scallions, parsley, and tarragon. You can substitute either fresh flounder or frozen flounder.

Chinese water chestnuts are not nuts at all but tubers of an aquatic plant. They come in cans in the Oriental foods section of most supermarkets. Because they retain their crispness after cooking, they are particularly good sautéed with fresh snow peas.

WHAT TO DRINK

Buy a good white Graves or a crisp California Sauvignon Blanc and use the same wine to make the sauce for the sole.

SHOPPING LIST AND STAPLES

4 skinless fillets of sole, flounder, or scrod (each about 8 ounces)
2 large baking potatoes, preferably Idaho (about 1¼ pounds total weight)
¾ pound snow peas
Small bunch scallions
Small bunch fresh parsley
Small bunch fresh tarragon, or ½ teaspoon dried
1 lemon
1 egg
½ pint heavy cream
4 tablespoons unsalted butter
8-ounce jar pimientos
8-ounce can water chestnuts
3 tablespoons vegetable oil
1 slice day-old white bread
Salt and freshly ground pepper
1 cup dry white wine, preferably same as dinner wine

UTENSILS

Food processor or blender
Large heavy-gauge skillet
2 medium-size saucepans, one with cover
13 x 9-inch baking dish
8 x 8-inch baking pan
2 medium-size bowls
Small bowl
Colander
Measuring cups and spoons
Paring knife
Chef's knife
Wooden spatula
Rubber spatula
Ricer or potato masher
Coarse sieve
Vegetable peeler

START-TO-FINISH STEPS

1. Prepare scallions and tarragon for sole recipe and parsley for sole and potatoes recipes. Chop pimiento for potatoes recipe.
2. Follow sole recipe steps 1 through 6.
3. Follow potato recipe step 1.
4. While potatoes are coming to a boil, follow sole recipe steps 7 and 8. Then follow potatoes recipe step 2.
5. While sole and potatoes are cooking, follow snow peas recipe steps 1 and 2.
6. Five minutes before sole and potatoes are done, follow snow peas recipe step 3.
7. Follow potatoes recipe step 3, sole recipe step 9, and serve with snow peas.

RECIPES

Fillets of Sole in Herb Butter

4 skinless fillets of sole, flounder, or scrod (each about 8 ounces)
1 lemon
1 egg
4 tablespoons unsalted butter
1 tablespoon chopped scallion
1 tablespoon chopped fresh parsley
1½ teaspoons chopped fresh tarragon, or ½ teaspoon dried
1 cup heavy cream
1 cup dry white wine (preferably same as dinner wine)
Salt
Freshly ground pepper
1 slice day-old white bread

1. Wipe fillets with damp paper towels.
2. In 13 x 9-inch baking dish, arrange fillets in single layer. Squeeze lemon juice over them and let stand.

3. Separate egg, dropping yolk into food processor or blender. Reserve white for another use. Combine butter with egg yolk and process until smooth. Add scallion, parsley, and tarragon, and blend well. With rubber spatula, scrape mixture into small bowl and set aside.

4. In medium-size saucepan, reduce cream by half over medium-high heat, about 10 to 15 minutes. Add wine and boil 1 minute. Season with salt and pepper to taste. Set aside.

5. Cut crust off bread and rub bread through coarse sieve onto piece of aluminum foil or wax paper.

6. Preheat oven to 450 degrees.

7. Fold each fillet in three, as if you were folding a letter, and place flat side down in 8 x 8-inch baking pan. Spread herb butter evenly over fillets and sprinkle with bread crumbs. Pour cream-wine mixture carefully into dish without touching top of fish, being careful not to disturb bread crumbs.

8. Bake until bread crumbs are golden-brown and fish is firm, 15 to 20 minutes.

9. Remove fish from oven. Using spatula, transfer fillets to dinner plates.

Riced Potatoes with Parsley

2 large baking potatoes, preferably Idaho (about
   1¼ pounds total weight)
Salt and freshly ground pepper
2 tablespoons minced fresh parsley
1 tablespoon chopped pimiento

1. Peel potatoes and cut in thirds. In medium-size saucepan, cover potatoes with 2 inches of cold water. Cover pan and bring to a boil over high heat.

2. Reduce heat to moderate and boil potatoes just until tender, 15 to 20 minutes. Drain thoroughly in colander and, off heat, return to saucepan to dry, 1 to 2 minutes.

3. With ricer, rice potatoes directly into medium-size bowl. Or, using potato masher, mash potatoes. Season with salt and pepper to taste, and sprinkle with parsley and pimiento. Divide among individual dinner plates.

Sautéed Snow Peas with Water Chestnuts

¾ pound snow peas
1 cup drained water chestnuts
3 tablespoons vegetable oil
Salt and freshly ground pepper

1. Snap off ends of snow peas and remove strings. In medium-size bowl, cover snow peas with cold water.

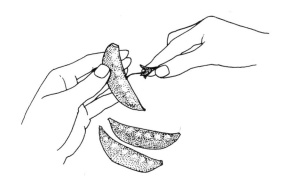

2. With chef's knife, cut water chestnuts into ¼-inch-thick slices. Pat dry with paper towels and set aside.

3. In colander, drain snow peas and pat dry with paper towels. In large heavy-gauge skillet, heat oil until hot but not smoking. Add snow peas and sauté, stirring with wooden spatula, about 2 minutes. Add water chestnuts and sauté mixture just until snow peas are crisp-tender, another 2 minutes. Season with salt and pepper to taste.

ADDED TOUCH

Gazpacho, the famous "liquid salad" of Spanish cuisine, requires a few minutes of peeling and chopping to ready the vegetables for the blender or food processor. Be careful not to overprocess the vegetables—the soup should have a crunchy texture.

Gazpacho

½ cup chopped scallions
½ cup chopped fresh tomato
½ cup chopped red bell pepper
½ cup chopped green bell pepper
½ cup chopped cucumber
Sprigs of parsley (optional)
16-ounce can whole peeled Italian plum tomatoes
2 tablespoons vegetable oil
2 tablespoons cider vinegar
Large clove garlic
1 teaspoon salt
1 teaspoon freshly ground pepper

1. Prepare fresh vegetables. If using parsley for garnish, separate sprigs, wash, and pat dry.

2. In food processor or blender, combine undrained canned tomatoes, oil, vinegar, garlic, salt, and pepper, and blend until smooth. Pour into large serving bowl.

3. In food processor or blender, combine scallions, fresh tomato, red and green bell peppers, and cucumber. Pulse or blend until vegetables are chopped but not mushy. With wooden spoon, stir chopped vegetables into tomato mixture and taste for seasoning. Cover bowl with plastic wrap and refrigerate until chilled, about 1 hour.

4. Divide soup among individual bowls and garnish each serving with parsley sprigs if desired.

Seafood Curry Chowder
Bibb Lettuce, Avocado, and Tomato Salad

For this informal meal, ladle the chowder into soup bowls set on dinner plates and serve the salad on the side.

Elisabeth Thorstensson combines two delicate lean fish with shrimp for this main-course chowder. Curry is a combination of several spices. A commercially blended curry powder, from the supermarket, which is suitable for this recipe, contains some combination of these spices: chili, turmeric, ginger, coriander, cumin, cloves, cinnamon, fenugreek, and black pepper.

WHAT TO DRINK

A dry Riesling from California, Alsace, or Germany would suit this menu.

SHOPPING LIST AND STAPLES

½ pound medium-size shrimp (10 to 12), shelled and deveined
1 fillet of flounder (about 11 ounces)
1 fillet of halibut, scrod, or cod (about 8 ounces)
4 tomatoes, preferably Italian plum (about 1 pound total weight)
2 heads Bibb lettuce
1 avocado
Small yellow onion
Medium-size clove garlic

Small bunch dill
2 lemons
½ pint heavy cream
4 tablespoons unsalted butter
10-ounce package frozen tiny peas
2 cups chicken stock, preferably homemade (see page 13), or canned
2 cups fish stock, preferably homemade, or two 8-ounce bottles clam juice
¾ cup vegetable oil
¼ cup red wine vinegar
1 teaspoon Dijon mustard
1 teaspoon chili sauce
¼ cup flour
1 teaspoon curry powder (approximately)
Salt
Freshly ground pepper

UTENSILS

Food processor or blender
Large heavy-gauge saucepan with cover
Medium-size bowl
Plate
Salad spinner (optional)
Measuring cups and spoons
Chef's knife
Paring knife
Wooden spoon
Ladle
Whisk
Juicer
·Medium-size jar with lid

START-TO-FINISH STEPS

1. For chowder recipe, transfer frozen peas from package to plate to defrost.
2. Juice lemon for chowder recipe and salad recipe.
3. Follow salad recipe steps 1 and 2.
4. Follow chowder recipe steps 1 and 2.
5. While stock simmers, follow salad recipe steps 3 through 5.
6. Follow chowder recipe step 3 and salad recipe step 6.
7. Follow chowder recipe steps 4 and 5, and serve with salad.

RECIPES

Seafood Curry Chowder

1 fillet of flounder (about 11 ounces)
1 fillet of halibut, scrod, or cod (about 8 ounces)
½ pound medium-size shrimp (10 to 12), shelled and deveined
2 tablespoons lemon juice
4 tablespoons unsalted butter
¼ cup flour
1 teaspoon curry powder, approximately

2 cups fish stock or clam juice
2 cups chicken stock
2 teaspoons salt
1 teaspoon freshly ground pepper
½ cup frozen tiny peas, thawed
½ cup heavy cream
2 tablespoons finely chopped dill

1. Wipe fish fillets with damp paper towels. With chef's knife, cut halibut into ½-inch pieces. Cut flounder into ¾-inch pieces. Cut shrimps in half lengthwise. Transfer fish and shrimps to medium-size bowl, sprinkle with lemon juice, and toss to combine. Set aside.
2. In large heavy-gauge saucepan, melt butter over medium-low heat. Add flour and curry powder to taste, and whisk until thoroughly blended. Cook, stirring with whisk, 3 minutes. Whisking constantly, slowly add fish stock and chicken stock. Add salt and pepper and, stirring occasionally, bring to a boil over medium-high heat. Reduce heat, cover, and simmer 10 minutes.
3. Add fish pieces, shrimps, peas, and cream, and stir to combine. Simmer 1 minute.
4. Remove pan from heat and whisk in dill.
5. Ladle chowder into individual soup bowls set on dinner plates.

Bibb Lettuce, Avocado, and Tomato Salad

Medium-size clove garlic
Small yellow onion
1 teaspoon chili sauce
1 teaspoon Dijon mustard
¼ cup red wine vinegar
¾ cup vegetable oil
½ teaspoon salt
½ teaspoon pepper
2 heads Bibb lettuce
4 tomatoes, preferably Italian plum (about 1 pound total weight)
1 avocado
2 tablespoons lemon juice
1 teaspoon finely chopped dill

1. Peel garlic and onion. Cut onion into quarters.
2. In medium-size jar, combine garlic, onion, chili sauce, mustard, vinegar, ¼ cup water, vegetable oil, salt, and pepper. Shake well to mix dressing and refrigerate until ready to serve.
3. Wash lettuce and dry in salad spinner or pat dry with paper towels. Wash tomatoes and cut crosswise into ¼-inch-thick slices. Set aside.
4. On individual dinner plates, arrange lettuce, leaving room for soup bowls.
5. Peel avocado and halve lengthwise. Twist to separate halves. Remove pit and discard. Cut each half lengthwise into 6 slices. Divide avocado and tomato slices among individual plates and arrange on lettuce. Sprinkle lemon juice over avocado slices.
6. Shake dressing to recombine and spoon over tomatoes and avocado. Sprinkle each serving with dill.

Chicken Liver Mousse
Fillets of Brook Trout with Mushroom Sauce
Spicy Rice

Serve the chicken liver mousse appetizer in small crocks with sliced pumpernickel bread. A garnish of lime slices and strips of red pepper provide a striking color contrast to the fillets of brook trout with mushroom sauce.

Fillets of brook trout are the entrée for this simple family meal. For the mousse appetizer, buy plump odorless chicken livers. To avoid any bitter taste, the cook recommends not cutting into the livers before sautéing them.

WHAT TO DRINK

Any dry white wine goes with trout; try a California Sauvignon Blanc or an Italian Pinot Bianco.

SHOPPING LIST AND STAPLES

1 pound chicken livers
8 fillets of brook trout, rainbow trout, or perch (1½ to
    2 pounds total weight)
1 pound small white mushrooms
Medium-size yellow onion
3 shallots
2 cloves garlic
Small bunch fresh parsley
Small bunch fresh thyme, or pinch of dried
2 lemons
½ pint heavy cream
2 sticks plus 2 tablespoons unsalted butter
2 cups chicken stock, preferably homemade (see page 13)
    or canned
2 tablespoons vegetable oil
1 cup long-grain white rice
1 cup flour
Small loaf pumpernickel bread
2 tablespoons pine nuts
1 teaspoon turmeric
1 teaspoon ground coriander
Salt and freshly ground pepper
1 cup dry white wine
2 tablespoons Cognac, brandy, or dry sherry

UTENSILS

Food processor or blender
Large heavy-gauge skillet
Small heavy-gauge skillet
2 medium-size saucepans, one with cover
13 x 9 x 2-inch baking pan
Medium-size bowl
Measuring cups and spoons
Chef's knife

Paring knife
2 wooden spoons
Wooden spatula
Rubber spatula
Slotted spatula
Juicer

START-TO-FINISH STEPS

1. Follow mousse recipe steps 1 through 3.
2. Follow mushroom sauce recipe steps 1 through 4.
3. Follow mousse recipe steps 4 and 5.
4. Follow rice recipe steps 1 and 2.
5. Follow trout recipe steps 1 through 3.
6. Follow rice recipe step 3.
7. Follow mousse recipe step 6 and serve.
8. Follow trout recipe steps 4 and 5, mushroom sauce recipe step 5, rice recipe step 4, and serve.

RECIPES

Chicken Liver Mousse

1 pound chicken livers
1 stick plus 3 tablespoons unsalted butter
2 tablespoons chopped shallots
½ teaspoon salt
½ teaspoon freshly ground pepper
2 tablespoons Cognac, brandy, or dry sherry
4 thin slices pumpernickel bread, halved

1. Remove membrane and fat from chicken livers, rinse under cold water, and gently pat dry with paper towels.
2. In large heavy-gauge skillet, heat 3 tablespoons butter over medium-high heat until slightly brown. Add livers and sauté 2 to 3 minutes. Add shallots, salt, and pepper, and cook, stirring, 2 minutes.
3. Transfer livers, shallots, and pan juices to bowl of food processor or blender and process until smooth. Add Cognac, brandy, or sherry and process briefly. Turn mixture into medium-size bowl and set aside to cool. Rinse skillet and dry.
4. In food processor or blender, cream remaining butter.
5. Add creamed butter to cooled liver mixture and stir until blended. Chill in freezer 15 minutes.
6. Remove mousse from freezer and divide among individual ramekins.

Fillets of Brook Trout

2 lemons
8 fillets of brook trout, rainbow trout, or perch
1 cup flour
2 teaspoons salt
1 teaspoon freshly ground pepper
1 teaspoon fresh thyme, or pinch of dried
4 tablespoons unsalted butter
Mushroom sauce (see following recipe)

1. Preheat oven to 200 degrees.
2. Juice 2 lemons and strain out pits. Wipe fish fillets with damp paper towels and arrange in single layer in baking pan. Pour lemon juice over fish. Set aside.
3. On sheet of foil, combine flour, salt, pepper, and thyme.
4. In large heavy-gauge skillet used for livers, heat 2 tablespoons butter over medium heat until lightly browned. While butter is browning, dredge 4 fillets in flour mixture. Fry fillets until golden brown, about 2 minutes on each side. Using slotted spatula, remove from pan and drain on paper towels. Transfer fillets to 2 dinner plates and keep warm in oven. Repeat process for remaining fillets.
5. When ready to serve, remove plates from oven and spoon sauce over fish.

Mushroom Sauce

1 pound small white mushrooms
1 clove garlic
3 tablespoons unsalted butter
1 cup dry white wine
1 cup heavy cream
Salt and freshly ground pepper

1. Wipe mushrooms clean with damp paper towels. Trim off stems and cut lengthwise into thin slices.
2. Peel garlic and crush with flat side of chef's knife.
3. In medium-size saucepan, melt butter over medium heat. Add garlic and sauté, stirring, 1 minute. Remove garlic and discard. Add mushrooms and cook, stirring, until liquid has almost evaporated, about 10 minutes.
4. Raise heat to medium-high. Add wine and cook, stirring occasionally, until reduced by half, about 5 minutes. Remove pan from heat and set aside.
5. Add heavy cream and cook, stirring, over medium heat until sauce has thickened slightly, 3 to 4 minutes. Do not boil. Season with salt and freshly ground pepper to taste. Keep warm over very low heat until ready to use.

Spicy Rice

2 tablespoons pine nuts
2 tablespoons vegetable oil
1 clove garlic, minced
Medium-size yellow onion, minced
1 cup long-grain white rice
2 cups chicken stock
1 teaspoon turmeric
1 teaspoon ground coriander
Salt and freshly ground pepper
1 tablespoon finely chopped parsley

1. In small heavy-gauge skillet, toast pine nuts over medium-high heat about 2 minutes, shaking skillet from time to time to keep pine nuts from scorching.
2. In medium-size saucepan, heat oil over medium-high heat. Add garlic and onion, and sauté, stirring frequently, until translucent, 3 to 4 minutes. Lower heat to medium, add rice, and cook, stirring, another 2 minutes.
3. Add stock, pine nuts, turmeric, and coriander, and stir until blended. Bring to a boil over high heat. Reduce heat to low, cover, and simmer 18 minutes.
4. Add salt and pepper to taste. With fork, fluff rice.

Bruce Cliborne

MENU 1 (Left)
Sautéed Scallops with White Wine Sauce
Spicy Spinach Sauté
Wild Mushroom Salad with Basil and Mint

MENU 2
Mussels and Shrimp in Coconut Cream with Mint
Stuffed Kohlrabi

MENU 3
Clams in Sesame-Ginger Sauce
Fettuccine with Garlic and Oil
Mixed Vegetables, Oriental Style

Bruce Cliborne spent his childhood summers on his grandparents' farm in rural Virginia, where they grew their own produce and raised their own beef, pork, and chicken. His grandmother's homemade sausages and freshly churned butter are some of the memories that inspire his own use of fresh, pure ingredients in cooking.

According to this cook, the culinary arts are analagous to the fine arts. As art students study the masters, beginning cooks should study the classic techniques of the world's finest chefs. With this solid grounding, cooks can be inventive. "Making good food should be challenging, intriguing, amusing, and hard work," says Bruce Cliborne.

He draws upon the cuisines of France (his major gastronomic influence), Japan, Italy, and China for inspiration, and his meals often contain elements of several, as in the menus here. In Menu 1, fresh basil, a favorite French and Italian herb, seasons the wild mushroom salad. To the French-inspired sautéed scallops, Bruce Cliborne adds hot dried chilies, which are common to Asian cooking. The two Oriental stir-fry dishes of Menu 3 are accompanied by an Italian specialty, fettuccine, with garlic as the unifying flavor for all three recipes.

The mussels and shrimp of Menu 2, an amalgam of European and Asian recipes, combines such diverse ingredients as coconut cream, mint, vermouth, olive oil, and snow peas.

For a festive meal, present scallops on a bed of sautéed spinach garnished with orange zest, and sautéed wild mushrooms on a bed of greens.

157

Sautéed Scallops with White Wine Sauce
Spicy Spinach Sauté
Wild Mushroom Salad with Basil and Mint

The salad for this company meal requires several unusual ingredients: arugula, lamb's tongue lettuce, and a choice of one of several varieties of fresh wild mushrooms. Arugula is a pungent Italian green that combines well with milder salad greens. Mild lamb's tongue lettuce, also known as *mâche*, grows in clumps of 10 to 15 tongue-shaped leaves. Rinse the greens well in cold water to remove any grit, wrap the clean leaves in paper towels, and refrigerate. Use them within a day or two. You can substitute Bibb or butter lettuce if you wish. If you cannot locate chanterelles, *shiitake*, or *enokitake*, substitute fresh cultivated mushrooms. Note: Unless you are an expert, under no circumstances should you use wild mushrooms picked on your own.

WHAT TO DRINK

A good-quality California Sauvignon Blanc or a good Graves would go well with the rich flavors here.

SHOPPING LIST AND STAPLES

1½ pounds plump sea scallops
⅔ pound fresh wild mushrooms, preferably chanterelles, shiitake, enokitake, or fresh cultivated mushrooms
1 pound spinach
Large bunch arugula
Large bunch lamb's tongue, or 1 head Boston or other young lettuce
Small bunch basil
Small bunch mint
4 shallots
3 cloves garlic
3 lemons
1 orange
3 eggs
2 sticks plus 2 tablespoons unsalted butter
1½ cups plus ⅓ cup olive oil
2 tablespoons white wine vinegar
1 tablespoon sherry vinegar
½ cup flour
6 whole dried chili peppers
¼ teaspoon Cayenne pepper, or ½ teaspoon red pepper flakes
Salt and freshly ground pepper
¼ cup dry white wine
1 tablespoon dry sherry

UTENSILS

2 large sauté pans
Medium-size non-aluminum saucepan with cover
Small non-aluminum saucepan
Heatproof platter
Large flat plate
2 large bowls, one heatproof
Medium-size bowl
2 small bowls
Sieve
Colander
Salad spinner (optional)
Measuring cups and spoons
Chef's knife
Paring knife
2 wooden spoons
Slotted spoon
Wooden spatula
Whisk
Juicer (optional)

START-TO-FINISH STEPS

1. Prepare clarified butter for scallops recipe (see page 20). You will need 1 stick plus 2 tablespoons to yield ½ cup clarified butter.
2. While butter is melting, mince garlic for spinach recipe, mince shallot for sauce recipe, and slice shallots for salad recipe. Juice orange for sauce recipe and julienne rind, if using, for scallops recipe. Juice lemons for salad and for scallops.
3. Follow sauce recipe steps 1 through 3.
4. Follow salad recipe step 1 and spinach recipe step 1.
5. Follow salad recipe steps 2 and 3, and wipe out pan.
6. Follow scallops recipe steps 1 through 7.
7. Follow spinach recipe steps 2 and 3.
8. Follow salad recipe steps 4 and 5, scallops recipe steps 8 and 9, and serve.

RECIPES

Sautéed Scallops with White Wine Sauce

1½ pounds plump sea scallops
3 eggs
½ cup flour
½ cup clarified butter

½ cup olive oil
6 whole dried chili peppers
Juice of 1½ lemons
White wine sauce (see following recipe)
1 tablespoon julienned orange peel for garnish (optional)

1. In colander, rinse scallops under cold running water. Drain and pat dry with paper towels. Preheat oven to 200 degrees.
2. Separate eggs into 2 small bowls. Reserve whites for another use. Lightly whisk yolks with 2 tablespoons cold water.
3. Place flour on large flat plate.
4. Dip each scallop in yolks, let excess drip off, then roll in flour, coating evenly. Gently shake off excess flour.
5. In large sauté pan, heat ¼ cup clarified butter and ¼ cup olive oil over medium-high heat.
6. When butter-oil mixture is hot, add 3 chili peppers to pan. Cook, stirring with wooden spatula, until peppers begin to brown, 3 to 4 minutes. Using slotted spoon, remove peppers from pan and discard.
7. Add half the scallops to the pan and sauté until golden, about 3 minutes per side. With slotted spoon, transfer scallops to paper-towel-lined heatproof platter and keep warm in oven. Repeat with remaining chilies, adding more butter and oil as necessary, for second batch of scallops.
8. Remove scallops from oven and sprinkle with lemon juice.
9. Using slotted spoon, arrange a portion of scallops on each bed of spinach and top with sauce. Garnish with orange peel, if desired.

White Wine Sauce

¼ cup dry white wine
1 tablespoon dry sherry
1 tablespoon sherry vinegar
¼ cup fresh orange juice
2 teaspoons minced shallot
1 stick unsalted butter, chilled
Salt and freshly ground pepper

1. In medium-size non-aluminum saucepan, combine wine, sherry, vinegar, orange juice, and shallots. Bring to a boil over medium-high heat and reduce, stirring with wooden spoon, until about 2 tablespoons of syrupy liquid remain, 3 to 4 minutes. Reduce heat to very low.
2. Whisk in chilled butter, 1 tablespoon at a time. Season with salt and pepper to taste.
3. Pour sauce through sieve to remove shallots. Cover and keep warm over very low heat until ready to serve.

Spicy Spinach Sauté

1 pound spinach
⅓ cup olive oil
1 tablespoon minced garlic
¼ teaspoon Cayenne pepper, or ½ teaspoon red pepper flakes
Salt and freshly ground pepper

1. Stem spinach leaves. Rinse thoroughly under cold running water, drain in colander, and dry in salad spinner or pat dry with paper towels.
2. In large sauté pan, heat half the oil over medium-low heat. Add half the spinach leaves and turn heat to medium-high. Add half the garlic and cook, tossing with 2 wooden spoons, until oil begins to crackle, about 1 minute. Add 4 tablespoons water and toss. Add half the Cayenne pepper and salt and pepper to taste and continue to toss until spinach is wilted, 4 to 5 minutes. Transfer to sieve and press with back of spoon to extract excess liquid. Place in large heatproof bowl and keep warm in 200-degree oven. Repeat with remaining ingredients.
3. Divide among individual plates, forming bed for scallops.

Wild Mushroom Salad with Basil and Mint

2 cups arugula leaves
2 cups lamb's tongue, Boston, or other young lettuce leaves
¼ cup basil leaves
2 tablespoons mint leaves
⅔ pound fresh wild mushrooms, preferably chanterelles, shiitake, enokitake, or fresh cultivated mushrooms
1 cup olive oil
3 shallots, peeled and thinly sliced
Juice of 1 lemon
Salt and freshly ground pepper
2 tablespoons white wine vinegar

1. Rinse arugula, lamb's tongue, basil, and mint, and dry in salad spinner or pat dry with paper towels. Place in large bowl and set aside.
2. Wipe mushrooms clean with damp paper towels. With chef's knife, slice mushrooms into ¾-inch strips.
3. In large sauté pan, heat ½ cup oil over medium-high heat. Add mushrooms and sauté, stirring with wooden spatula, just until lightly browned, 4 to 5 minutes. Reduce heat to low, add shallots, and sauté just until tender. Stir in lemon juice and season mixture with salt and pepper to taste. Transfer mushroom mixture to bowl.
4. Using 2 wooden spoons, toss the salad greens with the remaining ½ cup oil and the vinegar. Season with salt and pepper to taste.
5. Divide greens among 4 dinner plates, arranging them on one side of plate, and top each bed of greens with a portion of mushrooms.

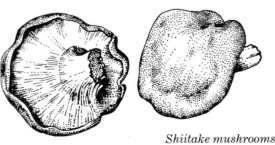

Shiitake mushrooms

Mussels and Shrimp in Coconut Cream with Mint
Stuffed Kohlrabi

For an attractive presentation, arrange the mussels and shrimp on a pinwheel of crisp snow peas and garnish each serving with a mussel shell. Serve the kohlrabi stuffed with chopped mushrooms, onions, and red bell pepper on the side.

Thick coconut cream, blended with heavy cream, vermouth, and water, makes a sweet base for this unusual seafood combination. You can buy canned coconut cream in Oriental groceries and many supermarkets. Select snow peas that are very crisp and fresh-looking, and refrigerate them unwashed in a perforated plastic bag until you are ready to cook them. If fresh mint is not available, the cook recommends fresh basil or parsley. See page 14 for instructions on cleaning shrimp.

Kohlrabi, a member of the cabbage family, is a green bulb with long leafy stalks and slightly sweet, crunchy flesh. Select unblemished bulbs and refrigerate them in a perforated plastic bag. To hollow out the kohlrabi after cooking, first cool the bulb under cold running water and then, holding it in the palm of one hand, carve out the center with a sharp paring knife.

For the wild mushrooms, choose one from among the following: Golden-colored chanterelles, shaped like slender curved trumpets, are delicately flavored. Dark-brown *shiitake* mushrooms have velvety, thick caps with edges that are curled under when fresh. *Enokitake* resemble tiny, creamy-white umbrellas.

There is no substitute for kohlrabi for this recipe. If kohlrabi is unavailable, make the ADDED TOUCH salad of Jerusalem artichokes and Brussels sprouts.

WHAT TO DRINK

A full-bodied white wine is in order; try a Chardonnay or Pinot Blanc from California.

SHOPPING LIST AND STAPLES

3 pounds mussels
1 pound shrimp
4 small kohlrabi (about 1 pound total weight)
1 red bell pepper
½ pound snow peas
¼ pound fresh wild mushrooms, preferably chanterelles, shiitake, enokitake, or 2 ounces dried porcini (fresh cultivated may be substituted)
Medium-size Spanish onion (about ½ pound)
3 large or 6 small shallots
Small bunch mint
Small bunch thyme, preferably, or parsley
½ cup milk (if using homemade coconut cream)
½ pint heavy cream
1 tablespoon unsalted butter
18-ounce can cream of coconut
4 tablespoons virgin olive oil
6-ounce package shredded unsweetened coconut (if using homemade coconut cream)
Salt
Freshly ground black pepper
Freshly ground white pepper
1½ cups dry vermouth

UTENSILS

Food processor or blender (if using homemade coconut cream)
Stockpot with cover
Large deep skillet with cover or wide, low casserole with cover
Medium-size saucepan
Large sauté pan
Heatproof platter
Large bowl
Medium-size bowl (if using homemade coconut cream)
4 small bowls
Colander
Fine sieve (if using homemade coconut cream)
Measuring cups and spoons
Chef's knife
Paring knife
Slotted spoon
Wooden spoon
Wooden spatula
Melon baller
Stiff scrubbing brush
Cheesecloth or cloth napkin

START-TO-FINISH STEPS

One hour ahead: If preparing homemade coconut cream, combine ½ cup packaged shredded coconut with ½ cup boiling milk in medium-size bowl. Soak 20 to 30 minutes. Transfer to food processor or blender and process 4 to 5 minutes, or until smooth. Strain through a very fine sieve set over soaking bowl. With your hand, squeeze the pulp left in the sieve until you have extracted as much liquid as possible. Discard pulp and set aside liquid.

Fifteen to 20 minutes ahead: If using porcini for kohlrabi recipe, place in small bowl and soak in warm water to cover.

1. Follow mussels recipe steps 1 through 4.
2. While mussels are steaming, mince thyme for kohlrabi recipe and chop mint for mussels recipe. Follow mussels recipe step 5.
3. Follow kohlrabi recipe step 1.
4. While water is coming to a boil, follow kohlrabi recipe steps 2 through 5.
5. While kohlrabi are cooking, follow mussels recipe steps 6 through 8.
6. While poaching liquid is reducing, drain kohlrabi and follow recipe step 6.
7. Follow mussels recipe step 9 and kohlrabi recipe steps 7 through 10.
8. Follow mussels recipe steps 10 through 15.
9. Follow kohlrabi recipe step 11, mussels recipe step 16, and serve together.

RECIPES

Mussels and Shrimp in Coconut Cream with Mint

3 pounds mussels
1 pound shrimp
1½ cups dry vermouth
2 to 3 tablespoons cream of coconut, preferably homemade, or canned
1 cup heavy cream
2 large or 4 small shallots
1 tablespoon chopped fresh mint
Freshly ground white pepper
Salt
½ pound snow peas
Fresh mint sprigs (optional)

1. Scrub mussels well with stiff brush and remove beards.
2. Peel and devein shrimp.
3. In stockpot, bring vermouth and ¾ cup water to a boil. Reduce to a simmer.
4. Add mussels, cover, and cook, stirring occasionally, until they open, 4 to 5 minutes.
5. With slotted spoon, transfer mussels to large bowl, discarding any that have not opened.
6. In colander lined with triple thickness of cheesecloth or cloth napkin, strain mussel poaching liquid over deep skillet.
7. Shell mussels, reserving 2 or 3 shells per serving for garnish. Set mussels aside.

8. Over high heat, reduce mussel poaching liquid to about ¾ cup, about 10 minutes. Reduce heat to medium-high.
9. For sauce, add coconut cream and heavy cream to reduced poaching liquid. Stirring with wooden spoon, reduce by one-third, about 10 to 15 minutes.
10. Add shrimp and poach until they turn pink, about 3 minutes.
11. While shrimp are poaching, peel shallots and slice thinly.
12. Add mussels to sauce. Add shallots, chopped mint, and pepper to taste, and stir to combine. Remove skillet from heat, cover, and keep warm until ready to serve.
13. In saucepan used for kohlrabi, bring 1 quart salted water to a boil.
14. While water is coming to a boil, rinse snow peas under cold running water. Snap off ends and remove strings.
15. Add snow peas to boiling water, return water to a boil, and immediately pour snow peas into colander to drain. Refresh snow peas under cold running water and drain.
16. With slotted spoon, remove shrimp and mussels from sauce. Divide shrimp and mussels among 4 dinner plates. Top each portion with sauce and surround with "pinwheel" of snow peas. Arrange a few reserved mussel shells, open side down, near mussels and shrimp and garnish with fresh mint sprigs, if desired.

Stuffed Kohlrabi

1 red bell pepper
¼ pound fresh wild mushrooms, preferably chanterelles, shiitake, enokitake, or 2 ounces dried porcini, reconstituted (fresh cultivated may be substituted)
Medium-size Spanish onion (about ½ pound)
1 large or 2 small shallots
4 small kohlrabi (about 1 pound total weight)
4 tablespoons virgin olive oil
1 tablespoon unsalted butter
Salt
Freshly ground black pepper
½ teaspoon minced fresh thyme, preferably, or parsley

1. In medium-size saucepan, bring 1½ quarts water to a boil.
2. Core, seed, halve, and dice red pepper.
3. If using fresh mushrooms, wipe clean with damp paper towels and mince. If using porcini, drain, discard soaking liquid, pat dry, and mince.
4. Peel and dice onion. Peel and mince shallots.

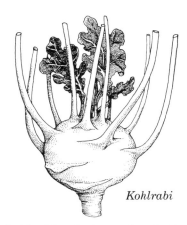

Kohlrabi

5. Trim kohlrabi and plunge into boiling water. Boil just until point of sharp knife pierces them easily, about 20 minutes.

6. Preheat oven to 200 degrees. In large sauté pan, heat 2 tablespoons oil over medium heat. Add red pepper and sauté until soft, 3 to 5 minutes. With slotted spoon, transfer to small bowl.

7. Add butter to pan. When butter has melted, add onion and sauté over medium heat until soft, about 5 minutes. With slotted spoon, transfer to another small bowl.

8. Add remaining 2 tablespoons oil to pan. Add mushrooms and shallots, and sauté over medium heat 3 to 4 minutes, or until shallots are translucent and mushrooms have softened slightly. With slotted spoon, transfer to third small bowl. Season each mixture with salt and pepper to taste.

9. With paring knife, cut concentric circles in top of each kohlrabi, about 1 inch deep. With knife and melon baller, dig out and discard insides of kohlrabi to make shell about ¼ inch thick, taking caring not to break sides or puncture bottom.

10. Fill each shell with layers of pepper, onion, and mushroom-shallot mixture. Transfer to heatproof platter and keep warm in oven until ready to serve.

11. With chef's knife, carefully halve kohlrabis lengthwise. Sprinkle with minced thyme and serve.

ADDED TOUCH

Jerusalem artichokes, also known as sunchokes, can be peeled, but for the best flavor, use them unpeeled. This artichoke salad resembles a potato salad, and if Jerusalem artichokes are out of season, use potatoes instead.

Jerusalem Artichokes and Brussels Sprouts Salad

1 pound Brussels sprouts
1 pound small Jerusalem artichokes
½ red bell pepper
Salt
3 scallions
2 cloves garlic
½ cup virgin olive oil
1 tablespoon walnut pieces
Freshly ground pepper
2 tablespoons white wine vinegar flavored with tarragon or other herbs
1 tablespoon chopped flat-leaved parsley, preferably, or curly parsley

1. With paring knife, trim Brussels sprouts and Jerusalem artichokes.

2. In 2 medium-size covered saucepans, bring 1½ quarts water and 1½ teaspoons salt to a boil. Cook sprouts and artichokes until just tender, 20 to 25 minutes. Drain, separately, in colander.

3. Core, seed, and dice red pepper. Rinse scallions, pat dry with paper towels, and slice into ⅛-inch-thick rounds. Peel and mince garlic.

4. While sprouts are still warm, slice in half and place in medium-size bowl. Add ¼ cup oil, walnut pieces, and salt and pepper to taste, and toss.

5. While artichokes are still warm, cut into ¼-inch-thick slices, discarding any nubby ends. Do not peel. Place slices in medium-size bowl. Add red pepper, scallions, garlic, remaining ¼ cup oil, vinegar, parsley, and salt and pepper to taste and toss.

6. Arrange Brussels sprouts in center of salad platter and surround with Jerusalem artichokes.

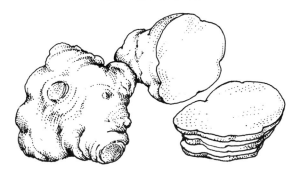

Jerusalem artichokes (sunchokes)

Clams in Sesame-Ginger Sauce
Fettuccine with Garlic and Oil
Mixed Vegetables, Oriental Style

This meal features two different Oriental-style recipes. The stir-fried clams, water chestnuts, and daikon are served on a bed of fettuccine and accompanied by a second stir-fry dish of snow peas, bean sprouts, and julienned vegetables.

aikon, a crisp Japanese white radish, is available year-round in Oriental groceries and some supermarkets. Look for canned lychees in Oriental groceries or specialty food shops. Buy only an Oriental brand of sesame oil; the cold-pressed Middle Eastern variety is not a substitute.

WHAT TO DRINK

A California or Alsatian Gewürztraminer would match the spiciness in this menu; a Riesling would harmonize with the slight sweetness of the sauce.

SHOPPING LIST AND STAPLES

24 clams, preferably Cherrystone (about 3 pounds total weight)
½-pound daikon, if available, or white radishes
½ pound snow peas
2 medium-size carrots (about ⅓ pound total weight)
Medium-size parsnip (about ¼ pound)
¼ pound bean sprouts
6 to 7 large cloves garlic
Medium-size leek (about ¼ pound)
Large bunch scallions
Small bunch fresh parsley
1½-inch piece fresh ginger
1 orange
1 egg
1 tablespoon unsalted butter
¼ pound Parmesan cheese
½ to ¾ pound fresh fettuccine, preferably, or dried
20-ounce can lychees
8-ounce can water chestnuts
½ cup plus 3½ tablespoons virgin olive oil
3 tablespoons Chinese sesame oil
3½ tablespoons soy sauce
1 tablespoon cornstarch
Salt and freshly ground pepper
¼ cup dry sherry

UTENSILS

Large stockpot with cover (if not using steamer unit)
Wok or large heavy-gauge skillet
Large saucepan
Steamer unit (optional)

Large heatproof bowl
2 small bowls
Colander
Measuring cups and spoons
Chef's knife
Paring knife
2 wooden spoons
Slotted spoon
Chinese wok spatulas (optional)
Grater
Wire scrub brush
Vegetable peeler

START-TO-FINISH STEPS

1. Follow clams recipe step 1.
2. Follow vegetables recipe steps 1 and 2.
3. Follow clams recipe step 2 and fettuccine recipe steps 1 and 2.
4. While pasta water is coming to a boil, follow vegetables recipe step 3 and clams recipe steps 3 through 6.
5. Follow fettuccine recipe steps 3 and 4, and vegetables recipe steps 4 and 5.
6. Follow fettuccine recipe step 5.
7. Follow clams recipe steps 7 through 10, vegetables recipe step 6, and serve.

RECIPES

Clams in Sesame-Ginger Sauce

24 clams, preferably Cherrystone
½-pound daikon, if available, or white radishes
12 scallions
8-ounce can water chestnuts
20-ounce can lychees
1 tablespoon cornstarch
3 tablespoons Chinese sesame oil
1 tablespoon finely grated ginger
1 tablespoon minced garlic
¼ cup dry sherry
2 tablespoons soy sauce

1. Scrub clams and rinse thoroughly to rid them of sand. In large stockpot or steamer unit, bring ½ inch water to a boil. Add clams and steam, covered, 5 to 7 minutes.
2. With slotted spoon, transfer clams to colander.
3. When clams are cool enough to handle, discard any that have not opened, and set remaining clams aside. Pour off cooking water from pot, return clams to pot, cover, and keep warm.
4. Peel daikon and cut into 2 x ⅛-inch strips.
5. Rinse scallions and pat dry. Trim off root ends and most of green. Slit each scallion in half lengthwise.
6. Drain water chestnuts and lychees, and set aside. In small bowl, blend cornstarch with 1 tablespoon cold water.
7. Heat wok or skillet used for vegetables over medium-high heat for 30 seconds. Add oil. When hot, add Daikon, scallions, and water chestnuts, and stir fry 4 minutes.

8. Add ginger, garlic, sherry, and soy sauce, and toss 1 minute. Add clams and lychees, and stir fry 1 minute.
9. Add cornstarch mixture to pan a few drops at a time, stirring constantly, until clam mixture reaches desired thickness. You may not need all the cornstarch.
10. Top each portion of fettuccine with a serving of clams in their shells.

Fettuccine with Garlic and Oil

Salt
½ cup plus 1 tablespoon virgin olive oil
1 egg
½ to ¾ pound fresh fettuccine, preferably, or dried
1 tablespoon finely minced garlic
¼ cup grated Parmesan cheese
1 tablespoon chopped parsley
Freshly ground pepper

1. Preheat oven to 200 degrees. In large covered saucepan, over high heat, bring 2 quarts water, 1 tablespoon salt, and 1 tablespoon olive oil to a boil.
2. In small bowl, beat egg with fork just until blended.
3. Add fettuccine to boiling water and cook 2 to 3 minutes for fresh, 8 to 12 minutes for dried, or just until *al dente*.
4. While pasta is cooking, warm 4 plates in oven.
5. Drain fettuccine in colander. Return hot pasta to pan. Add remaining ½ cup olive oil, and toss until evenly coated. Add egg, garlic, Parmesan, parsley, and salt and pepper to taste, and toss until combined. Divide among warmed plates and return to oven until ready to serve.

Mixed Vegetables, Oriental Style

½ pound snow peas
2 medium-size carrots (about ⅓ pound)
Medium-size parsnip (about ¼ pound)
Medium-size leek (about ¼ pound)
2½ tablespoons olive oil
¼ pound bean sprouts, rinsed and drained
2 teaspoons minced garlic
1½ tablespoons soy sauce
1 tablespoon grated orange peel
1 tablespoon unsalted butter

1. In colander, rinse snow peas, drain, and pat dry with paper towels. Pinch off stem ends and pull off strings.
2. Peel carrots and parsnip, and cut into ¼-inch-thick julienne strips.
3. Thoroughly rinse leek. Trim off root end and green part, and discard. With chef's knife, cut white part into ¼-inch-thick julienne strips.
4. Heat wok or large skillet over medium-high heat for 30 seconds. Add oil, tilting pan to coat surface evenly. When oil is hot, add the julienned vegetables and bean sprouts, and toss until well coated. Reduce heat to medium.
5. Add snow peas, garlic, and soy sauce, and stir fry just until vegetables are crisp-tender, 4 to 5 minutes. Turn into heatproof bowl and keep warm in oven. Wipe out pan.
6. Add orange peel and butter, and toss until blended.

Paul Neuman and Stacy Bogdonoff

MENU 1 (Right)
Poached Salmon with Green Sauce
Rice Pilaf with Scallions
Asparagus with Lemon Glaze

MENU 2
Mediterranean Fish Stew
Basil Toasts
Watercress and Endive Salad
with Warm Olive Oil Dressing

MENU 3
Broiled Swordfish with Herb Butter
Sautéed Spinach with Shallots
New Potatoes Braised in Broth with Leeks

Though Paul Neuman never trained as a cook, he has had extensive experience in the food business, including work at his family's Manhattan fish market. He and Stacy Bogdonoff, his wife, now run a Manhattan catering service. He believes that food preparation must be simple and direct. Most importantly, meals must be aesthetically appealing, with vivid, often contrasting, colors and textures—a concept he derived from Japanese cuisine.

With classical training in French cooking, Stacy Bogdonoff brings to this team the technical competence to produce *haute cuisine*. Nevertheless, she describes herself as an untraditional cook who, like her husband, prefers vivid, visual foods.

As they cook and plan menus together, they select a central element or ingredient, something they like to cook, and build the meal around that. They always follow a cardinal rule: Plan a meal for flavor and visual impact. The themes for Menu 1 and Menu 3 are similar: Pale-fleshed fish steaks—salmon and swordfish—play off the bright greens of the vegetables and the pale greens of the fish sauces.

The dramatic fish chowder of Menu 2 is richly textured and colorful. Served in a shallow bowl, the mussel shells and chunks of seafood are half-covered with the orange-red liquid. The endive and watercress salad and the basil toast create additional textures and colors.

When you serve this elegant spring or summer meal, arrange the salmon steaks on a platter with the warm green sauce, and garnish with watercress sprigs. Pass the asparagus spears and the rice pilaf in separate dishes. If you have them, use white serving pieces to emphasize the various shades of green and white in this meal.

166

Poached Salmon with Green Sauce
Rice Pilaf with Scallions
Asparagus with Lemon Glaze

In this menu the main-course fish is cooked by poaching, a low-calorie cooking method that uses no fat. The barely simmering poaching liquid can contain many seasonings or may be flavored only with lemon juice, as in this recipe. It must never boil because the rapid water movement would break the fish apart, marring both flavor and appearance. Firm-fleshed fish such as salmon (or its substitutes in this recipe, sea bass or striped bass) are best for poaching. Save half a cup of poaching liquid for the accompanying sauce, and store the rest in the refrigerator or freezer for future use. The green sauce calls for fresh dill, but you can substitute parsley or basil.

Select plump, bright-green asparagus with compact tips. Before storing the spears, cut a small piece from the bottom of each, then stand them upright in a container of cold water in the refrigerator. If fresh asparagus are not available, use any green vegetable in season—perhaps broccoli, green beans, or snow peas.

WHAT TO DRINK

To complement the delicate salmon and sauce, choose a subtle wine such as a Riesling.

SHOPPING LIST AND STAPLES

4 center-cut fillets of salmon, sea bass, or striped bass, or 1-inch-thick steaks (each about 8 ounces)
16 asparagus spears (about 1 pound total weight), or 1 pound green beans, broccoli, or snow peas
2 stalks celery
Large yellow onion
2 shallots
4 large lemons
Medium-size bunch watercress
Medium-size bunch scallions
Medium-size bunch parsley
Medium-size bunch chives
Small bunch dill
1 stick plus 2 tablespoons unsalted butter
½ pint heavy cream
1½ cups chicken stock, preferably homemade (see page 13), or canned (optional)
¾ cup long-grain white rice
3 tablespoons vegetable oil
1 tablespoon Dijon mustard
Salt

Freshly ground white pepper
Freshly ground black pepper
3 tablespoons dry white wine
3 tablespoons sweet vermouth

UTENSILS

Food processor or blender
3 large skillets, one with cover
1 small saucepan
2 small enamel-lined saucepans, one with cover
2 heatproof serving platters
Heatproof plate
Serving bowl
Colander
Salad spinner (optional)
Measuring cups and spoons
Chef's knife
Paring knife
1 or 2 slotted spatulas
Wooden spatula
Rubber spatula
Whisk
Vegetable peeler

START-TO-FINISH STEPS

1. Follow pilaf recipe steps 1 and 2.
2. While vegetables are cooking, follow green sauce recipe steps 1 and 2 and salmon recipe step 1.
3. Follow green sauce recipe step 3.
4. While cream is reducing, follow pilaf recipe steps 3 and 4.
5. While stock is coming to a boil, follow salmon recipe steps 2 and 3.
6. Juice lemons for salmon and asparagus recipes. Follow salmon recipe step 4 and pilaf recipe step 5.
7. While pilaf is cooking, follow asparagus recipe steps 1 and 2.
8. Follow salmon recipe step 5 and green sauce recipe step 4.
9. While sauce is reducing, place serving platters for salmon and asparagus and bowl for pilaf in oven to warm and follow asparagus recipe step 3.
10. Follow green sauce recipe step 5 and asparagus recipe step 4.

11. Follow green sauce recipe step 6.

12. Follow asparagus recipe step 5, green sauce recipe step 7, pilaf recipe step 6, salmon recipe step 6, and serve.

RECIPES

Poached Salmon with Green Sauce

4 center-cut fillets of salmon, sea bass, or striped bass, or
   1-inch-thick steaks (each about 8 ounces)
½ cup lemon juice
Green sauce (see following recipe)
8 sprigs of watercress (optional)

1. Wipe salmon with damp paper towels.

2. In each of 2 large skillets, bring 2 inches water and ¼ cup lemon juice to a boil over high heat. Reduce to a simmer.

3. Preheat oven to 200 degrees.

4. Add salmon in single layer, making sure fish is completely covered by liquid (add more water if necessary). Return water to a simmer and poach salmon, being careful not to boil, until fish turns light pink all the way through, 8 to 10 minutes. Using sharp stainless steel knife, make a small slit in center of salmon to check color.

5. With 1 or 2 slotted spatulas, transfer fish to heatproof plate and keep warm in preheated oven. Measure ½ cup poaching liquid and reserve for sauce. Discard remaining liquid. Rinse out 1 skillet.

6. Pour small amount of sauce on heated serving platter, top with salmon, and cover with remaining sauce. Garnish with sprigs of watercress, if desired.

Green Sauce

2 shallots
½ medium-size bunch watercress
Small bunch dill
1 cup heavy cream
3 tablespoons dry white wine
3 tablespoons sweet vermouth
½ cup reserved salmon poaching liquid
Salt and freshly ground black pepper
2 tablespoons unsalted butter

1. Wash, peel, and finely mince shallots. Set aside.

2. In colander, wash watercress and dill. Dry in salad spinner or pat dry with paper towels. Remove stems and discard. In food processor or blender, combine watercress and dill, and process until smooth. Set aside.

3. In small saucepan, reduce cream by half over medium-high heat, about 10 to 15 minutes.

4. In small enamel-lined saucepan, combine wine, vermouth, poaching liquid, and shallots. Bring to a boil over medium-high heat, and cook until liquid is reduced by half, about 8 to 10 minutes.

5. Reduce heat to medium. Add reduced cream to wine mixture, whisking until blended, and cook just until sauce thickens, about 3 to 5 minutes.

6. With rubber spatula, scrape processed watercress and

dill into sauce. Add salt and pepper to taste, and whisk until blended.

7. Remove pan from heat and add 1 tablespoon butter at a time, whisking until totally incorporated.

Rice Pilaf with Scallions

2 stalks celery
Medium-size bunch scallions
Large yellow onion
3 tablespoons vegetable oil
¾ cup long-grain white rice
1½ cups chicken stock or water
Salt and freshly ground white pepper
½ cup chopped parsley

1. Wash celery and scallions, and pat dry with paper towels. With chef's knife, trim off ends of celery and scallions and finely dice. Peel and dice onion.

2. In large skillet, heat oil over medium heat. Add celery and onion, and sauté, stirring frequently with wooden spatula, until vegetables are translucent, about 10 minutes.

3. Add scallions and rice, and sauté, stirring, another 3 to 5 minutes.

4. Add stock or water, stir, and bring to a boil over high heat.

5. Cover, reduce heat to medium, and cook until rice is tender and has absorbed liquid, about 18 minutes. Remove pan from heat and keep covered until ready to serve.

6. Fluff rice with fork and season with salt and white pepper to taste. Turn into warmed serving bowl and sprinkle with parsley.

Asparagus with Lemon Glaze

16 spears fresh asparagus (about 1 pound total weight), or
   1 pound green beans, broccoli, or snow peas
Medium-size bunch chives
1 stick unsalted butter
⅓ cup lemon juice
1 tablespoon Dijon mustard
Salt and freshly ground black pepper

1. Wash asparagus and break off ends. Peel stems and, if necessary, trim ends to make spears of uniform length. Set aside. Wash, pat dry, and mince ⅓ cup plus 1 teaspoon chives.

2. In small enamel-lined saucepan melt butter over low heat. Add lemon juice, ⅓ cup chives, mustard, and salt and pepper to taste. Cover partially and keep warm over very low heat.

3. In large skillet used for salmon, bring 2 inches water to a boil over high heat.

4. Place asparagus in skillet, return water to a boil, and cook spears 4 to 5 minutes, until bright green and tender but still firm.

5. Drain asparagus in colander and place on warmed serving platter. Pour lemon butter over asparagus and garnish with remaining chives.

Mediterranean Fish Stew
Basil Toasts
Watercress and Endive Salad with Warm Olive Oil Dressing

The richly seasoned Mediterranean chowder contains vegetables, herbs, and four varieties of seafood. The mackerel for the chowder is either king mackerel, an oily, strong-flavored fish, or Spanish mackerel, leaner and more delicately flavored. If neither is available fresh, use frozen, but not canned. When buying live mussels, check that their shells are tightly closed. For any with open shells, test if they are alive by trying to slide the two shells laterally across one another. Discard any with shells that move or that remain open and also discard any mussels

Garnish the appetizingly colorful Mediterranean fish stew with chopped parsley. To accompany this substantial entrée, pass crisp basil toasts and a salad of watercress and endive. Informal serving pieces are ideal.

that do not open during cooking. Raw shrimp should be firm and odor free. See page 11 for shelling and deveining instructions.

Since squid is usually sold whole, ask the fish dealer to clean it and cut it up. Otherwise, follow the directions on page 14.

Fresh fennel and saffron threads flavor the chowder base. Fennel has a delicate anise flavor; it is available in Italian groceries and some supermarkets. If fresh fennel is unavailable, use fennel seeds and four stalks of sliced celery. Grind saffron threads with a mortar and pestle or pulverize them with your fingers between two sheets of wax paper.

Basil toasts can be prepared up to five days in advance and stored in an air-tight container.

WHAT TO DRINK

Mediterranean flavors go with Mediterranean wines. Serve a French rosé, such as a Lirac or a Tavel, or a full-bodied Italian white, such as a Greco di Tufo.

SHOPPING LIST AND STAPLES

12 mussels
1 pound whole king or Spanish mackerel, boned
½ pound medium-size fresh shrimp
2 squid (about 1 pound total weight), cleaned and cut into rings
1 fennel bulb, or 1 tablespoon fennel seeds
2 large yellow onions
6 cloves garlic
2 or 3 shallots
2 bunches watercress
2 heads endive
Small bunch parsley
Small bunch fresh basil, or 3 teaspoons dried
1 orange
1 lemon
1 egg
1 stick unsalted butter
¼ pound Parmesan cheese
32-ounce can Italian plum tomatoes
6-ounce can tomato paste
¾ cup plus 2 tablespoons olive oil
¼ cup walnut oil
¼ cup sherry vinegar or balsamic vinegar
1 teaspoon saffron threads
1 long loaf crusty French bread
Salt and freshly ground pepper
½ cup white Burgundy wine

UTENSILS

Small skillet
Large heavy-gauge enamel or stainless steel saucepan or stockpot with cover
Small saucepan
17 x 11-inch cookie sheet
Salad bowl
Small bowl
Salad spinner (optional)
Measuring cups and spoons
Chef's knife
Serrated knife
Paring knife
Wooden spoon
Metal spatula

Wooden spatula
Ladle
Grater
Whisk
Pastry brush
Mortar and pestle (optional)
Stiff scrubbing brush

START-TO-FINISH STEPS

1. Follow fish stew recipe steps 1 through 3.
2. While onions are sautéing, wash, dry, and chop basil for fish stew and basil toasts recipes. Grate Parmesan for basil toasts recipe.
3. Follow fish stew recipe step 4.
4. While tomato mixture is cooking, follow fish stew recipe step 5, basil toasts recipe steps 1 through 4, and salad recipe steps 1 through 3.
5. Follow basil toasts recipe step 5 and fish stew recipe step 6.
6. While fish is cooking, follow salad recipe steps 4 and 5.
7. Warm serving bowl and platter under hot running water. Dry. Follow fish stew recipe step 7, salad recipe step 6, and serve with basil toasts.

RECIPES

Mediterranean Fish Stew

2 large yellow onions
6 cloves garlic
1 fennel bulb, or 1 tablespoon fennel seeds
1 teaspoon saffron threads
6 tablespoons olive oil
½ cup white Burgundy wine
32-ounce can Italian plum tomatoes
¼ cup tomato paste
1 tablespoon chopped fresh basil, or 1 teaspoon dried
12 mussels
½ pound medium-size fresh shrimp
1 pound whole king or Spanish mackerel, boned
1 orange
2 squid (about 1 pound total weight), cleaned and cut into rings
2 tablespoons chopped fresh parsley for garnish (optional)

1. With chef's knife, peel and slice onions, and peel and chop garlic. Wash and slice fennel bulb, if using.
2. Using mortar and pestle or with fingers, crush saffron.
3. In large heavy-gauge saucepan or stockpot, heat oil over medium-high heat until hot but not smoking. Add onions and fresh fennel, if using. Sauté, stirring with wooden spoon, until onions are soft but not transparent, about 5 minutes. Add garlic, saffron, and wine. Cook 1 minute.
4. Add tomatoes, tomato paste, basil, and fennel seed, if using. Break up tomatoes with spoon. Cover, reduce heat to low, and cook 30 to 35 minutes.

5. With stiff brush, scrub mussels under cold running water. Pull off any beards. Shell and devein shrimp. Cut mackerel into 1½-inch pieces. Finely grate enough orange rind to measure 2 tablespoons.
6. Stir in orange rind. Add mussels to tomato mixture and cook 2 minutes. Add shrimp and squid, then gently top with fish pieces. Cook 3 minutes. Turn off heat.
7. When ready to serve, gently ladle stew into serving bowl, so that fish pieces do not fall apart. If desired, garnish with chopped parsley.

Basil Toasts

2 or 3 shallots
1 long loaf crusty French bread
1 stick unsalted butter
2 tablespoons finely chopped fresh basil, or 2 teaspoons dried
¼ cup freshly grated Parmesan cheese

1. Preheat oven to 425 degrees.
2. With chef's knife, peel shallots and mince finely.
3. With serrated knife, cut bread into ¾-inch-thick slices and arrange in single layer on cookie sheet.
4. In small skillet, melt butter over low heat. Add shallots and sauté, stirring with wooden spatula, until just translucent, about 3 minutes. Add basil and stir to blend.
5. Brush bread slices with herb butter and sprinkle with cheese. Bake until lightly browned, 8 to 10 minutes.

Watercress and Endive Salad with Warm Olive Oil Dressing

2 bunches watercress
2 heads endive
1 lemon
½ cup olive oil
¼ cup walnut oil
¼ cup sherry vinegar or balsamic vinegar
1 egg
Salt
Freshly ground pepper

1. Wash watercress and remove stems. Dry in salad spinner or pat dry with paper towels.
2. Remove bruised outer leaves of endive. With chef's knife, cut endive into ¼-inch-thick diagonal slices, from tip to root end.
3. In salad bowl, combine watercress and endive. Cover and place in refrigerator. Squeeze enough lemon juice to measure 2 teaspoons.
4. In small saucepan, heat olive oil and walnut oil over medium heat just until warm. Off heat, add vinegar and lemon juice. Remove pits, if necessary.
5. In small bowl, separate egg, retaining yolk and discarding white. In a slow, steady stream, add oil and vinegar mixture, whisking constantly until sauce is smooth and thick. Season with salt and pepper to taste.
6. Remove greens from refrigerator, toss with dressing, and serve.

172

Broiled Swordfish with Herb Butter
Sautéed Spinach with Shallots
New Potatoes Braised in Broth with Leeks

Sautéed spinach with a twist of orange rind, together with new potatoes braised with leeks, provides an appealing color contrast to the swordfish topped with a generous amount of herb butter.

S wordfish has firm flesh and a flavor that can stand alone without elaborate sauces or seasonings. An uncomplicated herb butter is, in fact, the ideal sauce. Make the butter in advance, if you prefer, and store it, for up to 3 days in the refrigerator or up to 6 weeks in the freezer, rolled in a log shape and wrapped in wax paper. To serve, slice rounds from the roll and place on top of the fish steaks just before serving.

The sautéed spinach dish calls for shallots, considered the aristocrat of onions because of their very delicate flavor. The spinach is tossed with a medley of citrus juices—lemon, orange, and lime—which add a subtle flavor to the dish.

Buy straight, slender leeks, avoiding those that have become bulbous, as they may be woody and flavorless. Choose those with the greenest tops and wash them thoroughly. Coarse mustard, an essential flavoring ingredient in the stock, contains crushed mustard seeds, unlike Dijon mustards. Imported and domestic coarse mustards are sold in most supermarkets.

WHAT TO DRINK

These dishes are simple and direct, and the wine should match them; choose a California Pinot Blanc, a dry Vouvray from the Loire, or a white Burgundy.

SHOPPING LIST AND STAPLES

Four 1-inch-thick swordfish steaks (each about 8 ounces)
1½ to 2 pounds young spinach
1½ pounds new red potatoes
Medium-size leek
2 shallots
1 clove garlic
¼ cup mixed fresh herbs, such as watercress, parsley, dill, basil, marjoram, and rosemary, or 2 tablespoons dried
2 lemons
1 lime
1 orange
2 sticks unsalted butter
1 to 1¼ cups chicken stock, preferably homemade (see page 13), or canned
¼ cup olive oil
2 tablespoons coarse mustard
Salt

Freshly ground white pepper
Freshly ground black pepper
½ cup dry white wine

UTENSILS

Food processor or blender (optional)
2 large skillets, one with cover
Medium-size skillet
Broiler pan
Medium-size bowl, plus one additional if not using food processor
Small bowl
Measuring cups and spoons
Chef's knife
Paring knife
Wooden spoon
Slotted spoon
Metal spatula
Rubber spatula
Wooden spatula
Juicer (optional)
Pastry brush

START-TO-FINISH STEPS

At least 1 hour ahead: Follow herb butter recipe steps 1 through 3.

1. Follow spinach recipe steps 1 and 2.
2. Follow potatoes recipe steps 1 through 5.
3. Follow swordfish recipe steps 1 and 2.
4. Follow potatoes recipe step 6 and swordfish recipe step 3. Warm plates under hot running water.
5. Follow swordfish recipe step 4, potatoes recipe step 7, and spinach recipe steps 3 through 5.
6. Follow swordfish recipe step 5. While steaks finish broiling, dry plates.
7. Follow swordfish recipe step 6, potato recipe step 8, and spinach recipe step 6 and serve.

RECIPES

Broiled Swordfish with Herb Butter

Four 1-inch-thick swordfish steaks (each about 8 ounces)
¼ cup olive oil
Herb butter (see following recipe)

1. Preheat broiler. Place broiler pan 3 to 4 inches from heating element and heat 3 to 5 minutes.
2. Wipe swordfish with damp paper towels. Lightly brush both sides of steaks with oil.
3. Place steaks on broiler pan and broil 4 to 5 minutes.
4. Using metal spatula, turn steaks and broil 2 to 3 minutes longer.
5. Cut 1 or 2 generous slices herb butter for each steak. Top steaks with butter and broil 1 minute longer, or just until butter begins to melt.
6. Transfer steaks to warm plates.

Herb Butter

1 clove garlic
½ lemon
½ lime
¼ cup mixed fresh herbs (any combination, including watercress, parsley, dill, basil, marjoram, and rosemary), or 2 tablespoons dried
1 stick unsalted butter, at room temperature

1. Peel and finely chop garlic. Juice enough lemon to measure 2 tablespoons and enough lime to measure 1 tablespoon. Combine juices and remove pits. Wash fresh herbs, if using, pat dry, and chop finely.
2. In food processor or blender, combine butter, garlic, citrus juices, and chopped herbs, and process until well mixed. Or, in medium-size bowl, knead same ingredients together by hand.
3. Form herb butter into log-shaped roll 2 inches long and 2 to 2½ inches in diameter. Wrap snugly in wax paper and place in freezer for 1 hour or refrigerate for several hours.

Sautéed Spinach with Shallots

1½ to 2 pounds young spinach
2 shallots
1 lemon
½ orange
½ lime
4 tablespoons unsalted butter
Salt
Freshly ground white pepper
4 orange twists (optional)

1. Wash spinach thoroughly, remove stems, and place wet leaves in medium-size bowl. Peel shallots and chop enough to measure 2 tablespoons.

2. Squeeze ¼ cup lemon juice, 3 to 4 tablespoons orange juice, and 1 tablespoon lime juice. In small bowl, combine juices and remove pits.
3. In large skillet heat butter over medium-high heat until foamy. Add shallots and toss lightly with wooden spatula for 1 minute, removing skillet from heat to keep shallots from burning if necessary.
4. Add spinach and toss to combine thoroughly with butter and shallots.
5. While spinach is still bright green, push to one side of skillet and pour citrus juices into pan. Reduce juices over medium-high heat 30 seconds, then quickly toss spinach with juices and salt and pepper to taste.
6. Serve alongside swordfish steaks and, if desired, garnish each serving with an orange twist.

New Potatoes Braised in Broth with Leeks

1½ pounds new red potatoes
1 to 1¼ cups chicken stock
½ cup dry white wine
2 tablespoons coarse mustard
Medium-size leek
4 tablespoons unsalted butter
Salt
Freshly ground pepper

1. Wash potatoes but do not peel. Cut into quarters.
2. In large skillet, combine stock, wine, and mustard. Bring to a boil over medium-high heat, then reduce to a simmer.
3. Trim off root ends and upper leaves of leek, leaving some green, and split leek lengthwise. Gently spread leaves and rinse under cold running water, to remove any sand and grit. Pat dry with paper towel. With chef's knife, cut into ¼-inch slices.
4. Add potatoes to simmering broth. Cover and simmer 5 to 7 minutes.
5. In medium-size skillet melt butter over medium-low heat. Add leek and, stirring with wooden spoon, sauté 8 to 10 minutes.
6. Remove cover from potatoes and simmer uncovered 4 to 5 minutes.
7. Add leeks to potatoes, using rubber spatula to scrape out butter. Cook uncovered 5 minutes, turning occasionally, until broth is reduced and buttery leeks glaze the potatoes. Sprinkle with salt and pepper to taste.
8. With slotted spoon, transfer to dinner plates.

Kathleen Kenny Sanderson

MENU 1 (Right)
Seafood Soup Provençale
Chèvre Florentine
Garlic Bread

MENU 2
Rainbow Trout
Julienned Vegetables
Saffron Rice Mold

MENU 3
Sea Bass with Fennel-Butter Sauce
Warm Potato Salad
Garden Salad with Mustard Vinaigrette

As Kathleen Kenny Sanderson explains, "Most people are afraid of cooking with seafood because they do not understand how to handle it." But, in fact, preparing seafood should be a particular pleasure. In each of the menus here, the cook employs one of the standard French techniques—she poaches the fish and shellfish in Menu 1, sautés the trout in Menu 2, and both poaches and bakes the sea bass in Menu 3—then improvises to make each recipe her own. Consequently, all her menus have French overtones, even if she uses American products. If you cook all three of these menus, you will have mastered three essential techniques of fish cookery.

The fish stew of Menu 1 resembles the classic bouillabaisse of the Mediterranean city Marseilles. However, this version uses only four kinds of fish and shellfish rather than the traditional variety of twelve or more. The trout of Menu 2, served with lemon juice, butter, and parsley, is served with saffron rice rather than the more typical French accompaniment, boiled potatoes. For Menu 3, the sea bass, served with a fresh fennel-butter sauce, is accompanied by a garden salad of four distinctive greens.

Seafood soup Provençale makes an impressive main-course offering for this informal meal. Serve the spinach salad with goat cheese and a chunk of garlic bread on the same plate. Offer guests extra bread in a napkin-lined basket.

176

Seafood Soup Provençale
Chèvre Florentine
Garlic Bread

Kathleen Kenny Sanderson uses two varieties each of shellfish and fish for her substantial stew—a perfect cold-weather company meal. Of these, goosefish is probably the least familiar. The only edible section of the fish is the tail section, which contains a firm lobster-like meat. You can use sea bass in its place, and then select either cod or halibut for your other fish. Or use any combination you like, according to what is fresh in your market. Just be sure to use a firm, white-fleshed fish. You can also use frozen fish if you thaw it partially before adding it to the soup. This way it will not overcook and fall apart.

Pernod is often used in bouillabaisse because its delicate anise flavor enhances seafood. This yellowish French liqueur is sold in well-stocked liquor stores.

Chèvre Florentine, a goat's cheese and spinach salad, is unusual and simple to prepare. Chèvre is a generic name for goat's cheese, and Montrachet, a moderately mild variety, is shaped like a log and sometimes coated with a thin layer of edible black ash. Substitute any other goat cheese, or feta, if Montrachet is unavailable.

WHAT TO DRINK

A crisp, dry white wine like an Italian Verdicchio is the best selection, or choose a French Muscadet.

SHOPPING LIST AND STAPLES

½ pound fillet of cod, halibut, or sea bass, cut 1 inch thick
½ pound fillet of goosefish (also known as monkfish and angler fish)
12 littleneck clams or mussels
12 medium-size shrimp
1 pound spinach
3 large carrots
1 bunch celery
Medium-size red bell pepper
Large yellow onion
4 cloves garlic
2 shallots
Small bunch fresh basil, or 1 teaspoon dried
Small bunch fresh oregano, or 1 teaspoon dried
1 stick unsalted butter
½ pound chèvre, preferably Montrachet, or feta cheese
16-ounce can Italian plum tomatoes
¾ cup virgin olive oil
3 tablespoons white wine vinegar
1 loaf French or Italian bread, white or whole wheat

½ teaspoon crushed red pepper
1 bay leaf
Salt and freshly ground pepper
¾ cup dry white wine
2 tablespoons Pernod

UTENSILS

Large saucepan
Small saucepan
15½ x 12-inch cookie sheet
Plate
Salad bowl
2 small bowls
Salad spinner (optional)
Measuring cups and spoons
Chef's knife
Paring knife
Ladle
Wooden spoon
Stiff scrubbing brush
Vegetable peeler (optional)

START-TO-FINISH STEPS

1. For garlic bread recipe, remove butter from refrigerator.
2. Follow chèvre recipe steps 1 through 3.
3. Follow soup recipe steps 1 through 5. While vegetables are cooking, follow garlic bread recipe steps 1 and 2.
4. Follow soup recipe step 6. While soup is cooking, follow garlic bread recipe steps 3 and 4.
5. Follow soup recipe step 7 and chèvre recipe steps 4 through 6.
6. Follow soup recipe step 8 and chèvre recipe step 7.
7. Follow soup recipe step 9.
8. While fish is cooking follow chèvre recipe step 8 and garlic bread recipe step 5.
9. Follow chèvre recipe step 9, soup recipe step 10, and serve with garlic bread.

RECIPES

Seafood Soup Provençale

3 large carrots
Large yellow onion
2 stalks celery

178

12 medium-size shrimp
12 littleneck clams or mussels
½ pound fillet of goosefish (also known as monkfish and
    angler-fish)
½ pound fillet of cod, halibut, or sea bass, cut 1 inch thick
¼ cup virgin olive oil
¾ cup dry white wine
2 tablespoons Pernod
16-ounce can Italian plum tomatoes
1 bay leaf
Salt and freshly ground pepper

1. Peel carrots and onion and wash celery. Cut carrots, celery, and onion into ¼-inch slices. Cut through onion rings crosswise to separate them into semi-circles.
2. Shell and devein shrimp (see page 14).
3. With stiff scrubbing brush, scrub clams or mussels under cold running water. Debeard mussels if necessary. Rinse thoroughly and discard any that have open shells.
4. Wipe goosefish and cod with damp paper towels. With chef's knife, cut fish into 1½-inch squares.
5. In large saucepan, heat oil over medium-high heat. Reduce heat to medium. Add carrots, onion, and celery, and sauté, stirring with wooden spoon, until carrots and celery are bright in color, 2 to 3 minutes.
6. Add wine and Pernod, and cook over medium-high heat 2 to 3 minutes.
7. Add tomatoes with their juice, bay leaf, and salt and pepper to taste. Bring to a boil over medium-high heat, then reduce to a simmer and cook, uncovered, 4 to 5 minutes.
8. Add shrimp and clams or mussels, and simmer 3 minutes.
9. Add fish and simmer just until firm, about 5 minutes.
10. Remove bay leaf and ladle soup into 4 individual bowls. Place bowls on dinner plates and serve.

Chèvre Florentine

2 cloves garlic
½ cup virgin olive oil
½ teaspoon crushed red pepper
½ pound chèvre, preferably Montrachet, or feta cheese
1 pound spinach
Medium-size red bell pepper
2 shallots
3 tablespoons white wine vinegar

1. Pell garlic and mince finely.
2. In small saucepan, combine oil, garlic, and crushed red pepper, and sauté over medium heat just until garlic turns golden brown, about 2 minutes.
3. Slice chèvre evenly into 8 rounds or break feta into 8 pieces and place cheese on plate. Transfer 5 tablespoons oil to small bowl and spoon remaining oil, with garlic and red pepper, over chèvre. Set aside.
4. Wash spinach and remove and discard stems. Dry spinach in salad spinner or pat dry with paper towels.
5. Wash red bell pepper and pat dry with paper towels.

Core, halve, and seed pepper. Cut into ½-inch dice and set aside.
6. Peel and mince shallots.
7. In salad bowl, combine spinach, red pepper, and shallots.
8. Toss salad with reserved oil and then with vinegar.
9. Divide salad among 4 dinner plates, arranging on one-third of each plate, and top each serving with 2 slices marinated chèvre.

Garlic Bread

2 cloves garlic
1 stick unsalted butter, at room temperature
1 tablespoon minced fresh basil, or 1 teaspoon dried
1 tablespoon minced fresh oregano, or 1 teaspoon dried
½ teaspoon freshly ground pepper
1 loaf French or Italian bread, white or whole wheat

1. Preheat broiler.
2. Peel garlic and mince finely.
3. In small bowl, mash together butter, garlic, basil, oregano, and pepper until thoroughly combined.
4. Halve bread lengthwise and spread cut sides with butter mixture. Place on cookie sheet, buttered sides up.
5. Broil bread until butter is brown and bubbly and bread is lightly toasted, 1 to 2 minutes.

ADDED TOUCH

Sabayon is a sweet egg-custard sauce that can be served warm over fruit or eaten on its own.

Strawberries and White Wine Sabayon

2½ cups strawberries or raspberries
6 eggs
⅓ cup sugar
⅓ cup dry white wine
1 cup heavy cream, well-chilled
2 tablespoons Grand Marnier

1. In colander, rinse berries under cold running water and drain. Gently pat dry with paper towels. Hull, if necessary, and set aside.
2. Using 2 small bowls, separate eggs, reserving whites for another use, and set aside yolks.
3. In bottom of double boiler, over high heat, bring just enough water to a boil so that water level will be ½-inch below bottom of upper half of double boiler.
4. In upper half of double boiler, combine egg yolks and sugar, and whisk until pale yellow and creamy.
5. Add wine to egg yolk mixture and place top half of double boiler over simmering water in bottom half. Taking care that water never boils, whisk mixture constantly until thickened into fluffy custard, about 5 minutes.
6. Remove mixture from heat and continue whisking until cool.
7. In small stainless steel bowl, whip cream until stiff.
8. With rubber spatula, fold whipped cream into egg yolk mixture. Gently fold in liqueur. Spoon over berries.

Rainbow Trout
Julienned Vegetables
Saffron Rice Mold

Garnish the fish with parsley sprigs and halved lemon "wheels." Colorful saffron rice and julienned vegetables accompany the fish.

F resh rainbow trout is a delicacy and is at its best when just caught. Tank-bred trout are sold live in specialty food shops and good fish markets. Store fresh trout packed in ice in the refrigerator until you are ready to cook it. Frozen trout is commonly available but may have lost some of its delicate flavor. Defrost frozen trout overnight in the refrigerator.

WHAT TO DRINK

A good-quality white Burgundy, such as a Meursault, or a fine California Chardonnay, is right for this trout classic.

SHOPPING LIST AND STAPLES

4 whole rainbow trout, bluefish, or perch (8 to 10 ounces each), or eight ½-inch thick fillets (3 to 4 ounces each)
½ pound carrots
½ pound yellow squash
½ pound zucchini
Large red bell pepper (optional)
1 bunch scallions
Medium-size bunch fresh parsley
Small bunch fresh dill, or 1 teaspoon dried
2 lemons

1 stick plus 2 tablespoons unsalted butter
2¼ cups chicken stock, preferably homemade
    (see page 13), or canned
¼ cup plus 1 tablespoon vegetable oil
1 cup long-grain rice
⅓ to ½ cup flour
½ to 1 teaspoon saffron threads
Salt and freshly ground pepper
⅓ cup dry white wine

UTENSILS

2 large skillets
Medium-size sauté pan with cover
Small saucepan
Four ½-cup ramekins or custard cups
Large plate
Measuring cups and spoons
Chef's knife
Paring knife
Wooden spoon
Wooden spatula
Whisk
Vegetable peeler
Mortar and pestle

START-TO-FINISH STEPS

1. Follow rice recipe steps 1 through 5.
2. While rice is cooking, wash, dry, and chop parsley for trout and rice recipes, and follow trout recipe steps 1 through 5.
3. While first batch of trout is cooking, follow vegetables recipe step 1 and rice recipe step 6.
4. Follow trout recipe step 6.
5. Follow rice recipe step 7 and, after turning trout, vegetables recipe steps 2 and 3.
6. Follow trout recipe steps 7 through 9, rice recipe step 8, and serve with vegetables.

RECIPES

Rainbow Trout

2 lemons
4 whole rainbow trout, bluefish, or perch (8 to 10 ounces
    each), or eight ½-inch-thick fillets (3 to 4 ounces each)
⅓ to ½ cup flour
Salt and freshly ground pepper
¼ cup vegetable oil
⅓ cup dry white wine
⅓ cup chopped parsley, plus additional sprigs for garnish
1 stick unsalted butter

1. Preheat oven to 200 degrees.
2. Squeeze enough lemon to measure ⅓ cup juice and slice lemon "wheels" for garnish.
3. If using whole fish, remove fins and, with knife, gently scrape skin to remove scales. Wipe whole fish or fillets

with damp paper towels and pat dry.
4. On large flat plate, mix flour with salt and pepper to taste. Roll fish or dip fillets in flour to coat lightly.
5. In large skillet, heat 2 tablespoons oil over medium-high heat. Add 2 whole fish or 4 fillets. Cook whole fish 4 minutes per side, fillets 2 to 3 minutes per side, turning with spatula. Transfer to plates and place in oven.
6. Repeat cooking process with remaining fish.
7. Pour off excess oil. Add lemon juice, wine, and ⅓ cup parsley to skillet. Over medium-high heat, reduce liquid by about half, about 3 minutes.
8. Add butter, 1 tablespoon at a time, whisking constantly.
9. Remove plates from oven, pour sauce over fish, and garnish with parsley sprigs and halved lemon "wheels."

Julienned Vegetables

½ pound carrots, peeled
½ pound yellow squash
½ pound zucchini
Large red bell pepper, cored and seeded (optional)
2 tablespoons unsalted butter
¼ cup chicken stock
1 tablespoon chopped fresh dill, or 1 teaspoon dried
Salt and freshly ground pepper

1. With chef's knife, julienne all vegetables, cutting into 3-inch matchsticks.
2. In large skillet, melt butter over medium heat. Add vegetables and toss with wooden spatula until completely coated with butter. Add chicken stock and dill, and cook over medium-high heat, stirring, until just crisp tender, 2 to 3 minutes. Season with salt and pepper to taste.
3. Keep warm over very low heat.

Saffron Rice Mold

1 bunch scallions
2 cups chicken stock
½ to 1 teaspoon loosely packed saffron threads
1 tablespoon vegetable oil
1 cup long-grain rice
Salt and freshly ground pepper
1 tablespoon chopped parsley (optional)

1. Wash scallions and pat dry with paper towels. Trim scallions and dice enough to measure ½ cup.
2. In small saucepan, bring chicken stock to a boil over medium-high heat.
3. With mortar and pestle, pulverize saffron threads.
4. In medium-size sauté pan, heat oil over medium-high heat. Add scallions and sauté 1 minute. Add rice and saffron, and sauté, stirring, 1 minute.
5. Add boiling stock to rice mixture and add salt and pepper to taste. Return to a boil over medium-high heat, then reduce to a simmer. Cover and cook 18 minutes.
6. Turn off heat. Let sit 10 minutes.
7. Lightly butter four ½-cup ramekins or custard cups.
8. Pack rice into ramekins, and then invert and unmold onto plates. Garnish with parsley, if desired.

Sea Bass with Fennel-Butter Sauce
Warm Potato Salad
Garden Salad with Mustard Vinaigrette

Y ou can serve sea bass with the skin on, but the cook suggests that you skin it before eating, although the skin is edible. The butter sauce contains chopped fresh fennel, also know as *finocchio*. Fennel has a bulbous base and feathery green leaves. Select bulbs that are firm and have no soft or brownish spots. Fennel is sold in Italian groceries or well-stocked supermarkets during fall and winter. If fresh fennel is unavailable, substitute fennel or anise seeds and crush them to release their flavor.

A warm potato salad and a chilled garden salad accom-

Silvery sea bass topped with fennel-butter sauce and garnished with a sprig of watercress makes an elegant company dish. Serve the potato salad with the fish, and the garden salad separately.

pany the sea bass. For the warm salad, select evenly sized new red potatoes for uniform cooking. Be sure they are firm and have smooth unblemished skins. Pour the dressing on while the potatoes are still warm so that it soaks in.

The garden salad combines four leafy vegetables, watercress, radicchio, arugula, and endive, with contrasting colors and textures. Watercress should be crisp and bright green, and is available all year. Radicchio, an Italian wild chicory, has ruby red leaves, is shaped like a small head of lettuce, and is tightly packed like cabbage. You can buy it only at quality greengrocers, usually during the winter. Arugula, a popular Italian salad green, has long slender notched leaves that should look crisp and not wilted or discolored. Arugula is often sandy and must be rinsed thoroughly before use. Belgian endive grows in a compact

head consisting of long slender white leaves with pale yellow tips. All salad greens should be wrapped in plastic bags and refrigerated.

WHAT TO DRINK

A firm, acidic wine is what this menu calls for, and there are several candidates: a California Sauvignon Blanc, a small-château Graves from Bordeaux, a Pouilly Fumé from the Loire, or an Italian Greco di Tufo.

SHOPPING LIST AND STAPLES

4 fillets of sea bass, sea trout, or halibut (each about 8 ounces), with or without skin

1½ pounds new red potatoes
Medium-size fennel bulb, or 1 tablespoon fennel seeds or anise seeds
1 head radicchio or small head escarole
1 head endive
Small bunch arugula
Medium-size bunch watercress
1 bunch scallions
Medium-size bunch parsley
1 bunch chives
1 lemon
1 egg
2 sticks plus 1 tablespoon unsalted butter, approximately
1⅓ cups vegetable oil
¼ cup red wine vinegar or balsamic vinegar

1 tablespoon whole-grain mustard
Dash of Worcestershire sauce
Salt
Freshly ground pepper
2 cups dry white wine

UTENSILS

2 medium-size saucepans with covers
7 x 12-inch flameproof baking dish
Metal steamer
3 small bowls
Colander
Salad spinner (optional)
Measuring cups and spoons
Chef's knife
Paring knife
Wooden spoon
Metal spatula
Juicer (optional)
2 whisks

START-TO-FINISH STEPS

1. Follow potato salad recipe steps 1 through 3.
2. While potatoes are boiling, follow fennel-butter sauce recipe steps 1 and 2.
3. While wine is reducing, follow garden salad recipe steps 1 through 4 and sea bass recipe step 1.
4. Follow fennel-butter sauce recipe step 3 and potato salad recipe step 4.
5. Follow sea bass recipe steps 2 through 5.
6. While fish is baking, follow garden salad recipe steps 5 through 7 and potato salad recipe step 5.
7. Follow fennel-butter sauce recipe step 4, sea bass recipe steps 6 and 7, garden salad recipe step 8, potato salad recipe step 6, and serve.

RECIPES

Sea Bass with Fennel-Butter Sauce

4 fillets of sea bass, sea trout, or halibut (each about 8 ounces), with or without skin
1 tablespoon unsalted butter, approximately
½ cup dry white wine
Salt
Freshly ground pepper

Fennel-butter sauce (see following recipe)
Watercress sprigs for garnish (optional)

1. Preheat oven to 400 degrees.
2. Wipe fish with damp paper towels.
3. Butter flameproof 7 x 12-inch baking dish.
4. In baking dish, bring ½ cup water and wine to a boil over medium-high heat. Add fish and salt and pepper to taste, and cover tightly with aluminum foil.
5. Bake until fish flakes easily when tested with fork, 5 to 6 minutes.
6. While fish is baking, warm dinner plates under hot running water and dry.
7. With metal spatula, transfer fillets to warm dinner plates. Top with fennel-butter sauce and garnish with watercress sprigs, if desired. Skin fillets before eating, if desired.

Fennel-Butter Sauce

Medium-size fennel bulb, or 1 tablespoon fennel seeds or anise seeds
½ bunch scallions
1½ cups dry white wine
2 sticks unsalted butter

1. Rinse fennel, trim off ends and feathery greens, and dice enough of bulb to measure 1 cup. Rinse and trim scallions and finely chop enough to measure ⅓ cup.
2. In medium-size saucepan, combine fennel, scallions, and wine, and bring to a boil over high heat. Lower heat to medium-high and reduce liquid until wine is almost evaporated, 8 to 10 minutes, taking care that vegetables do not singe.
3. Reduce heat to very low, and whisk in butter, 1 tablespoon at a time, until completely incorporated. Cover pan partially and turn off heat, but leave pan on burner until ready to serve.
4. Whisk sauce to recombine.

Warm Potato Salad

1½ pounds new red potatoes
1 lemon
⅓ cup chopped parsley
¼ cup finely chopped chives or scallion greens
⅓ cup vegetable oil
Salt
Freshly ground pepper

184

1. Wash potatoes, but do not peel.
2. In medium-size saucepan fitted with steamer, bring 2 inches water to a boil. Place potatoes in steamer, cover, and steam just until potatoes can be easily penetrated with tip of sharp knife, 15 to 20 minutes, depending on size of potatoes.
3. Squeeze enough lemon to measure 2 tablespoons juice. Wash parsley and chives or scallions and pat dry. Chop enough parsley to measure ⅓ cup. Trim chives or scallion greens, and finely chop enough to measure ¼ cup.
4. Drain potatoes in colander and return to pan off heat.
5. In small bowl, combine parsley, chives, and lemon juice. Add oil, salt and pepper to taste, and whisk until blended. Set aside.
6. Slice potatoes and arrange on dinner plates alongside fish. Spoon dressing over warm potatoes.

Garden Salad with Mustard Vinaigrette

1 head radicchio or small head escarole
Medium-size bunch watercress
Small bunch arugula
1 head endive
1 egg
1 cup vegetable oil
1 tablespoon whole-grain mustard
¼ cup red wine vinegar or balsamic vinegar
Dash of Worcestershire sauce
Salt
Freshly ground pepper

1. Place salad bowls in freezer to chill.
2. Separate radicchio leaves and discard core. Remove stems from watercress. Trim arugula stems. Wash radicchio, watercress, and arugula, and dry in salad spinner or pat dry with paper towels.
3. Remove bruised outer leaves of endive. Slice ½ inch off base of endive, then slice endive in half crosswise and lengthwise, and separate leaves.
4. Remove salad bowls from freezer and divide greens among them. Cover and refrigerate until ready to serve.
5. Separate egg, placing yolk in small bowl and reserving white for another use. Whisk yolk until thick and lemon-colored, 1 to 2 minutes. Beating constantly, add oil in thin stream until completely incorporated.
6. In another small bowl, combine mustard, vinegar, and Worcestershire sauce, and stir until blended.
7. Slowly drizzle mustard mixture into egg mixture, whisk-

ing constantly. Season with salt and pepper to taste. Set aside.
8. Toss salad with mustard vinaigrette and serve.

ADDED TOUCH

Bosc pears are ideal for poaching, as in this recipe, and will soak up the color of the red wine. For a more intense flavor, prepare the pears a day in advance and let them steep in the wine overnight.

Spiced Pears in Red Wine

2 cups red wine
2 cups sugar
2 whole cloves
1 cinnamon stick, 1½ to 2 inches long
½ teaspoon grated lemon peel
½ teaspoon grated orange peel
4 Bosc pears (4 to 5 ounces each)
1 tablespoon cornstarch
4 mint sprigs for garnish (optional)

1. In medium-size saucepan, combine wine, sugar, cloves, cinnamon stick, and lemon and orange peels. Bring to a boil over high heat, then cover and reduce to a simmer.
2. Peel pears, leaving stems intact. Stand pears upright in wine, stem side up. If necessary, add water so that liquid barely covers pears.
3. Cover pan and poach pears until tender, 20 to 25 minutes.
4. Remove from heat. Uncover and allow pears to cool in liquid. With slotted spoon, transfer pears to dessert plates.
5. Bring wine mixture to a boil over medium-high heat and boil until reduced to 1 cup, 8 to 10 minutes.
6. In small bowl, mix cornstarch with ¾ cup cold water. In a slow, steady stream, add boiling wine, whisking until incorporated. Lower heat to medium and stir sauce until thick enough to coat spoon, 2 to 3 minutes.
7. Pour sauce through fine sieve set over bowl and let cool.
8. When sauce has cooled, pour ¼ cup around each pear, and garnish each serving with a mint sprig if desired.

LEFTOVER SUGGESTION

Use leftover raw fennel by chopping it up and adding it to salads, meat balls, or meat loaf. Or, braise the fennel and serve it with poultry or veal.

185

EGGS

Jean Anderson

MENU 1 (Right)
Eggs with Salt Cod, Onion, and Green Olives
Marinated Green Beans with Fresh Coriander
Cherry Tomatoes in Basil Butter

MENU 2
Baked Bell Peppers with Parmesan Soufflé
Shredded Zucchini and Leek Sauté
Anchovy Bread

MENU 3
Curried Eggs
Vegetable Pilaf
Stir-Fried Broccoli and Red Bell Pepper
with Fresh Ginger

World traveler, food writer, and cook Jean Anderson is a sort of culinary alchemist. Drawing upon her food-science training and her passion for exotic tastes and offbeat foods, she creates extraordinary meals from everyday ingredients. Menu 1 substantiates this: After rambling often through Portugal she discovered that the Portuguese are ingenious egg cooks with many egg recipes in their repertoire. For her entrée, she scrambles eggs with salt cod and olives—two Portuguese staples—to create a dish similar to one she ate at the Pousada do Castelo, a government inn north of Lisbon. Marinated green beans with coriander, a classic Portuguese salad, and cherry tomatoes in basil butter, an invention of her own, accompany the eggs.

Italy has inspired her Menu 2 dinner, which balances flavors, colors, shapes, and textures. Stuffed red peppers are an unexpected container for the individual maincourse cheese soufflés, served with sautéed shredded vegetables, and toasted Italian bread with herbed anchovy butter.

Her Menu 3 is reminiscent of India, where she was dazzled by the array of curry spices in the markets. In this eclectic meal, she serves a curried hard-boiled egg dish based on one she sampled in the southern town of Mahabalipuram, near Madras. The addition of a vegetable pilaf and a stir-fried broccoli, red bell pepper, and fresh ginger dish (more Chinese than Indian) makes this a memorable offering.

The colors and contrasting textures in this Portuguese-inspired meal are especially vivid against simple, dark tableware. Serve each guest a wedge of eggs with salt cod along with portions of crisp marinated green beans and plump cherry tomatoes glossy with basil butter.

188

Eggs with Salt Cod, Onion, and Green Olives
Marinated Green Beans with Fresh Coriander
Cherry Tomatoes in Basil Butter

S alt cod is sold in large, dried slabs—with or without the skin and bones—or in small fillets, boxed or wrapped in plastic. It is available at fishmarkets or at groceries that cater to Italian, Portuguese, Greek, or Hispanic customers. Choose thick, supple pieces, preferably from the tail end of the fish. To freshen it and to remove its saltiness, salt cod must be soaked in cool water (in a nonmetallic dish) in the refrigerator the day before you plan to cook it. Change the water several times until the fish no longer tastes salty. (A cup of milk added during the final soaking helps eliminate any trace of salt.) The soaking time will vary depending on the saltiness of the cod, and pieces containing bone will require slightly more time than fillets. Remove any bones before cooking and then treat the fish as you would any fresh fish.

Fresh coriander, which is in the marinade for the green beans, is also called Chinese parsley or cilantro. A pungent, aromatic herb, it has delicate green leaves and resembles flat-leafed parsley. Select fresh-looking bunches and refrigerate coriander with its roots and stems in water. It will keep about a week.

WHAT TO DRINK

The cook suggests a red Portuguese Vinho Verde with the main course and a good Port or Madeira after dinner.

SHOPPING LIST AND STAPLES

½ pound boneless dried salt cod
1 pound green beans
1 pint cherry tomatoes
Large Spanish onion
2 small cloves garlic
Large bunch fresh coriander, or large bunch fresh parsley and ½ teaspoon coriander seeds
Small bunch fresh basil, or 2 tablespoons dried
8 large eggs
1 pint half-and-half or ½ pint light cream
6 tablespoons unsalted butter
7-ounce jar pitted green olives, preferably pimiento-stuffed
¼ cup plus 3 tablespoons olive oil, preferably extra-virgin
3 tablespoons red wine vinegar
Salt
Freshly ground pepper

UTENSILS

Food processor (optional)
Large heavy-gauge skillet, preferably enamel-lined with flameproof handle
Medium-size skillet
Large heavy-gauge saucepan with cover
Medium-size saucepan, preferably enamel-lined
Small heavy-gauge saucepan
3 medium-size bowls, one glass or porcelain
Colander
Large sieve
Salad spinner (optional)
Measuring cups and spoons
Chef's knife
Paring knife
Wooden spoon
Metal spatula
Whisk

START-TO-FINISH STEPS

The day before: Place salt cod in medium-size glass or porcelain bowl. Add 6 cups cold water, cover, and refrigerate at least 12 hours. Change water several times.

1. Follow green beans recipe steps 1 through 5.
2. Follow cod recipe steps 1 through 3.
3. Follow tomatoes recipe steps 1 through 4.
4. Follow cod recipe steps 4 through 8.
5. Follow tomatoes recipe step 5.
6. Follow cod recipe step 9.
7. Follow green beans recipe step 6, cod recipe step 10, and serve with tomatoes.

RECIPES

Eggs with Salt Cod, Onion, and Green Olives

Large Spanish onion
Small clove garlic
3 tablespoons olive oil, preferably extra-virgin
½ pound boneless dried salt cod, soaked at least 12 hours
¾ cup pitted green olives, preferably pimiento-stuffed
8 large eggs
½ cup half-and-half or light cream
Freshly ground pepper

1. Preheat oven to 200 degrees.
2. Peel onion and garlic. Cut onion into 1½-inch chunks. Place onion and garlic in processor fitted with steel blade, and chop coarsely, pulsing 4 to 5 times. Or, coarsely chop onion and garlic with chef's knife.
3. Warm olive oil over medium-low heat in large non-cast-iron skillet. Add garlic and onion and sauté 10 to 12 minutes, stirring occasionally, until soft and golden. Remove from heat and transfer skillet to oven to keep warm.
4. Drain cod and rinse well in cold water. Check that no bones are present. Place cod in medium-size saucepan, add 4 cups water, and bring to a simmer over moderate heat. Cook, uncovered, 5 minutes, or just until fish flakes easily with tip of sharp knife. Transfer cod to sieve and drain. Flake coarsely and set aside.
5. Remove skillet from oven. Set broiler rack 4 to 5 inches from heat source and preheat broiler. Halve olives lengthwise.
6. In medium-size bowl, beat together eggs, half-and-half, and pepper to taste.
7. Return skillet to medium-low heat; spread onion-garlic mixture evenly across the bottom. Pour eggs into skillet and cook, without stirring, until edges begin to set, 2 to 3 minutes.
8. Sprinkle half of cod and of olives over eggs, then stir up eggs gently from bottom to blend. Top with remaining cod and olives.
9. Place skillet in broiler and cook just until eggs are lightly set and surface is touched with brown, about 2 minutes.
10. Cut egg dish into wedges and transfer to dinner plates.

Marinated Green Beans with Fresh Coriander

Salt
1 pound green beans
Large bunch coriander, or large bunch parsley and
    ½ teaspoon coriander seeds
Small clove garlic
¼ cup olive oil, preferably extra-virgin
Pinch of freshly ground pepper
3 tablespoons red wine vinegar

1. Bring 2 quarts water and 2 teaspoons salt to a boil in large covered saucepan.
2. Trim and wash beans in tepid water. Add beans to boiling water, cover, and simmer just until crisp-tender, 8 to 10 minutes.
3. Stem enough coriander leaves or parsley to measure 1 cup. Wash leaves and dry in salad spinner or pat dry with paper towels. Peel garlic.
4. Place coriander or parsley in processor fitted with steel blade. Add garlic and chop coarsely, pulsing 4 to 5 times. Or coarsely chop coriander and garlic with chef's knife. Transfer coriander and garlic to medium-size bowl. Add olive oil, pepper and coriander seeds, if using, and toss together.
5. Drain beans, add to coriander mixture, and toss lightly.

(Do not add vinegar.) Let stand at room temperature at least 10 minutes, or until ready to serve.
6. Drizzle vinegar over beans, add salt to taste, and toss. Divide among 4 dinner plates.

Cherry Tomatoes in Basil Butter

Small bunch fresh basil, or 2 tablespoons dried
6 tablespoons unsalted butter
1 pint cherry tomatoes

1. Rinse basil, dry with paper towels, and chop enough leaves to measure 6 tablespoons.
2. In small heavy-gauge saucepan, melt butter over medium-low heat. When butter has melted, turn heat as low as possible, add basil, and leave mixture to steep 10 minutes. (If butter begins to brown, let steep off heat.)
3. Rinse tomatoes and pat dry. Set aside.
4. Pour butter into medium-size skillet. Add tomatoes, stir gently to coat, and set aside.
5. Just before serving, set skillet over very low heat. Shaking skillet gently from time to time, warm tomatoes just until heated through, about 3 minutes.

———————

ADDED TOUCH

The garlic flavor in this rich appetizer is subdued by baking. Purée the mixture in a blender if you do not have a food processor.

Garlic-Cheese Spread with Toast Triangles

Medium-size head garlic (about 13 cloves)
½ pound Brie, Camembert, or Fontina cheese
4 tablespoons unsalted butter, chilled and cut in pats
6 slices firm-textured white bread

1. Preheat oven to 400 degrees.
2. Wrap head of garlic in double thickness heavy-duty foil and roast in oven until soft, about 35 minutes.
3. Remove garlic from oven and let cool in foil.
4. Reduce oven temperature to 325 degrees.
5. Trim rind from cheese and discard. Cut cheese into 1-inch cubes and place in top of double boiler. Set over simmering water until cheese melts, about 5 minutes.
6. Meanwhile, separate cooled garlic head into cloves. Holding a clove by pointed tip, squeeze pulp directly into food processor fitted with steel blade. Repeat with remaining garlic.
7. Start processor, add melted cheese, and then butter. Process 60 seconds nonstop. Or, combine ingredients in blender.
8. Spoon spread into a ½-cup ramekin or small crock, cover loosely, and let stand at room temperature about 1 hour before serving.
9. Stack 3 slices bread and trim off crusts. Cut slices diagonally into triangles. Repeat with remaining bread. Spread triangles on 13 x 9-inch baking sheet.
10. Place bread in oven and toast until golden brown, 5 to 7 minutes.
11. Serve toast with garlic spread.

Baked Bell Peppers with Parmesan Soufflé
Shredded Zucchini and Leek Sauté
Anchovy Bread

Fresh dill, one of the soufflé seasonings, is a feathery green herb available year-round in well-stocked supermarkets and greengrocers. Its flavor fades quickly, so it should be rinsed, then wrapped in a moist paper towel, put inside a plastic bag and refrigerated until ready to use.

WHAT TO DRINK

Dry white wine goes well with this Italian menu. The cook prefers Orvieto, Soave, or Pinot Grigio, served chilled.

Pale pottery with a primitive motif sets off the red peppers filled with Parmesan-cheese soufflé and the sauté of zucchini and leeks. Keep the slices of herbed anchovy bread warm in a napkin-lined bowl.

SHOPPING LIST AND STAPLES

4 large red bell peppers (each about ½ pound)
4 small zucchini (about 1 pound total weight)
4 small leeks (about 1 pound total weight)
Small yellow onion
2 medium-size cloves garlic
Small bunch fresh dill
4 large eggs
½ pint heavy cream
1 stick plus 4 tablespoons unsalted butter, approximately
½ pound Parmesan cheese
2-ounce can flat anchovy fillets packed in oil
¼ cup olive oil, preferably extra-virgin
½ teaspoon hot red pepper sauce

Long loaf Italian bread
5 slices firm-textured white bread
1 teaspoon dried oregano
1 teaspoon dried rosemary
Pinch of nutmeg, preferably freshly grated
Salt and freshly ground pepper

UTENSILS

Food processor or blender
2 large skillets
9 x 9-inch baking dish
2 small platters
2 medium-size bowls
Small bowl

Measuring cups and spoons
Chef's knife
Paring knife
Wooden spoon
Rubber spatula
Grater (if not using food processor)
Electric mixer or whisk

START-TO-FINISH STEPS

1. Follow baked peppers recipe steps 1 through 10.
2. Follow anchovy bread recipe steps 1 through 4.
3. Follow zucchini recipe steps 1 through 4.
4. Follow zucchini recipe step 5, baked peppers recipe step 11, anchovy bread recipe step 5, and serve.

Baked Bell Peppers with Parmesan Soufflé

½ pound Parmesan cheese
5 slices firm-textured white bread
4 large red bell peppers (each about ½ pound)
Small yellow onion
Pinch of nutmeg, preferably freshly grated
4 tablespoons unsalted butter, approximately
Small bunch fresh dill
½ teaspoon hot red pepper sauce
¾ cup heavy cream
Salt
4 large eggs

1. Preheat oven to 400 degrees.
2. If using food processor, cut Parmesan into 1½-inch cubes and process with steel blade 15 to 20 seconds to grate finely. Or, use grater to grate cheese finely. Measure 1¾ cups cheese and reserve remainder for another use.
3. Tear bread into chunks, place in processor fitted with slicing blade or in blender, and process until fine, 10 to 15 seconds. Measure 1¼ cups crumbs and reserve remainder for another use.
4. Wash peppers and pat dry with paper towels. Slice off tops; core, seed, and remove membranes. Stand peppers upright in lightly buttered baking dish. (If necessary, even bottoms by cutting off a small slice.)
5. Peel onion and mince finely. Grate nutmeg, if using fresh. Melt butter in large skillet over low heat. Add onion and nutmeg and cook, stirring occasionally, until onion is soft, about 5 minutes.
6. While onion is cooking, wash dill, dry, and chop enough to measure 2 tablespoons.
7. Remove onions from heat and add bread crumbs, cheese, red pepper sauce, cream, dill, and salt to taste, stirring to combine.
8. Separate eggs, dropping whites into medium-size bowl and blending yolks, one by one, into onion mixture.
9. Add pinch of salt to whites and, with electric mixer or whisk, beat until stiff but not dry. Fold half of whites into onion mixture, then gently but thoroughly fold in remainder. Carefully spoon about 1 cup soufflé mixture into each pepper, mounding top.
10. Bake peppers, uncovered, until soufflés are puffed and lightly browned, 20 to 25 minutes.
11. Carefully transfer peppers to platter.

Shredded Zucchini and Leek Sauté

4 small zucchini (about 1 pound total weight)
4 small leeks (about 1 pound total weight)
2 medium-size cloves garlic
¼ cup olive oil, preferably extra-virgin
Salt and freshly ground pepper

1. Wash zucchini and trim ends. Cut into 1½-inch chunks and shred, if using food processor, with medium-size shredding disk. Or, shred zucchini with grater. Turn zucchini into medium-size bowl and reserve.
2. Trim off roots and all but 1 inch of greens from leeks. Halve leeks lengthwise and wash thoroughly under cold running water. Dry with paper towels and slice crosswise. Peel garlic and mince finely.
3. Heat oil in large skillet over medium heat. Add leeks and sauté, stirring occasionally, until white part is translucent, about 3 minutes. Add zucchini and cook, stirring occasionally, just until crisp-tender, about 3 minutes.
4. Add garlic and salt and pepper to taste; toss to combine. Turn heat to very low and keep vegetables warm, uncovered, until ready to serve.
5. Transfer zucchini and leeks to platter.

Anchovy Bread

1 teaspoon dried oregano
1 teaspoon dried rosemary
2-ounce can flat anchovy fillets, undrained
1 stick unsalted butter, at room temperature
Long loaf Italian bread

1. Place oregano, rosemary, and anchovies with their oil in food processor fitted with steel blade; process 10 seconds. Scrape down sides of bowl, add butter, and process just until smooth, about 10 seconds. Or, place oregano and rosemary in a mortar and grind finely with pestle. Add anchovies and oil and mash to a paste. Transfer mixture to a small bowl, add butter, and blend with fork.
2. Using serrated knife, cut bread into 1-inch-thick slices, cutting down to—but not through—bottom crust.
3. Carefully spread slices with anchovy butter, coating both sides of each slice. Wrap loaf in aluminum foil.
4. To avoid disturbing soufflés, open oven slowly and carefully. Quickly place loaf in 400-degree oven, and then gently and slowly close door. Bake loaf 15 minutes.
5. Unwrap bread, break into clumps of several slices, and place in napkin-lined bowl.

Curried Eggs
Vegetable Pilaf
Stir-Fried Broccoli and Red Bell Pepper with Fresh Ginger

Fragrant with exotic Indian spices, the curried eggs complement the flavors of the vegetable pilaf, garnished with fresh coriander leaves and apple slices. Ginger-spiced broccoli and red pepper are a bright addition.

Curry powder is a blend of many different spices. Indian cooks grind their own spices daily in various combinations to suit the food being prepared. Here the cook uses cardamom, fennel seeds, and turmeric to season the eggs. Aromatic cardamom (with a faint lemon-eucalyptus flavor) is sold either as whole pods, which contain the flavorful seeds, or as ground seeds. The pods have a longer shelf life; remove the dark seeds and discard the pods before using. Ground cardamom is handy but loses both its flavor and aroma quickly. Fennel seeds have a mild licorice flavor. Bright orange-yellow turmeric has a slightly musky flavor, and must be used sparingly or it imparts a bitter taste. Ground cardamom, fennel, and turmeric are available in most supermarkets.

Fresh ginger, which is used to flavor the stir-fried broccoli and pepper, is a pale-brown gnarled root with a sharp, sweet taste and crunchy texture. Fresh ginger should be firm, taut-skinned, and even-colored, with no sign of shriveling; wrinkled ginger has dried out and lacks flavor. Powdered ginger is not a substitute.

Fresh ginger

WHAT TO DRINK

The best beverage with this spicy and fragrant dinner would be tea—either hot or iced—or ale.

SHOPPING LIST AND STAPLES

Large head broccoli
Large red bell pepper, or 2 medium-size pimientos
Small carrot
Small sweet potato
Small zucchini
Large yellow onion
3 small cloves garlic
3-inch piece ginger
Small bunch fresh coriander or fresh parsley for garnish
  (optional)

195

Small lemon (optional)
Medium-size Granny Smith or Yellow Delicious apple,
    plus 2 for garnish (optional)
8 large eggs
1 pint half-and-half or ½ pint light cream
1 stick unsalted butter
1¾ cups chicken stock, preferably homemade
    (see page 13), or canned
¼ cup vegetable oil
2 tablespoons cider vinegar
1 cup long-grain rice
1½ teaspoons ground cardamom, preferably freshly
    ground
1 teaspoon ground cinnamon
1 teaspoon ground cloves
1 teaspoon ground coriander
1 teaspoon fennel seeds
1 teaspoon ground cumin
½ teaspoon ground turmeric
½ teaspoon Cayenne pepper
Salt
Freshly ground pepper

UTENSILS

Food processor (optional)
2 large sauté pans or heavy-gauge skillets,
    one with cover
2 medium-size heavy-gauge saucepans with covers
Medium-size bowl
Colander
Measuring cups and spoons
Chef's knife
Paring knife
Vegetable peeler
Wooden spoon
Rubber spatula
Wooden spatula
Juicer
Grater (optional)
Mortar and pestle or rolling pin
Egg slicer (optional)

START-TO-FINISH STEPS

One hour ahead: Set out 1 cup half-and-half or light cream
to bring to room temperature.

1. Follow curried eggs recipe steps 1 through 4.
2. While onions are sautéing, follow broccoli recipe steps 1
through 3.
3. Follow curried eggs recipe steps 5 and 6.
4. Follow pilaf recipe steps 1 through 3.
5. While pilaf is cooking, follow curried eggs recipe steps 7
through 10.
6. Follow broccoli recipe steps 4 and 5.
7. Follow pilaf recipe step 4, curried eggs recipe step 11,
and serve with broccoli.

RECIPES

Curried Eggs

8 large eggs
3 small cloves garlic
Large yellow onion
1-inch piece ginger
Medium-size Granny Smith or Yellow Delicious apple,
    plus two for garnish (optional)
4 tablespoons unsalted butter
1 teaspoon fennel seeds
1 teaspoon ground cardamom, preferably freshly
    ground
1 teaspoon ground cinnamon
1 teaspoon ground cloves
1 teaspoon ground coriander
1 teaspoon ground cumin
½ teaspoon ground turmeric
½ teaspoon Cayenne pepper
Small bunch fresh coriander or fresh parsley for garnish
    (optional)
Small lemon (optional)
1½ teaspoons salt
2 tablespoons cider vinegar
1 cup half-and-half or light cream
Vegetable Pilaf (see following recipe)

1. Place eggs in medium-size heavy-gauge saucepan, add
enough cold water to cover them by 1 inch, and bring to a
boil over high heat. Cover pan, turn off heat, and let eggs
stand 15 minutes.
2. While eggs are cooking, peel garlic, onion, and ginger.
Quarter onion. Peel, core, and quarter apple. If using food
processor, fit with steel blade and process garlic and ginger 10 seconds; scrape down work bowl sides and process
10 seconds longer. Add onion and apple and chop coarsely,
pulsing 4 to 5 times. Or, if using chef's knife, mince garlic
and ginger and coarsely chop onion and apple. Combine
ingredients in medium-size bowl.
3. Melt butter in large sauté pan over medium heat. Add
onion mixture and sauté, stirring frequently, until lightly
browned, 8 to 10 minutes.
4. Meanwhile, crush fennel seeds with mortar and pestle
or rolling pin. Grind enough cardamom seeds to measure 1
teaspoon, if using fresh.
5. Drain eggs and plunge into cold water. Immediately
crack broad end of each egg. Peel them, cover with cold
water, and set aside.
6. Reduce heat under sauté pan to low and stir in fennel
seeds, cardamom, cinnamon, cloves, coriander, cumin,
turmeric, and Cayenne pepper. Cover and cook until flavors have blended, 2 to 3 minutes. Set aside.
7. Drain eggs and pat dry. Chop eggs with chef's knife or,
using egg slicer, slice each egg lengthwise and then width-
wise. Set chopped eggs aside.
8. Prepare garnish if using: Wash coriander sprigs or
parsley and pat dry with paper towels. If using apple
slices, squeeze enough lemon juice to measure 1 table-

spoon. Wash, dry, quarter, and slice 2 apples; toss with lemon juice. Set aside coriander and apples.

9. Stir salt and vinegar into onion mixture, raise heat to medium-high, and cook, stirring constantly, until almost all liquid has evaporated, about 5 minutes.

10. Add half-and-half or cream and cook, stirring to combine, until heated through, about 2 minutes. (Mixture may look curdled but will become smooth once eggs are added). Lower heat to medium and gently stir in chopped eggs. Heat briefly, just until eggs are warm, 1 to 2 minutes. Do not let mixture boil. Cover pan and remove from heat.

11. Top each serving of pilaf with curried eggs and garnish with apple slices and coriander or parsley, if desired.

Vegetable Pilaf

Small sweet potato
Small carrot
Small zucchini
4 tablespoons unsalted butter
1 cup long-grain rice
½ teaspoon ground cardamom, preferably freshly
    ground
1¾ cups chicken stock
½ teaspoon salt

1. Wash vegetables and dry with paper towels. Peel sweet potato and scrape carrot. Reserve one-half sweet potato for another use. Shred sweet potato, carrot, and zucchini in food processor fitted with steel blade, or on grater.

2. Melt butter in medium-size saucepan over medium heat. Add shredded vegetables and sauté, stirring and tossing, until vegetables are coated with butter and warm. Add rice and cardamom and cook, stirring, until rice is golden, 2 to 3 minutes.

3. Add chicken stock and salt, and bring to a boil over medium-high heat. Reduce heat to a gentle simmer, cover, and cook until rice is tender and all liquid is absorbed, about 18 minutes.

4. Fluff pilaf with fork and divide among 4 dinner plates.

Stir-Fried Broccoli and Pepper with Fresh Ginger

Large head broccoli
Large red bell pepper, or 2 medium-size pimientos
2-inch piece ginger
¼ cup vegetable oil
Salt
Freshly ground pepper

1. Cut broccoli into slim florets 1½ to 2 inches long. Reserve stems for another use. You should have about 4 cups florets. Wash and shake dry.

2. Wash bell pepper and pat dry with paper towels. Halve, core, and seed pepper, and cut lengthwise into ¼-inch strips. Set aside.

3. Peel ginger and grate enough to measure 1 tablespoon; set aside.

4. In large sauté pan or heavy-gauge skillet set over high heat, heat oil until almost smoking. Add broccoli and stir fry 3 minutes. Add bell peppers and ginger and stir fry until broccoli is crisp-tender, about 2 minutes.

5. Add salt and pepper to taste and toss well.

_____

ADDED TOUCH

Rose water, used to flavor many Indian sweets, is available at Middle Eastern stores, gourmet shops, and pharmacies.

Rose Water Pudding with Tangerine Crescents

3½ ounces marzipan
1 envelope plain gelatin
2 tablespoons superfine sugar
2 cups half-and-half or light cream
3 tablespoons rose water
1½ cups heavy cream
1½ cups fresh tangerine sections, or 11-ounce can
    mandarin oranges, drained
¼ cup minced blanched pistachio nuts
4 sprigs mint, washed and dried for garnish
    (optional)

1. Cut marzipan into small pieces. In food processor fitted with steel blade or in blender, combine marzipan, gelatin, sugar, 1 cup half-and-half or cream, and rose water. Process 20 seconds or until smooth. Add remaining half-and-half or cream and process until incorporated, 10 seconds.

2. Transfer mixture to medium-size heavy-gauge saucepan, and cook over medium-low heat, stirring often, 12 to 15 minutes, or until gelatin dissolves.

3. Chill bowl and beaters for whipping cream.

4. Fill a large bowl or saucepan with crushed ice or ice cubes and water. Set pan with marzipan mixture in ice bath for 10 to 15 minutes, being careful not to let any water spill into it. Whisk mixture frequently, until thick and syrupy.

5. With electric mixer at high speed, whip heavy cream to soft peaks, about 2 minutes, then fold into marzipan mixture. Cover pudding and chill several hours, until slightly firm, or overnight.

6. To serve, arrange tangerine sections around circumference of 4 dessert plates. Mound pudding in center of plates, scatter pistachios on top, and garnish with mint sprigs, if desired.

_____

LEFTOVER SUGGESTION

Broccoli is a perfect partner for eggs, and you can use the leftover broccoli stems as an omelet or quiche filling. Or, create a baked egg dish by cutting up and stir frying the broccoli stems, then seasoning them with soy sauce. Layer the broccoli on the bottom of buttered individual baking dishes, add leftover rice, if you have any, and two eggs. Top with cream, butter, and salt and pepper to taste, and bake.

Penelope Casas

MENU 1 (Right)
Eggs in Nests
Piparrada Salad
Spinach with Raisins and Pine Nuts

MENU 2
Pan-Set Eggs with Lima Beans and Artichokes
Catalan Garlic Bread
Salad Madrileño

MENU 3
Spanish-Style Soft-Set Eggs
Sauté of Red Bell Peppers
Watercress, Carrot, and Endive Salad
in Anchovy Vinaigrette

S panish cooking varies from region to region, but eggs are used throughout the country. According to Penelope Casas, who made her first visit to Spain over twenty years ago, "It is hard to imagine a Spanish meal that does not include eggs in several guises." All three of her menus feature Spanish-style eggs as the main course.

For Menu 1, she offers eggs in nests—hollowed-out rolls—a recipe handed down to her by her Spanish mother-in-law. A seasoned tomato sauce forms the bottom layer in the roll, an egg yolk the middle layer, and a crown of beaten egg whites the top. Two other Spanish dishes accompany the eggs: a salad version of *piparrada* (a Basque specialty combining peppers, onions, and tomatoes) and spinach with raisins and pine nuts.

The eggs in Menu 2 cook in covered skillets with lima beans and artichoke hearts and are served with a kind of garlic bread popular in Catalonia in northeastern Spain. The soft-set eggs in Menu 3 are similar to scrambled eggs, but are prepared in a double boiler fashioned from two skillets to give them a more delicate consistency. This meal also includes sautéed red pepper strips and a watercress, carrot, and endive salad dressed with an anchovy-flavored vinaigrette.

Set a bright fiesta table with flowers and colorful pottery to go with the Spanish-style ham-and-egg-filled rolls and piparrada *salad. The lightly cooked spinach is mixed with golden raisins and subtly sweet pine nuts.*

Eggs in Nests
Piparrada Salad
Spinach with Raisins and Pine Nuts

For the nests, you can use egg twist rolls, bow knot rolls, or any roll with a firm crust that will not become soggy when filled and baked. Store pine nuts *(pignoli)* in a jar in the refrigerator because they spoil quickly.

WHAT TO DRINK

Try a white Rioja with this menu or use it to make a wine punch. Mix 1 bottle of Rioja, 2 tablespoons of orange juice, and 1 tablespoon of sugar with orange and lemon slices. Chill until ready to serve, then stir in 1 cup of club soda.

SHOPPING LIST AND STAPLES

¼ pound cured ham, such as prosciutto
1½ pounds spinach
2 medium-size tomatoes (about 1 pound total weight)
Medium-size cucumber
Large green bell pepper
Small onion
Large shallot
Small bunch scallions
2 cloves garlic, 1 large and 1 small
Small bunch parsley
8 small eggs
6-ounce can tomato paste
4-ounce jar whole pimientos (optional)
½ cup olive oil, approximately
¼ cup plus 2 tablespoons vegetable oil
3 tablespoons white wine vinegar
8 medium-size rolls, such as egg twist or bow knot
3 tablespoons golden raisins
2-ounce jar pine nuts
Pinch of dried thyme
Salt and freshly ground pepper

UTENSILS

Electric mixer
Medium-size skillet
Large saucepan with cover
Small saucepan
15 x 10-inch baking sheet
Large bowl
Medium-size bowl
Small bowl
Colander
Measuring cups and spoons

Chef's knife
Paring knife
Wooden spoon
Metal spatula
Pastry brush
Whisk
Vegetable peeler (optional)

START-TO-FINISH STEPS

1. Peel garlic cloves: Mince large clove to measure 1 tablespoon for spinach recipe; mince small clove to measure 1 teaspoon for salad recipe. Rinse parsley and dry with paper towels; chop enough to measure 2 tablespoons for eggs recipe, for spinach recipe, and 1 tablespoon, if using, for salad recipe.
2. Follow salad recipe steps 1 through 3.
3. Follow eggs recipe steps 1 through 4.
4. While sauce cooks, follow spinach recipe steps 1 through 3 and eggs recipe step 5.
5. Follow spinach recipe steps 4 and 5, and eggs recipe steps 6 through 8.
6. Follow salad recipe step 4, eggs recipe step 9, and serve with spinach.

RECIPES

Eggs in Nests

Small bunch scallions
¼ cup, approximately, plus 2 tablespoons olive oil
¼ pound cured ham, such as prosciutto
¼ cup plus 2 tablespoons tomato paste
Salt and freshly ground pepper
8 medium-size rolls, such as egg twist or bow knot
8 small eggs
2 tablespoons chopped parsley

1. Preheat oven to 450 degrees.
2. Rinse scallions, dry with paper towels, and chop enough white part to measure ¼ cup. Reserve remainder of scallions for another use. Heat 2 tablespoons olive oil in small saucepan over medium heat. Add scallions and cook, stirring frequently, until soft, about 5 minutes.
3. Dice ham, add to pan, and sauté 2 to 3 minutes, or just until scallions are lightly browned.
4. Stir in tomato paste, ¾ cup water, and salt and pepper to taste. Bring mixture to a simmer and cook, stirring

occasionally, about 20 minutes. If mixture becomes too thick, add enough water to obtain desired consistency.

5. Cut a 1½-inch circular plug from middle of each roll, keeping bottom intact. Hollow out rolls, leaving bottoms about 1¼-inches thick and sides ½-inch thick. Discard bread from hollows or reserve for another use. Place hollow rolls on 15 x 10-inch baking sheet. Spoon about 1½ tablespoons of sauce into each roll.

6. Separate eggs, catching whites in large bowl and carefully slipping yolks into hollow rolls. Brush outsides of rolls with remaining olive oil.

7. Using an electric mixer, beat egg whites with a pinch of salt at high speed until stiff but not dry. Spoon egg white into hollow of each roll, making 2-inch-high dome. Reserve leftover egg white for another use.

8. Place nests in oven and bake 5 minutes, or until egg whites are lightly golden.

9. With spatula, transfer 2 nests to each dinner plate, garnish with parsley, and serve.

Piparrada Salad

Large green bell pepper
Medium-size cucumber
Small onion
1 whole pimiento (optional)
2 medium-size tomatoes (about 1 pound total weight)
¼ cup plus 2 tablespoons vegetable oil
3 tablespoons white wine vinegar
1 teaspoon minced garlic
Salt and freshly ground pepper
1 tablespoon chopped parsley (optional)

1. Rinse, core, halve, and seed bell pepper. Remove membranes and cut pepper into 1-inch-wide strips (see illustration below); cut strips in half crosswise. Peel cucumber, cut in half lengthwise; then cut halves crosswise into ½-inch-thick slices. Peel onion and chop enough to measure ¼ cup. If using pimiento, drain, and cut into julienne strips. Rinse tomatoes, dry with paper towels, and cut in half; cut halves into ½-inch-thick slices.

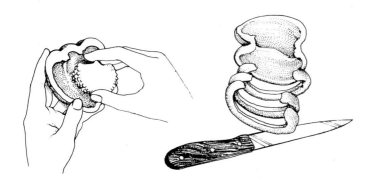

2. Whisk oil and vinegar together in medium-size bowl. Whisk in garlic and salt and pepper to taste.

3. Stir in bell pepper, cucumber, onion and tomatoes until coated with dressing. Cover bowl with plastic wrap and refrigerate until ready to serve.

4. Toss salad, divide among individual plates, and garnish with parsley and pimiento, if desired.

Spinach with Raisins and Pine Nuts

1½ pounds spinach
3 tablespoons golden raisins
Large shallot
Salt
2 tablespoons olive oil
1 tablespoon minced garlic
1 tablespoon chopped parsley
Pinch of dried thyme
3 tablespoons pine nuts
Freshly ground pepper

1. Remove and discard spinach stems. Wash leaves well and drain in colander; do not dry.

2. Place raisins in small bowl with enough warm water to cover. Peel and mince shallot to measure 2 tablespoons.

3. Place spinach in large saucepan and sprinkle lightly with salt. Cook spinach, covered, over medium-high heat about 5 minutes, or until wilted. Turn spinach into colander to drain.

4. Heat olive oil in medium-size skillet. Add shallots and garlic, and sauté about 5 minutes over medium heat until shallots are soft.

5. Drain raisins and add to skillet along with spinach, parsley, and thyme. Stir in pine nuts, salt and pepper to taste, and cook, stirring occasionally, until flavors are combined and spinach heated through, about 5 minutes.

ADDED TOUCH

This easy fruit and wine compote is a traditional Basque dessert. It will keep for weeks in a jar in the refrigerator, but warm it before serving to bring out the subtle flavors.

Dried Fruit Compote

1 lemon
1 orange
¾ cup red wine
¼ cup cream sherry
¼ to ½ cup packed light brown sugar
¼ cup honey
1 stick cinnamon
4 cups mixed dried fruits, such as pitted prunes, apricots, peaches, or apples (about 1 pound total weight)

1. Rinse lemon and orange and cut each in half; peel one half of each, removing as much white pith as possible; slice peels finely.

2. Combine lemon and orange peels with remaining ingredients and 1 cup water in medium-size saucepan. Bring mixture to a boil, reduce heat, and simmer, covered, 15 minutes, or until fruits are soft. Remove cinnamon stick; set compote aside in pan, covered.

3. When ready to serve, warm compote briefly over low heat. Immediately spoon fruit into large serving bowl or divide among individual dessert dishes.

Pan-Set Eggs with Lima Beans and Artichokes
Catalan Garlic Bread
Salad Madrileño

Eggs with lima beans and artichokes, garlic-tomato bread, and salad make a quick meal for unexpected guests.

oth saffron and ground cumin season the pan-set eggs. Although cumin is widely available pre-ground, it is best freshly ground. Lightly roast ¼ cup of cumin seeds in an ungreased skillet to intensify their flavor, stirring constantly over medium heat. When they have turned a light chocolate color, remove them from the pan and cool. Crush the seeds between two sheets of waxed paper with a rolling pin.

For the garlic bread, select a firm-textured Italian- or French-style loaf that will hold up when you rub it with the ripe tomato.

WHAT TO DRINK

Enjoy this Spanish meal with a good Spanish wine, such as a full-bodied red Rioja.

SHOPPING LIST AND STAPLES

3½-ounce can light-meat tuna
Small head Romaine lettuce
4 medium-size very ripe tomatoes
1¼ pounds lima beans or two 10-ounce packages frozen
Small white onion
Small red onion
6 to 7 medium-size cloves garlic
Medium-size bunch parsley
8 large eggs
10-ounce package frozen artichoke hearts
1-pound jar white asparagus (optional)
½ cup chicken stock, preferably homemade (see page 13), or canned
4¾-ounce jar small green Spanish olives, preferably without pimiento
½ cup plus 3 tablespoons olive oil
¼ cup plus 2 tablespoons white wine vinegar
1 teaspoon Dijon mustard
1 loaf Italian or French bread, preferably round
Pinch of sugar
Large pinch of saffron threads
1 teaspoon ground cumin
2 bay leaves
Salt and freshly ground pepper

UTENSILS

2 large skillets with covers
Baking sheet

2 small bowls
Salad spinner (optional)
Measuring cups and spoons
Chef's knife
Paring knife
Wooden spoon
Wide metal spatula
Small whisk
Pastry brush

START-TO-FINISH STEPS

One hour ahead: For eggs recipe, set out frozen artichoke hearts and lima beans, if using, to thaw. Set out eggs to bring to room temperature.

1. Prepare tomatoes, onions, and garlic.
2. Follow salad recipe steps 1 through 3.
3. Follow eggs recipe steps 1 through 4.
4. While vegetables cook, follow bread recipe steps 1 through 3.
5. Follow eggs recipe step 5 and bread recipe step 4.
6. Follow eggs recipe step 6, bread recipe step 5, and salad recipe step 4.

RECIPES

Pan-Set Eggs with Lima Beans and Artichokes

2 tablespoons olive oil
3 tablespoons chopped white onion
1½ tablespoons minced garlic
½ cup very ripe chopped tomato
Medium-size bunch parsley
8 frozen artichoke hearts, thawed
3 cups lima beans
½ cup chicken stock
2 bay leaves
Large pinch of saffron threads
1 teaspoon ground cumin
Salt and freshly ground pepper
8 large eggs

1. Place 1 tablespoon olive oil in each of 2 large skillets over medium heat. Divide onion and garlic between skillets and sauté until onion is translucent, about 5 minutes.
2. Add ¼ cup chopped tomato to each skillet and cook, stirring occasionally, until sauce is slightly thickened, about 3 minutes.

3. Wash parsley, dry with paper towels, and mince enough to measure 5 tablespoons. Halve artichoke hearts.
4. Divide the following ingredients, adding half to each skillet: artichokes, lima beans, chicken stock, bay leaves, saffron threads, and cumin. Add salt and pepper to taste to each skillet. Divide 3 tablespoons parsley between skillets. Stir mixtures to combine, add about 5 tablespoons water to each skillet, cover both, and cook vegetables over medium-low heat until almost tender, about 10 minutes.
5. One at a time, break eggs, and drop, 4 per skillet, on top of vegetable mixture, spacing evenly. Cover skillets tightly and continue cooking over medium-low heat until whites are just set and yolks are still soft, about 5 minutes.
6. With wide spatula, divide eggs with vegetables among dinner plates and sprinkle with remaining parsley.

Catalan Garlic Bread

1 loaf Italian or French bread, preferably round
¼ cup plus 2 tablespoons olive oil
4 teaspoons minced garlic
Medium-size very ripe tomato, halved

1. Preheat oven to 350 degrees.
2. From center of loaf, cut four ¾-inch-thick slices of bread. Lay bread on baking sheet and toast in oven, turning once, until lightly browned on both sides, about 10 minutes.
3. While bread toasts, combine olive oil and garlic in small bowl, stirring with fork.
4. Remove toasted bread from oven, leaving heat on. Rub both sides of bread slices with cut side of tomato; discard tomato. Using pastry brush, lightly spread olive oil-garlic mixture on toast.
5. Place toast on baking sheet and return to oven just to crisp, 3 to 4 minutes. Serve warm with eggs.

Salad Madrileño

Small head Romaine lettuce
4 white asparagus spears (optional)
2 medium-size very ripe tomatoes, cut in wedges
4 thin slices red onion
3½-ounce can light-meat tuna
16 small green Spanish olives, preferably without pimiento
3 tablespoons olive oil
¼ cup plus 2 tablespoons white wine vinegar
1 teaspoon Dijon mustard

Pinch of sugar
Salt
Freshly ground pepper

1. Separate lettuce into leaves, wash, and dry in salad spinner or with paper towels. Tear enough leaves to measure about 6 cups and divide lettuce among 4 salad plates. If using asparagus spears, cut off ends.
2. Arrange 2 tomato wedges, 1 slice onion, one quarter of tuna, 1 asparagus spear, and 4 olives on top of lettuce on each plate. Cover plates with plastic wrap and refrigerate.
3. Combine olive oil, vinegar, mustard, sugar, and salt and pepper to taste in small bowl and whisk well to combine. Set aside until ready to serve.
4. Just before serving, stir dressing to recombine and spoon over salad.

<hr>

ADDED TOUCH

Drambuie is a liqueur made from fine Scotch whiskey, herbs, and heather honey. Kirsch, or *kirschwasser*, is a clear cherry brandy. You may substitute any fruit liqueur for either one.

Strawberry "Soup" with Vanilla Ice Cream

3 pints fresh strawberries, or 6 cups whole frozen strawberries, thawed
Medium-size orange
¼ cup dry sherry
¼ cup kirsch
¼ cup Drambuie
2 sticks cinnamon
¼ cup sugar
Pinch of salt
1 pint vanilla ice cream

1. If using fresh strawberries, wash, hull, and coarsely chop enough to measure 6 cups. If using frozen, chop thawed berries. Halve orange and squeeze enough juice to measure ¼ cup.
2. Combine strawberries, orange juice, sherry, kirsch, Drambuie, cinnamon sticks, sugar, and salt in large saucepan. Bring liquid to a boil over medium-high heat, reduce to a simmer, and cook, uncovered, about 10 minutes, or until strawberries are soft.
3. Remove pan from heat and cover to keep warm. When ready to serve, divide strawberry mixture among 4 dessert bowls and top with a scoop of ice cream.

Spanish-Style Soft-Set Eggs
Sauté of Red Bell Peppers
Watercress, Carrot, and Endive Salad in Anchovy Vinaigrette

For a late-night supper or weekend brunch, serve soft-set eggs combined with crabmeat and prosciutto and red bell peppers sautéed with garlic. A salad of watercress, carrot, and endive is the colorful side dish.

Prosciutto, a dry-cured ham, is deep pink, moist, and only mildly salty; it is the best choice for this egg recipe. Commonly sold in Italian markets and some specialty food shops, prosciutto is also packaged presliced. You can substitute a cured or boiled ham—but not a smoked one.

If fresh crab is unavailable at your fish dealer, use either the canned variety that is labeled "fresh" or frozen crabmeat. Remove all bits of cartilage and shell before cooking.

WHAT TO DRINK

The cook suggests a dry white wine from the Penedes region of Catalonia. If unavailable, look for a white Rioja.

SHOPPING LIST AND STAPLES

¼ pound medium-size shrimp, or 8-ounce package frozen
2 ounces fresh crabmeat (about ⅓ cup), or 6-ounce package frozen, or 1-pound can pasteurized "fresh"
2 ounces prosciutto (1 thick slice)
5 large red bell peppers (2¼ pounds total weight)
8 spears asparagus (about ½ pound total weight)
2 medium-size carrots (about ½ pound total weight)
Small tomato (optional)
2 ounces mushrooms
Large bunch watercress
2 heads Belgian endive
Medium-size bunch parsley
Small bunch scallions
2 cloves garlic, 1 large and 1 small
8 large eggs
¼ cup milk
1 stick plus 4 tablespoons unsalted butter
1 tablespoon chicken stock, preferably homemade (see page 13), or canned
2-ounce can anchovy fillets
2-ounce jar pimientos
½ teaspoon capers
Small sour pickle
½ cup olive oil
3 tablespoons red wine vinegar
4 slices white bread
Pinch of sugar
Salt
Freshly ground pepper

Food processor (optional)
Extra-large skillet
2 large skillets, one with cover
Medium-size skillet with cover
2 medium-size bowls
Small bowl
Salad spinner (optional)
Measuring cups and spoons
Chef's knife
Paring knife
Wooden fork
Wooden spoon
Metal spatula
Metal tongs
Whisk
Vegetable peeler

■■■
START-TO-FINISH STEPS

Two hours ahead: If using frozen crabmeat or shrimp for eggs recipe, set out to thaw.

1. Rinse parsley and dry with paper towels: Chop 4 tablespoons for eggs recipe and reserve 4 sprigs for garnish, if desired; mince 2 teaspoons for salad recipe. Peel garlic: Thinly slice large clove for peppers recipe; mince small clove to measure ½ teaspoon for salad recipe.
2. Follow salad recipe steps 1 and 2.
3. Follow peppers recipe step 1.
4. Follow eggs recipe steps 1 through 4.
5. While asparagus cooks, follow salad recipe step 3.
6. Follow eggs recipe steps 5 and 6.
7. While bread is sautéing, follow salad recipe step 4.
8. Follow peppers recipe steps 2 and 3.
9. While peppers are cooking, follow eggs recipe steps 7 through 11.
10. Follow salad recipe step 5, eggs recipe step 12, and serve with peppers.

■■■
RECIPES

Spanish-Style Soft-Set Eggs

2 ounces fresh crabmeat (about ⅓ cup), or 6-ounce package frozen, or 1-pound can pasteurized "fresh"
¼ pound medium-size shrimp, or 8-ounce package frozen

2 ounces mushrooms
2 ounces prosciutto (1 thick slice)
2-ounce jar pimientos
4 tablespoons chopped parsley, plus 4 sprigs for garnish (optional)
8 asparagus spears (about ½ pound total weight)
Salt
4 slices white bread
4 tablespoons plus 1 stick unsalted butter
8 large eggs
¼ cup milk
Freshly ground pepper

1. Flake crabmeat with fork. If using fresh shrimp, peel and devein. Cut shrimp in half. Wipe mushrooms with damp paper towels; trim stems, reserving for another use. Cut prosciutto into quarters.
2. If using food processor, combine mushrooms and prosciutto, and mince; transfer to medium-size bowl. In same manner, mince shrimp and crab, and then pimientos. Or mince all ingredients with chef's knife and place in bowl. Add chopped parsley and stir to combine.
3. Trim stems from asparagus leaving 2-inch-long spears plus tips; reserve stems for another use. Bring ½ inch water and ½ teaspoon salt to a boil over medium-high heat in medium-size skillet. Add asparagus, cover, reduce heat to medium, and simmer until just tender, 5 to 10 minutes.
4. Meanwhile, remove crusts from white bread and slice diagonally into triangles.
5. With tongs transfer asparagus to plate and cover loosely to keep warm. Dry skillet thoroughly.
6. In large skillet, heat 4 tablespoons butter over low heat. Add bread triangles and sauté, turning once, until golden and crisp on both sides, 8 to 10 minutes.
7. Transfer triangles to plate and cover with foil.
8. Break eggs into medium-size bowl and beat lightly with fork. Beat in milk and salt and pepper to taste.
9. Half fill extra-large skillet with water and bring to a boil over high heat.
10. While water is heating, melt remaining stick of butter in medium-size skillet. Add shrimp-crab mixture and sauté about 1 minute, then remove from heat.
11. Reduce boiling water to a simmer. Stir beaten eggs into shrimp-crab mixture. Gently place skillet containing egg mixture into larger skillet of simmering water to form double boiler. Stir egg mixture constantly with wooden spoon until just set but still quite soft, about 3 to 4 minutes.

12. Divide eggs among 4 plates and garnish with asparagus and parsley sprigs, if desired. Place 2 bread triangles on each side of eggs and serve.

Sauté of Red Bell Peppers

5 large red bell peppers (about 2¼ pounds total
  weight)
2 tablespoons olive oil
1 tablespoon plus 1 teaspoon thinly sliced garlic
1 tablespoon chicken stock, preferably homemade
  (see page 13), or canned
Salt
Freshly ground pepper

1. Wash peppers, dry with paper towels, core and halve, remove seeds and membranes; cut into ½-inch strips. Set aside.
2. Heat oil in large skillet. Add peppers and stir fry with wooden fork over medium-high heat 2 to 3 minutes only.
3. Reduce heat to medium, stir in garlic, chicken stock, and salt and pepper to taste. Cover, reduce heat to medium-low, and cook until peppers are crisp-tender, about 10 minutes.

Watercress, Carrot, and Endive Salad in Anchovy Vinaigrette

3 anchovy fillets
½ teaspoon capers
Small sour pickle
Small tomato (optional)
Small bunch scallions
½ teaspoon minced garlic
2 teaspoons minced parsley
¼ cup plus 2 tablespoons olive oil
3 tablespoons red wine vinegar
Pinch of sugar
Salt
Freshly ground pepper
Large bunch watercress
2 heads Belgian endive
2 medium-size carrots (about ½ pound total
  weight)

1. For vinaigrette, mince anchovy fillets. Rinse, drain, and mince capers. Mince enough pickle to measure 1 tablespoon. If using, wash tomato and dry with paper towel. Halve, core, and seed tomato; mince enough to measure 1

tablespoon. Rinse scallions, dry with paper towels, and mince enough white parts to measure 3 tablespoons plus 1 teaspoon; reserve remainder of scallions for another use.
2. In small bowl, combine anchovies, capers, pickle, tomato, scallions, garlic, parsley, olive oil, vinegar, and pinch of sugar. Whisk ingredients to blend. Add salt and pepper to taste, whisking to combine. Set aside.
3. Trim watercress of stems, wash, and dry in salad spinner or with paper towels. Wash endive, separate leaves, and dry; stack 4 endive leaves and cut into long thin strips. Repeat with remaining leaves. Peel carrots and cut diagonally into ¼-inch-thick x 2-inch-long strips. Combine carrots with endive and set aside.
4. Divide watercress among 4 salad plates, placing on one half of each plate. Place carrots and endive on other halves of plates. Cover and refrigerate until ready to serve.
5. Just before serving, whisk dressing to recombine and pour over salads.

ADDED TOUCH

If you have a chafing dish, preparing this dessert at the table would be a lovely finale to any meal. You can also serve the bananas with vanilla ice cream.

Sautéed Bananas with Pine Nuts

Small lemon
Small orange
½ cup dark brown sugar
4 tablespoons unsalted butter
4 ripe bananas
3 tablespoons Grand Marnier
2 ounces pine nuts

1. Squeeze enough lemon and orange to measure 1 teaspoon juice each. In a small bowl, mix together dark brown sugar, lemon and orange juices, and 3 tablespoons warm water.
2. Melt butter in large skillet or chafing dish over medium heat. Peel and cut bananas in half lengthwise, and then slice crosswise. Add slices to skillet and sauté 1 minute, turning once.
3. Add brown sugar mixture to skillet, reduce heat to medium-low, and cook 1 minute.
4. Stir in Grand Marnier and cook another 2 minutes, stirring occasionally.
5. Add pine nuts and stir gently to combine.
6. Divide bananas among 4 dishes and serve immediately.

Douglas Oaks

W hen cooking for friends or for his own plea-sure, Douglas Oaks loves nothing more than to open the refrigerator and prepare a meal with what is on hand. For him the challenge is in being innovative on the spot. Although his meals can be unorthodox, he usually achieves what he sets out to do: create a unified menu from disparate elements. The menus here, although carefully planned, reflect his spontaneity in the kitchen.

In Menu 1, he cooks the eggs in prebaked potato shells, rather than in traditional ramekins. The eggs are en-hanced with three types of cheese and prosciutto. To accompany the main course, he offers honey-glazed Brussels sprouts and a salad of sliced tomatoes in a vin-aigrette dressing.

Menu 2 is an elegant spring dinner. The salmon fillets are molded into individual turbans, each filled with baked egg and a mixture of mushrooms and green pepper. As a finishing touch, the cook tops the turbans with Béarnaise sauce (made from egg yolk, butter, and a wine and vinegar reduction seasoned with tarragon). Although Béarnaise is generally served with red meat, it also goes extremely well with eggs. Menu 3 features a large omelet filled with an unexpected combination of red peppers, chicken, hearts of palm, and cheese. Eggs reappear in the topping for the snow pea and carrot side dish.

For a hearty brunch, serve potato shells filled with prosciutto, eggs, and cheese—topped with sautéed vegetables. Color-com-plement the main dish with glazed Brussels sprouts and a tomato salad flavored with basil, fennel, and capers.

Baked Eggs in Idaho Potatoes
Honey-Glazed Brussels Sprouts with Walnuts
Tomatoes Vinaigrette

Brussels sprouts resemble miniature cabbages but are more delicately flavored. Buy Brussels sprouts that are compact, firm, and have a bright green color. Refrigerated unwashed in a plastic bag, they will keep for several days, but for best results use them quickly.

A very fresh egg white whipped into the salad dressing acts as a frothy suspension for the herbs and spices and helps to blend the ingredients for a fuller flavor. Crush the fennel seeds to release their oils before adding them to the dressing.

WHAT TO DRINK

A full-bodied dry white wine or a light-bodied dry red would go well with these baked eggs. Try a California Chardonnay or French Mâcon for white; a California Merlot, French Saint-Émilion, or Italian Chianti for red.

SHOPPING LIST AND STAPLES

8 slices prosciutto (about ¼ pound total weight)
4 large Idaho potatoes (about ¾ pound each)
1 pound fresh Brussels sprouts, or 10-ounce package frozen
2 medium-size tomatoes (about 1 pound total weight)
Medium-size red bell pepper
Medium-size green bell pepper
Small head Bibb or leaf lettuce
2 ounces mushrooms
Small bunch scallions
Small bunch watercress (optional)
Small bunch dill
Small bunch basil
9 small eggs
1 stick unsalted butter
2 ounces Gruyère cheese
2 ounces Romano cheese
2 ounces Swiss cheese
½ cup olive oil
2 tablespoons vegetable oil
2 tablespoons red wine vinegar
¼ cup honey
1¼ teaspoons capers
4-ounce package walnut pieces
1 teaspoon caraway seeds (optional)
½ teaspoon fennel seeds
Salt and freshly ground white pepper

UTENSILS

2 medium-size skillets
Vegetable steamer
Baking sheet
Shallow glass baking dish
Medium-size bowl, preferably stainless steel
Salad spinner (optional)
Measuring cups and spoons
Chef's knife
Paring knife
Wooden spoon
Mortar and pestle
Grater
Whisk
Vegetable scrub brush
Pastry brush

START-TO-FINISH STEPS

One hour ahead: If using frozen Brussels sprouts, set out to thaw.

1. Follow eggs recipe steps 1 and 2.
2. While potatoes are baking, follow tomatoes recipe steps 1 through 4 and eggs recipe steps 3 through 5.
3. When potatoes are done, follow eggs recipe steps 6 through 8.
4. While eggs are baking in potato shells, follow Brussels sprouts recipe steps 1 and 2.
5. Follow eggs recipe step 9.
6. Follow tomatoes recipe step 5 and Brussels sprouts recipe steps 3 and 4.
7. Follow eggs recipe step 10, and serve with Brussels sprouts and tomatoes.

RECIPES

Baked Eggs in Idaho Potatoes

4 large Idaho potatoes (about ¾ pound each)
2 tablespoons vegetable oil
2 ounces Gruyère cheese
2 ounces Romano cheese
2 ounces Swiss cheese
1 teaspoon caraway seeds (optional)
Small bunch scallions
Medium-size red bell pepper
2 ounces mushrooms

4 tablespoons unsalted butter
8 slices prosciutto (about ¼ pound total weight)
8 small eggs

1. Preheat oven to 400 degrees.
2. Scrub potatoes and dry thoroughly with paper towels. Liberally brush each potato with vegetable oil and lay on baking sheet. Bake 35 to 40 minutes, or until potato yields to pressure, but is still firm.
3. Grate cheeses to measure about ½ cup each; toss together. Toss cheeses with caraway seeds, if desired, and set mixture aside.
4. Trim scallions; wash, dry, and slice thinly to measure about ½ cup. Wash red pepper; halve, seed, remove membranes, and dice to measure about ½ cup. Wipe mushrooms with damp paper towels and dice finely to measure about ⅔ cup.
5. Heat 4 tablespoons unsalted butter in skillet. Add scallions, pepper, and mushrooms and sauté over medium heat about 3 minutes, until scallions are translucent.
6. Halve cooked potatoes lengthwise. Scoop out flesh, leaving ¼-inch-thick shell. Reserve flesh for another use. Place shells on baking sheet.
7. Sprinkle 1 to 1½ teaspoons grated cheese mixture into each potato and line shell with 1 slice of prosciutto, folding to fit, if necessary. Then break 1 egg into each shell.
8. Bake 8 to 10 minutes, or until eggs are barely set.
9. Remove potatoes from oven and turn oven to broil. Sprinkle with remaining cheese and top with sautéed vegetable mixture. Set aside until ready to serve.
10. Just before serving, broil 1 minute, or just until cheese has melted. Transfer 2 potato halves to each of 4 dinner plates and serve.

Honey-Glazed Brussels Sprouts with Walnuts

Small bunch dill
1 pound fresh Brussels sprouts, or 10-ounce package frozen, thawed
4 tablespoons unsalted butter
⅓ cup walnut pieces
¼ cup honey

1. Wash dill, dry with paper towel, and chop enough to measure 1 teaspoon. If using fresh Brussels sprouts, trim off bottoms and discolored leaves, wash, and drain.
2. Steam Brussels sprouts, 8 to 10 minutes, or until slightly crisp-tender. Set aside.
3. Heat butter in skillet until foaming. Stir dill into butter,

then add Brussels sprouts and walnuts and sauté over high heat about 2 minutes, stirring constantly, just until edges of walnuts begin to brown.
4. Add honey, stir to coat, and cook 4 to 5 minutes, stirring constantly, until honey just begins to caramelize.

Tomatoes Vinaigrette

1¼ teaspoons capers
Small bunch basil
½ teaspoon fennel seeds
1 small egg
½ cup olive oil
2 tablespoons red wine vinegar
Salt and freshly ground white pepper
8 leaves Bibb or leaf lettuce
4 sprigs watercress (optional)
2 medium-size tomatoes (about 1 pound total weight)
Medium-size green bell pepper

1. Rinse and drain capers; dry with paper towel and mince. Wash basil; dry with paper towel and chop enough to measure 1 teaspoon. Crush fennel seeds. Separate egg; place white in medium-size bowl, preferably stainless steel, and reserve yolk for another use.
2. To egg white add olive oil, vinegar, capers, basil, fennel seeds, and salt and pepper to taste. Whisk vigorously 10 to 15 seconds, or until mixture becomes slightly frothy. Add 1 to 2 tablespoons water, if desired, to reduce acidity.
3. Wash lettuce and watercress, if using, and dry with paper towels or in salad spinner; refrigerate in plastic bags. Wash tomatoes; cut into ¼-inch rounds. Wash, dry, core, halve, seed, and remove membranes from green pepper; cut into 2 x ¼-inch strips.
4. Place tomato slices and green pepper strips in shallow glass dish. Beat vinaigrette dressing to recombine; pour over vegetables. Cover dish and refrigerate for approximately 30 minutes.
5. Just before serving, divide lettuce leaves among 4 salad plates and top with sliced tomatoes and peppers. Garnish each serving with sprig of watercress, if desired.

LEFTOVER SUGGESTION

Since only the potato shells are used in the main-course recipe, use the rest of the potato flesh as a thickener for any light soup or for making vichyssoise.

Salmon Turbans with Béarnaise Sauce
Wild Rice with Pecans
Buttered Asparagus Spears

Remove any visible fat from the salmon before cooking because it will give the fish an undesirable flavor. If you cannot find fillets of the recommended size, buy smaller pieces and mold them to the sides of the ramekins.

The filling for the turbans is a mixture of chopped mushrooms, shallots, green pepper, and garlic. Wrap the chopped mushrooms in cheesecloth or a towel and wring out any excess moisture before sautéing.

If the Béarnaise sauce begins to separate or thin, remove it from the heat and continue to whisk to lower its temperature. You might slowly add a few drops of cold water, milk, or cream to the sauce, then speed up whisking as soon as the eggs begin to accept the liquid.

Eggs in rolled salmon fillets are topped with vegetables and a Béarnaise sauce for a dazzling dinner. The asparagus spears are delicately flavored with a thyme butter and the wild rice is tossed with pecans.

WHAT TO DRINK

Choose a very dry, firm white wine such as an Alsatian Gewürztraminer or Riesling or a California Gewürztraminer or Sauvignon Blanc for this menu.

SHOPPING LIST AND STAPLES

Four ¾-inch-thick skinless salmon fillets (each about 5 ounces, measuring 2 x 6 inches), or Dover sole, lemon sole, or flounder

16 asparagus spears (about 1 pound total weight)
Small green bell pepper
2 ounces mushrooms
Small bunch fresh tarragon, or ½ teaspoon dried
2 large shallots
2 medium-size cloves garlic
Large lemon
7 large eggs
1 stick unsalted butter, plus 1 stick salted
2¼ cups chicken stock, preferably homemade (see page 13), or canned
2 tablespoons tarragon vinegar
¾ cup wild rice
3-ounce can pecan halves
Pinch of dried dill
Pinch of dried thyme, plus ½ teaspoon
Salt
2 peppercorns
Freshly ground white pepper
2 tablespoons dry white wine

UTENSILS

Medium-size heavy-gauge skillet
Small heavy-gauge skillet
2 medium-size heavy-gauge saucepans, 1 with cover
Small heavy-gauge saucepan
Double boiler or medium-size saucepan and stainless steel bowl
Vegetable steamer
Small bowl
Four 10- to 12-ounce ramekins or soufflé dishes
Colander
Fine sieve or cheesecloth
Measuring cups and spoons
Chef's knife
Paring knife
Wooden spoon
Rubber spatula
Whisk

START-TO-FINISH STEPS

1. Juice lemon to measure 2 tablespoons for salmon recipe, 1 teaspoon for Béarnaise recipe, and 1 tablespoon for asparagus recipe.
2. Follow wild rice recipe steps 1 through 3.
3. While rice is cooking, follow salmon recipe steps 1 through 3, asparagus recipe step 1, and Béarnaise recipe steps 1 through 6.
4. Follow wild rice recipe step 4 and salmon recipe steps 4 through 6.

5. While fish bakes, follow asparagus recipe steps 2 and 3, and wild rice recipe step 5.

6. Follow salmon recipe step 7 and asparagus recipe step 4.

7. Follow wild rice recipe step 6, Béarnaise recipe step 7, and serve with salmon turbans and buttered asparagus.

RECIPES

Salmon Turbans with Béarnaise Sauce

Four ¾-inch-thick skinless salmon fillets (each about 5
  ounces, measuring 2 x 6 inches), or Dover sole, lemon
  sole, or flounder
Salt and freshly ground white pepper
Pinch of dried dill
Pinch of dried thyme
2 tablespoons lemon juice
4 tablespoons unsalted butter
2 ounces mushrooms
Small green bell pepper
2 medium-size cloves garlic
2 large shallots
4 large eggs
Béarnaise Sauce (see following recipe)

1. Preheat oven to 350 degrees.

2. Season salmon fillets with salt, pepper, dill, thyme, and lemon juice to taste.

3. Melt butter in medium-size heavy-gauge skillet. Lightly brush inside of ramekins or soufflé dishes with melted butter and curl fillets around insides of dishes; cover and set aside. Set aside skillet.

4. Wipe mushrooms with damp paper towel and dice finely to measure about ½ cup. Wash pepper; halve, seed, remove membranes, and dice finely to measure about ½ cup. Peel garlic and mince to measure about 2 teaspoons. Peel shallots and dice to measure about ¼ cup.

5. Set skillet with remaining butter over high heat. Add vegetables and sauté 3 to 4 minutes, stirring constantly, until shallots begin to brown. Remove from heat.

6. Break 1 egg into each salmon-lined ramekin. Spoon in one quarter of sautéed vegetables. Cover with foil and bake turbans 10 to 12 minutes, or until salmon flakes easily.

7. With rubber spatula, carefully turn each turban out onto a dinner plate and top with Béarnaise Sauce.

Béarnaise Sauce

Small bunch fresh tarragon, or ½ teaspoon dried
2 tablespoons tarragon vinegar
2 peppercorns
2 tablespoons dry white wine
1 stick salted butter
3 large eggs
1 teaspoon lemon juice

1. If using fresh tarragon, rinse gently, dry with paper towels, and chop enough to measure 1 tablespoon. Combine half the tarragon with tarragon vinegar, pepper-

corns, and white wine in small heavy-gauge saucepan. Boil over medium-high heat about 7 minutes, or until mixture is reduced by one half. Strain mixture through fine sieve or cheesecloth into small bowl.

2. In same saucepan, heat butter until foaming. Remove pan from heat; set aside.

3. Bring 1 to 2 inches water to a boil in bottom of double boiler or medium-size saucepan.

4. Separate eggs, reserving whites for another use. Place yolks and lemon juice in top of double boiler or in stainless steel bowl; set over simmering water. Whisk mixture vigorously to the consistency of heavy cream, about 4 to 5 minutes. (Keep water at a simmer; if eggs become too hot they will separate.)

5. Remove bowl from heat and, whisking constantly, add small amounts of melted butter alternately with drops of tarragon mixture, incorporating each addition completely.

6. Combine sauce and remaining tarragon; cover to keep warm until ready to use.

7. Just before serving, whisk to recombine sauce.

Wild Rice with Pecans

2¼ cups chicken stock
¾ cup wild rice
2 tablespoons unsalted butter
½ cup pecan halves

1. Bring stock to a simmer in medium-size saucepan over medium-high heat.

2. Wash wild rice under cold running water and drain.

3. Stir rice into hot chicken stock. Bring to a simmer, cover, and cook 35 minutes, or until rice is tender, stirring occasionally.

4. Drain any excess stock from rice; cover and set aside until ready to serve.

5. Melt butter in small skillet over medium-high heat. Add pecans, and sauté about 3 minutes, until edges of pecans begin to turn golden brown.

6. Just before serving, toss pecans with wild rice.

Buttered Asparagus Spears

16 asparagus spears (about 1 pound total weight)
½ teaspoon dried thyme
¼ teaspoon salt
Freshly ground white pepper
1 tablespoon lemon juice
2 tablespoons unsalted butter

1. Wash asparagus, trim off woody ends, and peel, if desired. Set aside.

2. Combine thyme, salt, pepper to taste, lemon juice, and butter in small heavy-gauge saucepan. Warm, stirring, over medium heat just until butter melts. Set aside.

3. Steam asparagus 3 to 4 minutes in vegetable steamer over boiling water just until crisp-tender.

4. Divide asparagus among plates and drizzle with butter sauce.

California Omelets
Snow Peas and Carrots Polonaise

Hearty omelets filled with chicken, peppers, and hearts of palm are accompanied by snow peas and carrots with a crumb topping.

Hearts of palm are a primary ingredient in these quick omelets. This delicious but expensive vegetable is taken from the cream-colored interior of small palm trees, usually palmettos. The hearts are like velvety white asparagus stalks in appearance and texture; they taste something like artichokes. Fresh hearts of palm are rare, but they are widely available canned at specialty food shops. Refrigerate leftovers in a nonmetal container filled with water.

The carrots and snow peas are prepared with a Polish-style topping that contains chopped hard-boiled eggs, fresh parsley, and bread crumbs sautéed in butter and garlic. Select snow peas, also known as Chinese pea pods, that are very crisp and bright green. Refrigerate the pods, unwashed, in a paper bag inside a plastic bag. If fresh snow peas are unavailable, use peeled broccoli stems or green beans.

WHAT TO DRINK

A medium-bodied dry white Alsatian or Italian Pinot Blanc would be good here. The cook also suggests a light red Beaujolais.

SHOPPING LIST AND STAPLES

2 whole chicken breasts (about 1 pound total weight), skinned and boned
2 medium-size carrots (about ½ pound total weight)
½ pound snow peas
4 medium-size hearts of palm, or 14-ounce can water-packed artichoke hearts
Large red bell pepper
Small bunch parsley
Small bunch scallions
3 small cloves garlic
9 large eggs
1 stick plus 1 to 4 tablespoons unsalted butter
2 ounces Parmesan cheese
2 ounces Gruyère cheese
3 to 4 slices stale bread
Salt and freshly ground white pepper

UTENSILS

Food processor (optional)
2 medium-size skillets
Omelet pan
Small saucepan
Vegetable steamer
9 x 13-inch heavy-gauge baking sheet
8 x 8-inch flameproof baking dish
Medium-size bowl
Wooden bowl and chopper (if not using processor)
Colander
Measuring cups and spoons
Chef's knife
Paring knife
Wooden spoon
Metal spatula
Whisk
Grater (if not using processor)
Vegetable peeler
Scissors

START-TO-FINISH STEPS

1. Peel garlic and mince to measure 2 teaspoons for omelets recipe and 1 teaspoon for snow peas and carrots. Trim scallions and wash; dry with paper towels and chop green parts to measure ¼ cup for omelets recipe. Wash parsley, dry with paper towels, and chop 1 tablespoon for garnish for omelets recipe and 1 tablespoon for snow peas and carrots recipe.
2. Prepare snow peas and carrots recipe steps 1 through 4.
3. Follow omelets recipe steps 1 through 12.
4. Follow snow peas and carrots recipe steps 5 through 7.
5. Follow omelets recipe step 13.
6. Follow snow peas and carrots recipe step 8.
7. Follow omelets recipe step 14, snow peas and carrots recipe step 9, and serve.

RECIPES

California Omelets

2 whole chicken breasts (about 1 pound total weight), skinned and boned
Salt
Freshly ground white pepper
Large red bell pepper
4 medium-size hearts of palm or artichoke hearts
6 tablespoons unsalted butter
2 teaspoons finely minced garlic
¼ cup finely chopped scallion greens
2 ounces Parmesan cheese
2 ounces Gruyère cheese
8 large eggs
1 tablespoon chopped fresh parsley for garnish

1. Cut chicken breasts into 2 x ¼-inch strips. Season with salt and pepper to taste.
2. Wash red pepper; halve, remove membranes, and seed. Slice each half into twelve ¼-inch strips.
3. Drain hearts of palm; dry with paper towels and slice into 2 x ¼-inch strips.
4. Melt 2 tablespoons butter in medium-size skillet. Add chicken breast strips and sauté about 5 minutes over medium-high heat, until lightly browned on all sides. Remove strips from pan and keep warm.
5. Reserve 12 strips of red pepper for garnish and add remainder to skillet along with garlic and scallions. Stirring constantly, cook over high heat about 4 minutes, until peppers are just crisp-tender. Set aside.
6. In food processor fitted with grating disk, or with cheese grater, grate cheeses to measure about ½ cup each; toss together.

7. Preheat oven to 200 degrees.

8. Beat eggs and ½ cup water in medium-size bowl. Season lightly with salt and pepper.

9. Melt 1 tablespoon butter in omelet pan over medium-high heat. When butter foams, make first of 4 omelets, using one quarter of egg mixture (see page 11). When omelet has set, in 40 to 60 seconds, remove from heat, and sprinkle with 1 teaspoon grated cheeses.

10. Lay one quarter of chicken breast strips down one half of omelet and top with one quarter of sautéed vegetables. With spatula, fold omelet in half, transfer to baking sheet, and set in oven to keep warm.

11. Repeat steps 9 and 10 for remaining omelets.

12. Remove omelets from oven. Adjust broiler rack to 4 inches from heat and turn oven to broil. Garnish each omelet with one quarter of the remaining cheese and red pepper strips.

13. Broil omelets 1 minute, or just until cheese has melted and begins to brown.

14. Transfer to plates and garnish with chopped parsley.

Snow Peas and Carrots Polonaise

1 large egg
2 medium-size carrots (about ½ pound total weight)
3 to 4 slices stale bread
3 to 6 tablespoons unsalted butter
1 teaspoon minced garlic
½ pound snow peas
1 tablespoon coarsely chopped fresh parsley

1. Boil egg 8 to 10 minutes, until very firm (see page 11).

2. Scrape carrots and cut diagonally into ¼-inch-thick slices.

3. Steam carrots 5 minutes, until barely cooked. Set aside.

4. Drain and peel egg; set aside.

5. Cube bread to measure 1½ cups. Melt 3 tablespoons butter in medium-size skillet, over medium-high heat. Sauté bread cubes and garlic, stirring frequently, adding more butter if necessary, about 3 minutes, until cubes are golden brown.

Stringing pea pods

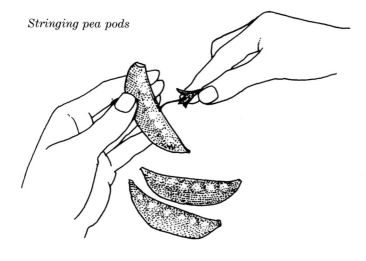

6. String pea pods and trim ends (see preceding illustration). Wash and drain. Place sautéed bread cubes and garlic, hard-boiled egg, and parsley in food processor fitted with steel blade and process until egg and parsley are chopped and mixed with the bread crumbs; or chop in wooden bowl with chopper. Set aside.

7. Add snow peas to carrots in vegetable steamer. Steam 2 to 3 minutes, or just until crisp-tender.

8. Transfer vegetables to baking dish and top with bread crumb mixture. Place under preheated broiler 2 to 3 minutes, or until crumbs begin to brown.

9. Divide snow peas and carrots among 4 dinner plates, arranging portions so that crumbs are on top.

ADDED TOUCH

Serve these crunchy, deep-fried morsels as an appetizer while you finish preparing the omelets and vegetables.

Vegetable Fritters with Garlic Butter

1 tablespoon vegetable oil, plus additional for deep frying
1½ to 2 cups flour
½ cup buttermilk
4 large eggs, lightly beaten
½ cup stale beer
Freshly grated nutmeg
Salt
2 cups fennel in julienne strips, or 1 cup grated carrot
1 stick unsalted butter
4 teaspoons minced garlic
½ cup finely chopped scallions
½ cup grated Cheddar cheese

1. Combine 1 tablespoon vegetable oil, 1½ cups flour, buttermilk, eggs, beer, and nutmeg and salt to taste. Whisk thoroughly to blend ingredients. If batter seems thin (it should be the consistency of muffin batter), beat in a little more flour. Let batter stand 1 hour.

2. Steam fennel 4 to 6 minutes, until slightly undercooked. Transfer to platter, allow to cool slightly, and refrigerate.

3. Melt butter over medium heat until foaming. Add minced garlic, reduce heat to low, and cook, stirring occasionally, about 3 minutes. Remove from heat and let stand until serving time.

4. Stir steamed fennel, finely chopped scallions, and grated Cheddar cheese into batter.

5. Preheat oven to 200 degrees.

6. Heat oil for deep frying to 375 degrees on a deep fat thermometer.

7. Drop batter by heaping tablespoons into hot oil. Cook fritters, a few at a time, about 2 to 3 minutes, until golden brown.

8. Drain fritters on paper towels. Keep warm in oven while remaining fritters are cooked.

9. Strain garlic butter through fine sieve or cheesecloth. Set briefly over medium-high heat just to warm.

10. Remove fritters from oven and serve immediately accompanied by garlic butter.

PASTA

Ed Giobbi

MENU 1 (Right)
Spaghettini with Salad Greens
Veal Chops in Paper Bags
Baked Asparagus

MENU 2
Macaroni Country Style
Orange and Olive Salad

MENU 3
Spaghettini Primavera
Fillet of Sole with Vegetables
Baked Spinach

Y ears ago, as an art student on a meager budget, Ed Giobbi—rather than eating inferior restaurant food—cut costs by cooking family-style, regional Italian meals at home. These menus were based on fresh seasonal vegetables, seafood, and pasta and seasoned simply with herbs—thus he learned that the appeal of authentic Italian cooking lies in its economy and its use of fresh foods. Now an internationally known painter, he still makes time in his day for cooking.

Contrary to the image many Americans have of most Italian food, when properly prepared it requires a minimum of oil and is a particularly low-fat (and even a low-calorie) cuisine. Ed Giobbi's three menus highlight both the seasonality and wholesomeness of Italian cooking. Menu 1 and Menu 3 are suitable for spring and summer dining: they feature vegetables that reach their flavor peak during warm weather. The salad in Menu 2, an ample winter meal, calls for fresh oranges, which are at their best in Italy in winter. The pasta, meat, and fresh produce in each menu are carefully balanced for nutrition, color, and flavor.

A native of Connecticut, Ed Giobbi is a first-generation American who nonetheless has lived many years in Italy, traveling throughout the country to familiarize himself with various regional favorites. He specializes in those from central Italy, particularly Abruzzo and the Marches, where seafood stews, grilled meats, and exceptionally good pasta are characteristic.

Dark linens and coordinated dinnerware make an appropriate, home-style backdrop for spaghettini with salad greens, veal chops, and asparagus spears. For a dramatic presentation, leave the veal chops in their paper wrapping and snip each bag open when you serve them. Garnish the baked asparagus with lemon crescents.

Spaghettini with Salad Greens
Veal Chops in Paper Bags
Baked Asparagus

Spaghettini with salad greens is really an appetizer, not a salad, but because it is a light dish, you can feature it as a main luncheon course with an accompanying platter of bread and cheese. If you wish to increase the pasta quantity to provide second helpings, Ed Giobbi suggests you prepare this recipe—as you should all pasta recipes—several times as it is. That way you know what taste to strive for when you increase quantities. Unlike other recipes, pasta with sauce cannot simply be doubled—larger quantities of hot cooked pasta will absorb more liquid, and you must adjust the sauce to provide that moisture.

Cooking food wrapped in paper is an excellent way to retain moisture in delicate lean meats such as veal and chicken. Before paper wrapping the chops, trim off any excess fat, then shake them in a sealed paper or plastic bag with flour to coat them. When you are ready to fill the paper bags for baking, place them in a baking dish in case the bags leak in the oven. Place a chop in each bag, ladle in the sauce, then crimp the tops of the bags closed. Rubbing the bags with oil helps to prevent their scorching. As the meat cooks, excess steam evaporates, causing the bags to rise and puff up. Serve the meal with the bags intact; snipping them open at the table releases an appetizing aroma. Paper bags are readily available and easy to use, but make sure you use clean, brown ones. You can use kitchen parchment instead, but avoid using foil, which traps the steam.

The asparagus bakes in an olive oil-based sauce. Since the distinctive flavor of the oil is important to the success of this recipe, select an imported extravirgin olive oil.

WHAT TO DRINK

The richly flavored sauce on the veal chops here calls for a light and elegant red wine—a young Taurasi or a young Barbaresco, or a light Cabernet or Merlot from California. A good white Graves is another alternative.

SHOPPING LIST AND STAPLES

4 veal chops, each about 1 inch thick
3 shallots
½ pound fresh mushrooms
1 bunch scallions
1 bunch fresh Italian parsley
1 pound fresh asparagus
1 lemon
1 tablespoon chopped fresh rosemary, or 1 teaspoon dried
5 cloves garlic
1 head Bibb lettuce
1 head escarole
1 head Belgian endive
1 bunch arugula
3 tablespoons butter
¾ pound spaghettini
3 tablespoons chicken broth
10 tablespoons olive oil
¼ cup red wine vinegar
½ cup flour
Salt and pepper
¾ cup Marsala, or ½ cup sweet sherry

UTENSILS

Large stockpot or kettle with cover
1 large or 2 medium-size skillets
Large baking dish
Medium-size oval or rectangular baking dish
Cup or small mixing bowl
Colander
Measuring cups and spoons
Chef's knife
Tongs
Salad spinner
4 lunch-size brown paper bags

START-TO-FINISH STEPS

1. Slice mushrooms and chop shallots, scallions, and rosemary for veal recipe. Chop parsley and mince garlic for veal and asparagus recipes. Follow veal recipe steps 1 through 6.
2. Follow pasta salad recipe steps 1 and 2.
3. Wedge lemon for asparagus recipe. Follow asparagus recipe steps 1 and 2.
4. As asparagus bakes, follow veal recipe step 7.
5. As veal bakes, follow pasta salad recipe steps 3 through 5.
6. Follow veal recipe step 8, and follow asparagus recipe step 3. Serve both with pasta salad.

RECIPES

Spaghettini with Salad Greens

1 head Bibb lettuce
1 head escarole

1 head Belgian endive
1 bunch arugula
¾ pound spaghettini
3 tablespoons olive oil
¼ cup wine vinegar
½ teaspoon minced garlic (optional)
Freshly ground black pepper
Salt

1. Bring water to a boil in large stockpot or kettle for pasta.
2. Wash greens, drain, and spin dry. Tear into bite-size pieces. There should be approximately 6 cups torn salad greens. Greens should be at room temperature.
3. Cook pasta in boiling salted water 5 to 7 minutes, or until *al dente*.
4. Mix oil, vinegar, and garlic, if desired, in cup or bowl.
5. When pasta is cooked, drain well in colander and put in serving bowl with salad greens. Pour dressing over pasta and toss to mix well. Add salt and pepper to taste.

Veal Chops in Paper Bags

4 veal chops, each about 1 inch thick
Salt
Freshly ground black pepper
¼ cup flour, for dredging
¼ cup olive oil
3 tablespoons butter
3 cups sliced fresh mushrooms (about ½ pound)
1½ tablespoons chopped shallots
2 cloves garlic, minced
½ cup coarsely chopped scallions
1 tablespoon chopped fresh rosemary, or 1 teaspoon dried
¾ cup Marsala, or ½ cup sweet sherry
3 tablespoons chicken broth
4 tablespoons chopped fresh Italian parsley

1. Preheat oven to 400 degrees.
2. Sprinkle chops with salt and pepper and dredge in flour, shaking off excess.
3. Heat oil and butter in skillet large enough to hold chops in 1 layer, or use 2 skillets. When oil is very hot, add chops and cook over high heat about 3 minutes, turning constantly until browned. Remove chops from skillet.
4. Lower heat under skillet and add mushrooms, shallots, garlic, scallions, rosemary, salt, and pepper. Stir constantly until mixture begins to brown.
5. Add Marsala, chicken broth, and chops. Cook over high heat until sauce thickens slightly, about 5 minutes. Turn chops over occasionally. When sauce has thickened, turn off heat.
6. Using paper towel, completely grease outside of 4 lunch-size clean, brown paper bags to prevent bags from charring.
7. Gently place 1 chop in each bag, and then put mushrooms and sauce on top of each chop. Sprinkle 1 tablespoon of the parsley on each chop. Crimp bags and place in

baking dish. Bake 10 to 15 minutes, depending on how pink you like veal.
8. Serve chops in paper bags, opening bags at table.

Baked Asparagus

1 pound fresh asparagus
2 small cloves garlic, minced
Salt
Freshly ground black pepper
4 tablespoons chopped fresh Italian parsley
3 tablespoons olive oil
4 lemon wedges

1. Preheat oven to 400 degrees.
2. Wash and drain asparagus. Cut off and discard tough ends. Place asparagus tightly together in baking pan. Sprinkle with garlic, salt, pepper, parsley, and oil. Bake uncovered until asparagus is firm to the bite, 15 to 20 minutes, depending on thickness.
3. Serve with lemon wedges.

ADDED TOUCH

This cake, which takes about an hour to make—including baking time—calls for fresh seasonal fruit, and you can vary the fruit combination to suit your taste.

Torta di Frutta

The filling:
½ cup milk
1 egg
⅓ cup vegetable oil
⅓ cup sugar
1 cup flour
1½ teaspoons baking powder
½ teaspoon salt

The topping:
½ cup sugar
¼ cup flour
⅛ teaspoon salt
¼ cup dried lemon peel
2 tablespoons vegetable oil
1 teaspoon lemon juice
1½ cups fresh seasonal fruit, washed, peeled, and cut into bite-size pieces

1. Preheat oven to 375 degrees.
2. For filling, mix together egg, milk, and vegetable oil. Add sugar, and mix until well blended. In separate bowl, mix flour, baking powder, and salt. Add mixture to egg-milk mixture and blend.
3. Grease medium-size baking dish, and add mixture to dish.
4. Make topping by combining sugar, flour, salt, dried lemon peel, vegetable oil, and lemon juice. Mix until well blended.
5. Sprinkle topping on cake batter, then add 1½ cups of fresh fruit. Place cake in oven and bake 30 minutes, or until done.

Macaroni Country Style
Orange and Olive Salad

Pass the macaroni country style on a large, plain platter. Put the orange and olive salad in a glass bowl to add bright color.

The pasta, potato, broccoli, mushrooms, cheese, herbs, and wine in Ed Giobbi's macaroni country-style recipe make an ideal one-pot meal—a gratifying lunch or dinner for a brisk day. Besides being rich in texture and color, it is nutritionally complete—the broccoli contains vitamin A, and the cheese and ham are rich in protein and together contribute vitamins A, B, and D. The potato adds only a few calories and also contributes calcium and vitamin C.

The combination of potato with pasta is by no means unusual. The idea comes straight from a turn-of-the-century northern Italian cookbook. As practical Italian cooks

have always known, pasta cooked in the same water with potato acquires an invisible starchy coating that makes any sauce adhere better. The sauce in this recipe is based on white wine, rather than the more conventional tomato or cream.

The orange and olive salad is a southern Italian specialty from Ed Giobbi's uncle's kitchen. It may have originated centuries ago in Greece and may also owe something to Arab cooking. Southern Italian cooking has ancient connections from all around the Mediterranean—North Africa and the Mideast, as well as Greece. Leaving the oranges unpeeled not only saves preparation time but adds the pungency of the peel to the salad flavors. You will need a sharp knife and fork for the salad. The cured black olives—Mediterranean favorites—have a wrinkled, almost dried appearance. Additionally, they have a slightly bitter aftertaste that, in this salad, counterbalances the sweetness of the sliced oranges.

WHAT TO DRINK

Serve this meal with simple wines of good quality to show off the virtues of the down-to-earth ingredients. Try a good bottle of Valpolicella or a Beaujolais if you want red wine, Soave or Muscadet if you prefer white.

SHOPPING LIST AND STAPLES

¼ pound boiled ham, sliced ½ inch thick
1 bunch broccoli
2 medium-size potatoes
1 medium-size onion
⅛ pound fresh mushrooms
1 bunch fresh Italian parsley
1 clove garlic
4 navel oranges
1 bunch watercress (optional)
½ pound dried-cured black olives, preferably Italian or Greek
2 tablespoons butter
¼ pound Parmesan cheese
½ pound rigatoni or other tubular pasta
¼ cup olive oil
1½ teaspoons chopped fresh marjoram, or ½ teaspoon dried
Salt and pepper
½ cup dry white wine

UTENSILS

Large stockpot or kettle with cover
Heavy skillet with cover
Small bowl
Colander
Measuring cups and spoons
Chef's knife
Potato peeler or small knife
Grater

START-TO-FINISH STEPS

1. Follow salad recipe steps 1 through 3.
2. Slice mushrooms and onion, chop herbs, grate Parmesan cheese, and cube ham for pasta recipe.
3. Follow pasta recipe steps 1 through 6.
4. Follow salad recipe step 4.
5. Serve pasta and salad.

RECIPES

Macaroni Country Style

Salt
1 bunch broccoli, cut into flowerets
2 medium-size potatoes
2 tablespoons olive oil
2 tablespoons butter
1 medium-size onion, thinly sliced
¼ pound boiled ham, sliced ½ inch thick and cut into cubes
½ cup sliced mushrooms (about ⅛ pound)
Freshly ground black pepper
½ pound rigatoni or other tubular pasta
½ cup dry white wine
1½ teaspoons chopped fresh marjoram, or ½ teaspoon dried
2 tablespoons chopped fresh Italian parsley
½ cup freshly grated Parmesan cheese

1. In large stockpot or kettle, bring salted water to a boil for pasta.
2. Trim broccoli. Peel potatoes and cut them into ¼-inch dice. There should be about 1 cup.
3. Heat oil and butter in skillet and sauté onion until wilted. Add ham, mushrooms, and pepper, and cook, stirring, 3 or 4 minutes.
4. Add pasta to boiling water.
5. Add wine, marjoram, and 1 tablespoon of the parsley to ham mixture. Cover and simmer over low heat.
6. When water has reached a rolling boil, add potatoes and broccoli. Cook until pasta is *al dente*. Drain pasta and vegetables in colander and put in large serving bowl. Add ham sauce and toss well. Add cheese and the remaining parsley.

Orange and Olive Salad

4 navel oranges
1 cup dried-cured black olives
1 clove garlic
¼ cup olive oil
1 bunch watercress for garnish (optional)

1. Wash skins of oranges thoroughly and cut whole oranges into thin slices. Do not peel.
2. Pit olives and cut into about 4 pieces. Set aside.
3. Rub salad bowl with peeled garlic and then discard garlic. Arrange orange slices in bowl.
4. Just before serving, add olives and sprinkle with olive oil. Toss gently. Garnish with watercress, if desired.

ADDED TOUCH

Since the main dish is filling, the best dessert is a bowl of fresh fruit—even though the salad features fruit. Serve pears and apples and, for a nice contrast, try adding some Italian cheeses. Gorgonzola (akin to Roquefort) is traditional with pears, and Bel Paese goes well with tart apples.

Spaghettini Primavera
Fillet of Sole with Vegetables
Baked Spinach

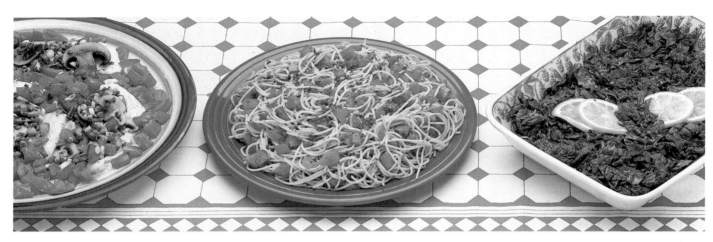

Serve the pasta primavera with the meal or, if you prefer, as a first course while the fillet of sole and the spinach finish cooking.

Spaghettini primavera is a popular late-spring, early summer dish in the central regions of Italy. It combines two Italian favorites: pasta and fresh raw tomatoes. The American version of this pasta dish can include—in addition to or instead of the tomatoes—a combination of garden-fresh vegetables, available from spring through the fall. (The vegetables for pasta primavera should always be blanched until they are crisp-tender before you add them to the cooked pasta.) Ed Giobbi, who helped to popularize pasta primavera in the United States, says that you should make this dish only when you can purchase the very best, freshest seasonal vegetables.

Sweet and tender fillets of sole take careful handling during and after cooking because they tend to fall apart easily. If fresh sole is not available in your market, you can use other thin white-fleshed fish, such as small red snapper or small bass fillets. Try to avoid using frozen fish — the texture and the taste do not compare to fresh.

A casserole of baked spinach rounds out this well-balanced nutritious meal. Use fresh rather than frozen spinach if possible. You can buy fresh spinach in bulk by the pound or prewashed in plastic bags. In either case, pick out spinach with crisp, dark-green leaves. Do not buy any that looks wilted. Raw spinach, stored in a plastic bag, keeps for up to five days in the refrigerator. Before cooking the spinach, immerse it in cold water, rinse it thoroughly, and repeat the process two or three times, tasting a leaf or two at random to make sure the grit is gone. Lemon juice, garlic, and freshly ground black pepper—as in this recipe—are perfect partners for spinach.

WHAT TO DRINK

The pronounced tomato flavor in this menu requires bright, fruity, acidic white wines to match it. Your best choice is from the young Italian white wines, especially the northern Pinot Grigio or the southern Greco di Tufo.

SHOPPING LIST AND STAPLES

4 fillets of sole or other white-fleshed fish
   (about 7 inches long)
8 medium-size tomatoes
2 pounds fresh spinach
1 bunch fresh basil
1 bunch fresh Italian parsley
½ pound fresh mushrooms
1 bunch scallions
4 cloves garlic
2 lemons
1½ tablespoons butter
¾ pound spaghettini or linguine
10½ tablespoons olive oil
Salt and pepper

UTENSILS

Food processor or blender
Large stockpot or kettle with cover
Oven-proof casserole
Shallow baking tray

Medium-size skillet
Colander
Measuring cups and spoons
Chef's knife
Long metal turner

START-TO-FINISH STEPS

1. Chop garlic, tomatoes, and parsley for pasta recipe.
2. Follow pasta recipe steps 1 and 2.
3. Slice mushrooms, chop scallions and parsley, and cube tomatoes for sole recipe, and follow sole recipe steps 1 through 3.
4. Wash spinach and mince garlic for spinach recipe, and follow spinach recipe steps 1 and 2.
5. As spinach bakes, follow sole recipe step 4.
6. As sole bakes, follow pasta recipe steps 3 and 4.
7. Slice lemons for spinach recipe, and follow spinach recipe step 3; serve with sole and pasta.

RECIPES

Spaghettini Primavera

2 tablespoons salt
1½ teaspoons coarsely chopped garlic
3 tablespoons olive oil
¼ cup loosely packed fresh basil
3 cups coarsely chopped ripe tomatoes (about
    4 medium-size)
1½ tablespoons chopped fresh Italian parsley
Freshly ground black pepper
¾ pound spaghettini or linguine

1. Bring water to a boil in stockpot or kettle for pasta. Add 2 tablespoons salt.
2. Puree garlic, olive oil, and basil in blender or food processor. Fold in tomatoes and parsley. Or, if you prefer, puree all ingredients together for smoother sauce. Season to taste.
3. Cook pasta in rapidly boiling water, stirring often.
4. When pasta is cooked *al dente*, drain in colander and put in warm serving bowl. Add sauce and blend well. Or put pasta in individual bowls and spoon sauce over, letting each person mix his or her own at table.

Fillet of Sole with Vegetables

1½ tablespoons butter
4½ tablespoons olive oil
2 cups thinly sliced fresh mushrooms (about ½ pound)
4 fillets of sole or other white-fleshed fish
    (about 7 inches long)
1 lemon
Salt
Freshly ground black pepper
1½ cups chopped scallions
2 tablespoons chopped fresh Italian parsley
3 cups cubed ripe tomatoes (about 4 medium-size)

1. Preheat oven to 500 degrees.
2. Heat butter and 1½ tablespoons oil in skillet and sauté mushrooms until all moisture cooks out.
3. Arrange fish fillets on baking tray in 1 layer. Squeeze lemon juice on each fillet and season with salt and pepper. Sprinkle with dash of olive oil. Spread each fillet with layer of mushrooms, scallions, and parsley and mound of tomatoes. Season again with salt and pepper and then sprinkle with remaining olive oil.
4. Place fish in oven and cook about 6 minutes. Do not overcook. As soon as fish separates, it is done. Remove with long metal turner to be certain fillets remain intact.

Baked Spinach

3 tablespoons olive oil
2 small cloves garlic, minced
2 pounds fresh spinach, well washed and trimmed
Salt
Freshly ground black pepper
4 lemon slices

1. Preheat oven to 500 degrees.
2. Pour oil into oven-proof casserole. Add garlic, spinach, salt, and pepper. Cover and bake about 10 minutes, stirring once or twice.
3. Serve with lemon slices.

ADDED TOUCH

Potato balls make an extra vegetable dish to round out the meal. This recipe calls for pine nuts, which are expensive and often difficult to find. If you wish, you can substitute your favorite nuts for them.

Potato Balls

2 medium-size Idaho potatoes (1 pound)
2½ tablespoons pine nuts, chopped
½ tablespoon olive oil
1½ tablespoons chopped Italian parsley
Salt
Freshly ground black pepper
Lightly beaten egg white from 1 small egg
Dry unflavored bread crumbs (about 1 cup)
Corn oil (about 2 cups)
1 lemon, wedged

1. Boil potatoes; peel and mash them.
2. Add pine nuts, olive oil, parsley, salt, and pepper and mix well. Form balls about size of walnuts (1 heaping tablespoon). Roll each ball in egg white, then in bread crumbs.
3. Heat ¾ inch of corn oil in skillet. When very hot, place some of the potato balls in oil with tongs. If oil is not hot enough, potato balls will fall apart. Cook balls, turning gently with tongs, until golden brown. Drain on paper towels. Repeat process until all potato balls are cooked. Serve with lemon wedges.

Diane Darrow and Tom Maresca

D iane Darrow and Tom Maresca, a husband-wife team living in New York City, favor the Italian custom of eating several small courses rather than building their meal around one large main course. Their at-home suppers may consist of only an antipasto and pasta or only a pasta and a salad and perhaps a loaf of Italian bread. Their desserts are usually seasonal fruits served with a platter of cheese—also an Italian custom.

The Darrow-Maresca approach to dining is reflected in their menus, which progress through several balanced courses, all suitable for informal meals. Menu 2, an elegant party dinner, is the only exception, with its unusual first course of veal tartare and a delicate second course of capelli d'angelo, or "angel's hair" pasta. Menu 1 is an economical meatless meal, and its pasta course is spaghetti, teamed here with peppers, eggplant, and tomatoes. These vegetables are simmered together and seasoned with garlic, capers, anchovies, and a grating of sharp Romano cheese. Menu 3, which features rigatoni dressed with a sauce of mushrooms and chicken livers, does not call for any seasonal produce, so you can serve it at any time of year. Menu 4, a satisfying Italian country-style meal, is designed for cold-weather dining.

You can serve the antipasto dish of sliced tomatoes and tuna sauce—garnished with black olives, Italian parsley, and crossed lemon slices—while you heat a loaf of Italian bread. Then bring on the main course of spaghetti with peppers, eggplant, and tomatoes, served in a rimmed platter, and the hot bread. Pass the freshly grated Romano separately.

229

Sliced Tomatoes with Tuna Sauce
Spaghetti with Peppers, Eggplant, and Tomatoes

This economical meatless summer menu features two seasonal favorites—ripe tomatoes and eggplants. The first course of tomatoes in tuna sauce is a variation of *vitello tonnato*, a classic dish that features thinly sliced veal steeped in a creamy tuna and anchovy-based sauce. By substituting sliced tomatoes for veal, Diane Darrow and Tom Maresca have created something much lighter. If vine-ripened tomatoes are not in season, they suggest that you use slices of peeled and thinly sliced raw celery root, roasted and peeled green peppers, or raw crisp zucchini. To crisp fresh zucchini, place whole zucchini in a bowl of ice water in the refrigerator early in the morning and leave them to chill for the day. At serving time, remove the zucchini from the water, dry them thoroughly, and slice thinly. For a richer tuna flavor, buy canned Italian tuna packed in olive oil.

Like many Italian recipes, this one calls for fresh basil, generally available only in the summer season. Rather than using dried basil, which does not have the same mild minty flavor, they recommend that you freeze batches of fresh basil for year-round use. See the sidebar on basil in the introduction for instructions and suggestions.

The first course should be garnished with imported Moroccan or Sicilian olives. If you cannot find them, substitute any kind of oil-cured ripe olive. A decorative trick for garnishing this dish—and one that is simple to do—is to slice and arrange the lemons in the following manner. Take center-cut, round lemon slices and cut them in half. Notch the center of one half through the flesh and almost through the rind. Slip uncut halves into the notches so the pieces will stand up at right angles forming an arched X. Add an olive or a sprig of parsley.

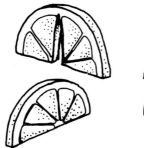 

The spaghetti recipe is a variation of a traditional Sicilian dish. If possible, buy small Italian or Oriental eggplants, about the length of a finger, which are sweeter and have fewer seeds than the larger ones.

WHAT TO DRINK

Summer flavors like these call for a cold white wine with some body and depth. Try an Italian Greco di Tufo or a Cortese, or a California Sauvignon or Fumé Blanc. Marsala—sweet or dry—goes well with the fruit dessert.

SHOPPING LIST AND STAPLES

1½ pounds ripe tomatoes
½ pound eggplant, preferably long slender small ones
2 large red or yellow bell peppers (about ¾ pound)
2 lemons plus 1 lemon (optional)
1 bunch fresh basil
2 large cloves garlic
1 egg
¼ pound pecorino Romano cheese
14-ounce can Italian plum tomatoes
3 anchovy fillets, preferably salt packed
2 tablespoons plus 2 teaspoons capers
8 Sicilian or Moroccan black olives, not brine packed
7-ounce can dark-meat tuna packed in olive oil
1 pound spaghetti
1 loaf Italian or French bread
1 cup plus 5 tablespoons olive oil
1 teaspoon Dijon mustard
Salt and pepper

UTENSILS

Food processor or blender
Large stockpot or kettle with cover
Nonaluminum sauté pan or casserole with cover
Colander
Measuring cups and spoons
Chef's knife
Wooden spatula
Grater
Juicer

START-TO-FINISH STEPS

1. Juice 2 lemons and slice third lemon for garnish, if desired, for tomato recipe. Grate cheese and chop 2 teaspoons basil for pasta recipe. Measure out 1 cup of the canned tomatoes with their juice for pasta recipe.

2. Follow pasta recipe steps 1 through 5. When water comes to a boil, preheat oven to 350 degrees.
3. Follow pasta recipe step 6.
4. Follow tomato recipe steps 1 through 3.
5. Follow pasta recipe steps 7 and 8. Warm bread in oven.
6. Follow tomato recipe steps 4 through 6.
7. Follow pasta recipe steps 9 and 10. Serve with tomatoes.

RECIPES

Sliced Tomatoes with Tuna Sauce

1 egg
2 tablespoons lemon juice
1 teaspoon Dijon mustard
⅛ teaspoon salt
1 cup olive oil
7-ounce can dark-meat tuna packed in olive oil
1 anchovy fillet
2 tablespoons capers
1½ pounds ripe tomatoes
8 Sicilian or Moroccan black olives, not brine packed
Lemon slices for garnish (optional)
1 loaf Italian or French bread

1. Put egg, 1 tablespoon of the lemon juice, mustard, and salt into bowl of blender or food processor. Process 1 minute with metal blade.
2. With machine running, add ¼ cup of the olive oil in stream of droplets. Then gradually add the remaining oil.
3. Add tuna and all its oil, anchovy, the remaining 1 tablespoon of lemon juice, and capers. Blend until sauce is smooth.
4. Slice tomatoes ¼ inch thick.
5. Choose serving platter large enough to hold all tomato slices in 1 or 2 layers with minimal overlap. Spread platter with thin layer of the tuna sauce. Place tomato slices on sauce and spoon the remaining sauce over. Refrigerate until ready to serve.
6. At serving time, garnish platter with black olives and slices of lemon, as desired. Serve with loaf of fresh Italian or French bread, warmed 5 minutes in 350-degree oven.

Spaghetti with Peppers, Eggplant, and Tomatoes

½ pound eggplant
2 anchovy fillets
2 teaspoons capers
5 tablespoons olive oil
2 large cloves garlic, unpeeled
2 large red or yellow bell peppers (about ¾ pound)
2 teaspoons chopped fresh basil, or 2 teaspoons frozen
1 cup canned Italian plum tomatoes, coarsely
    chopped, with juices
Salt
Freshly ground black pepper
1 pound spaghetti

⅔ cup freshly grated pecorino Romano cheese

1. Peel eggplant and chop into ½-inch pieces.
2. Rinse salt from anchovy fillets, pat dry, and cut each into 2 or 3 pieces. Rinse and drain capers. Set aside.
3. Warm olive oil in nonaluminum sauté pan or casserole. Add eggplant, anchovies, and unpeeled garlic cloves. Sauté over moderate heat, stirring occasionally, 5 to 8 minutes, or until eggplant is soft.
4. Wash peppers, slice in half, and remove seeds and membranes. Cut crosswise into ¼-inch strips. Roughly chop tomatoes.
5. Bring stockpot or kettle of water to a boil for pasta. Add 2 tablespoons salt and bring to a rolling boil.
6. When eggplant is soft, add peppers, tomatoes, capers, and basil to sauté pan. Stir well. Bring to a simmer, cover, and cook over medium heat, stirring occasionally, 12 to 15 minutes, or until peppers are tender.
7. Meanwhile, cook spaghetti in boiling water until *al dente*.
8. Remove garlic cloves from sauce and discard. Taste for seasoning and add salt, if necessary, and generous amount of pepper. Set sauce aside until pasta is ready.
9. Drain spaghetti in colander and then return it to stockpot. Add half of the sauce and toss to coat thoroughly; then add half of the cheese and toss again. Keep warm in turned-off oven while serving first course.
10. When ready to serve, heat the remaining sauce and add to spaghetti, tossing well. Serve the remaining cheese at table.

ADDED TOUCH

For a light, elegant dessert for this meal, use sweet fresh peaches. Slice them in half and fill with crumbled *amaretti*—Italian macaroons—brandy, and unsweetened cocoa, all of which are complementary flavors for summer-ripe peaches.

Baked Stuffed Peaches

4 large firm ripe freestone peaches
3 ounces *amaretti* cookies (about 14)
1½ tablespoons sugar
1½ teaspoons unsweetened cocoa
1 teaspoon brandy
1 tablespoon butter

1. Preheat oven to 350 degrees.
2. Wash and dry peaches, but do not peel. Cut in half and remove stones. With teaspoon, scoop out some of the pulp to enlarge cavities, but leave wall about ½ inch thick all around.
3. Mince removed pulp and place in small bowl. Crumble *amaretti* cookies into bowl, and stir into peach pulp along with sugar, cocoa, and brandy. Stuff peaches with mixture.
4. Butter 4 individual oblong gratin dishes, and set 2 stuffed peach halves in each. Bake 30 minutes. Serve hot, warm, or at room temperature.

Veal Tartare
Capelli d'Angelo with Asparagus Sauce

Asparagus and mushrooms tossed with prosciutto and served on a bed of slender pasta follow the first course of veal tartare.

For veal tartare, you must use good-quality lean veal, preferably ground at the very last moment. The best cuts of veal for this recipe come from the leg or the more economical shoulder cut. If you have a food processor or meat grinder, grind the veal at home just before serving the meal. Otherwise, have it ground at the meat counter the same day you serve it. Be sure that the grinding equipment is very clean in either case. If the butcher is doing the grinding, tell him you intend to serve the meat raw. Keep the veal well chilled until you use it and do not save any leftovers, since ground raw meat spoils quickly. (Note: most doctors now advise pregnant women to eat no raw meat at all.) The lemon juice, which you sprinkle over the veal, does all the "cooking" necessary for the raw meat dish.

The pasta is a springtime dish since it features fresh asparagus. Capelli d'angelo, or "angel's hair," is the slenderest of all Italian pastas. Because it cooks quickly, you must watch it carefully. Fresh angel hair pasta will cook in just under one minute, the dried in one to two minutes.

WHAT TO DRINK

A full-bodied white wine or a light red is the right wine to accompany this elegant meal: either a good-quality California Chardonnay or an Italian Cabernet would be best. In either case, the younger the better.

SHOPPING LIST AND STAPLES

1 pound lean veal shoulder or tenderloin
2 slices prosciutto (about 1 ounce)
1 pound fresh asparagus, preferably no more than ½ inch thick
¾ pound fresh mushrooms
1 yellow or red Bermuda onion
2 lemons
1 bunch fresh parsley (optional)
4 tablespoons butter
2 eggs
½ pound Parmesan cheese

1 pound capelli d'angelo
1 cup chicken or beef broth
2-ounce jar capers (optional)
1 small loaf firm white sandwich bread
½ cup plus 3 tablespoons olive oil
2 tablespoons flour
2 teaspoons chopped fresh thyme, or ½ teaspoon dried
Salt and pepper

UTENSILS

Food processor or meat grinder
Large stockpot or kettle with cover
Large skillet with cover
Small skillet
Medium-size saucepan
3 small mixing bowls
Colander
Measuring cups and spoons
Chef's knife
Grater

START-TO-FINISH STEPS

1. Grate cheese for pasta and veal recipes.
2. Follow pasta recipe steps 1 through 4.
3. Mince onion and parsley for veal recipe. Juice lemons for veal recipe.
4. Follow veal recipe steps 1 through 4. Refrigerate.
5. Follow pasta recipe steps 5 through 9.
6. Follow veal recipe steps 5 and 6 and serve.
7. Follow pasta recipe step 10 and serve.

RECIPES

Veal Tartare

1 pound lean veal shoulder or tenderloin
2 teaspoons salt
3 tablespoons lemon juice
2 tablespoons finely minced onion
½ teaspoon freshly ground black pepper
½ cup olive oil
¼ pound fresh mushrooms
¼ cup freshly grated Parmesan cheese
Minced parsley and/or capers for garnish (optional)
3 slices firm white bread, crusts trimmed, cut into
   triangles

1. Carefully trim veal and discard any sinew and fat.
2. In bowl, dissolve salt in lemon juice. Add onion, pepper, and olive oil. Mix well.
3. Slice mushrooms very thin. In bowl, toss with 3 tablespoons of the dressing from step 2.
4. Grind veal in food processor or meat grinder. Add cheese and mix in well. Pour in dressing and process briefly until mixed.

5. Mound veal on individual plates. Surround with decorative ring of mushroom slices and garnish with parsley and/or capers, as desired.
6. Just before serving, toast bread triangles. Serve with veal and pass pepper mill at table.

Capelli d'Angelo with Asparagus Sauce

1 pound fresh asparagus
½ pound fresh mushrooms
3 tablespoons olive oil
Salt
3 tablespoons plus 2 teaspoons butter
Freshly ground black pepper
2 teaspoons chopped fresh thyme, or ½ teaspoon dried
2 tablespoons flour
1 cup chicken or beef broth
2 eggs
1 cup freshly grated Parmesan cheese
2 slices prosciutto (about 1 ounce)
1 pound capelli d'angelo

1. Preheat oven to 200 degrees.
2. Bring water to a boil in stockpot or kettle for pasta. Also bring saucepan of water to a boil for asparagus.
3. Snap off and discard tough bottoms of asparagus. Wash spears and cut into 1-inch lengths. Blanch in boiling water 1 minute, then run under cold water to stop cooking. Separate tips from stalks, and set both parts aside.
4. Wipe mushrooms and cut into ¼-inch slices.
5. Heat olive oil in large skillet. Add mushrooms and sauté over high heat about 1 minute, stirring constantly, until they take up all oil. Turn heat to low, sprinkle mushrooms lightly with salt, and continue cooking—stirring—until they begin to exude juices, about 1 more minute. Turn heat to medium-high, and cook about 1 minute more, stirring, until slices are tender.
6. Add 3 tablespoons of the butter to saucepan and, when melted, add cut-up asparagus stalks (not tips) and thyme. Add salt and pepper to taste and sauté over moderate heat 3 to 4 minutes, depending on thickness of asparagus. Sprinkle flour over vegetables, and stir 1 minute. Add broth, bring to a boil, and simmer 1 minute. Cover sauce and set aside until ready to use.
7. In bowl, mix eggs, cheese, ½ teaspoon salt, and ½ teaspoon pepper.
8. Cut prosciutto slices into ¼-inch strips and warm together with asparagus tips in small skillet with the remaining 2 teaspoons of the butter. Keep warm in turned-off oven.
9. Plunge capelli d'angelo into boiling water and watch it very carefully—it cooks quickly. When *al dente*, drain well, turn back into stockpot, and toss thoroughly with half of the asparagus sauce. Keep warm in turned-off oven.
10. When ready to serve, toss with egg-and-cheese mixture and the remaining asparagus sauce. Turn into warm serving bowl and scatter prosciutto and asparagus tips over top.

Mozzarella Tart
Rigatoni with Mushroom and Chicken Liver Sauce
Spinach and Chicory Salad

This is an economical family meal, suitable for any time of year. The rigatoni dish, of Neapolitan origins, takes advantage of the affinity between chicken livers and mushrooms. The two are sautéed together, then simmered in a light tomato sauce. A large tubular pasta such as rigatoni is a logical choice for this thick, chunky sauce.

The mozzarella tart, which may sound complicated, is actually a quick-to-assemble dish. Treat the bread slices as if you were making French toast, and once they have soaked up the egg dip, layer the cheese over the bread.

Chunky rigatoni, served with a mushroom and chicken liver sauce, accompanies the mozzarella tart appetizer. A mixed green salad, a brightly colored table setting, and an ivy plant centerpiece make the meal even more appealing.

WHAT TO DRINK

For this meal you will need a hearty wine with some degree of complexity in its flavor: a Barbera or Dolcetto from the Piedmont in northern Italy would be fine. You can also try a full-bodied Zinfandel from California. If you decide to make the dessert, save some Marsala to sip after dessert along with your coffee.

SHOPPING LIST AND STAPLES

½ pound chicken livers
2 ounces prosciutto
2 ounces prosciutto fat, or fat from
    any good cured ham
½ pound fresh mushrooms

1 large yellow Bermuda onion
6 ounces crisp fresh spinach
6 ounces chicory
1 lemon
1 bunch fresh basil, or ¾ teaspoon frozen
14 tablespoons butter (1¾ sticks)
1 bunch fresh parsley (optional)
1 egg
½ cup milk
½ pound mozzarella cheese
¼ pound Parmesan cheese
1 pound rigatoni
14-ounce can Italian plum tomatoes
8 anchovy fillets, preferably salt packed
1 loaf French or Italian bread
3 tablespoons olive oil
1 teaspoon fennel seeds or dried oregano,
    or ½ teaspoon each
Salt and pepper
1 cup dry red wine

Small bowl (optional)
Colander
Measuring cups and spoons
Chef's knife
Wooden spatula
Grater
Food mill
Salad spinner
Whisk or blender

UTENSILS

. Large stockpot or kettle with cover
Large heavy-bottomed casserole with cover
Shallow baking dish (about 9 by 12 inches)
Medium-size mixing bowl

START-TO-FINISH STEPS

1. Chop herbs for pasta recipe. Juice lemon for salad.
2. Follow pasta recipe steps 1 through 7. As water comes to a boil and sauce simmers, follow tart recipe steps 1 through 6. As tart bakes, follow pasta recipe step 8 and salad recipe step 1.
3. Serve mozzarella tart.
4. Follow pasta recipe step 9.
5. Follow salad recipe step 2, and serve with pasta.

RECIPES

Mozzarella Tart

2 tablespoons butter, softened
1 egg yolk

½ cup milk

8 anchovy fillets

8 slices French or Italian bread, about ½ inch thick (crusts trimmed, if desired)

½ pound mozzarella cheese

1 teaspoon fennel seeds or dried oregano, or ½ teaspoon each

2 tablespoons freshly grated Parmesan cheese

1. Preheat oven to 400 degrees.

2. Generously grease baking dish.

3. Put egg yolk, milk, and anchovy fillets into blender and blend until smooth, or mash anchovy with egg yolk in small bowl and beat in milk with whisk.

4. Arrange bread slices in 1 layer in baking dish and moisten each slice with 1½ tablespoons of the blended liquid. Try not to let mixture spill over onto bottom of pan. If bread is reluctant to take up liquid, pierce it here and there with fork to hasten absorption. You can dip bread slices into blended liquid, but you do not want them too soggy.

5. Cut mozzarella into thin slices and lay evenly over bread. Sprinkle fennel or oregano over top; or put fennel on half of the slices and oregano on the other half. Sprinkle Parmesan evenly over all.

6. Bake uncovered 20 minutes, or until cheese is bubbly and just starting to brown on top. Let sit 5 minutes before serving.

Rigatoni with Mushroom and Chicken Liver Sauce

⅔ cup chopped onions

2 ounces prosciutto fat, or fat from any good cured ham

½ pound fresh mushrooms

4 slices prosciutto (about 2 ounces)

½ pound chicken livers

12 tablespoons butter (1½ sticks)

1 cup dry red wine

2 cups canned Italian plum tomatoes, drained

Freshly ground black pepper

¾ teaspoon chopped fresh basil, or ¾ teaspoon frozen

Salt

1 pound rigatoni

½ cup freshly grated Parmesan cheese

¾ teaspoon chopped fresh parsley for garnish (optional)

1. Finely chop onion together with prosciutto fat.

2. Wipe mushrooms and cut into thin slices. Cut prosciutto into ¼-inch strips.

3. Trim chicken livers, removing and discarding any bits of fat or membrane, and cut each into pieces no larger than 1 inch.

4. Put salted water on to boil for pasta in stockpot or kettle.

5. Set casserole over low heat. Melt 4 tablespoons of the butter and sauté onion and prosciutto fat until fat is rendered and onion is translucent—about 2 minutes. Add mushrooms and chopped prosciutto and continue to simmer, stirring often, another 2 minutes. Add livers and

sauté, stirring 1 minute, or until they have just lost raw red color.

6. Raise heat, pour in wine, and cook, stirring, until wine is completely evaporated. Set food mill fitted with medium-size blade over casserole, and mill in tomatoes. Add generous amount of pepper. If using frozen basil, add it to sauce now.

7. Bring sauce to a boil, reduce heat to maintain gentle simmer, and cook, covered, 15 to 20 minutes, or until tomatoes have completely dissolved and sauce is slightly thickened. Taste for salt. If prosciutto is very salty, none may be needed.

8. Meanwhile, cook rigatoni in boiling water until *al dente*, 15 to 18 minutes. Drain pasta in colander and return to stockpot. Toss with the remaining 8 tablespoons butter, cut into several pieces. Add grated Parmesan cheese and half of the sauce, tossing well after each. Keep warm in turned-off oven.

9. When ready to serve, add the remaining sauce and toss well. Turn into large warm serving bowl and sprinkle chopped fresh basil over top. If you used frozen basil in sauce, garnish with chopped parsley, if desired.

Spinach and Chicory Salad

6 ounces crisp fresh spinach

6 ounces chicory

Scant ¼ teaspoon salt

2 teaspoons lemon juice

2 to 3 tablespoons olive oil

1. Remove and discard spinach stems. Wash spinach and chicory carefully; drain and spin dry. Tear leaves into bite-size pieces and put in large salad bowl. There will be about 4 cups torn salad greens.

2. At serving time, put salt and lemon juice into bowl of salad serving spoon. Stir with salad serving fork to dissolve salt. Sprinkle this over greens, and then sprinkle olive oil over. Toss thoroughly.

ADDED TOUCH

Zabaglione, a rich egg custard, is a favorite Italian dessert that you can serve at room temperature or chilled. Its classic flavoring is Marsala, a sweetish Italian dessert wine. You can also make this dessert with **Madeira**.

Zabaglione

3 egg yolks

3 tablespoons sugar

⅓ cup dry Marsala

1. Put yolks and sugar in top of double boiler but not over water. With whisk or hand-held electric mixer, whip until they become pale cream color.

2. Set double-boiler top over simmering water, add **Marsala**, and continue beating, about 3 minutes, until cream foams and mounds into smooth custard.

3. Scoop into individual serving dishes and serve at once, preferably with crisp nut cookies.

Roasted Peppers and Anchovies on Italian Bread
Pappardelle alla Contadina
Fennel and Red Onion Salad

Country-style noodles look best on a bright pottery plate. Pass the peppers before or during the meal, and serve the salad separately.

The appetizer in this country-style, cold-weather meal combines three classic Italian flavors—roasted peppers, anchovies, and garlicky bread. Just before serving the layered roasted peppers, anchovies, and bread, drizzle a flavorful olive oil over the top—the recipe calls for extra-virgin, the finest available.

Pappardelle, a pasta easy to make at home, is a broad egg noodle with fluted edges; Diane Darrow and Tom Maresca suggest using fettuccine as a substitute. In Tuscany, pappardelle usually accompanies a rich sauce made with hare; Diane Darrow and Tom Maresca pair it with sautéed sausage meat, mushrooms, Parmesan, and heavy cream. The hot sausage goes very well with the milder ingredients, enhancing them rather than over-powering them. To crumble the sausage links, slit open the casings and scoop out the meat. If you like things extra spicy, grind a generous portion of black pepper over the noodle dish just before serving.

WHAT TO DRINK

A full-bodied red wine should accompany this meal—for example, a Dolcetto from the Piedmont or a young Taurasi from the Italian south. A California Zinfandel, medium bodied, will also combine well with these robust flavors.

SHOPPING LIST AND STAPLES

½ pound Italian-style hot sausage (5 links)
4 large red or green bell peppers
1 large fennel bulb (about 1 pound)
1 red onion (about ½ pound)
2 medium-size onions
¾ pound fresh mushrooms
1 clove garlic
¼ pound Parmesan cheese
1 cup heavy cream
6 tablespoons butter
1 pound pappardelle or fettuccine
4 whole anchovy fillets, preferably salt packed
1 loaf Italian bread
4 tablespoons extravirgin olive oil
8 tablespoons olive oil
2 tablespoons vegetable oil
4 teaspoons red wine vinegar
Salt and pepper

UTENSILS

Food processor or blender
Large stockpot or kettle with cover
Large enamel sauté pan or casserole with cover
Medium-size saucepan with cover
Small saucepan
Medium-size baking pan
Colander
Measuring cups and spoons
Paring knife
Bread knife
Wooden spatula
Grater
Tongs

START-TO-FINISH STEPS

1. Grate Parmesan cheese for pasta.
2. Follow pepper recipe steps 1 through 3.
3. Follow pasta recipe steps 1 through 8.
4. Follow fennel salad recipe steps 1 and 2.
5. Follow pasta recipe step 9 and pepper recipe step 4.
6. To serve, follow pepper recipe step 5, fennel salad recipe step 3, and pasta recipe step 10.

RECIPES

Roasted Peppers and Anchovies on Italian Bread

4 large red or green bell peppers
4 whole anchovy fillets
1 loaf Italian bread
Salt
Freshly ground black pepper
1 clove garlic
8 tablespoons olive oil

1. Turn 2 front burners of gas stove to high. Set 1 pepper directly onto each grate. Watch closely and, as skin blackens in flame, turn peppers with tongs until entire surface is black. As each pepper is finished, put it into paper bag and close mouth of bag. Roast the remaining 2 peppers the same way.
2. Remove from paper bag and, under running water, scrape away all blackened skin of each pepper with paring knife. Cut peppers in half, remove all seeds and mem-

brane, and blot dry with paper towels.

3. Also under running water, fillet anchovies, scraping off skin and any large bones. Pat anchovies dry with paper towels.

4. Slice bread into eight ¾-inch-thick slices and toast under broiler until light golden brown. Rub each slice with garlic clove and set slices on individual serving dishes.

5. Place 1 pepper half over each slice of bread. Salt and pepper to taste. Top each with 1 anchovy fillet. Drizzle 1 tablespoon of the olive oil over each pepper.

Pappardelle alla Contadina

¾ pound fresh mushrooms
2 medium-size onions
½ pound Italian-style hot sausage (5 links)
Salt
6 tablespoons butter
2 tablespoons vegetable oil
1 cup heavy cream
Freshly ground black pepper
1 pound pappardelle or fettuccine
½ cup freshly grated Parmesan cheese

1. Wash and slice mushrooms, using slicing blade of food processor. Scrape onto plate. Do not wash processor bowl, but fit it with steel blade.

2. Mince onions in processor.

3. Remove sausage meat from casings and chop it roughly.

4. Put salted water on to boil in stockpot or kettle for pasta.

5. In enamel sauté pan or casserole, melt 2 tablespoons of the butter with oil. Add sausage meat and onions. Sauté over medium heat, stirring often and breaking up pieces of sausage, about 5 minutes, until onions are translucent and sausage has lost its raw red color.

6. Turn heat to medium-high. Add mushrooms and continue) sautéing, stirring often, another 5 minutes. Mushrooms will begin to exude liquid after 1 or 2 minutes.

7. Meanwhile, melt the remaining 4 tablespoons of butter in ½ cup of the cream. When cream is just at simmer, turn off heat and set aside until ready to use.

8. After mushrooms have sautéed in sauce 5 minutes, lower heat, add ¼ teaspoon salt, 6 or 8 generous grinds of pepper, and the remaining ½ cup of the cream. Cook gently, uncovered, until liquid thickens somewhat—about 5 minutes. Set aside, covered, until ready to use.

9. Cook pasta in boiling salted water until just *al dente*.

10. Drain and turn into warm serving bowl. Toss with butter-cream mixture, then sauce, then cheese. Pass additional cheese and pepper mill at table.

Fennel and Red Onion Salad

1 large fennel bulb (about 1 pound)
1 red onion (about ½ pound)
4 tablespoons extravirgin olive oil
4 teaspoons red wine vinegar

1. Wash and trim fennel bulb, discarding feathery leaves. Cut into even, vertical slices, about ¼ inch thick. Remove core at base of slices if it is hard and woody.

2. Peel and slice red onion into disks about ⅛ inch thick.

3. Arrange alternating slices of fennel and onion on individual plates, dressing each portion with 1 tablespoon olive oil and 1 teaspoon vinegar (or more to taste). If desired, salt and pepper can be added.

ADDED TOUCH

Fresh strawberries in a ricotta cheese parfait make a lovely, festive dessert for this party meal. You can use sliced peaches, or, for a tropical touch, sliced mangoes instead. If you prefer, you can use fresh raspberries, substituting a raspberry-flavored liqueur for the almond-flavored Amaretto.

Ricotta Strawberry Parfait

1 pound ricotta cheese
1 egg yolk
3 tablespoons Amaretto
4 teaspoons sugar
1 pint fresh strawberries
½ lemon
1 ounce slivered almonds for garnish (optional)

1. Put ricotta in bowl and beat until smooth. Add egg yolk, Amaretto, and sugar. Mix well. Chill in refrigerator until ready to serve.

2. Hull strawberries and rinse briefly. Drain and pat dry. Halve them if large and toss them in bowl with juice of ½ lemon. Chill until ready to serve.

3. Distribute strawberries in 4 parfait dishes. Spoon ricotta mixture over top and sprinkle with slivered almonds, if desired.

Alfredo Viazzi

L iguria, on the Gulf of Genoa on the northernmost coast of western Italy, claims credit for the creation of two internationally popular and classic dishes—the rich vegetable-and-pasta soup called minestrone, and ravioli, in particular the special ones filled with minced veal, pork, egg, and Parmesan cheese. A famous culinary center, Liguria has a rich local cuisine based on a liberal use of herbs. Basil, which flourishes in the hills of the region, is a familiar flavoring in many Ligurian dishes.

Alfredo Viazzi, who lives in New York, acquired both his love of food and his basic training in his native Liguria, which glorifies a simple, hearty way of cooking and eating. He was taught that there really is no such thing as a dish too plain to be good and that even a well-cooked meal of potatoes and onions can be delicious. Now, as a restaurant owner, he believes that above all, good food should entertain people and be pleasing to look at as well as to taste. And, without being overwhelming, his menus have a certain lavish quality, either in the richness of ingredients or the—to us—unusual combinations of such ingredients as fresh beans, nutmeg, nuts, and cream (see Menu 1), that makes them festive indeed.

Each of his menus is as suitable for guests as for home-style meals. In the manner of Ligurian cooking, recipes in Menu 1 and Menu 3 call for basil, which should be fresh to capture its authentic flavor. Menu 2 features fresh scallops with linguine, served with a rich creamy sauce.

This meal will taste best when zucchini and green beans are at their prime, in mid- to late summer. Serve the spaghettini, topped with crumbled sausage and mushroom and zucchini slices, and the green beans with nuts and cream on the side.

Spaghettini with Sausage and Zucchini
Green Bean Salad with Nuts and Cream

The main dish here is spaghettini with sausage and zucchini in an olive oil-based tomato sauce. This taste is refreshingly light when paired with a thin spaghetti. Italian parsley, also an ingredient in the sauce, is the ubiquitous herb that Italians use liberally for seasoning. Also known as plain leaf or flat parsley, Italian parsley is more fragrant and flavorful than the familiar curly parsley. If your market does not carry Italian parsley, you can substitute curly parsley, but, for an extra touch of flavor, add a bit of the tender stems, finely minced.

During tomato season, you may want to use fresh rather than canned Italian, or plum, tomatoes. To peel them quickly, drop them in boiling water for several seconds, then scoop them out with a large slotted spoon and rinse them under cold water. When the tomatoes are cool enough to handle, peel them with a sharp knife and proceed with the recipe.

The string bean salad calls for walnuts, and a sprinkling of freshly grated nutmeg, as popular in Italy as elsewhere, gives the salad zest. Look for whole nutmegs on the spice shelves of your supermarket. As good cooks know, freshly grated nutmeg is more pungent than preground—and the grating takes almost no time.

For delicious fresh green beans, select only those that are unblemished, tender, young, and crisp enough to snap when you bend them. Rinse them under cold water after cooking and then be sure to let the cream with nuts and spices cool before you add the beans. The salad tastes best either warm or at room temperature.

WHAT TO DRINK

The harmony of flavors here allows a wide range of choice of red wine. From the north and south of Italy, respectively, a good Chianti or a young Taurasi, or a reasonably priced Merlot from California, would all offer the right degree of fruitiness and dryness.

SHOPPING LIST AND STAPLES

1 pound sweet Italian sausages
3 medium-size zucchini (about 1 pound)
1 pound fresh green beans
4 fresh mushrooms
1 lemon
1 onion
1 bunch fresh Italian parsley
1 clove garlic
3 to 4 fresh basil leaves, or ¼ teaspoon chopped dried
2 tablespoons plus 2 teaspoons butter
½ cup heavy cream
¼ pound Parmesan cheese
1 pound spaghettini
20-ounce can Italian peeled tomatoes
1 tablespoon chopped walnuts
⅓ cup olive oil
¼ cup vegetable oil
Pinch of marjoram
Whole nutmeg
Salt and pepper
3 tablespoons red wine

UTENSILS

Large stockpot or kettle with cover
8-inch skillet
Medium-size saucepan
Medium-size nonaluminum saucepan
Small saucepan
Colander
Measuring cups and spoons
Chef's knife
Slotted spoon
Nutmeg grater

START-TO-FINISH STEPS

1. Chop parsley for pasta recipe, and grate nutmeg for pasta and salad recipes. Follow pasta recipe steps 1 through 10.
2. Chop nuts and juice and peel lemon for salad recipe, and follow salad recipe steps 1 through 3.
3. Follow pasta recipe step 11.
4. Grate Parmesan cheese and follow pasta recipe step 12.
5. Follow salad recipe step 4, and serve with pasta.

RECIPES

Spaghettini with Sausage and Zucchini

½ small onion
1 clove garlic
⅓ cup olive oil
2 tablespoons butter
1 tablespoon chopped fresh Italian parsley

2½ cups Italian peeled tomatoes
Pinch of marjoram
Salt
Freshly ground black pepper
3 to 4 fresh basil leaves, or ¼ teaspoon chopped dried
3 medium-size zucchini (about 1 pound)
4 fresh mushrooms
1 pound sweet Italian sausages
¼ cup vegetable oil
Pinch of freshly grated nutmeg
3 tablespoons red wine
1 pound spaghettini
5 tablespoons freshly grated Parmesan cheese

1. Chop both onion and garlic finely.
2. Heat half of the olive oil in nonaluminum saucepan over medium flame. Add butter, wait 1 minute until it melts, and add onion, garlic, and parsley. Lower flame, stir, and cook about 5 minutes, or until softened.
3. Set stockpot or kettle of salted water over low flame to bring to a boil for spaghettini.
4. To saucepan with onion-and-garlic mixture, add tomatoes and break them up. Mix well. Add marjoram, salt, and pepper, and taste for seasoning. Add basil. Cook over low flame 25 minutes, stirring often.
5. Wash zucchini under cold water and pat dry. Slice into ⅛-inch rounds. Set aside.
6. Lightly rinse mushrooms and pat dry. Thinly slice caps and stems.
7. Take sausage meat out of casings and loosen it with your hands.
8. Heat vegetable oil in skillet over medium flame and sauté zucchini, stirring until golden brown. Drain on paper towels. Wipe out skillet.
9. Add the remaining olive oil to same skillet and sauté sausage meat until brown, stirring with spoon to crumble into small pieces. Add mushrooms, salt, pepper, and nutmeg. Mix gently. Add wine and let it evaporate. Taste for seasoning.
10. Add zucchini and sausage mixture to tomato sauce and blend well. Taste. Let sauce simmer over low flame.
11. Drop spaghettini into boiling water and loosen it up with long fork. Cook about 7 minutes, or until done. Drain well in colander.
12. Remove sauce from flame and pour half of it into large serving bowl. Transfer spaghettini to bowl and toss well. Add the remaining sauce to pasta and toss again. Pass Parmesan cheese and pepper mill.

Green Bean Salad with Nuts and Cream

Juice and rind of ½ lemon
Salt
1 pound fresh green beans
2 teaspoons butter
1 tablespoon coarsely chopped walnuts
½ cup heavy cream
Pinch of freshly grated nutmeg
White pepper

1. Bring small amount water to a boil in medium-size saucepan to which lemon juice, rind, and pinch of salt have been added.
2. Trim beans and cook 8 minutes, or until just tender. Drain well and cool under cold water. Drain again.
3. Melt butter in small saucepan and cook chopped nuts 5 minutes, stirring and shaking pan so they do not stick to bottom. Add cream and nutmeg and bring to a boil. Remove from heat and keep warm.
4. When ready to serve, add salt and pepper to cream dressing and pour over string beans. Mix well.

_____

ADDED TOUCH

If you have some extra time and wish to make an elegant appetizer, try peppers stuffed with cubed lamb, pine nuts, and other savory ingredients. Although it is easy to follow, it is a lengthy recipe that requires about an hour of preparation time.

Stuffed Peppers Saturnia

6 small sweet red or yellow peppers
6 tablespoons butter
2 tablespoons dry vermouth
Salt
Freshly ground black pepper
Rind of ½ lemon, chopped very fine
1½ pounds boneless lean lamb
1 egg yolk
3 tablespoons heavy cream
2 tablespoons freshly grated Parmesan cheese
½ packet saffron
2 tablespoons water
Pinch of turmeric
2 tablespoons chopped pine nuts
½ tablespoon freshly chopped Italian parsley
½ cup chicken stock

1. Preheat oven to 375 degrees.
2. Core and seed peppers. Rinse and let drain, open side down.
3. Melt butter over low flame and mix in vermouth. Simmer 2 minutes. Turn peppers cut side up, shaving off thin slice from bottoms so they stand flat. Pour mixture evenly into peppers, swirl around to coat insides of peppers, and allow to marinate for ½ hour.
4. Drain excess butter-and-vermouth mixture into skillet. Heat, and add salt and pepper. Add lamb and lemon rind. Cook over medium flame, about 20 minutes. Remove lamb and chop into small pieces. Let cool.
5. In medium-size bowl, combine chopped lamb, egg yolk beaten into heavy cream, Parmesan cheese, saffron diluted in 2 tablespoons of warm water, turmeric, parsley, and chopped pine nuts. Mix well, taste, and set aside.
6. Place peppers, open side up, in baking pan, and add chicken stock. Bake 10 minutes. Remove peppers and stuff with mixture. Arrange peppers, stuffed side up, in same baking pan. Replace in oven. Bake additional 15 minutes. Remove and place under broiler 1½ minutes.

Linguine with Scallops
Broccoli Salad

A dish of linguine, tossed together with scallops and garnished with chopped parsley, and a side dish of broccoli flowerets make an attractive meal. For an elegant touch, serve the wine from a glass decanter.

Recipes with shellfish are characteristic of Ligurian cooking, but such seasonings as nutmeg, ginger, and white pepper are untypical. Here, as Alfredo Viazzi inventively combines them in the scallop marinade and the linguine sauce, these spices add a piquant and distinctive flavor to the pasta dish.

The scallops we eat are thick muscles that open and close the familiar rippled shells. Scallops come in two varieties: the often preferred tiny, tender bay scallop and the larger, firmer sea scallop. When selecting scallops, check them for a clean sea-air odor and firm flesh.

The success of the salad depends upon your using broccoli that is both very fresh and crisp. When you shop for this recipe, select a bunch of broccoli with a rich green color, compact buds in the head, and firm stalks. Anchovies, tiny fish with a pungent flavor, are available packed in either salt or oil. Salt-packed anchovies, usually found in Italian groceries, are preferable, but must be cleaned under cold water, skinned, and boned before use. However, you can certainly use oil-packed anchovies, which are sold in tins or jars. When a recipe calls for using only a few anchovy fillets—as this one does—remove the required amount, drain the fillets on paper towels, and store the rest in the closed jar in the refrigerator.

WHAT TO DRINK

Scallops need a rich, dry white wine to complement them. A dry California Gewurztraminer or a good Chardonnay (from Italy or California) or a white Burgundy (a Rully or a Saint-Véran) would all do nicely. Serve the wine very cold. A sparkling mineral water also makes a pleasant accompaniment, whether or not you serve wine.

SHOPPING LIST AND STAPLES

1 pound fresh bay scallops
1 bunch broccoli
1 bunch fresh Italian parsley
2 cloves garlic
1 lemon
5 tablespoons butter
¼ cup heavy cream
¼ pound Parmesan cheese (optional)
1 pound linguine
5 anchovy fillets

244

½ teaspoon Dijon mustard
½ cup olive oil
1 tablespoon red wine vinegar
Pinch of ground ginger
Whole nutmeg
Salt and pepper
White pepper

Large stockpot or kettle with cover
Large saucepan
Large skillet
Medium-size bowl
Colander
Measuring cups and spoons
Chef's knife
Grater
Nutmeg grater

START-TO-FINISH STEPS

1. Peel lemon for salad recipe and juice lemon for pasta and salad recipes.
2. Follow pasta recipe steps 1 through 3.
3. Follow broccoli recipe steps 1 and 2.
4. Chop garlic, parsley, and anchovies for broccoli recipe and follow broccoli recipe step 3.
5. Grate Parmesan cheese, if using, and follow pasta recipe steps 4 through 8. Serve with broccoli salad.

RECIPES

Linguine with Scallops

1 pound fresh bay scallops
Juice of ½ lemon (about 2 tablespoons)
1 bunch fresh Italian parsley
1 large clove garlic
Pinch of freshly grated nutmeg
Pinch of ground ginger
Salt
Freshly ground white pepper
1 pound linguine
5 tablespoons butter
¼ cup heavy cream

¼ cup freshly grated Parmesan cheese for garnish (optional)

1. Set stockpot or kettle of salted water over low flame to bring to a boil for pasta.
2. Wash scallops thoroughly under cold water and drain well. Place scallops in bowl and add lemon juice.
3. Chop enough parsley to yield ½ tablespoon. Chop garlic. Grate nutmeg. Add parsley, garlic, nutmeg, ginger, salt, and white pepper to mixing bowl. Toss well. Taste marinade and adjust seasonings. Let scallops sit in marinade until ready to cook.
4. When water boils, drop linguine into water and loosen up with fork. Cook 7 or 8 minutes, or until done.
5. While pasta is cooking, melt butter in skillet. Drain scallops from marinade and sauté them 3 to 4 minutes, making sure to coat well with butter. Add cream and reduce, 1 minute. Taste. Add salt and pepper if needed.
6. Drain linguine when cooked *al dente*.
7. Set skillet over medium flame and wait 1 minute; then add linguine to scallop sauce. Blend thoroughly. Stir about 2 minutes.
8. Serve hot, distributing scallops as evenly as possible. Serve Parmesan cheese on the side, if desired, and pass pepper mill.

Broccoli Salad

1 bunch broccoli
Juice and rind of ½ lemon
½ cup olive oil
1 tablespoon red wine vinegar
½ tablespoon chopped fresh Italian parsley
5 anchovy fillets, finely chopped
½ teaspoon Dijon mustard
¼ teaspoon chopped garlic
Freshly ground black pepper

1. Cut broccoli into flowerets with 1-inch stems. Wash and drain them.
2. Cook broccoli about 4 minutes in boiling salted water to which lemon juice and rind have been added. Keep broccoli gently pressed down in water. Drain in colander and run under cold water. Shake broccoli gently to remove all water.
3. Mix the remaining ingredients in serving bowl and add broccoli. Toss gently to coat flowerets. Let stand at room temperature until ready to serve.

Pasticcio di Lasagnette
Arugula Salad

The baked pasticcio—lasagnette that is layered with meat, cheese, and vegetables—with an arugula salad is an informal meal.

Outside an Italian kitchen, *pasticcio* means "mess." To an Italian cook, a pasticcio is a dish that combines cooked pasta with cheese, vegetables, or meat, all bound together by eggs or a cream sauce. Often a pasticcio bakes without a crust, but this recipe calls for a layering of cheese slices, which form a bubbly crust when they melt. Though the dish is basically uncomplicated, it has a multiplicity of ingredients. Before you begin to follow the recipe, collect all the ingredients from the pantry and refrigerator and line them up in order on your work surface. Then proceed with making the recipe.

Arugula (see drawing) is an Italian salad green that recently has become a popular green in American homes. It has narrow frilled leaves and a distinctive peppery bite, not unlike watercress. If you have difficulty finding arugula, you can use either watercress or any field salad greens. Before using, arugula must be rinsed thoroughly to remove any sand, then drained, and gently patted dry.

WHAT TO DRINK

This interesting version of a classic Italian dish calls for a classic Italian wine—a full-bodied Chianti Classico *riserva*. As an alternative, try a young, medium-priced Barbaresco, a red wine from the Piedmont, or a California Merlot.

SHOPPING LIST AND STAPLES

1 pound lean chopped beef
¾ pound fresh spinach
2 bunches arugula
1 small onion
1 carrot
1 stalk celery
1 bunch fresh Italian parsley
1 bunch fresh basil, or ½ teaspoon dried
1 clove garlic (optional)
1 lemon
8 tablespoons butter (1 stick)
1 cup plus 2 tablespoons heavy cream
¼ pound Fontina, mozzarella, or other mild soft cheese
¼ pound Parmesan cheese
¼ pound mortadella or boiled ham, thinly sliced
1 pound lasagnette, fresh or dried
½ cup beef broth
2 tablespoons tomato paste
6 pieces imported dry *porcini* mushrooms
¼ cup flour

¼ cup plus 4 tablespoons olive oil
Pinch of ground ginger
Whole nutmeg
Salt and pepper
3 tablespoons red wine

UTENSILS

Food processor or blender
Large stockpot or kettle with cover
Medium-size baking pan
2 small saucepans
Vegetable steamer
Small bowl
Colander
Measuring cups and spoons
Chef's knife
Wooden spatula
Nutmeg grater
Whisk

START-TO-FINISH STEPS

1. Chop parsley and basil, grate nutmeg and Parmesan cheese, and wash and scrape carrot and celery for pasta recipe. Slice Fontina for pasta recipe.
2. Follow pasta recipe steps 1 through 13.
3. As pasta bakes, chop garlic if using it, and follow salad recipe steps 1 and 2.
4. Serve pasta and salad.

RECIPES

Pasticcio di Lasagnette

6 pieces imported dry *porcini* mushrooms
½ cup beef broth
1 small onion
1 carrot, washed and scraped
1 stalk celery, washed and scraped
2 tablespoons salt
¼ cup plus 2 tablespoons olive oil
8 tablespoons butter (1 stick)
½ tablespoon chopped fresh Italian parsley
1½ teaspoons chopped fresh basil, or ½ teaspoon dried
3 tablespoons red wine
¼ cup flour
1 cup plus 2 tablespoons heavy cream
Salt
Pinch of freshly grated nutmeg
Pinch of ground ginger
¾ cup freshly grated Parmesan cheese
1 pound lean chopped beef
2 tablespoons tomato paste
2 tablespoons water
Freshly ground black pepper
1 pound lasagnette, fresh or dried
¾ pound fresh spinach
¼ pound mortadella or boiled ham, thinly sliced
¼ pound Fontina, mozzarella, or other soft cheese, thinly sliced

1. Preheat oven to 375 degrees.
2. Wash mushrooms well under lukewarm water, and then soak them in beef broth until ready to use.
3. Puree onion, carrot, and celery together in food processor.
4. Bring water and 2 tablespoons salt to a boil in stockpot or kettle over medium flame for pasta.
5. Heat ¼ cup of the olive oil in saucepan and melt 1 tablespoon of the butter in it. Add vegetable mixture, parsley, and basil. Cook 5 to 6 minutes, stirring, or until vegetables are softened. Add red wine and cook until it evaporates, about 2 minutes.
6. Add chopped beef and amalgamate well with all other ingredients. Cook over low flame, stirring occasionally.
7. Melt 5 tablespoons of the butter in another saucepan over medium flame. Add flour and blend well with whisk. Cook until it becomes deep yellow mixture. Add cream, a bit at a time, and keep blending. Add pinch of salt, nutmeg, and ginger. Add ¼ cup of the Parmesan cheese. Blend well and keep warm. This is called béchamel sauce.
8. Remove mushrooms from their soaking liquid and coarsely chop them. Then add mushrooms and beef broth to chopped beef. Mix. Add tomato paste diluted in 2 tablespoons warm water. Blend well. Lower flame and let sauce simmer. Add salt and pepper. Taste and adjust seasonings if necessary. This is called Bolognese sauce.
9. At this point, water for pasta should be boiling. Drop in lasagnette. Cook fresh lasagnette 2 to 3 minutes or dry lasagnette about 7 minutes.
10. Wash spinach thoroughly under cold water and cut off tough stems. Steam spinach in small amount of water 2 minutes. Drain well and chop coarsely.
11. Drain pasta well in colander. Put back in pot and add the remaining 2 tablespoons olive oil. Toss to coat well.
12. Coat baking pan with the remaining 2 tablespoons butter. Lay half of the lasagnette in pan and pour Bolognese sauce over it. Shower with ¼ cup of the Parmesan cheese. Place slices of mortadella or ham over cheese. Lay the remaining lasagnette over mortadella. Cover with chopped spinach; smooth top. Pour béchamel sauce over spinach. Smooth. Sprinkle with the remaining ¼ cup Parmesan cheese. Arrange slices of Fontina or other cheese over béchamel.
13. Place pan in oven and bake 15 to 20 minutes. Cut into 4 portions to serve.

Arugula Salad

2 bunches arugula
2 tablespoons olive oil
½ lemon
Salt
Freshly ground black pepper
Touch of chopped garlic (optional)

1. Cut off tough stems and wash arugula thoroughly under cold water. Drain well and arrange in serving bowl.
2. Pour olive oil over salad and squeeze lemon juice on it. Add salt, pepper, and garlic if desired. Toss well.

VEGETABLES

Madhur Jaffrey

MENU 1 (Right)
Rice Pilaf with Black-Eyed Peas
and Green Beans
Eggplant in Spicy Tomato Sauce

MENU 2
Persian-Style Rice with Lima Beans and Dill
Cauliflower with Garlic and Sesame Seeds
Yogurt with Tomato and Cucumber

MENU 3
Brown Rice with Mushrooms
Peas and Tomatoes with Cumin Seeds
Yogurt with Mint

Cooking with vegetables and grains is an observance of Hindu religious tradition, which reveres all animal life. Madhur Jaffrey, who is an actress as well as a food writer and cook, learned vegetable cookery in her native India. Vegetables please her spirit and sustain her, she explains. Her three menus guide those who want vegetarian meals that are authentic, simple, and nutritionally balanced. At the heart of Indian cooking is rice—the main dish in each of these menus. As accompaniments, Madhur Jaffrey serves eggplant in a tomato sauce in Menu 1, seasoned cauliflower and a chilled, yogurt-based salad in Menu 2, and a bright mixture of peas and tomatoes along with a minty yogurt in Menu 3.

Like the best Indian cooks, Madhur Jaffrey prepares her vegetables to underscore their natural essence rather than to make them look and taste like meat. She balances her vegetarian meals with nuts, yogurt, and fruits—only a few of the elements in the almost endlessly rich and varied repertoire of Indian cooking—and adds dimension to her recipes by using spices and seasonings, such as whole or ground cumin and coriander seeds, which are an integral part of the cuisine.

The main dish in this festive, all-vegetable Indian meal is rice pilaf with black-eyed peas and green beans, accompanied by a casserole of broiled sliced eggplant in a spicy tomato sauce.

250

Rice Pilaf with Black-Eyed Peas and Green Beans
Eggplant in Spicy Tomato Sauce

India is famous for rice pilaf, which is rice fried and then braised with vegetables and seasonings. Here Madhur Jaffrey mixes the rice with black-eyed peas and green beans and serves a fennel-flavored eggplant dish on the side.

Frozen black-eyed peas are almost as good as fresh ones and much easier to handle. If you want to use dried peas, you must cook them ahead: Pick through the dried peas to remove unwanted particles, then wash them. Set them to simmer in about 3 inches of water in a large pot. After 2 minutes of simmering, turn the heat off, cover the pot, and let the peas sit for an hour. Then cook them 10 to 20 minutes.

Turmeric, a bright yellow spice in the ginger family, is common on American supermarket shelves, but you may need to shop for whole cumin, coriander, and fennel seeds in a specialty shop or Indian grocery. Fennel seeds have a pleasant, mild licorice taste, like anise, which you can substitute if you reduce the quantity. Frying spices, as in this recipe, helps release and intensify their flavor.

Eggplant soaks up oil when you fry it so broiling the slices with a light brushing of oil cuts down on fat. Broiling also helps eliminate the sometimes bitter taste of eggplant skin. The cook recommends white eggplant for this recipe, or the small Oriental eggplants, but you can use any of the several varieties you may find at the greengrocer.

The tomato sauce for the eggplant slices calls for coarsely chopped fresh ginger. The cook's technique for coarse-chopping ginger is to peel a section of fresh ginger and then slice it thinly. Use a potato masher to smash the ginger slices, then drag them across the surface of the cutting board to break up the fibers.

To make this meal nutritionally complete, include a dessert of fresh fruit with a dairy product. This could be either a platter of fruit, accompanied by a selection of various cheeses, or a bowl of peeled and sliced fresh fruit folded into sweetened yogurt or ice cream.

WHAT TO DRINK

The cook suggests a dry red wine with character, such as an Italian Montepulciano d'Abruzzo, to accompany this lively meal. Cold beer or light ale would also be good.

SHOPPING LIST AND STAPLES

1 large eggplant (about 1½ pounds)
3 medium-size tomatoes
¼ pound green beans
1 medium-size onion
1 lemon
7 medium-size cloves garlic
Fresh ginger
10-ounce package frozen black-eyed peas
¾ cup plus 1 tablespoon vegetable oil
2 cups long-grain rice, preferably basmati
1 tablespoon plus 2 teaspoons ground coriander
1 teaspoon whole cumin seeds
1 teaspoon ground cumin
1 teaspoon whole fennel seeds
¾ teaspoon ground turmeric
½ teaspoon Cayenne pepper
Dash of cinnamon
Salt
Freshly ground pepper

UTENSILS

Food processor or blender
Large skillet with lid
Large, heavy-gauge saucepan or skillet with tight-fitting lid
Medium-size saucepan with lid
Large broiling tray
Large bowl
Small cup
Colander
Measuring cups and spoons
Chef's knife
Paring knife
Wooden spatula
Metal spatula
Pastry brush

START-TO-FINISH STEPS

1. Follow rice pilaf recipe steps 1 through 3. Squeeze enough lemon to measure 2 tablespoons juice, peel and mince garlic, peel and finely chop onion, trim green beans and cut crosswise into ½-inch pieces.
2. Follow rice pilaf recipe steps 4 and 5.
3. Drain rice and follow rice pilaf recipe steps 6 and 7.
4. For eggplant recipe, peel and coarsely chop ginger, peel garlic cloves, and chop tomatoes.

RECIPES

Rice Pilaf with Black-Eyed Peas and Green Beans

2 cups long-grain rice, preferably basmati
10-ounce package frozen black-eyed peas
2 teaspoons ground coriander
1 teaspoon ground cumin
½ teaspoon ground turmeric
⅛ to ¼ teaspoon Cayenne pepper
¼ teaspoon coarsely ground black pepper
Dash of cinnamon
2 tablespoons lemon juice
4 tablespoons vegetable oil
1 medium-size clove garlic, peeled and minced
1 medium-size onion, peeled and finely chopped
¼ pound green beans, trimmed and cut crosswise into ½-inch pieces
1¼ teaspoons salt

1. Place rice in large bowl with cold water to cover. With your hands, swish the rice around quickly; pour off most of the water. Repeat 6 to 8 times, or until little water is no longer cloudy. Cover rice with water; set aside 25 minutes.
2. In medium-size saucepan, bring 1½ cups of water to a boil. Add black-eyed peas and return to a boil, breaking up frozen block of peas with fork as they are heating. Cover, turn heat to low, and simmer 10 minutes. Drain peas in colander.
3. While peas are cooking, combine coriander, cumin, turmeric, Cayenne, black pepper, cinnamon, lemon juice, and 1 tablespoon of water in small cup. Mix thoroughly and set aside.
4. In large, heavy-gauge saucepan or skillet, heat oil over medium heat. When hot, add garlic and onion. Cook, stirring with wooden spatula, until onion turns brown at edges.
5. Add spice mixture and stir well to combine. Fry about 1 minute.
6. Add the drained rice, black-eyed peas, green beans, and salt. Cook over medium heat 2 to 3 minutes, stirring carefully so as not to break the grains of rice. Lower heat if rice begins to stick to bottom of pan.

Eggplant in Spicy Tomato Sauce

1 large eggplant (about 1½ pounds)
9 tablespoons vegetable oil (approximately)
1 piece fresh ginger (1½ inches by 1 inch), peeled and coarsely chopped
6 medium-size cloves garlic, peeled
1 teaspoon whole fennel seeds
1 teaspoon whole cumin seeds
3 medium-size tomatoes, chopped
1 tablespoon ground coriander
1 teaspoon salt
¼ teaspoon ground turmeric
⅛ to ¼ teaspoon Cayenne pepper

1. Preheat broiler.
2. Halve eggplant lengthwise and then cut crosswise into ½-inch slices.
3. Brush slices on both sides with about 3 tablespoons of the oil and arrange them in a single layer in large broiling tray. Broil 3 inches from heat source, about 7 minutes; turn with spatula and broil another 7 minutes, or until eggplant is nicely browned.
4. While eggplant is broiling, purée ginger, garlic, and 3 tablespoons of water in food processor or blender. Set aside. In large skillet, heat remaining 6 tablespoons of oil over medium heat. When hot, add fennel and cumin seeds, and let sizzle 30 seconds, or until seeds turn a shade darker. Add ginger-garlic purée and cook, stirring, 1 minute. Stir in chopped tomatoes, coriander, salt, turmeric, and Cayenne, and bring to a simmer. Cook, still stirring, over medium heat 2 to 3 minutes. Cover, turn heat to low, and cook 5 minutes.
5. Fold the browned eggplant slices into the tomato sauce and bring to a simmer. Cover and cook over low heat another 3 to 5 minutes. Turn into serving dish.

LEFTOVER SUGGESTIONS

If you have leftover eggplant slices, serve them folded into some lightly fork-beaten plain yogurt. To reheat the rice pilaf, sauté it in hot oil with scallions and serve it as a snack or light lunch.

5. Follow eggplant recipe steps 1 through 5.
6. Toss rice and serve with the eggplant.

7. Add 3 cups water and bring to a boil. Cover lightly, first with aluminum foil and then with a lid. Turn heat very low and cook 25 minutes. Keep pilaf tightly covered until ready to serve.

Persian-Style Rice with Lima Beans and Dill
Cauliflower with Garlic and Sesame Seeds
Yogurt with Tomato and Cucumber

Colorful plates highlight the muted tones of the Persian rice, sautéed cauliflower, and yogurt-vegetable mixture.

Y ou can buy *basmati* rice in an Indian grocery or specialty food shop; it is aromatic, with delicate, long slender grains. Pick through it carefully before rinsing to remove unwanted particles.

The cauliflower recipe calls for unhulled sesame seeds, which you can buy in a health food store or in an Indian or Chinese market. Be sure to sift through the seeds to

remove any grit before you use them. A precautionary note: when dropped into hot oil, sesame seeds will pop; have a lid or spatter guard handy to hold them in the skillet.

WHAT TO DRINK

A dry white wine is needed for this menu: a French

Mâcon, a California Sauvignon Blanc, or an Italian Chardonnay would all be appropriate choices.

SHOPPING LIST AND STAPLES

1 medium-size cauliflower
1 medium-size ripe tomato
1 medium-size cucumber
1 small onion
5 cloves garlic
Large bunch fresh dill
Small bunch fresh thyme or ½ teaspoon dried
16-ounce container plain yogurt
10-ounce package frozen baby lima beans
½ cup vegetable oil
2 cups long-grain rice, preferably basmati
¼ ounce unhulled sesame seeds
Cayenne pepper
Salt
Freshly ground pepper

UTENSILS

Large skillet
2 large, heavy-gauge saucepans, 1 with tight-fitting lid
Small saucepan
Large bowl
Colander
Measuring cups and spoons
Chef's knife
Paring knife
2 wooden spatulas or spoons
Rubber spatula
Whisk

START-TO-FINISH STEPS

1. Follow Persian-style rice recipe step 1.
2. Follow cauliflower recipe step 1.
3. Follow Persian-style rice recipe step 2.
4. Follow yogurt recipe steps 1 through 3. Refrigerate until ready to serve.
5. Drain rice and follow Persian-style rice recipe steps 3 through 4.
6. Trim cauliflower and break into small flowerets. Follow cauliflower recipe steps 2 through 4.
7. Toss rice and serve with the cauliflower and the yogurt.

RECIPES

Persian-Style Rice with Lima Beans and Dill

2 cups long-grain rice, preferably basmati
10-ounce package frozen baby lima beans
1¼ teaspoons salt
4 tablespoons vegetable oil
1 small onion, peeled and thinly sliced
¾ cup firmly packed chopped fresh dill
1½ teaspoons chopped fresh thyme, or ½ teaspoon dried

1. Place rice in large bowl and wash in several changes of water. Drain in colander. Return rice to bowl and cover with 5 cups of water; set aside 25 minutes.
2. While rice is soaking, cook lima beans in small saucepan in ½ cup water with ¼ teaspoon salt for 8 minutes. Drain in colander.
3. In large, heavy-gauge saucepan, heat oil over medium heat. When hot, add onion. Cook, stirring, until onion is lightly browned. Add drained rice, lima beans, dill, thyme, and remaining salt. Stir gently and cook 2 to 3 minutes, taking care not to break the grains of rice. If rice begins to stick to bottom of pan, turn down heat a bit.
4. Pour in 2⅔ cups of water and bring to a boil. Cover tightly, first with aluminum foil and then with lid. Turn heat to very low and cook 25 minutes. Keep covered until ready to serve.

Cauliflower with Garlic and Sesame Seeds

Salt
1 medium-size cauliflower, broken into small flowerets
4 tablespoons vegetable oil
4 to 5 cloves garlic, peeled and minced
1½ tablespoons unhulled sesame seeds
Dash Cayenne pepper
Freshly ground black pepper

1. In large, heavy-gauge saucepan, bring 3 quarts of water to a boil. Stir in 1 tablespoon salt.
2. Add cauliflower and return water to a rolling boil. Boil rapidly 1 to 1½ minutes, or until cauliflower is crisply tender. Drain in colander and set aside.
3. In large skillet, heat oil over medium heat. When hot, add garlic. Fry, stirring, until garlic turns light brown.
4. Add sesame seeds. When sesame seeds turn a few shades darker or begin to pop, add the cauliflower. Stir cauliflower gently until evenly coated with sesame seeds. Add Cayenne, a generous amount of black pepper, and about ¼ teaspoon salt, and stir once more. Turn into serving bowl.

Yogurt with Tomato and Cucumber

1 medium-size ripe tomato
1 medium-size cucumber
1½ cups plain yogurt
½ teaspoon salt
Freshly ground black pepper
Dash Cayenne pepper

1. Core tomato and cut into ¼-inch dice. Peel cucumber and cut into ½-inch dice.
2. Turn yogurt into serving bowl and beat lightly with fork or whisk until smooth and creamy.
3. Add vegetables and seasonings and mix. Taste and adjust seasonings if necessary.

Brown Rice with Mushrooms
Peas and Tomatoes with Cumin Seeds
Yogurt with Mint

This informal Indian vegetarian meal features brown rice with sliced mushrooms, peas and chopped tomatoes spiced with cumin, and yogurt with chopped mint. Pass the yogurt separately and, if you wish, garnish with sprigs of fresh mint.

Not many Asians eat brown rice. They prefer white because its bland taste does not compete with other savory ingredients. But brown rice, which is unmilled white rice, has a distinctive nutty flavor that appeals to many Westerners. Madhur Jaffrey prefers the texture of long-grain brown rice, but you can use the short-grain variety. To soften it quickly, soak it for 20 minutes in hot water to cover. Remember that brown rice requires a longer cooking time than white, so plan accordingly. The cooked rice dish can stand for a half hour without being ruined. Just remove the foil and replace it with a clean dish towel, which helps to absorb the extra moisture, and set the lid on top of the towel. You can vary this menu and still keep it balanced by substituting whole wheat pita bread for the rice recipe.

The combination of seven spices together with peas and tomatoes is a traditional Delhi dish. In Menus 1 and 2, you fry the spices to bring out their taste, but here you mix them with water into a paste before you fry them.

Mint probably came from Turkey originally, but Indians have adopted it universally. Chopped mint and yogurt, stirred together, cool and refresh the palate after a spicy meal.

If you like, serve fresh fruit, such as melon, berries, mangoes, or pineapple, for dessert.

WHAT TO DRINK

The flavors in this menu would blend best with a small, accommodating red wine, such as an Italian Valpolicella or California Pinot Noir.

SHOPPING LIST AND STAPLES

4 pounds fresh peas
3 ripe tomatoes (about 1¼ pounds total weight)
8 medium-size mushrooms
2 small onions
1 clove garlic
Small bunch parsley
Small bunch mint
16-ounce container plain yogurt
8 tablespoons vegetable oil
1½ cups long-grain brown rice
1 teaspoon brown sugar
2 teaspoons ground coriander
2 teaspoons ground cumin

1 teaspoon whole cumin seeds
½ teaspoon ground turmeric
¼ teaspoon ground ginger
¼ teaspoon freshly grated nutmeg
Cayenne pepper
Salt
Freshly ground black pepper

UTENSILS

Large sauté pan
Large, heavy-gauge saucepan with tight-fitting lid
Large bowl
Small cup
Colander
Measuring cups and spoons
Chef's knife
Paring knife
2 wooden spatulas or spoons
Rubber spatula
Whisk
Nutmeg grater

START-TO-FINISH STEPS

1. Follow brown rice recipe step 1. Peel and mince garlic, peel and chop onion, clean mushrooms with damp paper towels and slice thinly, and mince enough parsley to measure 2 tablespoons.
2. Follow brown rice recipe steps 2 through 5.
3. For peas and tomatoes recipe, grate enough nutmeg to measure ¼ teaspoon, peel and finely chop onion, and core and finely chop tomatoes.
4. Follow peas and tomatoes recipe steps 1 through 7.
5. Prepare yogurt with mint.
6. Toss brown rice and serve with the peas and tomatoes and the yogurt with mint.

RECIPES

Brown Rice with Mushrooms

1½ cups long-grain brown rice
4 tablespoons vegetable oil
1 clove garlic, peeled and minced
1 small onion, peeled and finely chopped
8 medium-size mushrooms, wiped clean and thinly sliced
2 tablespoons minced parsley
1 teaspoon salt

1. Place rice in large bowl and wash in several changes of water. Drain in colander. Return rice to bowl and cover with 3 cups of hot water; set aside 20 minutes.
2. In large, heavy-gauge saucepan, heat oil over medium heat. When hot, add garlic and onion. Fry, stirring, until onion turns brown at edges.
3. Stir in mushrooms and fry them until they wilt.
4. Sprinkle parsley over mixture and stir a few seconds.
5. Add rice with its soaking liquid and salt. Bring to a boil.

Cover tightly, first with aluminum foil and then with lid. Turn heat down to very low and cook 35 minutes. Turn off heat and let pan sit in warm spot, covered and undisturbed, another 5 minutes.

Peas and Tomatoes with Whole Cumin

4 pounds fresh peas (approximately)
2 teaspoons ground cumin
2 teaspoons ground coriander
⅛ to ¼ teaspoon Cayenne pepper
½ teaspoon ground turmeric
¼ teaspoon coarsely ground black pepper
¼ teaspoon ground ginger
¼ teaspoon freshly grated nutmeg
4 tablespoons vegetable oil
1 teaspoon whole cumin seeds
1 small onion, peeled and finely chopped
3 ripe tomatoes, cored and finely chopped (about 1¼ pounds total weight)
1 teaspoon salt
1 teaspoon brown sugar

1. Shell enough peas into a quart measure to make 4 cups. Set aside.
2. In small cup, mix cumin, coriander, Cayenne, turmeric, black pepper, ginger, and nutmeg with 5 tablespoons warm water, and set aside.
3. In large sauté pan, heat oil over medium heat. When hot, add whole cumin seeds. Let them sizzle about 20 seconds.
4. Add chopped onion and fry, stirring, until edges begin to brown.
5. Stir in spice paste and fry with the onion 2 minutes.
6. Add tomatoes. Bring to a vigorous simmer over slightly higher heat. Stir and cook 3 to 4 minutes, or until the tomatoes soften and reduce.
7. Stir in peas, salt, and brown sugar. Bring to a simmer. Cover, turn heat to low, and cook 5 minutes, or until peas are just tender. Turn into serving dish.

Yogurt with Mint

1½ cups plain yogurt
½ to ¾ teaspoon salt
Freshly ground black pepper
Dash Cayenne pepper (optional)
3 tablespoons finely chopped mint

Turn yogurt into serving bowl. Beat lightly with fork or whisk until smooth and creamy. Add remaining ingredients and mix well.

LEFTOVER SUGGESTIONS

Leftover peas and tomatoes become a kind of stew when you add 2 boiled beets, peeled and cut into ½-inch pieces, and some stock or water. Turn the brown rice with mushrooms into a pilaf by heating it in a skillet and adding diced cooked chicken or meat from another meal.

Richard Sax

L ike other zealous cooks, Richard Sax believes that beautiful food adds pleasure to life. Trained professionally in French and American kitchens where chefs spend money lavishly to prepare rich, complex recipes, he manages to streamline elegant concoctions into foods that even untrained home cooks can produce economically and quickly. He calls this "bringing food down to earth," yet his cooking is neither skimpy nor slapdash.

Because he is not a dogmatic cook, he likes to shift the emphasis of a meal, turning an appetizer or first course into a substantial entrée, especially when such a recipe features vegetables. He does this with the vegetable chowder of Menu 1 and with the leek and mushroom tart of Menu 2.

Another facet of his style—particularly in his soups, stews, and composed dishes—is his use of chunky ingredients to highlight their flavors and bright colors. He also likes strong, intense flavors such as mustard, vinegar, and hot peppers; a subtle version of this approach is his use of the nearly forgotten practice of seasoning pumpkin with pepper in his light pumpkin soufflés.

In this array of fresh vegetables—(clockwise from lower left) carrots, green beans, leeks, red peppers, onions, potatoes, corn, tomatoes, and peas—are some of the ingredients for the main-course chowder. Served with a tossed green salad and hot buttermilk biscuits, this is a substantial meal, suitable for any time of the year.

259

Hearty Vegetable Chowder
Herbed Buttermilk Biscuits
Tossed Green Salad

This hearty vegetable chowder uses vegetables that are available year round, but Richard Sax's vegetable choices are not mandatory. Instead of broccoli and beans, you may wish to use asparagus in season or snow peas; instead of corn, chick peas. There are numerous vegetables to cut up for the chowder, but, since it is the main course, you have little else to prepare. Vegetarians can omit the bacon and substitute vegetable stock for the chicken stock.

Most cooks would use a flour-fat roux to thicken this vegetable version of a traditional New England chowder recipe. Instead, Richard Sax thickens his chowder with some puréed onions, carrots, celery, and potatoes. Not only does this vegetable thickener produce a lighter soup, but it also intensifies the vegetable flavors.

WHAT TO DRINK

Try a light red wine, such as a Beaujolais or a California Gamay, to complement the robust chowder.

SHOPPING LIST AND STAPLES

½ pound bacon, thickly sliced
Small bunch broccoli
4 to 5 medium-size potatoes (about 1½ pounds)
¼ pound green beans
¼ pound mushrooms
2 red peppers
1 zucchini (optional)
½ pound fresh peas or 10-ounce package frozen (optional)
1 ear corn-on-the-cob or 10-ounce package frozen corn
3 carrots
2 stalks celery
3 medium-size onions
3 radishes (optional)
1 head soft leaf lettuce, such as Boston or Bibb
Small head Romaine lettuce
1 bunch fresh herbs (parsley, chives, tarragon, or mixture)
1 clove garlic
1 stick plus 2 tablespoons butter (approximately)
1 cup milk
½ cup buttermilk
½ pint heavy cream
3 cups chicken stock, preferably homemade (see page 13), or canned

16-ounce can whole tomatoes
3 tablespoons olive oil
1½ tablespoons red wine vinegar
1 teaspoon Dijon mustard
2 cups flour
2 teaspoons baking powder
½ teaspoon baking soda
½ teaspoon sugar
Paprika
Mixed dried herbs (thyme, rosemary, and marjoram)
Salt and freshly ground black pepper

UTENSILS

Food processor or blender
Stockpot with cover
Small saucepan
Large baking sheet
Plate
Large salad bowl
Large mixing bowl
Small bowl
Colander
Strainer
Measuring cups and spoons
Chef's knife
Paring knife
Slotted spoon
Wooden spoon
Rubber spatula
Small whisk
Vegetable peeler
Pastry brush
Pastry blender (optional)
2- or 2½-inch biscuit cutter or round drinking glass
Salad spinner (optional)
Sifter (if not using food processor)

START-TO-FINISH STEPS

1. Cut bacon into ½-inch pieces and follow chowder recipe step 1.
2. Prepare vegetables for chowder: peel and dice onions; peel and slice carrots; slice celery; peel and dice potatoes; rinse broccoli, trim stem, and break into small flowerets; cut green beans; core, seed, and dice red peppers; scrub zucchini, if using, and slice; clean mushrooms with damp paper towel and slice. If using fresh corn, trim base, stand

corn on base end, and with sharp paring knife vertically slice kernels off cob. If using fresh peas, shell enough to make ½ cup. Drain canned tomatoes in strainer and chop.

3. Follow chowder recipe step 2.

4. For salad, slice radishes and mince garlic, if using. Chop herbs for biscuits.

5. Follow chowder recipe step 3.

6. Follow salad recipe step 1.

7. Follow chowder recipe step 4.

8. Follow herbed biscuit recipe steps 1 through 4.

9. Follow chowder recipe step 5.

10. Make dressing for salad, step 2.

11. Follow chowder recipe step 6, salad recipe step 3, and serve with hot biscuits.

RECIPES

Hearty Vegetable Chowder

½ pound bacon, thickly sliced, cut in ½-inch pieces
3 medium-size onions, peeled and diced
3 carrots, peeled and sliced
2 stalks celery, sliced
4 to 5 medium-size potatoes (about 1½ pounds), peeled and diced
3 cups chicken stock
Salt
Pinch of dried thyme
1 to 1½ cups small broccoli flowerets
¾ cup green beans, cut in 1½-inch lengths
2 red peppers, cored, seeded, and diced
1 zucchini, sliced (optional)
½ cup corn kernels
½ cup peas, preferably fresh, or frozen (optional)
¾ cup canned whole tomatoes, drained and chopped
1 cup sliced mushrooms
⅔ cup heavy cream
½ to 1 cup milk
Freshly ground black pepper
2 tablespoons butter (approximately)
Paprika

1. In stockpot, brown bacon over medium-low heat until golden but not crisp. With slotted spoon, transfer to paper-towel-lined plate; drain.

2. Add onions, carrots, and celery to bacon fat and sauté until onions are wilted, about 8 minutes.

3. Add potatoes, stock, salt to taste, and thyme, and stir to combine. Bring to a simmer and cook until potatoes are tender, about 15 minutes. Using slotted spoon, transfer about half of the vegetables to food processor or blender; reserve.

4. Add broccoli, green beans, red peppers, and zucchini, if using, to pot. Simmer, uncovered, until broccoli is just tender. Meanwhile, purée reserved vegetable in food processor or blender until smooth.

5. Return purée to soup; add corn, peas, if using, tomatoes, mushrooms, cream, ½ cup of milk, and bacon, and stir to combine. Simmer, uncovered, 5 minutes. If you like thinner chowder, add milk to desired consistency.

6. Taste soup and correct seasoning with salt and pepper if necessary. Top each serving with pat of butter and a sprinkling of paprika.

Herbed Buttermilk Biscuits

2 tablespoons butter (approximately)
2 cups flour
2 teaspoons baking powder
¾ teaspoon salt
½ teaspoon baking soda
½ teaspoon sugar
6 tablespoons cold butter
¼ cup chopped fresh herbs (parsley, chives, tarragon, or mixture)
½ cup buttermilk (approximately)

1. Preheat oven to 450 degrees. In small saucepan, melt butter and set aside. Lightly butter baking sheet. Sift together flour, baking powder, salt, baking soda, and sugar into mixing bowl. With 2 table knives or pastry blender, cut in cold butter until mixture is crumbly.

2. Add fresh herbs and about ⅓ cup of buttermilk. Using fork, stir mixture very gently, until it is soft but not sticky. Add more buttermilk as needed.

3. Gently turn out dough onto lightly floured surface, scraping sides of bowl with rubber spatula to loosen any clinging bits of dough. Pat to about ½-inch thickness. Using biscuit cutter, cut into 2- to 2½-inch rounds, and place on baking sheet. You should have about 12 biscuits.

4. Brush biscuits with melted butter and bake 12 to 14 minutes, until puffed and lightly golden. Serve hot, with additional butter.

Tossed Green Salad

1 head soft leaf lettuce, such as Boston or Bibb
Small head Romaine lettuce
3 radishes, thinly sliced (optional)
1½ tablespoons red wine vinegar (approximately)
Pinch dried herbs, including thyme, rosemary, and marjoram, or ½ teaspoon fresh herbs, including parsley
1 teaspoon Dijon mustard
1 clove garlic, minced (optional)
¼ teaspoon salt
½ teaspoon freshly ground pepper
3 tablespoons olive oil

1. Core lettuce and discard any bruised or discolored outer leaves. Wash lettuce under cold running water and dry in salad spinner or pat dry with paper towels. Tear into bite-sized pieces and place in salad bowl. Add radishes, if using. Cover and refrigerate until ready to serve.

2. In small bowl, whisk or stir together vinegar, herbs, mustard, garlic, salt, and pepper until smooth. In a slow, steady stream, add olive oil, whisking vigorously to combine. Correct seasoning, if necessary. Set dressing aside.

3. Just before serving, whisk or stir dressing to recombine and pour over salad; toss.

Leek and Mushroom Tart
Mixed Vegetable Slaw

Serve each guest a wedge of leek and mushroom tart, with a portion of the colorful vegetable slaw on the side.

The French *flamiche* and the Italian *porrata*, which are leek tarts, were the models for Richard Sax's savory and substantial leek and mushroom tart. Leeks, unknown in many American kitchens, are staples in Europe. Prized for their subtle, delicate flavor and versatility, they have a gentle onion taste that enhances rather than overpowers other ingredients.

WHAT TO DRINK

To complement the leek tart try a Chablis or a white Burgundy.

SHOPPING LIST AND STAPLES

6 thin slices ham (about 3 ounces)
8 slender leeks (about 1¾ pounds)
½ to ¾ pound mushrooms
½ cup snow peas (optional)
2 red bell peppers
2 carrots
1 large cucumber
4 radishes
Small bunch fresh parsley
2 eggs

1 stick plus 3 tablespoons unsalted butter
½ pint heavy cream
½ cup milk
¼ pound Swiss cheese
2 tablespoons vegetable oil
¼ cup vinegar, preferably rice wine vinegar
1½ cups flour
1 cup dried beans or rice
1 teaspoon sugar
Freshly grated nutmeg
Cayenne pepper
Salt and freshly ground pepper

UTENSILS

Food processor or grater
Large skillet with cover
9-inch tart or pie pan
3 large mixing bowls
Medium-size bowl
Small bowl
Measuring cups and spoons
Chef's knife
Paring knife
2 wooden spoons
Whisk
Nutmeg grater
Vegetable peeler
Rolling pin
Cooling rack

START-TO-FINISH STEPS

1. Follow tart shell recipe step 1.
2. Clean leeks and trim off tops and roots. Split lengthwise in half and rinse well under running water. Cut crosswise into slices. Clean and quarter mushrooms.
3. Complete tart shell recipe, steps 2 through 4.
4. Follow leek tart recipe steps 1 and 2. Sliver ham and, using food processor or grater, grate Swiss cheese. Chop parsley. Separate eggs and grate nutmeg.
5. Continue leek tart recipe, steps 3 through 5.
6. Prepare slaw vegetables; follow recipe steps 1 and 2.
7. When tart has rested, serve with slaw.

RECIPES

Leek and Mushroom Tart

8 slender leeks (about 1¾ pounds), trimmed, washed, halved lengthwise, and cut into 1-inch slices
3 tablespoons butter
Salt
1½ cups quartered mushrooms
1 cup slivered ham (about 6 slices)
½ cup freshly grated Swiss cheese
3 tablespoons chopped parsley
½ cup milk
½ cup heavy cream (or use more milk)

2 egg yolks
Pinch each of Cayenne pepper and grated nutmeg
Freshly ground pepper
1 partly baked 9-inch tart shell (see following recipe)

1. Preheat oven to 400 degrees.
2. Place leeks, 1 tablespoon of butter, 1 tablespoon cold water, and a little salt in large skillet. Cook over medium heat, covered, until leeks are slightly limp, about 10 minutes. Uncover and toss until liquid has evaporated, 1 to 2 minutes. Transfer to large mixing bowl.
3. Heat remaining butter in skillet and sauté mushrooms. Add mushrooms, ham, cheese, and parsley to mixture in bowl; toss to combine.
4. In medium-size bowl, whisk together milk, cream, egg yolks, Cayenne, nutmeg, and salt and pepper to taste.
5. Spread leek mixture in tart shell; place in oven and pour custard mixture over leeks. Bake 8 minutes, then lower heat to 375 degrees. Bake until set and lightly golden, 25 to 30 minutes. Let sit 5 minutes; cut into wedges.

Tart Shell

1½ cups flour
1 teaspoon salt
8 tablespoons cold butter
2 tablespoons cold water (approximately)
1 cup dried beans or rice (for weighting down pastry shell)

1. In large bowl, mix flour and salt, and cut in butter with 2 knives until mixture is crumbly. Stir in enough cold water so that pastry can be gathered into a ball. Wrap in wax paper and chill briefly.
2. Preheat oven to 400 degrees.
3. Roll out pastry, fit into 9-inch tart pan, and trim. Line with aluminum foil and fill with dried beans or rice. Bake shell until sides are set, 6 to 8 minutes.
4. Carefully remove foil and beans, and return shell to oven for about 8 minutes, until very pale gold. Remove from oven and set on cooling rack.

Mixed Vegetable Slaw

2 red bell peppers, seeded, cored, and cut into long, thin strips
1 large cucumber, peeled, halved lengthwise, seeded, and cut into long, thin strips
2 carrots, peeled, trimmed, and cut into long strips
4 radishes, thinly sliced
½ cup snow peas, cut lengthwise into strips (optional)
¼ cup vinegar
2 tablespoons vegetable oil
1 teaspoon sugar
½ teaspoon salt
Freshly ground pepper

1. Combine prepared vegetables in large mixing bowl.
2. In small bowl, stir together vinegar, oil, sugar, salt, and pepper. Correct seasonings to taste; use plenty of pepper. Pour dressing over vegetables and toss. Chill.

Individual Pumpkin Soufflés
Oven-Roasted Chicken Breasts
Rice Pilaf with Fresh Vegetables

Pumpkin soufflé is a light complement to this autumn meal of browned chicken breasts and vegetable-studded pilaf.

The pumpkin soufflés here are made without a flour-butter base, so they are exceptionally fragile. These do not rise as high as other soufflés, nor do they stay puffed once out of the oven.

If you use canned pumpkin purée, make sure it is the unsweetened variety, not the pie filling. To prepare fresh purée, split a pumpkin in half crosswise and scrape out the seeds and stringy material. Place halves cut-side down on a foil-lined baking sheet. Cover with foil and bake at 350 degrees, until tender, about 1½ hours. Cool, then scrape the flesh from the pumpkin shells and purée through a sieve or in a food processor.

WHAT TO DRINK

With this menu, the cook suggests a sprightly fruity white wine, such as an Italian Pinot Grigio or Tocai.

SHOPPING LIST AND STAPLES

2 large whole boneless chicken breasts with skin
2-pound fresh pumpkin, or 16-ounce can pumpkin
¼ pound green beans
¼ pound mushrooms
1 carrot

2 medium-size onions
2 scallions
Small bunch parsley
1 clove garlic
5 eggs
5 tablespoons unsalted butter
1¾ cups chicken stock, preferably homemade (see page 13), or canned
3 tablespoons maple syrup
2 tablespoons olive oil
1¼ cups long-grain rice
Flour or ground nuts
Freshly grated nutmeg
Cinnamon
Allspice
Salt and freshly ground pepper
2 tablespoons dry white wine

UTENSILS

Food processor (if using fresh pumpkin)
Large ovenproof skillet
Small skillet
Medium-size heavy-gauge saucepan with cover
Small baking pan
4 individual soufflé dishes or custard cups
2 large mixing bowls, 1 copper (if using whisk for soufflés)
Measuring cups and spoons
Chef's knife
Paring knife
Wooden spoon
Rubber spatula
Nutmeg grater
Electric hand mixer or whisk
Metal tongs

START-TO-FINISH STEPS

1. For soufflé recipe, peel and finely chop onion, separate eggs, grate nutmeg, and follow recipe steps 1 through 4.
2. Prepare vegetables for pilaf and follow recipe steps 1 through 4.
3. Follow soufflé recipe steps 5 and 6.
4. With flat side of chef's knife, crush garlic lightly and peel. Follow chicken recipe steps 1 through 3.
5. Follow pilaf recipe step 5, chicken recipe step 4, and serve with soufflés.

RECIPES

Individual Pumpkin Soufflés

1 tablespoon butter
Flour or ground nuts
3 tablespoons finely chopped onion
1½ cups pumpkin purée, fresh or canned
3 egg yolks
3 tablespoons maple syrup
½ teaspoon salt

¼ teaspoon freshly grated nutmeg
Pinch each of cinnamon, allspice, and freshly ground pepper
5 egg whites

1. Preheat oven to 425 degrees.
2. Butter 4 individual soufflé dishes or custard cups. Dust bottom and sides with flour or nuts; shake out excess.
3. In small skillet, heat 1 tablespoon butter over medium-low heat and sauté onion briefly, just until wilted.
4. In large mixing bowl, blend sautéed onion, pumpkin purée, egg yolks, maple syrup, salt, and spices.
5. In another large bowl, beat egg whites until stiff but not dry. Gently fold about one fourth of the whites into the pumpkin mixture; fold in remaining whites. Gently pour into dishes and smooth tops with spatula.
6. Bake until soufflés have puffed, 18 to 20 minutes.

Oven-Roasted Chicken Breasts

2 large whole boneless chicken breasts with skin (about 1 to 1¼ pounds each), halved
Salt and freshly ground pepper
1 clove garlic, lightly crushed and peeled
1 tablespoon butter
2 tablespoons olive oil

1. Trim off all fat and excess skin from chicken. Sprinkle lightly with salt and pepper. Rub with garlic.
2. Heat butter, oil, and garlic clove in ovenproof skillet large enough to hold chicken in single layer. When butter stops foaming, add breasts, skin side down. Sauté chicken over medium heat until skin is golden, about 5 minutes.
3. Place skillet in oven (after soufflés have cooked about 10 minutes). Open and shut oven door gently. Roast 5 minutes. Using tongs, turn breasts and roast 5 minutes.
4. Remove to dinner plates.

Rice Pilaf with Fresh Vegetables

2 tablespoons butter
1 tablespoon finely chopped onion
2 scallions, green and white portions, sliced
1 carrot, peeled and sliced
½ cup green beans, cut into 1- to 1½-inch lengths
½ cup sliced mushrooms
1¼ cups long-grain white rice
2 tablespoons dry white wine
1¾ cups chicken stock
2 tablespoons chopped parsley
Salt and freshly ground pepper

1. In medium-size heavy-gauge saucepan, heat butter over medium-low heat. Cook onion briefly until wilted.
2. Add vegetables and sauté about 3 minutes.
3. Add rice and toss to coat with butter. Cook, stirring, about 2 minutes. Add wine and boil briefly.
4. Add stock, stirring, and bring to a boil. Lower heat and simmer, partly covered, about 17 minutes, or until rice is tender. Remove from heat, cover, and keep warm.
5. Add parsley and salt and pepper to taste; fluff with fork.

Barbara Tropp

Most Westerners assume that Chinese cuisine accentuates meats and fish, but, according to Barbara Tropp, China scholar turned cook: "In the Chinese world, vegetables have preeminence. The Chinese love to keep the character of the vegetable intact." They never serve raw vegetables. Instead, the Chinese cook them until just crisp-tender to bring out their full, natural flavor, as she does with the red peppers in the stir-fried recipe of Menu 1.

Traditionally, the Chinese prize freshness, which is why Barbara Tropp does not include canned vegetables in her recipes. If a vegetable is unavailable fresh, she advises you to select another. You must think of your recipe as a mixture of contrasting tastes and textures, then include a vegetable you enjoy. One dish in Menu 3 is stir-fried spinach and glass noodles. If perfectly fresh, crisp spinach is not available, try kale or an Oriental spinach-like green such as *bok choy*.

When Chinese cooks prepare produce for a multi-vegetable recipe, they slice each differently. For the Hunan-style vegetables of Menu 2, for instance, the cook directs you to slice the zucchini and carrots in different widths, so that they cook evenly. For the entrée in that meal, she uses sliced pork loin or—in an alternate version—an exotic ingredient, gluten, as a centerpiece for the vegetables. Also known as "mock meat," this high-protein product is made from wheat gluten and formulated to have a meaty texture.

Fresh ginger, almonds, tofu, mushrooms, red pepper, egg, green pepper, scallions, and carrots are ubiquitous Chinese ingredients. They are combined in this menu to produce a savory tofu stew, shown here in a Chinese sand pot, as well as a colorful stir-fried rice dish with green and red peppers and whole almonds.

Savory Tofu Stew
Stir-Fried Rice with Bell Peppers and Almonds

The combination of the tofu stew and stir-fried rice provides enough color, texture, and complementary proteins to comprise a complete dinner without any meat. Tofu is a soybean product that is low in fat. Often used in Oriental cooking, it is available in supermarkets.

You can find black soy sauce in Chinese markets or specialty food shops. You will also need either a Chinese black vinegar or balsamic vinegar for the stew. Black vinegar is usually available in Chinese markets.

WHAT TO DRINK

Chinese flavors are best accompanied by good German wine—a Riesling, for instance. But the cook, a red wine lover, also recommends a robust Italian or French red: a Côtes du Rhône or a Barbera.

SHOPPING LIST AND STAPLES

6 squares white Chinese-style tofu (about 1½ pounds)
1 pound slender carrots
⅓ pound medium-size or large white mushrooms
2 large bell peppers, preferably red
1 bunch medium-size scallions
4 large cloves garlic
2-inch length fresh ginger
3 large eggs
1¾ cups unsalted chicken or vegetable stock, preferably homemade (see page 13), or canned
5 to 6 cups plus 5 to 6 tablespoons corn or peanut oil
3 tablespoons black soy sauce
1½ to 2 tablespoons Chinese black vinegar or balsamic vinegar
1 cup rice
8 medium-size or 6 large dried Chinese black mushrooms, preferably the flower variety
2½-ounce package blanched whole almonds
1 tablespoon light brown sugar
Kosher salt and freshly ground black pepper
Freshly ground white pepper
2 teaspoons Chinese rice wine or dry sherry

UTENSILS

14-inch wok
    or Dutch oven with cover (for frying tofu)
    and large cast-iron skillet (for stir frying rice)
12-inch Chinese sand pot
    or 12-inch heavy casserole with cover
Medium-size saucepan with tight-fitting lid
2 baking sheets
Large dinner plate
Large bowl
6 small bowls
2 large strainers
Measuring cups and spoons
Thin-bladed Chinese cleaver or chef's knife
Paring knife
Metal wok spatula or metal spatula
Slotted metal spoon or Chinese mesh spoon
16-inch chopsticks or wooden spoon
Wooden tongs (optional)
Vegetable peeler
Deep-fat thermometer
Scissors

START-TO-FINISH STEPS

The night before or in the morning: Prepare rice for stir-fried rice recipe, steps 1 through 6.

1. Preheat oven to 300 degrees.
2. Trim and cut scallions into 1-inch lengths, slice ginger into 4 quarter-size rounds, and follow tofu stew recipe steps 1 through 15.
3. Wipe out wok, if using. In small bowl, beat eggs with fork and set aside until ready to use. Follow rice recipe steps 7 through 16. Heat serving bowl for rice in oven.
4. Follow tofu stew recipe step 16, stir-fried rice recipe step 17, and serve.

RECIPES

Savory Tofu Stew

8 medium-size or 6 large dried Chinese black mushrooms
6 squares white Chinese-style tofu (about 1½ pounds)
5 to 6 cups corn or peanut oil
1 pound slender carrots
⅓ pound medium-size or large fresh white mushrooms
4 medium-size whole scallions, cut into 1-inch lengths
4 quarter-size slices fresh ginger
4 large cloves garlic
1¾ cups unsalted chicken or vegetable stock
3 tablespoons black soy sauce
1 tablespoon light brown sugar, firmly packed

1½ tablespoons Chinese black vinegar or balsamic vinegar
Kosher salt and freshly ground black pepper

1. In small bowl, soak dried mushrooms in hot water to cover until fully soft and spongy, 20 to 30 minutes.
2. Cut tofu into large triangles by cutting across both diagonals of each square to yield 24 triangles.
3. Place tofu, cut sides down, on baking sheet lined with a triple layer of paper towels.
4. Set wok or Dutch oven over high heat. Add oil to a level 1¼ inches below rim and heat.
5. Peel carrots. Cut on diagonal at 1-inch intervals, rolling carrot a third of a turn away from you after each cut.
6. Clean fresh mushrooms and trim any woody stems. Halve or quarter mushrooms, including stems.
7. Smack scallions and ginger lightly with broad side of cleaver. Smack each clove of garlic similarly and discard peel. In small bowl, combine scallions, ginger, and garlic. In another small bowl, combine stock, soy sauce, brown sugar, and vinegar.
8. Line another baking sheet with a double layer of paper towels and set beside baking sheet with tofu.
9. When oil registers 375 degrees on deep-fat thermometer, hot enough so that a bit of tofu bobs to surface within 2 seconds, carefully add tofu triangles to oil one by one. Shield yourself from any spattering; do *not* cover pot. With chopsticks or wooden spoon, poke triangles gently to separate them. Adjust heat to maintain temperature: there will be a crown of white bubbles around each triangle. If necessary, fry tofu in 2 batches, being certain to let oil reheat to 375 degrees before frying second batch.
10. Fry tofu triangles until evenly golden brown, about 4 minutes, turning them with chopsticks or wooden tongs. With slotted metal spoon or Chinese mesh spoon, remove them to drain on prepared paper-towel-lined baking sheet.
11. Turn off heat and carefully move pot to a back burner. (When it has cooled, you can strain oil and store for reuse.)
12. Drain black mushrooms, snip off stems with scissors, and rinse caps briefly under cool water to dislodge any sand trapped in gills. If caps are very large, cut them in half with scissors.
13. Stir stock mixture, then pour into sand pot or heavy casserole. If you are using a sand pot, bring liquids to a simmer over low heat. Otherwise, simmer over high heat.
14. Add black mushrooms and scallion mixture to pot. Cover and simmer 5 minutes.
15. Add tofu, carrots, and fresh mushrooms. Stir gently to baste them with sauce, cover, and simmer until carrots are tender, 20 to 30 minutes. Lift lid after 10 minutes to check simmer and gently stir stew to redistribute ingredients.
16. Turn off heat and stir stew. Taste and adjust seasonings, adding a dash more vinegar or sugar to obtain a rich flavor. Add Kosher salt and pepper to taste.

Stir-Fried Rice with Bell Peppers and Almonds

1 cup rice
½ cup blanched whole almonds
2 large bell peppers, preferably red

5 to 6 tablespoons corn or peanut oil
3 large eggs, beaten
2 teaspoons Chinese rice wine or dry sherry
1 teaspoon Kosher salt
Freshly ground white pepper

1. Place rice in large bowl with cold water to cover. With your hand, stir in circles 15 to 20 seconds. Drain in strainer. Dry bowl.
2. Transfer rice to saucepan. Add 1½ cups water for short- or medium-grain rice, 1¾ cups for long-grain rice, and bring to a rolling boil over medium-high heat.
3. When starchy bubbles climb nearly to rim, in about 30 seconds, cover and reduce heat to maintain a slow, bubbly simmer. Do not lift lid until removing rice from pan.
4. Simmer rice 15 minutes. Remove from heat and let rest 20 minutes.
5. Remove cover and gently fluff rice with fork to separate grains. Spread rice in thin layer on baking sheet to cool.
6. When thoroughly cool, transfer to the large bowl used for soaking, cover, and refrigerate until needed.
7. Spread almonds on baking sheet and toast in oven until golden, about 5 minutes, shaking sheet occasionally. Transfer to small bowl and set aside. Turn off oven.
8. Cut peppers in half lengthwise; core, seed, and remove white ribs. Cut lengthwise into ½-inch strips. Holding strips together, cut them crosswise into ½-inch squares.
9. Using your fingers, toss the cold rice. Have all ingredients plus dinner plate within easy reach.
10. Heat wok or skillet over high heat until hot enough to evaporate a bead of water on contact. Coat bottom and lower sides of pan with 2½ tablespoons of oil, then reduce heat to medium-high. When oil is hot enough to puff 1 drop of egg on contact, beat eggs again and add to pan. They should puff and bubble around the edge immediately. Pause until film of cooked egg sets on bottom. With spatula, push cooked egg to far side of pan, so liquid egg will flow into center. Continue until just set, then scrape onto plate and break into small bits.
11. Wipe pan with wet paper towel, leaving thin film of oil, and return it to high heat.
12. When pan is hot enough to evaporate a bead of water on contact, add 2 tablespoons oil, swirl to coat bottom, and reduce heat to medium-high. When hot enough to sizzle a pepper square, add peppers and, using spatula, toss to glaze and heat through, 15 to 20 seconds, adjusting heat so peppers sizzle without scorching.
13. Add wine to pan, pause several seconds, then stir briskly to glaze peppers with wine essence.
14. Add rice and toss to combine. Heat about 1 to 2 minutes; lower heat if rice begins to scorch. If necessary, drizzle in more oil from side of pan to prevent sticking.
15. When rice is hot, add salt and toss to combine. Taste for seasoning; add salt and pepper to taste.
16. Add eggs, tossing gently to combine, and heat through, about 10 seconds. Turn off heat; keep covered.
17. Just before serving, add almonds and stir to combine. Turn rice into heated serving bowl.

Pot-Browned "Noodle Pillow"
Stir-Fried Curried Pork with Onions
Hot-and-Sour Hunan-Style Vegetables

Barbara Tropp's name for the pan-fried noodles in this menu is "noodle pillow." Quickly cook the noodles and drain them. Form a pillow by coiling noodle strands in a hot skillet. Brown pillow on each side, as you would a pancake. If possible, use fresh, Chinese egg noodles, which come in one-pound bags. You can refrigerate extra noodles for up to a week or freeze them for several months. If you cannot find the Chinese variety, substitute fresh or dried Italian vermicelli. You can prepare this recipe a day

or two ahead: just boil, drain, and toss the noodles with oil and salt; then store them in a covered container in the refrigerator.

Both Northern and Southern Chinese use curry in a limited number of stews, favoring a flavor that is fruitier than that of the more familiar, sharp-and-spicy Indian curries. The pork recipe here calls for curry paste, an oil-based mixture of spices, turmeric, and hot chilies. Available in Chinese groceries, it will keep indefinitely in your pantry. If you use the gluten alternate, pay careful attention to the recipe directions for this version. Some of the steps and techniques are different, and you will not need the curry paste. The "Companion" brand of canned, curry-braised gluten is the one Barbara Tropp recommends. You

Serve the curried pork on a bed of crisp pan-fried noodles, which have been pre-cut for easier handling. The hot-and-sour vegetables, displayed in a shallow dish, offer a variety of taste, color, and texture.

can buy it at many large Chinese markets. In either case, you will need regular soy sauce and black sesame seeds. A regular, or thin and light, soy sauce is mild tasting and ideal for adding both color and taste to cooking liquids. Black sesame seeds are a standard Chinese garnish, desirable for their flavor and texture. Toasting them first, which is optional, intensifies the nutty flavor. They are available in Chinese markets and should be stored in airtight jars in your refrigerator.

For the vegetable recipe, you need two other typically Oriental ingredients: salted black soybeans and rice vinegar. The black beans are a popular seasoning agent used in many kinds of sauces. They come in plastic bags, bottles, or jars and, once opened, last indefinitely in an airtight container on your pantry shelf. Avoid brands that contain Chinese five-spice powder; these are too potent for most recipes. A white rice vinegar, whether Chinese or Japanese, has a clean, refreshing taste that is fuller than that of a Western white vinegar. Rice vinegars are sold in the gourmet section of many supermarkets.

WHAT TO DRINK

The cook favors a hearty red wine for this menu, either a Petite Syrah or a Zinfandel. Ice-cold beer or ale are traditional beverages served with highly seasoned Chinese dishes; either one would be a good accompaniment to the lively spices featured here.

SHOPPING LIST AND STAPLES

¾-pound well-trimmed boneless pork loin, or 10-ounce can Curry-Braised Gluten (Curry Chai Chi Jou), preferably Companion brand
¾-pound Chinese cabbage (with broad, tightly wrapped, light green leaves)
1 head cauliflower (to yield ¾ pound flowerets)
1 pound firm, slender zucchini
½ pound carrots
2 large yellow onions
3 cloves garlic
1-inch length fresh ginger
1 cup plus 1½ tablespoons unsalted chicken or vegetable stock, preferably homemade (see page 13), or canned
1 cup plus 6 tablespoons corn or peanut oil
¼ cup plus 2½ tablespoons light soy sauce
2 tablespoons unseasoned Chinese or Japanese rice vinegar
2 teaspoons Oriental sesame oil

3 to 4 teaspoons curry paste
¾ pound thin, fresh or frozen Chinese egg noodles, or
   Italian vermicelli
2 tablespoons Chinese salted black beans (not the variety
   seasoned with five-spice powder)
2 tablespoons black sesame seeds
2 tablespoons cornstarch
¾ teaspoon dried red pepper flakes
2 teaspoons sugar
Kosher salt

UTENSILS

Stockpot or kettle with cover
2 woks or 2 twelve-inch heavy-gauge skillets with covers,
   preferably cast iron
Heatproof serving bowl
Large plate (optional)
2 large bowls
Medium-size bowl
2 small bowls plus additional bowl (if using alternate
   recipe)
Large colander
Strainer (if using alternate recipe)
Measuring cups and spoons
Thin-bladed Chinese cleaver or chef's knife
Paring knife
Metal spatula or metal wok spatula
Wooden spoon
16-inch chopsticks or wooden spoon
Vegetable peeler

START-TO-FINISH STEPS

1. If using frozen noodles, thaw and follow noodle pillow recipe step 1.
2. While water comes to a boil, follow stir-fried curried pork recipe steps 1 through 4.
3. Follow noodle pillow recipe steps 2 through 6.
4. Follow Hunan-style vegetables recipe steps 1 through 5.
5. Preheat oven to 250 degrees. Heat serving platters or bowl for vegetables and for noodle pillow.
6. Follow noodle pillow recipe steps 7 and 8.
7. In small bowl or cup, dissolve cornstarch in stock or water. Cook hot-and-sour vegetables, steps 6 through 12, and keep warm in oven.
8. Cook other side of noodle pillow, steps 9 through 11.
9. Follow curried pork recipe steps 5 through 8.
10. Remove vegetables and noodle pillow from oven. Follow noodle pillow recipe step 12, curried pork recipe step 9, and serve at once with vegetables.

RECIPES

Pot-Browned "Noodle Pillow"

¾ pound thin Chinese egg noodles, fresh, or frozen
   and thoroughly defrosted, or Italian vermicelli

2 teaspoons Oriental sesame oil
1½ teaspoons Kosher salt
5 to 7 tablespoons corn or peanut oil

1. In covered stockpot or kettle, bring 3 to 4 quarts of warm, unsalted water to a boil over high heat.
2. In large colander, gently fluff noodles with your fingers to separate strands.
3. Add noodles to pot and cook 3 to 4 minutes until still firm but just cooked through, swishing occasionally with chopsticks or handle of wooden spoon.
4. Drain immediately in colander, then refresh under cold running water until chilled, turning noodles with your hands, once they have begun to cool, to chill them evenly. Shake colander several times to remove excess water from noodles.
5. Spread noodles on large, lint-free towel, then roll it up into loose tube and gently pat to dry noodles, just as you would dry a sweater.
6. Remove noodles to large bowl, sprinkle with sesame oil and salt, then gently toss strands with your fingers, glazing and separating them. Be careful not to break noodles as you toss them.
7. Heat skillet or wok over high heat until hot enough to evaporate a bead of water on contact. Add 4 or 5 tablespoons vegetable oil, depending on size of pan, then swirl to glaze sides and bottom of pan. Reduce heat to medium.
8. When oil is hot enough to sizzle a single noodle, add noodles, coiling them evenly in pan and working from outer perimeter to the center. Press down with spatula, cover pan, and cook until bottom is evenly golden brown, 5 to 7 minutes. Check after a minute and adjust heat if required so that noodles sizzle gently in oil and begin to steam.
9. With spatula, loosen browned noodles, then flip pillow over with sharp jerk of your wrist, or slide pillow onto inverted pot lid or large plate; invert holder and slip noodles back into pan, browned side up.
10. Drizzle remaining oil in from side of pan, then shake gently to distribute oil underneath noodles. Press pillow down with spatula, cover pan, and cook until browned, 5 to 7 minutes more.
11. With spatula, loosen noodles, if needed, then slip them onto round, heated serving platter. If necessary, you can hold noodle pillow in preheated 250-degree oven.
12. For easy serving, cut noodle pillow into wedges with knife, before topping with stir-fried curried pork or gluten. It will not appear cut and will be very easy to serve.

Stir-Fried Curried Pork with Onions

¾-pound well-trimmed boneless pork loin, or 10-ounce
   can Curry-Braised Gluten (Curry Chai Chi Jou)
1 tablespoon cornstarch
1½ or 1¾ teaspoons sugar
4 tablespoons light soy sauce
2 large yellow onions
¾ pound Chinese cabbage (with tightly wrapped, light
   green leaves)

3 to 4 teaspoons curry paste
½ cup unsalted chicken or vegetable stock
7 to 9 tablespoons corn or peanut oil
Kosher salt
2 tablespoons black sesame seeds

1. For pork recipe, using cleaver or chef's knife, cut meat against grain into even slices a scant ⅛-inch thick and 2 inches wide. In large bowl, combine cornstarch, 1½ teaspoons sugar, and 3 tablespoons soy sauce, stirring well to blend. Add pork, then toss well with your fingers to coat each slice.

For alternate recipe: Omit cornstarch mixture. Drain the gluten in strainer set over small bowl; reserve liquid. Cut gluten into ⅛-inch strips.

2. Using either Chinese cleaver or chef's knife, halve onions lengthwise, peel, then cut crosswise into arcs ¼-inch thick.

3. Leaving cabbage intact for quick cutting, slice crosswise into strips ½ inch wide. Cut base piece(s) where strips do not separate into pie-type wedges, then combine wedges and strips in medium-size bowl.

4. For pork recipe, in small bowl, combine curry paste, stock, ¼ teaspoon sugar, and 1 tablespoon soy sauce, stirring to blend. For alternate recipe, omit this entire step and all these ingredients.

5. Heat wok or skillet (that is deep enough to accommodate onions and cabbage) over high heat until hot enough to evaporate a bead of water on contact. Add 4 tablespoons oil, swirl to glaze pan, then reduce heat to medium-high. When hot enough to sizzle a piece of onion, add onions and toss gently to glaze and separate pieces, adjusting heat to maintain a sizzle without scorching onion; drizzle in a bit more oil from side of pan if onions become too dry. Continue to toss until onions soften, 3 to 4 minutes.

6. Add cabbage and toss briskly to combine with onions. Sprinkle with salt and continue to toss until cabbage is lightly glazed and hot, about 1 minute, adjusting heat to maintain a sizzle and drizzling in a bit more oil from side of pan if needed.

7. For pork recipe, transfer vegetables to medium-size bowl, cover, and keep warm. Wipe pan clean and return it to high heat until hot enough to evaporate a bead of water on contact. Add 3 tablespoons oil, swirl to coat bottom of pan, then reduce heat to medium-high. Add pork and toss briskly to separate slices. When pork is 90 percent gray, add curry mixture and vegetables, and toss 1 minute to combine thoroughly.

For alternate recipe: Leave vegetables in pan, add gluten strips, and toss to combine. Add reserved gluten liquid, stirring to blend. Raise heat to bring liquids to a simmer. Cover pan and simmer 2 to 3 minutes, until onions and cabbage have absorbed the liquid's color and flavor and liquid is reduced by about two thirds.

8. Turn off heat, stir, and sprinkle with 1 tablespoon of sesame seeds. Stir to combine. Taste and adjust seasoning, if necessary.

9. Mound on pot-browned noodle pillow and sprinkle with remaining sesame seeds.

Hot-and-Sour Hunan-Style Vegetables

1 head cauliflower (to yield ¾ pound flowerets)
½ pound carrots
1 pound firm, slender zucchini
1 tablespoon finely minced ginger
1 tablespoon finely minced garlic
2 tablespoons Chinese salted black beans (not seasoned with five-spice powder)
¾ teaspoon dried red pepper flakes
½ cup unsalted chicken or vegetable stock
2½ tablespoons light soy sauce
2 tablespoons unseasoned Chinese or Japanese rice vinegar
¼ teaspoon sugar
4 to 6 tablespoons corn or peanut oil
1 tablespoon cornstarch dissolved in 1½ tablespoons cold stock or water

1. Tear off leaves from base of cauliflower. Using paring knife, cut flowerets from cauliflower. Cut any large flowerets into walnut-size pieces.

2. Trim and peel carrots. Using Chinese cleaver or chef's knife, cut carrots on diagonal into thin coins, ⅛ inch thick.

3. Trim tips from zucchini, then cut crosswise into rounds ¼ inch thick. (The quickest way to do this is to line several zucchini up side by side, then cut them crosswise at once using cleaver or long chef's knife.)

4. Combine ginger, garlic, salted black beans, and pepper flakes in small bowl. With wooden spoon, combine stock, soy sauce, vinegar, and sugar in another small bowl, and leave spoon in bowl.

5. Have all ingredients within easy reach of your stovetop.

6. Heat wok or skillet over high heat until hot. Add 4 tablespoons oil, swirl to glaze pan, then reduce heat to medium-high. When oil is hot enough to sizzle a bit of ginger mixture, add it to pan. With wooden spoon, stir gently until fragrant, about 15 seconds, adjusting heat so mixture foams without scorching.

7. Add cauliflower and toss briskly about 1 minute, to glaze flowerets evenly and start them cooking. Lower heat if they begin to scorch, and drizzle in a bit more oil from side of pan if cauliflower becomes dry.

8. Add carrots and toss about 1 minute more, until evenly glazed, hot, and edges curl slightly; adjust heat and add more oil if needed.

9. Add zucchini and toss about 30 seconds, drizzling in a bit more oil if slices look dry.

10. With wooden spoon, stir sauce ingredients and add them to pan. Toss well to combine, then raise heat to bring liquids to a simmer. Adjust heat to maintain a steady simmer, cover pan, and simmer 1 minute. Stir, test for doneness, then cover and simmer another 30 to 60 seconds, if zucchini is not quite tender-crisp.

11. Reduce heat to low when zucchini is done. Stir cornstarch mixture to recombine, add it to pan, then toss until mixture turns glossy, about 15 seconds.

12. Remove vegetables to heatproof serving bowl and keep warm in oven until ready to serve.

Wine "Explosion" Mushroom Soup with Sweet Peas
"Old Egg" with Scallion and Shrimp
Stir-Fried Velvet Spinach with Glass Noodles

Wine "explosion" soup with mushrooms and peas precedes the light entrée—a Chinese-style soufflé and spinach with noodles.

In this light meal, suitable for a mild spring evening, the soup functions as a fragrant beverage for the soufflé and the vegetables. Serve all three dishes at once, just as a Chinese family would do.

The Chinese delight in whimsical names for their recipes. Here, wine "explosion" describes the sizzle in the classic Chinese technique of adding wine to hot oil. This evaporates the alcohol and traps the wine essence as the base for the soup. Barbara Tropp uses a mixture of dried and fresh mushrooms to give the broth its dusky character. Dried black mushrooms, highly valued in Chinese cooking, have a fragrant, smoky taste and, after soaking, a velvety texture. The soaking also makes them spongy enough to cut into pieces. Dried mushrooms are available from Chinese groceries or specialty food shops; they keep indefinitely on your pantry shelf.

A variety of fresh mushrooms is now available at several types of outlets. Western button mushrooms can be bought all year in most supermarkets—look for perfect,

white or cream-colored caps. Mild Japanese *enokitake*, which look like miniature umbrellas, *shiitake* (the Japanese term for the Chinese dried black mushroom in its fresh form), and pearly oyster mushrooms can be found in Oriental markets and in some Western markets. Golden trumpet-shaped chanterelles grow wild, but, unless you are a trained mycologist, you should look for them at quality greengrocers.

"Old egg," another Chinese whimsy, describes the Chinese version of soufflé, cooked for a long time (hence, old) on top of the stove. Unlike the French soufflé, this version puffs best when you chill the eggs before you beat them. Beat them only slightly; beat whites and yolks together. This recipe takes only a few minutes to assemble and about a half hour to cook.

Glass noodles, more commonly called bean threads, are sold in cellophane packets in Chinese markets or in the gourmet food section of some supermarkets. Made from mung-bean starch, they turn transparent when cooked.

Bean threads require soaking in either hot or boiling water, depending on where they were manufactured. Bean threads from Taiwan or Thailand need hot water; boiling water makes them gelatinous. Those from the People's Republic of China need boiling water. Regardless of the brand, soak bean threads still wrapped in their rubber-band or string binding; otherwise they become too unmanageable to cut.

Oriental sesame oil, used for seasoning rather than cooking, has the rich nutty aroma of toasted sesame seeds. For this recipe, do not buy the Middle Eastern, cold-pressed sesame varieties, which have a very different flavor.

If you wish to prepare this meal partly beforehand, you can make the soup, blanch the spinach, and soak the bean threads and the dried mushrooms a day in advance.

WHAT TO DRINK

The cook's preference here is for a light red wine with character, such as a Beaujolais. If you prefer tea with Chinese dishes, try a slightly acidic imported variety like Water Goddess or Dragon Well.

SHOPPING LIST AND STAPLES

½ cup tiny bay shrimp or ¼ pound small shrimp
2 pounds spinach, preferably with stems and rosy root ends intact
½ pound fresh mushrooms (choose 1 or 2 types: white button, enokitake, shiitake, oyster, or chanterelles)
½ pound unshelled peas, or 10-ounce package frozen peas
1 bunch scallions
4 shallots (optional)
8 large eggs
4⅓ cups unsalted chicken or vegetable stock, preferably homemade (see page 13), or canned
½ cup plus 1 tablespoon corn or peanut oil
2 teaspoons Oriental sesame oil
1½ teaspoons light soy sauce
2 ounces bean threads (glass noodles)
8 large dried Chinese black mushrooms, preferably thick-capped flower variety
2 teaspoons sugar
Kosher salt
Freshly ground pepper
2 tablespoons Chinese rice wine or dry sherry (approximately)

UTENSILS

2½- or 3-quart heavy Dutch oven, casserole, or small stockpot with tight-fitting cover
Wok or large, heavy-gauge skillet
Large saucepan with cover
Medium-size non-aluminum saucepan with cover
Small saucepan with cover
Large bowl

Medium-size bowl
2 small bowls
Colander
Strainer
Measuring cups and spoons
Thin-bladed Chinese cleaver or chef's knife
Paring knife
Chinese metal wok spatula or metal spatula
Wooden spoon
Whisk (optional)
Scissors

START-TO-FINISH STEPS

1. If using fresh peas for soup, shell enough to measure ½ cup; if using frozen peas, set them out to thaw. Mince shallots or scallions to measure 2 tablespoons. Follow mushroom soup recipe step 1.
2. Follow stir-fried spinach recipe step 1.
3. Follow old egg recipe step 1. Slice scallion rings to measure 4 tablespoons.
4. Heat 3 to 4 cups of water in teakettle to required temperature for soaking bean threads. Follow stir-fried spinach recipe steps 2 through 8.
5. Follow old egg recipe steps 2 through 6.
6. Follow mushroom soup recipe steps 2 through 9.
7. Follow stir-fried spinach recipe steps 9 and 10, old egg recipe step 7, and serve with the soup.

RECIPES

Wine "Explosion" Mushroom Soup with Sweet Peas

8 large dried Chinese black mushrooms
½ pound fresh mushrooms (choose 1 or 2 types: white button, enokitake, shiitake, oyster, or chanterelles)
4 cups unsalted chicken or vegetable stock
½ cup green peas, fresh or frozen and defrosted
2 to 4 tablespoons corn or peanut oil
2 tablespoons finely minced shallots or thinly cut scallion rings, from green and white sections
1½ tablespoons Chinese rice wine or dry sherry
Pinch of sugar
Kosher salt

1. In small bowl, soak dried mushrooms in hot water to cover until fully soft and spongy, 20 to 30 minutes.
2. Drain mushrooms, snip off stems with scissors, and rinse caps briefly under cool water to dislodge any sand trapped in gills. Using Chinese cleaver or chef's knife, cut caps into large strips about ⅛ inch thick.
3. Prepare fresh mushrooms: Clean button mushrooms by bobbing them briefly in small bowl of cool water. With paring knife, remove any woody stem tips, then cut mushrooms into umbrella-shaped slices 1/16 inch thick. Enokitake, shiitake, and oyster mushrooms do not need to be washed. Separate enokitake into small clusters and remove any very spongy stem ends. Separate oyster mush-

rooms into small clusters. Using paring knife, remove any tough shiitake stems, then cut caps into ⅛-inch slivers. With damp paper towel, wipe chanterelles clean, then cut into thin arcs or strips, following natural trumpet-like curve of mushroom.

4. In small saucepan, combine dried mushrooms, stock, and fresh peas, if using. (Do not add frozen peas until later.) Cover, bring to a slow simmer over high heat, and adjust heat to maintain a steady simmer. Simmer, covered, 5 minutes.

5. Heat non-aluminum saucepan over high heat until hot enough to evaporate a bead of water on contact. Add 2 tablespoons oil, swirl to coat bottom, then heat until hot enough to sizzle a pinch of shallot. Add shallots or scallions and stir with wooden spoon until fully fragrant, 10 to 15 seconds, adjusting heat so they foam without browning. Splash in wine, pause a second or two for it to explode in a fragrant hiss, then add fresh mushrooms. Stir fry until soft, about 4 minutes, drizzling in more oil from side of pan only if mushrooms are sticking. There should be no excess liquid in pan.

6. When mushrooms are soft, add simmering stock mixture to the pan. Bring to a simmer, stirring with wooden spoon, then cover and simmer 5 minutes.

7. Reduce heat to low and taste soup. Add sugar to enrich wine flavor, then season carefully with salt to bring out flavor of mushrooms.

8. Add frozen peas, if using, and stir several times until heated through.

9. Turn off heat and keep covered until ready to serve. The soup keeps perfectly, growing richer as it sits. If required, reheat it over low heat before serving.

"Old Egg" with Scallion and Shrimp

½ cup tiny bay shrimp or cubed small fresh shrimp (about ¼ pound)
1 teaspoon Chinese rice wine or dry sherry
Several twists freshly ground pepper
8 chilled large eggs
4 tablespoons thinly cut scallion rings, from green and white sections
⅓ cup unsalted chicken or vegetable stock
1½ teaspoons light soy sauce
Kosher salt
2 tablespoons corn or peanut oil

1. If using small shrimp, shell, devein, and cube them with sharp paring knife. In small bowl, toss shrimp and wine. Sprinkle with pepper and toss again.

2. In large bowl, lightly beat eggs with whisk or fork. Add scallion rings, stock, and soy sauce. Taste and add salt if necessary. Add shrimp mixture and stir gently to blend.

3. Heat Dutch oven, casserole, or stockpot over high heat until hot enough to evaporate a bead of water on contact. Add oil, swirl to coat bottom and sides of pot, then use oil-soaked paper towel to wipe oil film around sides of pot up to lip.

4. When oil is hot enough to slowly bubble a drop of egg in

about 30 seconds, stir egg mixture gently, swirl pot to redistribute oil, then add egg mixture to pot.

5. Cover tightly and cook over low heat 25 minutes.

6. After 25 minutes, peek quickly under lid. If egg is not puffed to within 1½ inches of lip, *gently* replace cover and cook 5 to 10 minutes more.

7. Bring pot swiftly to the table, lid still on (the soufflé will usually sink once lid is lifted). Call for attention, lift lid to display soufflé, then cut into wedges for serving.

Stir-Fried Velvet Spinach with Glass Noodles

2 pounds spinach
2 ounces bean threads (glass noodles)
3 tablespoons corn or peanut oil
1¼ teaspoons Kosher salt
½ to 1 teaspoon sugar
2 teaspoons Oriental sesame oil

1. In large covered saucepan, bring 2 to 2½ quarts of unsalted water to a boil over high heat.

2. Discard any straggly spinach leaves and white roots, then use scissors to cut stems and large leaves into 2-inch sections. Cut bulky stem clusters into 2 or 3 pieces through base; leave small stem clusters and any red root tips intact. In large bowl, plunge cut spinach into several changes of cold water, gently pumping up and down to remove grit. Drain in colander and shake off excess water.

3. Plunge spinach into boiling water.

4. After 1 minute, drain spinach in colander, flush with cold running water until chilled, then press lightly with palms of hands to remove excess water. Fluff spinach gently to loosen mass.

5. In medium-size bowl, cover bean threads with 3 to 4 cups of heated water, without removing binding of rubber bands or strings. If bean threads are from Taiwan or Thailand, use hot water; if they are from the People's Republic of China, use boiling water.

6. When pliable, after about 10 seconds, use scissors to cut through loop ends or center of skein, thereby cutting bean threads into manageable 4- to 5-inch lengths. Cut rubber bands or strings and discard them, then swish bean threads to disperse in water.

7. After another 10 to 15 seconds, when bean threads are firm—like rubber bands to the touch—rinse briefly with cool water and drain again.

8. Have all ingredients within easy reach of your stovetop.

9. Heat wok or skillet over high heat until hot enough to evaporate a bead of water on contact. Add oil, swirl to coat pan, then reduce heat to medium-high. When hot enough to sizzle a bit of spinach on contact, add spinach and toss briskly to separate leaves and glaze them with oil, 15 to 20 seconds. Sprinkle with salt and sugar, then continue to toss briskly another minute. Add noodles and, using spatula, blend with several quick stirs until heated through. Add sesame oil, toss briskly to combine, then remove from heat.

10. Arrange several rosy-tipped spinach stems on top, if desired, and serve at once.

Meet the Cooks

Acknowledgments

Index

Meet the Cooks

Stevie Bass, a food stylist and recipe developer, runs her own consulting firm, Food Concepts, which works with advertising and public relations agencies, photographers, filmmakers, and food companies in the San Francisco area.

Victoria Fahey is the chef for Curds & Whey, a specialty food store, charcuterie, and catering service in Oakland, California, and is also in charge of product development for the New Oakland Food Company.

Norman Weinstein, an instructor at the New York Cooking Center, has written two books on Chinese cooking—*32 Wok Dishes* and *Chinese Cooking: The Classical Techniques Made Easy*. He has also edited a newsletter focusing on Chinese cooking.

Victoria Wise has been cooking professionally since 1971, when she became the first chef at the famed restaurant Chez Panisse in Berkeley, California. Since 1973 she has owned and operated Pig by the Tail, a charcuterie, in Berkeley.

Lucy Wing was food and equipment editor for *American Home* magazine and contributing food editor for *Country Living* magazine. She has written articles for *Self* and *Family Circle* and is presently food editor at *McCall's*.

Meryle Evans, a writer and food historian, edited *The American Heritage Cookbook* and *American Manners and Morals*. She regularly contributes articles on food to the *New York Times* and *Food & Wine* magazine.

Dennis Gilbert combines two careers: cooking and writing. His short stories have appeared in numerous publications and he is now *chef de cuisine* at the Vinyard Restaurant in Portland, Maine.

Holly Garrison has been interested in cooking and fine food for most of her life and has attended cooking classes in the United States and in Europe. She is food editor at *Parents* magazine.

Perla Meyers attended classes at the Ecole Hotelier in Lausanne, Switzerland, and the Cordon Bleu in Paris. She is the author of *The Seasonal Kitchen, The Peasant Kitchen*, and *Perla Meyers' From Market to Kitchen Cookbook*. She writes for *Food & Wine* and other cooking magazines.

Anne Byrd studied cooking at L'Ecole de Cuisine La Varenne in Paris, the Cordon Bleu in London, and the Culinary Institute of America. She appears on a TV cooking show in Charlotte, North Carolina.

Mary Beth Clark is the founder of the Food Consulting Group, a research and consulting firm for the food, wine, and cookware industries. She developed the first cooking course in America to cover all seven regions of China and now runs her own cooking school in New York City.

Paula Wolfert is a journalist, cooking instructor, and former chef specializing in Mediterranean cuisine. She is the author of *Mediterranean Cooking, Couscous and Other Good Food From Morocco*, and *The Cooking of Southwest France*.

Elisabeth Thorstensson, a native of Sweden, once worked as a private cook at Mary Martin's ranch in Brazil. Currently, she is chef for the executive dining room of the Seagram Company in New York City.

Bruce Cliborne is chef at the Exile Restaurant in New York City. He was dinner chef at the Soho Charcuterie and was contributing editor for the *Soho Charcuterie Cookbook.*

Paul Neuman and **Stacy Bogdonoff,** a husband and wife cooking team, own and operate a New York City food store and catering service. He apprenticed with a private caterer and has taught fish and seafood cookery at the New York Restaurant School. She graduated from the Culinary Institute of America and attended classes at L'Ecole de Cuisine La Varenne in Paris.

Kathleen Kenny Sanderson was personal chef for the Robert Kennedy family. Formerly food editor at *Restaurant Business* magazine, she is now a freelance food consultant and teaches professional courses at the New York Restaurant School.

Jean Anderson is the author of more than ten cookbooks, including *Unforbidden Sweets* and *Jean Anderson Cooks.* She was food editor at *Ladies' Home Journal* and a contributing editor at *Family Circle* and now writes for *Food & Wine* and *Gourmet.*

Penelope Casas, who lived in Spain for many years, wrote the award-winning *Food and Wines of Spain.* She teaches at the New York Cooking Center, lectures on Spanish cuisine, and writes about food and travel for the *New York Times.*

Douglas Oaks, certified as an executive chef and culinary educator by the American Culinary Federation, has been awarded top prizes at the National Culinary Competition held annually in Chicago. He is executive chef at Litton Microwave Cooking in Minneapolis.

Ed Giobbi, a painter of international reputation and a specialist in Italian regional cooking, travels frequently to Italy. He is the author of *Italian Family Cooking.*

Diane Darrow and **Tom Maresca,** who are husband and wife, contribute articles to *Food & Wine, Bon Appétit,* and other magazines. He is the author of *Mastering Wine a Taste at a Time;* she has taught wine appreciation classes.

Alfredo Viazzi, a native of Savona, Italy, is the owner of and executive chef at several Italian restaurants in New York City. He is the author of *Alfredo Viazzi's Italian Cooking* and *Alfredo Viazzi's Cucina e Nostalgia.*

Madhur Jaffrey, born in Delhi, India, is an actress, writer, and cooking teacher. She is the author of *An Invitation to Indian Cooking* and *Madhur Jaffrey's World-of-the-East Vegetarian Cooking,* which won a Tastemaker Award.

Richard Sax, a food journalist and cooking instructor, was trained in New York and at the Cordon Bleu in Paris. He is the author of *Cooking Great Meals Every Day, Old Fashioned Desserts,* and *New York's Master Chefs,* a companion volume to the television series of the same name.

Barbara Tropp, who reads and speaks fluent Mandarin, is a scholar turned Chinese cook and the author of the highly acclaimed *Modern Art of Chinese Cooking.* She plans to open a Chinese restaurant in San Francisco.

Acknowledgments

Cover photo: John Burwell. *Frontispiece:* baskets—Primitive Artisan, Inc.; quilt and ceramics—Museum of American Folk Art Shop. **BEEF.** *Page 25:* platters—Richard-Ginori; board, utensils—WMF of America. *Pages 26–27:* dishes, trays—Katagiri; linens—China Seas, Inc. *Page 30:* flatware—Wallace Silversmiths; dishes—Pottery Barn; mat, napkin—Urban Outfitters. *Page 32:* bowls, utensils—Dean & DeLuca; handpainted cloth—Peter Fasano. *Page 34:* flatware, napkin, dishes—Frank McIntosh at Henri Bendel; paper—Four Hands Bindery. *Pages 36–37:* flatware—Wallace Silversmiths; wooden spoons—Dean & DeLuca; dishes, glass, linens—Pierre Deux. *Pages 40–41:* napkins—Williams-Sonoma; plate, baskets—Broadway Panhandler; rug—Pottery Barn. *Page 44:* dishes—Dean & DeLuca; napkins—Fabindia. *Pages 46–47:* dishes—The Museum Store of the Museum of Modern Art; paper—Four Hands Bindery. *Page 50:* utensils—Wallace Silversmiths; dishes—Far Eastern Arts, Inc.; vase—The Museum Store of the Museum of Modern Art. *Page 53:* platters—Pottery Barn; cloth—Brunschwig & Fils. *Pages 56–57:* flatware—Wallace Silversmiths; dishes—Mottahedeh & Co., Inc. *Page 60:* flatware—The Lauffer Company; dishes—Broadway Panhandler; white bowl—Dean & DeLuca; linens—Fabindia. *Page 63:* flatware—The Lauffer Co.; platters—Patrick Loughran Ceramics; countertop—Formica® Brand Laminate by Formica Corp. **PORK.** *Page 67:* pan—Bon Marché; tiles—Country Floors. *Pages 68–69:* chopsticks—Five Eggs; napkin—Leacock & Co.; plates—Haviland & Co. *Page 72:* utensils, plates, mugs, pitcher—The Museum Store of the Museum of Modern Art; tablecloth—Conran's. *Page 74:* tablecloth—Conran's; platters—Rose Gong; teapot—Japan Interiors Gallery. *Pages 76–77:* flatware—Ercuis; dishes, glass—Baccarat, Inc. *Page 80:* plates—Wedgwood; utensils—Gorham; napkin—Leacock & Co.; tabletop—Formica® Brand Laminate by Formica Corp.; glass—Conran's. *Page 82:* dishes—Haviland & Co.; utensils—Gorham; napkin—Pierre Deux. *Pages 84–85:* utensils, tray, plates, glass—Wolfman-Gold & Good Co. *Page 88:* platter, bowl, napkin—Pottery Barn; tablecloth—Conran's. *Page 91:* utensils—Gorham; placemat, napkin, plate—Ludwig Beck of Munich. *Pages 94–95:* plate—Mark Anderson; utensils—Wallace Silversmiths; napkins—Leacock & Co.; basket—Be Seated. *Page 98:* plates—Dan Bleier; glass—Gorham; paper—Four Hands Bindery; napkin—Ad Hoc Softwares; flatware—Frank McIntosh at Henri Bendel. *Page 101:* platter—Dan Bleier; dishes—Harlequin, courtesy of Columbus Avenue General Store; tablecloth—Conran's.

CHICKEN. *Page 105:* tablecloth—Katja; platter—Longchamps; bowl—Pottery Barn. *Pages 106–107:* tiles—Country Floors; butter bowl—Cecily Fortescue; napkin—Fabrications; dinner plates—Conran's; au gratin pan—Charles Lamalle. *Page 110:* beige bowl—New Country Gear; plate—Pottery Barn. *Page 112:* platter—Dansk International Designs, Ltd.; beige bowl—New Country Gear; blue bowl—Laura Ashley; napkin—Fabrications. *Pages 116–117:* mats, napkins—Leacock & Co.; pitcher, glass—Orrefors, Inc.; utensils—Dansk International Designs, Ltd.; white platter—The Pfaltzgraff Co.; dishes—International China Co. *Page 120:* tablecloth—Laura Ashley; dinner plate—Dansk International Designs, Ltd.; utensils, glass, salad plate—Conran's. *Page 122:* tablecloth—D. Porthault, Inc.; silver—Oneida Silversmiths; dishes—Richard-Ginori; serving pieces—Christofle Silver, Inc. *Pages 126–127:* tablecloth—D. Porthault, Inc.; china—Haviland & Co.; bowl—Orrefors, Inc. *Page 130:* flatware—The Lauffer Co. *Pages 132–133:* plate—Signature; tablecloth—Brunschwig & Fils. *Pages 136–137:* tablecloth, napkins, dishes—New Country Gear; utensils, salad bowl and servers—Dansk International Designs, Ltd.; *Page 140:* tablecloth—Leacock & Co.; napkins—New Country Gear; servers—Dansk International Designs, Ltd.; platter—Mayhew; plate, bowl—Conran's. *Page 143:* servers—Georg Jensen Silversmiths; plates—Mayhew. **FISH.** *Page 147:* flatware—Buccellati Silversmiths. *Pages 148–149:* flatware—Wallace Silversmiths; napkins—Leacock & Co.; plates—Rorstrand; glasses—Kosta Boda; handpainted cloth—Peter Fasano. *Page 152:* flatware—The Lauffer Co.; china—Hornsea. *Page 154:* flatware—The Lauffer Co.; dinner plate, cloths—New Country Gear. *Pages 156–157:* flatware—Wallace Silversmiths; plate—Beth Forer. *Page 160:* napkin—Leacock & Co.; cloth—Conran's; plate—Dorothy Hafner. *Page 164:* flatware—Buccellati Silversmiths; cloth—Handloom Batik Importers; plates—The Museum Store of the Museum of Modern Art. *Pages 166–167:* flatware—Wallace Silversmiths; platters, cloth—St. Rémy. *Pages 170–171:* bowl—Claudia Shwide, courtesy of Creative Resources; cloth—China Seas, Inc. *Page 173:* flatware—Wallace Silversmiths; crystal, china—Wedgwood; napkin—Leacock & Co. *Pages 176–177:* flatware—The Lauffer Co.; china, linens—Pierre Deux. *Page 180:* platter—Buffalo China, Inc.; linens—Ad Hoc Softwares. *Pages 182–183:* flatware—The Lauffer Co.; china—Dan Bleier, courtesy of Creative Resources; napkin—Conran's; countertop—Formica® Brand Laminate by Formica Corp. **EGGS.** *Page 187:* fork—Gorham;

plates—Columbus Avenue General Store; tablecloth, napkin—Conran's. *Pages 188–189:* plate—Ad Hoc Housewares; glass—Gorham; napkin—Leacock & Co. *Pages 192–193:* dishes—Dan Bleier; rug—Conran's. *Page 195:* flatware—Gorham; dishes—Dan Bleier; tablecloth—Conran's; napkin—Leacock & Co. *Pages 198–199:* napkins—Leacock & Co.; linens—Ad Hoc Softwares; service plates—Conran's; dishes—Broadway Panhandler. *Page 202:* flatware—Gorham; dishes, mat, glass—Ad Hoc Housewares; napkin—Ad Hoc Softwares. *Page 205:* napkin—Leacock & Co.; rug—Bowl & Board. *Pages 208–209:* fork—Gorham; tablecloth—Conran's; dishes, napkin—Ad Hoc Softwares. *Pages 212–213:* flatware—Gorham; napkins, rug—Museum of American Folk Art Shop. *Page 215:* flatware—Gorham; napkin, mat, plate—Columbus Avenue General Store. **PASTA.** *Page 219:* plate—Arabia; *Pages 220–221:* tablecloth—Saint Rémy; napkin—Mosseri Industries; utensils—The Lauffer Co.; plates—Rorstrand. *Page 224:* tablecloth—Brunschwig & Fils; napkin—Fabrications; bowl—Kosta Boda; platter—Rorstrand. *Page 226:* tablecloth—Conran's; baking dish—Hummelwerk. *Pages 228–229:* tabletop—Formica® Brand Laminate by Formica Corp.; spoon—Georg Jensen Silversmiths; oval platter—Royal Copenhagen Porcelain; octagonal platter—Haviland & Co. *Page 232:* napkin—The Lauffer Co.; carafe, glasses—Charles Lamalle; salad bowl—Feu Follet; platter, plates—Conran's. *Pages 234–235:* tiles—Laura Ashley; glasses—Conran's; bowls—Terrafirma Ceramics. *Page 237:* tablecloth, napkin—Fabindia; tableware—Arabia of Finland. *Pages 240–241:* tablecloth, napkin—Leacock & Co.; back cloth—Saint Rémy; small white plate—Buffalo China, Inc.; platter, plate—Wedgwood; utensils—The Lauffer Co. *Page 244:* napkin—Mosseri Industries; utensils—Buccellati Silversmiths; china—Hutschenreuther Corp.; carafe—Orrefors, Inc. *Page 246:* bowl—Dean & Deluca. **VEGETABLES.** *Page 249:* cloth—The Basket Handler; platter—Mayhew; quiche pan—Pottery Barn. *Pages 250–251:* aluminum pan—Farberware; red pan—Copco. *Page 254:* handpainted cloth—Peter Fasano; napkin—Katja; basket—F.O. Merz; plates—Metlox; flatware—Conran's. *Page 256:* cloth—Brunschwig & Fils; napkin—Leacock and Co.; basket—F.O. Merz; dish—Far Eastern Arts, Inc. *Pages 258–259:* pot—Farberware; bowls—Buffalo China, Inc. *Page 262:* countertop—Formica® Brand Laminate by Formica Corp.; napkins, trays, plates, glasses—Pottery Barn; flatware—The Lauffer Co. *Page 264:* cloth—Leacock and Co.; mat, napkin—D. Porthault Inc.; plate—Baccarat.

Pages 266–267: grill—Pottery Barn; blue bowl—Dean & DeLuca. *Pages 270–271:* hand-painted cloth—Peter Fasano; platter—Dean & DeLuca; bowl—Williams-Sonoma. *Page 274:* glass, dishes—Dean & DeLuca; flat-ware—Williams-Sonoma. *Kitchen equipment courtesy of:* White-Westinghouse, Commercial Aluminum Cookware Co., Robot-Coupe, Caloric, Kitchen-Aid, J.A. Henckels Zwillingswerk, Inc., and Schwabel Corp. Microwave oven compliments of Litton Microwave Cooking Products.
Illustrations by Ray Skibinski.
Production by Giga Communications.

Index

284